THE JAPANESE PRODUCTION SYSTEM

The Japanese Production System

Hybrid Factories in East Asia

Edited by
Hiroshi Itagaki

First published 1997 by
MACMILLAN PRESS LTD
Houndmills, Basingstoke, Hampshire RG21 6XS
and London
Companies and representatives
throughout the world

ISBN 0–333–63226–5

A catalogue record for this book is available
from the British Library.

This book is printed on paper suitable for recycling and
made from fully managed and sustained forest sources.

10	9	8	7	6	5	4	3	2	1
06	05	04	03	02	01	00	99	98	97

Printed and bound in Great Britain by
Antony Rowe Ltd
Chippenham, Wiltshire

Contents

v

Notes on the Contributors

Tetsuo Abo is Professor in the Institute of Social Science, University of Tokyo.

Du-Sop Cho is Associate Professor in the Graduate School of International Development, Nagoya University.

Yanshu Hao is Lecturer in the School of Business Administration, Meiji University.

Kunio Kamiyama is Professor in the Faculty of Economics, Josai University.

Nobuo Kawabe is Professor in the Graduate School of Commerce, Waseda University.

Tetsuji Kawamura is Professor in the Department of Economics, Teikyo University.

Hiroshi Kumon is Professor in the Faculty of Sociology, Hosei University.

Jaw-Yann Twu is Professor in the Economic Research Center, School of Economics, Nagoya University.

Acknowledgements

A great many people in the companies studied gave their time and experience, providing valuable information in interviews and in documents. The project and this book would have been impossible without their co-operation and assistance. I cannot mention every one by name, because they were too numerous. I would like to express our appreciation by listing the names of companies.

AUTOMOBILE INDUSTRIES (ASSEMBLY AND PARTS)

CALSONIC Corporation, Daewoo Public Motors Company Ltd, Fuji Heavy Industries Ltd, Hino Motors Ltd, Hirotech Company Ltd, Honda Motor Company Ltd, Hyundai Motor Company Ltd, Isuzu Motors Ltd, KAYABA Industry Company Ltd, Kia Motors Corporation, Mitsubishi Motors Corporation, NHK Spring Company Ltd, Nippondenso (the company name has been changed to Denso) Company Ltd, Nissan Motor Company Ltd, PROTON (Persahaan Otomobile Nasional Bhd.), Toyoda Gosei Company Ltd, Toyota Motor Corporation, Atsugi Unisia (the company name has been changed to UNISIA-JECS) Corporation, Yazaki Sogyo Company Ltd

ELECTRIC AND ELECTRONICS INDUSTRIES (ASSEMBLY AND PARTS)

ALPS Electric Company Ltd, FUJITSU Ltd, Hitachi Ltd, Leechun Electric Mfg. Company Ltd, L.G. Electronics Incorporated, Matsushita Electric Industrial Company Ltd, MINEBEA Company Ltd, Mitsubishi Electric Corporation, Motorola Incorporated, Murata Manufacturing Company Ltd, NEC Corporation, Onamba Company Ltd, Philips Ltd, Sam Sung Electronics Company, Sanyo Electric Company Ltd, Sharp Corporation, Sony Corporation, Tabuchi Electric Company Ltd, Taiyo Yuden Company Ltd, Tatung Company, TDK Corporation, TOKO Electric Corporation, TOSHIBA Corporation, Texas Instruments Incorporated, Victor Company of Japan Ltd.

Outside the companies there were several people who participated in the field studies, helped to analyse data, and contributed to this book. The editor and contributors are particularly indebted to Professor Toshio Tajima of Tokyo University, Professor Akira Suehiro of Tokyo University, Professor C. C. Chen of National Taiwan University and Associate Professor Norma Mansor of University of Malaya. Mr Herbert E. Brauer and Mr Robert Langridge helped tremendously in proof-reading and improving the English.

HIROSHI ITAGAKI

List of Abbreviations

Introduction

Hiroshi Itagaki

I IMPLICATIONS OF THE EMERGENCE OF JAPANESE MULTINATIONALS

How and why do the developmental processes and characteristics of multinationals differ according to their home countries? This question, posed by numerous scholars, seems to be becoming more and more important. Not only is it an interesting theme for discussions regarding multinational enterprises, but it is also directly related to the question of whether capitalism, market economies or corporate systems do, in fact, differ from country to country. While this question was raised by Ronald Dore in the early 1970s, when he contrasted Japanese welfare corporatism with Anglo-American market individualism,[1] it has drawn renewed attention in the wake of the collapse of socialist regimes. There is also no doubt that the emergence of Japanese multinationals and the strong international competitiveness of Japanese manufacturing companies have provided a powerful stimulus its subsequent debate.

Yoshino (1976) tries to answer this question as it applies to Japanese multinationals at their early stage of development, by applying the analytical framework supplied by Harvard's project for studying multinational corporations. He concludes that Japanese multinationals are a subcategory that follows the developmental pattern of American multinationals. He also argues that Japanese multinationals embody particular elements that stem from the characteristics of Japanese-style management based upon a homogeneous and group-orientated society. He speculates that these elements will prevent Japanese multinationals from fully developing their offshore activities. With the benefit of hindsight it is easy to observe that his arguments and conclusions are limited by the period in which they were formulated. Nevertheless, his position does provide a platform upon which ensuing studies on the characteristics and behavior of Japanese multinationals are based, and they still merit serious attention today.

Takamiya (1979) presents the following view: 'In the case of manufacturing industries, technology developed at the home country needs to be transferred to the host country.' However, 'Technology . . . is typically

1

intertwined with various human, organizational and institutional elements of the home society' and 'transferring such human and organizational elements of production is not at all a trivial task' . . . 'operation of foreign manufacturing subsidiaries, therefore typically shows blended mixtures of home- and host-country practices, modified to suit each other'. From this perspective, Takamiya surveys the colour television plants of Japanese, American and British companies in Great Britain and concludes that there are three major areas in which Japanese companies enjoy advantages: first is production management characterised by quality control through 'sheer effort and meticulous attention to details' and by flexible work practices; second is flexible inter-organisational co-ordination based on training and job rotation; and third is co-operative industrial relations represented by so-called single union practices. These are all 'organizational skills, which can be practiced through individual internalization of norms'. This book shares this understanding, and in a sense, is an attempt to further enrich and develop it.

Recently, several scholars have examined the salient differences between American, European and Japanese multinationals. Bartlett and Ghoshal (1989) and Humes (1993) argue that companies' managerial characteristics are strongly affected by the social environment of their home countries, and that such characteristics and resulting advantages define the multinational enterprise. These characteristics can be summarised as follows: American-based companies, established on the basis of a multicultural and individualistic society, are characterised by divisionalised and standardised structures, and strong leadership from professional management. European-based companies, founded on societies that emphasise personal relationships, accentuate personal trust, and endeavour to foster the development of trusted key persons. Japanese-based companies, built on a group-orientated and homogenous society, highlight intensive communications and culturally dependent systems.

Some of the assumptions underlying their arguments coincide with those of this book. In particular, we agree with Bartlett and Ghoshal's position that multinational enterprises should satisfy two, often incompatible, demands: one, to integrate and manage world-wide subsidiary networks; and the other, to respond to the different conditions of the host countries in which the subsidiaries operate. We also agree with their observation that Japanese multinationals have certain disadvantages, namely the over-concentration of information and authority at headquarters. Although we concur with the general thrust of these arguments, we must be careful to avoid the trap of stereotyping and convenient cultural determinism. Indeed, we suspect that their interpretation of

Japanese multinationals reveals such a tendency to stereotype. Nevertheless, it is necessary to study multinational enterprises empirically from the respective analytical standpoints of these researchers, and to formulate the salient features of multinational enterprises according to their different home countries.

II THE THEME OF THIS BOOK

This book will examine the salient features of foreign production carried out by Japanese companies in East Asia. Our research group has already completed field studies on Japanese affiliated plants in the United States, in 1986 and 1989.[2] Therefore, the theme of this book is to shed light on the characteristics of local production by Japanese companies in East Asian countries in comparison with those in the United States.

After the 1970s, Japanese companies expanded their foreign production rapidly. Since the early 1990s, however, they have halted that expansion, particularly in the United States and Europe, in the wake of the slump triggered by the bursting of the 'bubble economy'. Japanese companies have entered a phase of restructuring, or disinvestment of foreign subsidiaries. Of course, trade friction and the appreciation of the yen, which have been the main factors facilitating foreign production, have not disappeared. Japanese companies will inevitably face problems in reorganising and strengthening production networks, abroad as well as in Japan, in order to adapt to the continuing trend of yen appreciation.

Japanese production plants in the Asian region are becoming more important than may seem to be the case on a purely quantitative basis, for three reasons: first, Japanese affiliated plants in Asia, particularly electrical machinery plants, figure more prominently as export bases to Japan, the United States and Europe, as a consequence of the stronger yen. Second, as the Asian region is itself becoming more attractive as a consuming market for many products, including automobiles, Japanese affiliates are pressed to make an earnest response to this situation. And third, when Japanese affiliates raise funds for the expansion and renewal of their plants from local sources, such as the reinvestment of profits, such investment is not included in statistics compiled by the Ministry of Finance. Japanese investment in Asia is also important for reasons extending beyond those that apply to the companies themselves. Foreign direct investment by Japanese manufacturing industries, closely connected with trade, will play a major and dynamic role in facilitating the formation of a large economic sphere consisting of countries and areas that are in different stages of development, from Japan to the newly industrialised economies (NIE)s, the ASEAN (Association of South East Asian Nations) countries, and the coastal regions of China.[3]

This rapid regional development and the formation of an industrial society, known as 'the East Asian miracle',[4] has been achieved primarily through the efforts and wisdom of the people in these countries.[5] At the same time, there is no doubt that the transfer of production and management technology, as well as of high-quality capital goods accompanied by local production on the part of Japanese affiliates, are indispensable reinforcements for the rapid industrialisation of the East Asian region.[6] The process of industrialisation that began with labour-intensive industries in the NIEs resulted in increased income and technological progress, and this enabled the NIEs to introduce higher technologies and more advanced capital goods. Industrial development in the NIEs brought about a division of labour with Japan and stimulated Japan to develop higher added value products and to function as a supply base for more sophisticated capital goods, in turn facilitating a further transfer of technology. This cycle of positive reinforcement is not confined to the NIEs, but extends to a broader area encompassing the ASEAN countries and, more recently, China. This is a significant aspect of the 'geese formation' type of development seen in Asian countries.[7]

Taiwan and Korea, to be discussed in Chapter 3, were leading host countries, together with Hong Kong and Singapore, of Japanese foreign direct investment in Asia. However, the economies of these two countries, which had achieved a rapid growth rate through a conspicuous reliance upon exports, and the Japanese affiliates operating in them, now stand at critical turning points resulting from a drastic rise in wage levels led by democratisation in the late 1980s, a sharp increase in exchange rates against the US dollar, and the rise of ASEAN countries and China as exporters. Yet there is no doubt that Taiwan and Korea remain two of the most important countries for foreign investment by Japanese manufacturing countries. Taiwan in particular, along with Hong Kong, may become an intermediary for investment between Japan and China.

Nevertheless, there are few in-depth studies focusing on direct investment in Taiwan or Korea by Japanese companies. Nor are there many studies providing a detailed examination of such Japanese affiliates. The few notable works that exist include Ichimura (1988), which examines to some extent the management of Japanese affiliates in Taiwan and Korea, and Sasaki and Esho (1987), which surveys Japanese electronics firms in Taiwan. In addition, case studies of individual plants in Taiwan and Korea are also represented in Tokunaga *et al.*, (1991),

Ogawa and Makito (1990), Kumazawa (1989), and Maruyama (1994). Some of these are instructive in their scrutiny of the practical management of individual companies; however, the number of companies surveyed in this way is limited.

Investment by Japanese manufacturing companies in the ASEAN area also began to take place as early as the 1960s. Automobile and electrical assembly companies set up plants that produced various kinds of products or models to overcome trade barriers, such as high tariffs. However, it was not until the 1980s that Japanese investment there became significant in quality and quantity. New types of investment have been facilitated by the rapid and structural appreciation of the yen, an increase in domestic production costs associated with the strong yen, and trade friction between Japan and other industrially advanced countries. In the electrical industry, ASEAN plants have functioned as significant export bases to Japan and to the United States. Domestic markets in the ASEAN countries are expanding rapidly as a result of increased incomes, to the extent that Japanese affiliates in the automobile and other industries are launching new plants, or expanding existing ones. As is well known, recent investment to China has increased dramatically, sometimes in competition with those to ASEAN countries.

Yamashita (1991) offers a comprehensive examination of Japanese affiliated plants in ASEAN countries, and Koike and Inoki (1987) and Kobayashi (1992) also conduct some interesting case studies on Japanese companies in Taiwan and Korea in addition to their other publications focusing on Taiwan and Korea. Koike and Inoki, however, offer only a limited number of corporate examples, and the studies by Yamashita and by Kobayashi both suffer from the lack of a systematic analytical framework. The authors cited above also fail to provide a compelling international comparison, since they neglect to describe the salient features of Japanese affiliated plants in Asia.

This book will arrange and examine data obtained through field studies on Japanese plants in five East Asian countries, namely: Taiwan, Korea, Thailand, Malaysia and Singapore. This study represents the Asian part of our ongoing research. Our research group (The Japan Multinational Enterprise Study Group, under the direction of Professor Tetsuo Abo) has already carried out field studies in North America, including the United States. Consequently, we are able to examine and compare the results of these two field studies by applying a common analytical framework, the Hybrid Evaluation Model, which will be discussed below. That model is the centrepiece of this book.

Four industries, namely the auto assembly, auto parts, electronics assembly, and electronics parts (including semiconductors) industries have been targeted for this survey, since they have led exports and foreign investment by the Japanese manufacturing sector. It is common knowledge that not all Japanese manufacturing industries are highly competitive. The sector that has achieved excellent international competitiveness comprises mainly the so-called processing and assembly industries, of which the auto and electronics industries are typical. These industries are always referred to and cited as models when various features of Japanese management and production systems are discussed. We consider the production system in the processing and assembly industry itself to be an important source of competitive strength, and for this reason we examine in this book the international transfer of that system. We shall focus on the international transfer of the system of management and technology, noting, in particular, 'human elements' on the shop floor of the plants.[8] To clarify the viewpoint put forward in this book, we shall begin by explaining our understanding of the main characteristics of the Japanese-style production system.[9]

III THE AMERICAN SYSTEM VERSUS THE JAPANESE SYSTEM

Scholars, ranging from S. H. Hymer, to internalisation theorists, have pointed out that firms operating subsidiaries abroad must transfer the advantages of their own managerial resources from the home to the host countries.[10] The characteristics of production systems in home countries are thus more or less imprinted upon the managerial practices of multinational enterprises.

It is also well known that the competitive advantages enjoyed by Japanese manufacturing industries such as the automobile or electronics industries do not reside primarily in hardware technology such as innovative products or newly developed production equipment. Rather, the advantages are to be found in how most effectively to produce existing products or utilise existing equipment. This is, in other words, 'human and organisational elements' or 'organisational skills'. Recently, of course, the product development system through which Japanese automobile companies have been able to develop new models in short periods by co-operating with many parts suppliers has attracted considerable attention.[11] It also appears that there is a considerable number of products that only Japanese companies are able to develop and supply to the world market, particularly certain electronics components such as the liquid crystal display (LCD).[12] Even in such cases, the focal point of these systems are the organisational skills; that is, how to develop or create new products by combining and improving existing technologies.

The main features of the Japanese corporate system, in comparison with the American system, can be summed up as follows:[13] Japanese companies are characterised by workplace (production) orientated management and participatory decision-making. In contrast, American firms typically embrace a hierarchy-orientated management and top-down decision-making.

In traditional-type American companies, semi-skilled workers are allotted to many clearly demarcated job categories, and plant management is under the control of professional managers and engineers. However, job control unionism, under which seniority takes precedence over management discretion, has a strong affect upon who is allocated to what job, and determines the order in which employees are laid off. Factors that determine wages (salaries) and promotion differ between blue-collar and white-collar employees and there is a wide gap between the ways that these respective groups are treated. In the case of blue-collar employees, job categories almost exclusively determine wage rates, and seniority receives priority as a determining factor in the promotion to a higher grade of job-title. In contrast, white-collar employees receive on-the-spot individual performance evaluations that influence the amount of their salaries, and talented employees are sometimes instantly promoted to much higher positions in the corporate hierarchy.

In Japanese companies, the shop floor plays a relatively important role. Each work site itself, consisting of multiskilled and long-term employees, 'quasi-autonomously' assumes the responsibilities for job allotment and problem solving. Of course, product development and production technology departments also play important roles. Even so, these departments co-operate and communicate with the shop floors frequently and effectively. Blue-collar and white-collar employees are treated in almost the same way. Wages are characterised by a 'person-centred' as opposed to a 'job-centred' system, since there is no fixed concept of 'job'. Major factors determining wages are *nenkō* (length of service), and *jinji kōka* (performance evaluations). Employees are selected and promoted slowly, based upon evaluations that take place over a long term, corresponding to long-term employment.

Japanese and American production control systems function on the basis of the characteristics of their respective organisations. The traditional American system is characterised by, and gains its competitive advantage through the total pursuit of economies of scale, where specialised plants produce a limited number of models or products with the help of large, single-purpose machines. In contrast, Japanese companies are characterised by small-lot production on a diverse product line, where plants produce various products or models on the same production line by mixing products or switching among them so that companies can respond quickly and flexibly to fluctuating market needs. To make this system function effectively, Japanese companies have developed techniques of thorough in-process inventory and quality control (although the initial forms of these production control technologies were introduced by American companies). Thus Japanese firms have caught up and become tough rivals for American companies.

It goes without saying that these companies did not create their production systems by planning the consistency and rationality of the system from the very beginning. Both the Japanese and American systems have evolved as a result of various natural and historical factors, economic factors such as market scale, and accidental events. In addition to these causal factors, we venture to suggest that each system is suitable to the nature of its respective society. The American type of organisational principle, in which a rigid hierarchical mechanism is preferred and where each person's responsibility and authority is made clear, is required to organise people in a society where multicultural elements and diverse patterns of behaviour coexist and where people have much greater inter-regional and interorganisational mobility. In contrast, in Japan, society is homogenous and people are inclined to behave in concert with their colleagues and co-workers, and are able to communicate with each other more smoothly. Therefore, in the Japanese system, characterised by vague barriers between individual job tasks, inter-work place co-ordination and participatory management can function effectively. We can say, therefore, that the American system inclines to being artificially imposed upon society, while the Japanese system is a more spontaneous outgrowth of society.

Although it may seem more difficult to transfer the Japanese system abroad than it is to transplant the American system, this does not mean that the Japanese system is so unique and different from world standards that its international transfer is inherently problematic. The reason that specific industries of a specific country exhibit international competitive strength is that their respective management systems are affected strongly by their distinctive economic structure, values, culture, institutions and history.[14] As Takamiya (1979) points out, the international transfer of production systems, not only of Japan but also those of any other country, is always difficult, because each system is only completely rational within the context of its own society.[15] The important point is that the American system is also unique, because it has evolved as an adaptation to a society which contains diverse global elements. However, it is precisely this type of uniqueness that is able to create a 'universal' mechanism to absorb and neutralise diverse regional features. In contrast, the Japanese system is characterised by a strong reliance on human factors related to the Japanese social context, so that its international transfer is bound to be a more difficult task.

Of course, every society is in the process of changing, just as present American society has changed from that of the 1950s, when the traditional American system was at the height of its prosperity. Although such change is a matter of degree, what is of basic significance is that changes in social environments do affect corporate systems. But, conversely, we must also not neglect the potential for transformation in corporate practices to stimulate change in society.

IV   AN ANALYTICAL FRAMEWORK: THE HYBRID EVALUATION MODEL

The economic rationality of a system does not guarantee its survival and successful operation in every society. Moreover, the rationality itself may differ according to its social environment. It is natural that some elements of the Japanese system are extremely difficult to transfer to foreign countries, where social conditions are different from Japan, while other elements are less difficult to transfer. In some cases, the transfer may bear various costs or generate friction with the host societies. Therefore, we can talk about degrees of international transferability, which are determined by attributes of the elements in question. In other cases, it may not be the attributes or the elements themselves, but rather the combination of elements and the social environment of the host countries that may pose a problem. Finally, it is also important to note that the extent to which the transfer of elements is necessary or desirable in the first place, is determined by corporate strategy corresponding to the technological characteristics of specific industries and competitive conditions such as customers' requirements and the degree of competition offered by rivals in host countries.

In our analytical framework, 'application' refers to the aspect of transplanting Japanese elements, and 'adaptation' refers to the act of introducing elements native to the host countries. We are concerned with identifying the elements that have been transferred to the host countries, and those that have not. We wish to understand what kinds of application–adaptation 'hybrids' have been created as a result, and why. In this book, we shall examine this problem by making international comparisons based on a common analytical framework. The international transferability of a production system can be examined in great detail through international comparisons focusing on the points raised above. Also, surveying how the Japanese system has been modified outside Japan will contribute to examining the universality and peculiarity of the system itself.[16] Furthermore, it may offer insights as to whether hybrid systems abroad are merely products of a compromise with environments in the host countries, or whether they offer the possibility of giving rise to entirely new systems, just as Japanese companies have created a different system modelled after the American production system.

Our 'Hybrid Evaluation Model' functions as a common analytical framework for evaluating the degree of hybridisation between application and adaptation. The model was originally constructed after surveying over a hundred domestic plants of Japanese companies during our field studies in the United States. Its framework consists of twenty-three items, considered key elements in the international transfer of Japanese production system, which will be described in detail in Chapter 1. Those twenty-three items are grouped as follows: six items relate to work organisation as core human factors; four items concern production control as core functional factors; three items concern parts procurement (the quasi-core of the system); three items, including small group activities, are considered as subpart of the system that sustains the core; four items concern labour relations; and three items concern the relationship between parent companies and subsidiaries.

We applied basically the same analytical framework in our studies in East Asian countries, to enable a comparison between the hybrid configuration in use in East Asia and that in the United States. However, as will be mentioned in Chapter 1, there is a problem in applying that framework to Japanese affiliates in East Asia. The crucial point is that it is difficult to identify clearly the established systems in the host countries and therefore to compare them with the Japanese system. Taking this into consideration, the hybrid evaluation model was partially modified in applying it to East Asia.

V AN OUTLINE OF OUR SURVEY

We visited a total of thirty-four plants in Taiwan and Korea in 1992, including twenty-five Japanese affiliates and nine non-Japanese plants.

Seventeen of the plants visited in Taiwan are Japanese affiliates, one is a local capital company and another is a European affiliate. In Korea, eight are Japanese affiliates and seven are local capital enterprises. Among companies classified as Korean capital, some include Japanese capital investment without influence on management.

In 1993, we surveyed thirty-seven plants in three ASEAN countries, namely Thailand, Malaysia and Singapore. Thirty-five of those are Japanese affiliates, including one Japanese–European joint venture, and two plants are non-Japanese affiliates. In Thailand, we visited sixteen Japanese affiliates; in Malaysia, fifteen Japanese affiliates and two American-owned companies; and in Singapore, four Japanese-owned plants.

Yanshu Hao visited Japanese affiliated electronics plants in China independently, after separating from the other members of our group, who left Korea for Taiwan. Japanese affiliates in China are interesting to study in that they enable a comparison between their characteristics and those of Japanese affiliates in other East Asian countries. They are also interesting as they suggest the future relationships between East Asian countries, particularly Taiwan and China. For these reasons, her analysis in Chapter 6 is included in this book, although the survey was not executed as a group study.

We employed the same survey methods that were applied during the US field study, which consisted of one-day plant observations, and interviews with plant managers. We also made a point of including local people as interviewees as often as possible.

This kind of survey typically divides into two alternative approaches: one is cross-sectional – a questionnaire approach that targets numerous plants, sometimes sampled randomly; and the other is longitudinal – targeting a very limited number of plants, and staying there for a long time to collect specific data. A disadvantage of the former approach is that the validity and reliability of the data and information gathered may be quite limited. However, an advantage is that it is possible to get an overview of a more general situation. In contrast, a disadvantage with the latter approach is that it is difficult to draw meaningful inferences from specific data to general trends, while an advantage is that the quantity of data, its accuracy and reliability, rise dramatically.

Our one-day plant interview method is midway between these two approaches. The advantages of our approach, we believe, are that we can increase the number of subjects considerably over that obtainable through the specific plant observation approach, and, at the same time, we can gather extensive, detailed data and firsthand information complete with subtle nuances only the people at the workplace know, which is impossible to obtain by questionnaire. Of course, there may be some scepticism concerning our ability to understand the realities of plant management that comprises many diverse aspects and which is the product of long-term experience, through just one-day observation. We believe, however, that by utilising an interview format consisting of detailed check points to evaluate twenty-three elements in our analytical framework can significantly reduce that problem.

VI THE OUTLINE OF THE TEXT

In Chapter 1, Hiroshi Itagaki examines the characteristics of the Japanese production system and, in particular, practices such as flexible work organisation and skill formation. This chapter also introduces our international transfer model for the Japanese production system, called the 'Hybrid Evaluation Model' or the 'Application–Adaptation Model'. This model consists of twenty-three items grouped into six categories, which we consider to be the focal elements in the transfer of the Japanese production system.

In Chapter 2, Hiroshi Itagaki analyses Japanese affiliates in five East Asian countries and evaluates the extent to which elements of the Japanese production system can be transplanted into the host countries. The analysis employs a five-point scale and compares data from five Asian countries with data gathered in the United States during our field study in 1989. This chapter also reports on the performance of Japanese affiliates regarding profitability, production efficiency and product quality.

In Chapter 3, Jaw-Yann Twu begins by examining the reasons behind the rapid growth experienced by the East Asian economies, and provides a new angle for understanding this, namely, the Asian Growth Triangle framework. Secondly, Nobuo Kawabe outlines Japanese manufacturing foreign direct investment in Asian countries and considers its prospect for the future.

In Chapter 4, characteristics of the four industries targeted in our field study are explored by Hiroshi Kumon (auto assembly), Nobuo Kawabe and Kunio Kamiyama (auto parts), Tetsuo Abo (electronics assembly), and Du-Sop Cho (electronics components and semiconductors).

In Chapter 5, nine representative Japanese multinationals are studied by Kunio Kamiyama (Toyota Motor Corporation and Yazaki Corporation), Hiroshi Kumon (Nissan Motor Co. Ltd and Mitsubishi Motors Corporation), Du-Sop Cho (Nippondenso Co. Ltd), Tetsuji Kawamura

(Matsushita Electric Industrial Co. Ltd and Sony Corporation), Nobuo Kawabe (Sharp Corporation), and Yanshu Hao and Tetsuo Abo (Murata Mfg Co. Ltd).

In Chapter 6, Yanshu Hao analyses Japanese electrical appliance plants in South China, comparing the data gathered in her own research excursions with those gathered in the other five East Asian countries. In Chapter 7, Hiroshi Itagaki summarises the findings of this research, and examines briefly the implications and prospects for the application–adaptation hybridisation of the Japanese production system.

Notes

1. Dore (1973).
2. See The Institute of Social Science (1990) and Abo (1994a).
3. See, for example, JETRO (1989a).
4. The World Bank (1993).
5. Suehiro (1995), Watanabe (1979) and Amsden (1989).
6. Taniura (1990).
7. The term, 'geese formation' type of development, was first used in Akamatsu (1956).
8. Shimada (1988) characterises the Japanese production system as the humanware model.
9. For our basic angle to the Japanese production system, see Abo (1994a), chs 1 and 2, and Itagaki (1994b). Also Dore (1973), Shirai (1982), Koike (1988), Aoki (1988), Tanaka (1988), Imai and Komiya (1994) and Aoki and Dore (1994) are useful to understand the Japanese corporate system.
10. Hymer (1976) and Buckley and Casson (1985).
11. Clark and Fujimoto (1991).
12. Recently, Korean electronics companies have entered the market and Japanese monopoly was broken.
13. For a comparison between the Japanese corporate system and the American system, see Cole (1979), Abegglen and Stalk (1985), Aoki (1988), Koike (1988), Dertouzos *et al.* (1989), Womack *et al.* (1990), Kenney and Florida (1993), Suzuki (1991), Kogut (1993) and Itagaki (1994).
14. Porter (1990).
15. Lewchuk (1987) describes the process by which Ford tried to import its mass production system into Great Britain, faced various difficulties, and finally created a 'hybrid system'; that is, 'the British system of mass production'.
16. Abo (1994c) and Abo (1992).

1 Basic Characteristics of the Japanese Production System and the Hybrid Evaluation Model

Hiroshi Itagaki

I CHARACTERISTICS OF THE JAPANESE PRODUCTION SYSTEM

Functional Core

Functionally, the Japanese production system is characterised by small-lot production on a diverse product line, achieved through techniques including just-in-time procurement practices, and based on mass-production technology. It enables companies to achieve high production efficiency and high product quality on the shop floor, while responding quickly to fluctuating and diverse market needs (see Figure 1.1).

It is well known that the processing and assembly sector of manufacturing industries, represented here by the auto industry, which took root in Japan after the Second World War and which grew dramatically during the period of high economic growth, learned various systems from US companies such as production management and quality control. Its model was the mass production system, often referred to as the Ford production system. The basic characteristic of that system was its intensive pursuit of economies of scale. In such as system, one, or a few kinds of, product(s) or component(s) are produced en masse at specialised factories equipped with large-scale, single-purpose machines and conveyor belts. Semi-skilled and unskilled workers, whose task areas are extremely narrow and fixed, are assigned to those machines or conveyors. An ample inventory of parts is produced and stocked for every manufacturing process in every factory so that defective products or missing parts do not delay the production schedule.[1]

It was impossible, however, for Japanese companies to introduce the US system in its original form, since Japan had much smaller markets in

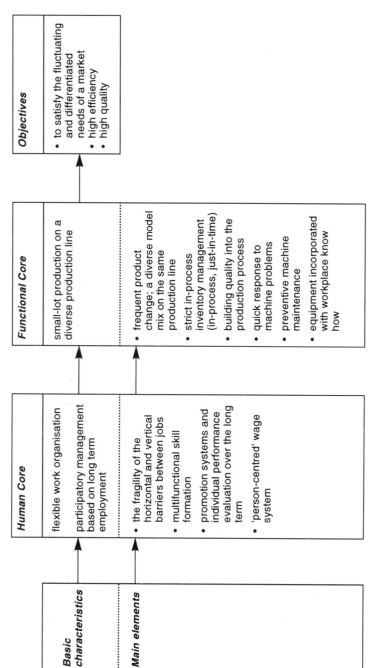

Figure 1.1   The core of the Japanese production system (within plants)

which numerous manufacturers (for example, over ten companies in the case of the auto industry) were in competition. They were compelled either to produce several models simultaneously on each production line, or to make small lots of each model and make frequent changes to the models produced on a line. If a large inventory had been carried for each model, profits would undoubtedly have been consumed by the costs of managing and providing space for this. Therefore, 'just-in-time practices' (or 'producing and procuring only what is necessary and just when it is necessary') was needed as a method of exercising thorough control over inventories.[2] Also, companies had to devise ways of changing dies, jigs and tools quickly, in order to accommodate different models produced on the same line.

Japanese manufacturing industries, particularly their processing and assembly sectors, have shown international competitive strength since the 1970s. This is not only because small, light, energy-efficient products that were adapted to Japanese conditions succeeded in penetrating US and European markets, where resource restrictions and environmental problems captured the public attention. Nor was it only because Japanese manufacturers were able to supply low-priced, mass-produced goods. Although these factors are not negligible, what is more important is that the production system was able to satisfy completely the fluctuating and differentiated needs of a mature market in advanced, high-income countries. Moreover, if total demand remained stable, companies could standardise their production volume by changing model mix proportions in accordance with demand fluctuation in the market. In this way, companies were able to secure a certain level of sales, and decrease excess inventory and equipment.[3]

Quality competitiveness is also crucial. As inventories are minimised, the entire production system is exposed to the danger of being paralysed by quality defects among in-process products or among parts procured externally. Japanese manufacturers have adopted quality control methods that differ from those of US companies, where workers devote themselves solely to production and where defective products are rejected during final product inspection. In contrast to this, Japanese companies have tried to achieve the type of quality control called 'building quality into the process.' This is a method by which not only quality control specialists but also ordinary production workers pay meticulous attention to product quality to avoid producing defective products. Ordinary production workers themselves try to maintain quality and not pass defective products on to the next stage in the manufacturing process by following standard work procedures that include quality checks on specific items. If defective products are discovered, the quality control division, production workers and inspectors determine the causes, and divisions from the shop floor to production equipment, and even to product design, co-operate in taking measures to ensure that such defects do not recur. As a result, know-how and product quality devices are built into the production equipment and incorporated into product design. The quality competitiveness of Japanese manufacturing companies has advanced remarkably under this type of strict quality control.

Superior machine maintenance has also contributed to the competitive strength of Japanese manufacturing firms. Long downtime of production equipment cannot be tolerated any more than defective products. To guard against such downtime, Japanese companies have developed preventive maintenance practices through which employees pay constant, meticulous attention to equipment. They have also established a maintenance system in which the maintenance division and the shop floor co-operate closely and respond quickly to machine breakdown. Maintenance technicians, whose expertise is cultivated internally over a long period of time, and who are well acquainted with the characteristics and dispositions of the various machines, are free to enter the shop floor at any time, and they play important roles ranging from preventive maintenance to trouble-shooting. One of the factors behind efficient maintenance is ordinary workers constantly cleaning and inspecting their machines, and, in the case of minor breakdowns, sometimes being able to solve problems. Based on these practices, the wisdom and know-how accumulated on the shop floor have been incorporated into machines and products, where they improve machine operating capacity (as well as product quality) as a result of close communication between the shop floor, production engineering, and design and development divisions.

Finally, the competitiveness of Japanese manufacturing industries has also benefited from the vigorous application of microelectronics (ME) devices. Since the 1970s, the utilisation of ME devices in Japanese plants has progressed more rapidly than in the United States or European countries. This has occurred because multifunctional skill formation and flexible work organisation, which are discussed in the following section, are well-suited to the application of these devices to production equipment and products. Machines equipped with ME devices are associated with a dramatic increase in labour productivity and remarkably fewer errors than those which require manual operation. The full utilisation of ME components has also yielded higher functionality in products and reduced the number of product parts, resulting in trends towards fewer problems and lower energy consumption.

The Human and Organisational Core of the System

Flexible Work Organisation and General and Multiskill Formation

The organisational core of the production system lies in the work organisation and methods of skill formation cultivated on the shop floor. Problem-solving methods illustrate well the characteristics of plant management and work organisation in Japanese companies. All problems that arise in the workplace, whether minor or serious, are solved by the many different employees involved in plant operations and through close co-operation among the various departments concerned.

To paraphrase, the important point is the fragility of the horizontal and vertical barriers between jobs. While vertical barriers exist in a formal sense, their fragility in practical terms means that there is relatively little difference between the levels of authority that exist at different positions in the organisational hierarchy at Japanese companies. In other words, a wide range of employees, including those stationed in the lower part of the hierarchy, actively participate in plant management. It is through their participation that information and knowledge accumulated on the shop floor feed directly or indirectly back into the improvement of product quality and production efficiency. Managers and engineers also enter the shop floor regularly and try to solve whatever problems occur, in close co-operation with production workers. This is often referred to as 'workplace-orientated' management.

The fragility of horizontal barriers signifies that job areas assigned to individual workers are not rigidly fixed. Job tasks are assigned to *han* or *kumi*, which represent the work team as the smallest unit of work organisation on the shop floor. This makes it possible to expand or contract the range of job tasks set for each worker according to the extent of his/her skills. Also, job tasks for individual workers can be reassigned flexibly in response to changes in the model mix or to the introduction of new models or machines. Moreover, the fragility of horizontal barriers between jobs facilitates job rotation so that workers can experience different but related jobs in succession, not only on the same production line but frequently beyond. Job rotation, in turn, creates multiskilled workers whose existence is necessary for the flexible work organisation mentioned above, and it promotes employees' understanding about and interest in the overall production process.

There is a frail partition between 'direct work' – namely, the operation of production machinery – and 'indirect work' – jobs such as quality control and machinery maintenance. To some extent, therefore, direct workers often participate in indirect work, and communication and co-ordination between direct and indirect workers is smooth and effective. Therefore, multiskilled workers have not only mastered a broad variety of job tasks at a given level, but have also acquired diverse skills enabling them to participate, to some extent, in job areas that require a more sophisticated problem-solving ability. Furthermore, some companies select ordinary shop-floor workers to be groomed as maintenance specialists. This illustrates how the existence of weak horizontal barriers between job categories themselves also facilitates the dismantling of vertical barriers. Such general and multifunctional skills are crucial for the Japanese production system.

Companies emphasise job rotation, especially for key employees whom they wish to cultivate as *sagyōchō* (first-line supervisors) and who require a broad understanding of the conditions existing on the shop floor. These first-line supervisors play important roles as intermediaries between managers and ordinary workers, conveying managers' intentions to the shop floor and transmitting workers' demands and views to managers. They also play critical roles in achieving co-ordination on the shop floor as well as between the shop floor and other sections, and they play a leading role in *kaizen* (improvement) activities, which are a key element of the Japanese production system.

It should be noted, however, that the elements introduced above, namely small-lot production on a diverse product line, workplace-orientated management with fragile vertical and horizontal barriers between job areas, and multifunctional skill formation, do not always function effectively, nor do they always succeed in strengthening the competitiveness of the manufacturing industries. In fact, workplace-orientated management is most effective in the processing and assembly sector of manufacturing industries, as demonstrated by their keen international competitive edge. It is not so effective in certain other industries, such as the chemical industry, which, despite sharing similar characteristics of organisation and skill formation, lag behind in international competition.[4]

'Co-operation and Competition' and 'Hierarchy and Egalitarianism'

Organisational mechanisms are required to create flexible work organisation and promote general and multifunctional skill formation over the long term. These mechanisms are the wage and promotion systems. A framework for the wage system is illustrated in the wage table of an in-house qualification system.[5] This table is composed of a series of *kyū* (ranks), subdivided into *gō* (steps). The starting *kyū* of new employees are mainly determined by academic background, and later they advance up the *gō* and *kyū* according to length of service and *jinji kōka* (individual performance evaluation). This is a 'person-centred' wage system, in contrast to a 'job-centred' wage system where jobs determine wage rates. Since wages are not determined by jobs, they do not impede job rotation or the overlapping of job demarcations. This system encourages employees to serve for an extended period at one company, since a greater proportion of the wages of Japanese workers is determined by length of service than is the case in other countries. Another characteristic of the Japanese wage system is the equal treatment accorded to white-collar and blue-collar employees. For example, individual performance evaluations are carried out on both types of employee, and the wage–salary distinction is generally not present. Another salient feature of the Japanese wage system is the narrower gap in the wage level between white-collar and blue-collar employees and, accordingly, the smaller wage differences overall among employees in the entire corporate hierarchy. This is one of the factors that facilitate participation in management on the part of a wide range of employees.

The key points of the Japanese wage and promotion systems are that, not only length of service but also performance evaluation are determining factors, and that employees are evaluated and promoted over a long period of time. Therefore, until a certain age, usually the early thirties, rank and wage differences among same-age employees are not very large. Later these differences increase although, as mentioned above, never to the extent observed in other countries. This is another mechanism that encourages management participation by a wide range of employees. Also, unlike the faulty stereotyped understanding of *nenkō-sei* (seniority system), there is considerable competition among employees on the basis of their long-term evaluation. Elements evaluated include not only individual skills and knowledge, but also co-operation with colleagues, instruction offered to younger co-workers, and co-ordination with employees in other divisions. In this way, 'co-operation and competition' intertwine within the system.

Because of the existence of in-house qualifications and multiple ranks (*kyū*), the gaps between vertical ranks within the hierarchy of a Japanese company are sometimes misinterpreted as being fairly wide. In fact, these ranks have nothing to do with job categories, nor are they necessarily linked with authority. Rather, compared with other countries, large Japanese corporations are characterised by egalitarian systems with regard to both wages and authority. Of course, minute differences among in-house qualifications are usually regarded as being important in terms of prestige. It is in this sense that 'hierarchy and egalitarianism' also intertwine within the Japanese system. There is also no formal ceiling for promotion from the shop floor. Production workers may 'naturally' become promoted to first-line supervisors in the course of time or, but less frequently, to middle or even upper positions in the corporate hierarchy. These promotion practices help to narrow the gap between the authority of different positions in the hierarchy, and maintain the workplace-orientated nature of the operation that produces close co-operation between management and the shop floor.

Some Objections to the Japanese System

The Japanese production system is not without its critics. Some question whether the system does in fact incorporate rational factors or offer internationally competitive advantages. Or, they argue, if these factors and advantages existed in the past, they are rapidly disappearing today. Particularly during the economic slump since the early 1990s, this negative appraisal of the Japanese system has prevailed among many scholars as well as among the mass media. Their arguments commonly point out that the characteristics (and at the same time, problems) of the Japanese system are lifetime (long-term) employment, the *nenkō* (seniority) system, and employees' strong sense of belonging to a company, as well as group-orientated management stemming from the lifetime employment/*nenkō* system, in-house labour unions, cross shareholdings, and the *keiretsu* (enterprise groupings).[6] With regard to the basic characteristics of the Japanese production system discussed above, they insist that lifetime employment and the *nenkō* system have lost their rationale and it is now impossible to maintain them.

The weakness of such arguments is, firstly, that they overlook or play down the advantages of a flexible work organisation and a broad and multifunctional skill formation within the context of long-term employment. They maintain that the international competitive strength of Japanese manufacturing companies is attributed to nothing more than hard work and long hours of labour, sustained by employees' loyalty and sense of belonging to a company or enterprise group, itself created by lifetime employment and the *nenkō* system. It is difficult, however, for these arguments to explain the considerable disparities that exist between the average labour productivity of auto plants in Japan and those in the United States or Europe, pointed out by Womack *et al.* (1990), and to explain why high productivity and high quality co-exist in many Japanese plants.

These arguments are unable to pinpoint the factors that lead Japanese auto companies in the United States to achieve better performance, in terms of productivity and product quality, than US companies.[7] Another difficulty with these arguments, as Takanashi (1994) points out, is that they fail to account for the fact that the fundamental structure of long-term employment and of the *nenkō* system have remained unchanged since the period of low economic growth following the first oil shock in the mid-1970s, although their demise has been predicted during every economic downturn since the early 1960s, when the Japanese economy was at the peak of its 'miracle' years. Of course, certain aspects of the corporate system, as well as of the overall economic system, have not adjusted to changes in the social environment, and have been maintained in their original state for a considerable period of time. Calls for the drastic reform of Japanese management and for deregulation, based on faith in the market mechanism, reveal a sense of crisis in the face of such situations. For these reasons, long-term employment and the *nenkō* system will also inevitably experience some revision, although certainly not to any radical extent. The basic characteristics of the Japanese system with its broad, multifunctional skill formation methods based on long-term employment and participatory management will be maintained far into the future, and rightly so.

Another weakness of the simple 'cultural approach' argument is its attempt to attribute the international competitive strength of Japanese companies to cultural features such as groupism and employees' sense of belonging to a company. These cultural features are indeed pervasive among Japanese organisations, ranging from private firms to government offices and universities so, at first glance, this approach seems to offer a persuasive explanation of the characteristics of the Japanese organisation. However, on closer examination, it becomes apparent that features of Japanese organisations such as groupism do not lead directly to the efficient operation of an organisation or to strong international competitiveness. This is well demonstrated by the inefficiency of the former National Railroad Corporation, or of universities in Japan, setting aside the question of whether efficiency is required in universities. Such Japanese organisations lack the competitive aspect of 'co-operation and competition', which is connected more strongly with institutional elements such as performance evaluations than with cultural elements. Moreover, the cultural approach shares a weakness with the critical views of the Japanese management system mentioned above; namely, its neglect of flexible work organisation and multifunctional skill formation.

The second type of criticism emphasises the dark side of the Japanese system by arguing that the admitted flexibility and efficiency of the Japanese production system are sustained by long hours of highly intensive labour and close (formal and informal) human relations, which keep employees disciplined within the 'community' of the workplace. Such arguments contend that the reason workers comply with management's efforts to achieve flexibility and efficiency, often at their own great expense, is that managerial 'supervision' and 'compulsion' compel workers to participate in plant operation. This is because the management system puts workers who move from company to company at a disadvantage, thus effectively tying workers to a single company. Second, the arguments maintain that labour unions, which should normally curb the power of management, only have a small degree of regulating power against management because they are in-house unions.[8]

It has never been the intention of this writer to suggest that Japanese companies have created workplace paradises brimming with solidarity, fraternity and voluntarism. There is no doubt that, for example, *jinji kōka* (performance evaluation) and the promotion system based on it, the favourite targets for this type of criticism, are shrewd mechanisms that allow companies to take advantage of the competitive spirit of employees', as well as their co-operative and voluntary attitudes. However, in terms of a 'compulsory' nature of such participation, such arguments are far removed from the realities that exist within Japanese companies.

In the first place, Japanese corporate systems are not maintained solely by voluntary 'sacrifices' offered by employees. Employee participation in and co-operation with management, sometimes accompanied by long hours of overtime, should be regarded as part of a package that includes opportunities to acquire knowledge and skills, job security, opportunities for promotion based on such knowledge and skills, and fringe benefits such as employee welfare programmes. A broader give-and-take relationship that cannot be calculated in monetary terms alone exists between a company and its employees. Studies of Japanese corporate systems that neglect to consider these aspects of this relationship deserve to be criticised as biased interpretations.[9]

Second, the manner of posing the problem itself, namely debating whether participation is 'voluntary' or 'compulsory and managed', or contrasting 'democratic' behaviours with 'controlled' procedures, relies excessively upon 'Westernised' dichotomies produced by a society wherein a managerial class and a labour class are in confrontation. It is difficult for this kind of dichotomous approach to deal with the issue of participation in the Japanese system that is characterised by the intertwining of 'co-operation and competition' or of 'hierarchy and the egalitarianism'.[10]

Third, this second type of criticism plays down the significance of the fact that in the Japanese system, not only the elite within the corporate hierarchy but also ordinary workers at the shop floor, and others, participate in management and develop innovative ideas that contribute to achieving high efficiency and high quality. Furthermore, as was the case with the first type of criticism, it fails to explain how Japanese affiliates in the United States achieve a high level of management performance.[11] Some insist, of course, that Japanese affiliates in the United States share many problems with factories located in Japan.[12] However, they cannot shed light on why many blue-collar workers in the United States and Great Britain, as opposed to many managerial personnel, basically accept and welcome management by Japanese affiliates, even though it is much easier for employees to change companies in these countries than in Japan.[13]

The problem with Japanese companies is to be found in a style of management that relies on and endeavours to maintain and enhance employee homogeneity rather than enforce compulsory participation. This mechanism is both the precondition and result of the co-operation–competition system or the give-and-take relationship between a company and its employees. This can be called a management system that shuns heterogeneity or, in more moderate terms, a system that is poor at managing heterogeneous elements. However, not only is this possibly unethical, but from a strategic point of view it may also be unwise. In Japanese companies in the future, it is reasonable to anticipate an increase in the number of highly specialised people who move from company to company in search of higher salaries, and the existence of employees with more diversified lifestyles, unlike 'company-centered people.' Increasing heterogeneity will therefore inevitably force Japanese companies to face the problem of maintaining the nucleus of their system; namely, the multifunctional skill formation based on long-term employment in core parts of their organisations. In that sense, the operation of foreign subsidiaries is a valuable experience for Japanese companies as they prepare to manage Japanese systems in the near future.

II   HYBRID EVALUATION MODEL OF THE JAPANESE PRODUCTION SYSTEM

One of the basic propositions of the theory of multinational enterprises, as expressed by scholars ranging from Steven Hymer to internalisation theorists, is that companies must transfer their own competitive advantages to their foreign subsidiaries.[14] Needless to say, in order to achieve their competitive strength, Japanese companies must also, to some degree, transfer the advantages of their managerial resources, which consist of human and organisational elements, to their foreign operations. Such local production systems are strongly influenced by the economic structures, value systems, cultures, institutions and histories, of their respective home countries, and in particular, the organisational aspects of such systems are closely intertwined with the behavioural patterns, attitudes and value systems existing in those societies.[15]

Various economic, historical and international factors such as government control during the Second World War, high economic growth in the civilian sector along with a de-emphasis on the military sector in the period immediately following the war, and the sharp decline of economic growth rates after the first oil shock, have contributed to the formation of the Japanese management and production system. Also, the characteristics of Japanese society – in other words, a homogeneous, co-operative society whose people share a common sense of values and behavioural patterns and where interpersonal understanding is achieved with relatively little effort – have undoubtedly played a certain role in constructing the Japanese production system. This homogeneous, co-operative society can be paraphrased as follows: it is a society without notable ethnic or religious diversity. There is no clear manifestation of social class, and disparities between value systems and incomes have rapidly narrowed, particularly since the end of the Second World War. It is a society where a belief that people should emphasise harmony and trust over individual freedom (including the freedom to take advantage of others for short-term profits) governs behaviour within and among organisations to a remarkable degree.

It is doubtful whether work organisation characterised by flexible job assignment and job rotation, and by interorganisational co-ordination and co-operation, a give-and-take relationship between a company and its employees through long-term employment, and long-term transactions between companies, frequently referred to as *keiretsu*, can be formed in the absence of the characteristics of Japanese society.[16]

It is true, as Aoki (1988) remarks, that the preconditions for a system are not necessarily indispensable for that system to function effectively. However, as Takamiya (1979) points out, neither is it a trivial task to transfer a production system to a country that has a different managerial environment. The combination of elements in the system and conditions in host countries makes it easier for some elements to be transferred than others. In some cases the transfer may result in tangible or intangible costs, including friction with local employees. The degree of necessity for transferring a particular element depends on corporate strategy, which may be determined by the specific features of the managerial advantages of a company and/or industry, the motivation behind pursuing local production, competitive conditions in the host countries and so on. A company may have to transfer certain elements, even at the risk of incurring costs. In contrast, a company will have to abandon transferring elements when costs outweigh benefits. In some cases it may be more beneficial for a company's local production to introduce elements native to the host country. Conversely, it may be preferable not to transfer certain other elements, no matter how necessary they may be considered.

The arguments put forward in this book are based on an analytical framework for the Japanese production system overseas called the 'Hybrid Evaluation Model' or 'Application–adaptation Analysis Model'. In this model, application refers to the behaviour of transplanting Japanese elements of the Japanese production system into the host countries, and adaptation refers to the act of introducing elements native to the host countries. The Hybrid Evaluation Model is an analytical framework used to compare the configurations of application and adaptation among different countries.

This model was originally constructed as an analytical framework to evaluate application and adaptation of the Japanese production system at Japanese affiliates in the United States. This model comprises twenty-three items, considered key elements in the international transfer of a Japanese production system characterised by small-lot production on a diverse product line and based upon flexible, participatory work organisation, with weak vertical and horizontal barriers separating job categories. These items are divided into six groups, according to attribute, and each item is submitted to a five-point evaluation concerning the extent of its application and adaptation (see Table 1.1 and Figure 1.2). Note that this is sometimes referred to as the '23-element, 6-group evaluation' in order to distinguish it from the '4-perspective evaluation' mentioned later. Five points are awarded if a Japanese affiliate abroad introduces almost the same practices or materials as does the parent plant in Japan, and one point if it adopts systems or practices that resemble those of the host countries. An award of three points for degree of application indicates that practices or elements are adopted that stand midway between these two extremes. Thus, the degree of application illustrates the extent of the mixture; that is, the hybridisation of the Japanese and host country systems. The main research theme for the study that was carried out in the

Table 1.1 Hybrid Evaluation Model

Item	1	2	3	4	5		
I Work Organisation and Administration							
① Job classification							
② Multifunctional skills							
③ Education and training							
④ Wage system							
⑤ Promotion							
⑥ First-line supervisor							
II Production Control							
⑦ Equipment							
⑧ Maintenance							
⑨ Quality control							
⑩ Process management							
III Procurement							
⑪ Local content							
⑫ Suppliers							
⑬ Procurement method							
IV Group Consciousness							
⑭ Small-group activities							
⑮ Information sharing							
⑯ Sense of unity							
V Labour Relations							
⑰ Hiring policy							
⑱ Long-term employment							
⑲ Harmonious labour relations							
⑳ Grievance procedure							
VI Parent–Subsidiary Relations							
㉑ Ratio of Japanese expatriates							
㉒ Delegation of authority							
㉓ Position of local managers							
Average of 23 items							

United States was the application of this analytical tool in examining precisely how and why a particular hybrid configuration was formed.

A few words should be added with regard to application and adaptation. As mentioned, five points reflects a situation that is almost the same as that of a parent plant in Japan. However, it is quite natural that practices and systems in Japan differ in emphasis among industries, among

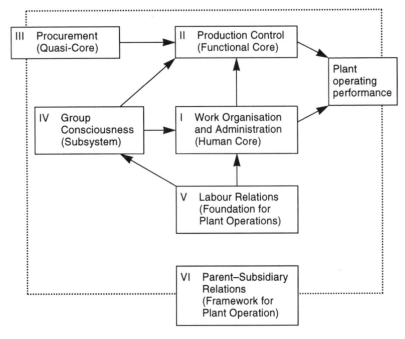

Figure 1.2   Hybrid Evaluation Model

companies in the same industry, and even among plants of the same company. In that sense, the Japanese production system that serves as a criterion for determining a five-point application is an ideal abstraction of various characteristics that exist at individual companies and in their respective industries. However, though it is an idealisation, it should be emphasised that extensive plant observations in Japan were carried out (more than a hundred plants were visited) in order to construct the Hybrid Evaluation Model.

The same holds for adaptation, which refers to the act of adapting to environmental conditions and systems native to the host countries. The ideal case of adaptation in the context of the United States is that of a traditional mass production system, often called the Ford production system, which matured and reached its peak of prosperity in the 1950s and 1960s. In fact there are differences between companies or industries, and moreover, recent production systems in the United States are being overhauled through the partial introduction of elements of the Japanese system – as seen, for example, in auto companies such as GM's Saturn plant, or in the product development processes at Chrysler, or in general innovation processes referred to as the re-engineering revolution. Therefore, adaptation, in the case of the research carried out in the United States, also employed an idealisation as its criterion, rather than concrete, individual cases that exist at present.

In the course of this research in Asia, which is the subject of this book, basically the same Hybrid Evaluation Model was applied for the analytical framework as during the research that was carried out in the United States. This was done to permit an examination of Japanese affiliates in Asian countries from a consistent perspective. However, environmental differences in the host countries surveyed did necessitate certain revisions in the Hybrid Evaluation Model. Revisions concerning the basic evaluation criteria will be discussed here, while those concerning specific individual items will be explained in the notes to the respective sections dealing with those items.

As mentioned above, adaptation is defined as the act of introducing practices native to the host countries. However, it is difficult to identify an established production system in a specific Asian host country, such as 'a Korean production system' or 'a Malaysian production system', unlike in the United States, for example, and therefore the criteria for evaluating adaptation are extremely vague. Even assuming that specific systems in individual host countries could be recognised through repeated and detailed surveys, it would be too complicated to establish different criteria corresponding to each of the five host countries. Therefore, the degrees of application in this book reveal solely the extent of the penetration of Japanese elements in Japanese affiliates, so that five points means the introduction of the same elements that exist at plants in Japan, and one point indicates an absence of Japanese elements.

Those areas where Japanese elements cannot be identified are considered simply as examples of adaptation, even though, strictly speaking, there should be an examination of specifically what elements are being adapted to. Perhaps they are elements of the US system, which, since the mid-twentieth century, has had a strong influence on many countries as a method of organising modern industries. In the case of Malaysia and Singapore, they might be elements of a British system of organisation that was transferred during the colonial era. Also, some countries may have developed their own production systems for organising modern industries, at least partially, just as in Japan, where a system initially modelled after US and European systems ultimately developed a unique flavour. Furthermore, as is often the case in countries that have only recently embarked on the path of industrialisation, company organisations may be affected directly by mechanisms and practices that existed in its own pre-industrialised society. In any case, the concept of adaptation as it is applied throughout this book is based on a combination of the various elements mentioned above.

By the same token, since the system of the host country is not clear, it is impossible to determine conclusively whether the elements that are the same as those in Japan are, in fact, transferred from Japan, or whether practices native to the host country happen to coincide with Japanese elements. Particularly in the case of Taiwan and Korea, which share historical and cultural characteristics with Japan, there is a strong possibility that practices that are the same as those at plants in Japan, do not originate from Japan. The influence of the period of Japanese colonisation also cannot be neglected. Although leftovers from the colonial period are certainly elements that came from Japan, they differ from the application of the Japanese system at issue at present. While exploring and classifying such differences may be a task worthy of subsequent research, in this book, the degrees of application are scored according to the extent to which Japanese elements are transferred.[17]

Application is also divided into two types. One type is where companies transfer elements of the Japanese system, unmodified, to the host countries. Though this is the usual type of application, it has the potential for creating friction with the local environment and even for reducing managerial performance. The other type of application is that where companies transfer the spirit or essence of the Japanese system by shrewdly utilising, but altering, the form of local elements. This latter type may be referred to as 'revised application', to distinguish it from the former variety. This type of revised application, although not seen that frequently yet, is likely to become increasingly significant in transplanting and establishing Japanese systems among Japanese local operations abroad.

The following sections will briefly introduce aspects of the Hybrid Evaluation Model, along with some additional elaboration about those elements of the Japanese production system that have not yet been explained. Readers can refer to the table appended to this chapter for more detailed item evaluation criteria.

I   Work Organisation and Administration

The group entitled 'Work Organisation and Administration' comprises six core human factors of the Japanese production system, which is characterised by flexible work organisation and multifunctional skill formation through long-term employment. The degree of application for ① *Job classification* corresponds to whether or not obvious institutional and formal barriers between job categories exist, such that the absence of barriers enables flexible assignment of employees to individual job tasks. Of course, the weaker the barrier separating job categories, the higher the score for degrees of application. It should be noted, therefore, that the degree of application is determined not by the actual rigidity of job assignments but by the existence of institutional and formal barriers. ② *Multifunctional skills* is evaluated on the basis of the variety and versatility of employee skills. ③ *Education and training* corresponds to the extent to which in-house education and training systems emphasising OJT (on-the-job training) are introduced so that employees are able to acquire skills by experiencing various jobs. Sending key personnel to Japan for training and sending Japanese trainers to the local plants are also considered as raising the degree of application for this item. ④ *Wage system* is evaluated in consideration of whether the system adopts a person-centred or job-centred approach. ⑤ *Promotion* involves appraising the extent of internal promotion and determining the factors of promotion for production workers. First-line supervisors, referred to as *sagyōchō* or *hanchō*, manage shop-floor work teams and play important, diverse roles for the production processes, labour management and *kaizen* activities in Japan. The degree of application for ⑥ *First-line supervisor* is determined by considering their roles and abilities and whether they are promoted internally or recruited from outside.

II Production Control

'Production Control' consists of four core functional elements of the Japanese production system. In ⑦ *Equipment*, the issue is whether Japanese affiliates utilise the same kind of equipment that parent plants utilise at the same time in Japan. If the equipment comes from Japan but is of an older generation and no longer used in Japan, then the application for this item is scored lower. If advanced machinery equipped with sophisticated electronics devices is utilised, then machine maintenance, including preventive maintenance to keep machines running smoothly and measures that allow rapid response to problems, become more crucial. Application scores for ⑧ *Maintenance* are determined by considering whether plants cultivate maintenance workers through in-house training or recruit experienced technicians from outside. The extent to which ordinary production workers participate in activities such as preventive maintenance, and plant maintenance records as reflected by the ratio of machine stoppage to operating hours, are also taken into consideration. Application for

⑨ *Quality Control* is evaluated by examining whether plants introduce methods for building quality into the production process or adopt procedures for rejecting defective products during final product inspection. Other factors are the way ordinary production workers participate in securing quality, and differences in in-process defect ratios or product quality at the shipment stage, between plants in Japan and plants of affiliates abroad, as well as the extent of such differences. In judging application for ⑩ *Process management*, it is necessary to examine the frequency of product change, the extent of product mixing, operating efficiency, *kaizen* activities, inventory management and so on. This makes it possible to determine whether or not small-lot production on a diverse product line is carried out smoothly, whether or not plants characteristically mass-produce a few models, and whether or not production lines operate efficiently.

III   Procurement

The relationship between the companies that assemble final products and those that supply the necessary parts and materials is a crucial element that sustains the Japanese production system and which has not yet been mentioned. Although the subcontracting system is often cited as an example of such a relationship, the pecking order of this hierarchy is not necessarily one of its salient points. Rather, the vital element is that high-quality parts and materials, which are indispensable for small-lot production on a diverse product line, are supplied in timely co-ordination with the activity of the production lines at the assembly companies (just-in-time or multiple daily deliveries). Such co-ordination is achieved on the basis of a long-term, trusting relationship, and technical exchange between assembly companies and their suppliers of materials and parts or components. In addition, in Japan, co-operation with the assembly companies and participation in the development of new product models by component suppliers also helps to bring about the advantages of the so-called design-in practice.[18]

The performance of Japanese affiliates in foreign countries is completely dependent upon their ability to procure parts and materials of good quality and reasonable price, and upon the extent to which they can transfer their supplier relationships, mentioned above, to the host countries. On the other hand, in consideration of matters concerning employment, the balance of trade, and technology transfer, host countries usually require Japanese affiliates to increase local content. Even Japanese companies themselves need to raise local content because of cost increases brought about by the strength of the yen. In examining procurement, it is also necessary to look at the roles played by Japanese affiliated component suppliers that accompanied assemblers when they first embarked on local overseas production, or which, at the request of the assembly companies, came later and began production in the host countries in order to allow the assembly companies to procure highly functional, quality parts, and at the same time to increase local content. The group Procurement is considered to be a quasi-core of the system because, although crucial, it concerns relationships that extend outside of the plants. In this group, application for ⑪ *Local content* is evaluated according to the proportion of parts produced locally and procured (the higher the proportion, the lower the application). Application for ⑫ *Suppliers* is determined by the extent to which a plant relies upon plants in Japan or their affiliates in host or third countries; and for ⑬ *Procurement method*, is based on how special long-term transaction relations between parts suppliers and just-in-time practices are transferred.

IV   Group Consciousness
Practices such as small-group activities or ritual gatherings at the start of the working day, which are dealt with in Group Consciousness, facilitate employees' participation in management and enhance their sense of unity. Although these practices are often considered to be typical of Japanese management, they are seen as a subsystem that makes preparations for transplanting core elements of the Japanese system into the host countries. The application of ⑭ *Small-group activities* is evaluated by considering the following questions: Are small group activities such as QC circles or ZD (zero defect) movements carried out? If a Japanese affiliate does practice such activities, what is the rate of employee participation? What is the motivation and what are the incentives for employee participation in small group activities? And, finally, what are the effects of these activities? ⑮ *Information sharing* is evaluated by considering communication within the company, the perception of employees' opinions by managers, and the disclosure of managerial information through meetings and gatherings at all levels. ⑯ *Sense of unity* is evaluated by considering the following items: cafeterias open to all employees; uniforms; open-style offices; and company-wide social events such as picnics, parties or sports activities.

V   Labour Relations
The issue is whether and how well labour relations are maintained. The elements in this group are thought to constitute the necessary foundation

for the transfer of core and subsystems. Application for ⑰ *Hiring method* is evaluated by examining whether plants select employees carefully, including ordinary production workers, who are willing to participate in management and willing to implement ideas and devices necessary for the Japanese-style production system. ⑱ *Long-term employment* concerns the stability of employees' relationships with the company, and the types of measure adopted to motivate employees to remain with the company for a long time. These comprise the foundation of broad, multifunctional skill formation and employees' sense of belonging to the company. ⑲ *Harmonious labour relations* is evaluated by considering whether the plant succeeds in creating good labour relations, what type of things the company pays attention to in order to achieve good relations, and what kinds of resources it commits to this. Evaluating application for ⑳ *Grievance procedure* concerns the extent of the efforts that are made to perceive and understand employees' complaints and demands such as for improvements in the work environment.

VI   Parent-Subsidiary Relations
This group is evaluated by examining the extent to which the parent companies delegate authority to the Japanese affiliates, and how such authority is shared between local managers and Japanese expatriates within the company. The elements of this Parent–Subsidiary Relations group constitute the framework for plant operation. Application for ㉑ *Ratio of Japanese expatriates* is determined through a simple calculation of the ratio of Japanese personnel to the total number of employees at the local production plant. ㉒ *Delegation of authority* concerns aspects of decision-making in areas including product, market, investment, local personnel and R&D activities. If major decisions are made at the local plants of the Japanese affiliates, this is evaluated as low application. Application for ㉓ *Position of local managers* is evaluated by considering whether local managers or Japanese expatriates have more decision-making authority, and how they share responsibility. The stronger the authority of local managers, the lower the application, and vice versa.

III   FOUR-PERSPECTIVE EVALUATION

As mentioned above, the Hybrid Evaluation Model provides the analytical framework for examining the hybridisation of application and adaptation

Table 1.2   Items of four-perspective evaluation

	Methods	*Results*

Human	Human–methods
	All items in I: 'Work
	  Organisation and Administration'
	All items in IV: 'Group
	  Consciousness
	⑱ Long-term employment
	⑳ Grievance procedure
		Human–results
		㉑ Ratio of Japanese expatriates
		㉓ Position of local managers

Material	Material–Methods ⑧ Maintenance ⑨ Quality control ⑬ Procurement method	Material–Results ⑨ Equipment ⑪ Local content ⑫ Suppliers

by local plants as managerial entities, from six perspectives including core human and functional factors, quasi-core factors, and the subsystem. An additional tool to analyse the international transfer of the Japanese production system by four element attributes called 'method', 'result', 'human', and 'material', is the 'Four-Perspective Evaluation'. The Hybrid Evaluation Model is first divided into two major categories: 'method' and 'result'. 'Method' refers to the application of the management methods and institutions which are themselves characteristic of the Japanese production system. 'Result' refers to bringing directly in from Japan existing elements such as personnel, equipment and parts. Each of these categories is then subdivided into two further categories: 'human' and 'material'.

'Human–method' consists of all the items in Work Organisation and Administration, and Group Consciousness, plus two items, Long-term employment and Grievance procedure from the group Labour Relations. 'Material–method' consists of three items: Maintenance, Quality control, and Procurement method. 'Human–result' includes two items: Ratio of Japanese expatriates and Position of local managers, and 'material–result' has three items: Equipment, Local content, and suppliers (see Table 1.2). Both of these analytical frameworks, namely the Hybrid Evaluation Model and the Four-Perspective Evaluation are applied throughout the following chapters.

Appendix Table 1.1 Criteria for Application (Hybrid) Evaluation

I WORK ORGANISATION AND ADMINISTRATION

① Job classification (JC)
This is concerned with the existence of overt institutional barriers between jobs, such as job classifications. It is evaluated not by considering the flexibility of actual job assignment, but by considering the presence of institutional and formal barriers. If no such barriers exist, then five points are assigned for this item. If barriers are found, criteria for assigning points are as follows:
5: Number of JC is 2 or less
4: 3–5
3: 6–10
2: 11–50
1: 51 or more

② Multifunctional skills
5: Job rotation (JR) is normally implemented within work teams and also planned and carried out beyond work teams in order to develop multiskilled workers (for example, a training table is kept and utilised by supervisors). Ordinary production workers participate actively in ensuring product quality, carrying out preventive maintenance, and dealing with various emergencies that arise.
4: JR is normally implemented within work teams, but beyond the work teams it is limited. Ordinary workers participate in ensuring product quality and carrying out preventive maintenance, but the extent of their participation is somewhat limited.
3: JR is normally implemented within work teams, but it is seldom planned and carried out beyond the level of the work teams. Ordinary production workers participate in ensuring product quality and in dealing with various emergencies, but the extent of their participation is considerably limited.
2: JR is not normally implemented. However, jobs are reassigned when the product mix is changed, a new model is introduced, or an unusual situation arises. Ordinary production workers basically do not participate in ensuring product quality or in carrying out preventive maintenance.
1: JR is absent and job assignment is rigid. There is a strict separation between ordinary production operations, and product quality assurance or preventive maintenance.
Note: Where cycle times are long, or the model mix is changed frequently, the application is evaluated a little higher.

③ Education and Training
5: The plant actively encourages skill formation in a wide variety of employees including ordinary production workers, maintenance personnel, first-line supervisors, engineers, and managers. This is based on long-range and systematic training programs that emphasise OJT and that utilise an in-house training center. Key personnel are sent to Japan for training, and Japanese trainers are invited to the local plant. Maintenance personnel and first-line supervisors are mainly trained within the company.

4: The plant actively implements an education and training program and sends key personnel such as maintenance workers and first-line supervisors to Japan for training. However, the program is a little less planned and systematic.

3: The plant does carry out employee training that emphasises OJT, but the program is not systematic. Inadequate in-house training is compensated for by sending employees to Japan, by inviting trainers from Japan, and by relying upon external education and training.

2: The plant attaches little importance to education and training. It manages with spontaneous skill development, and at best it sends some of its key personnel to Japan or utilises external training centers. Many key personnel are recruited externally.

1: The plant is not eager to educate and train its employees. It relies upon the external recruitment of key personnel.

④ **Wage system**

5: The plant adopts a 'person-centred' wage system, the main determinants of which are length of service (*nenkō*) and performance evaluation (PE). Basic wages correspond to in-house qualifications and each employee receives an annual rise. PE is carried out efficiently and is reflected in the wages of all employees, including ordinary production workers. Wage gaps between white-collar and blue-collar employees are not wide. Bonuses are equivalent to several months' wages.

4: The plant adopts basically the same wage system as in the case of five points; however, there are some functional problems with PE, or gaps between wage levels are slightly wider.

3: The plant basically adopts a 'person-centred' wage system, however, it lacks a systematic framework, or there are functional problems with PE. There are fairly large gaps between wage levels and there are certain job-specific allowances.

2: The plant adopts a 'job-centred' wage system where wages are determined on the basis of a few job grades, or a large proportion of the wage results from a job-specific allowance. Or the wage system is unsystematic, and wage levels are determined haphazardly. There are large gaps between wage levels.

1: The plant adopts a 'job-centred' wage system where wages are determined by multi-layered job grades. Or the wage system is unsystematic, and wage levels are determined haphazardly. There are very large gaps between wage levels.

⑤ **Promotion**

5: The plant adopts an internal promotion system where production workers, including technicians, can be promoted to first-line supervisors and sometimes to middle management positions according to ability. Receiving a promotion is also partly determined by length of service, so that long-term employees can rise to the upper ranks (*kyū*) of in-house qualifications, whereas even talented employees must remain at particular ranks for a specified number of years. The speed of promotion is, however, affected by the PE.

4: The plant adopts almost the same type of internal promotion system as described above; however, production workers are unable to be promoted any higher than the position of first-line supervisor.

3: Managers, including first-line supervisors, are partly promoted from within the company, and partly externally recruited. Ordinary production workers and technicians can rise to higher wage grades based on their length of service and PE.

2: Internal promotion is only partially implemented, and there is a basic separation between the promotion of shop-floor workers and that of managers, including first-line supervisors. Promotion is influenced by academic background, or state or community qualifications. In societies where labour union regulations exist, seniority has priority over PE in determining production workers' promotion to higher wage grades.

1: There is a clear separation between the promotion of shop-floor workers and the promotion of managers. Promotion to different jobs or to higher wage grades is determined by academic background, or community or state qualifications. In societies where labour union regulations exist, the promotion to higher wage grades is determined by seniority.

⑥ **First-line supervisor**

5: First-line supervisors are promoted internally and they participate actively not only in labour management (maintaining workplace discipline and carrying out PE) but also in the management of work teams (examination of daily production plans, workers' job assignments, analyzing operational situations, securing parts and materials, and education and training), and in the technical control of production processes (setting up work standards, maintenance of equipment, quality control, *kaizen* activities). They also play important roles in co-ordinating different workplaces. Their management abilities are equivalent to those of their Japanese counterparts.

4: First-line supervisors have slightly inferior management skills compared with their Japanese counterparts.

3: First-line supervisors are partly internally promoted and partly externally recruited. They participate in the management of work teams and in the technical control of production processes, but there are weaknesses in their management skills and they require technicians for support.

2: First-line supervisors considerably lack skill in the management of work teams or the technical control of production processes.

1: First-line supervisors only deal with labour management. The plant does not adhere to internal promotion of first-line supervisors.

II PRODUCTION CONTROL

⑦ **Equipment**

5: 100 per cent of the equipment is the same as in Japan.

4: 75 per cent of the equipment is the same as in Japan. Or, 100 per cent but older, perhaps less automated machines are utilised.

3: 50 per cent of the equipment is the same as in Japan.

2: 25 per cent of the equipment is the same as in Japan.

1: Equipment bears no resemblance to that used in Japan.

⑧ **Maintenance**

5: Shop-floor maintenance personnel are chosen from among production workers and trained internally, or enter as new, inexperienced employees, hired separately from ordinary workers. Ordinary production workers participate actively in preventive or other easy maintenance operations. Without the support of Japanese expatriates, the skills of maintenance personnel are so high that the stoppage ratios (downtime-to-operating ratios), even for new types of machines, are almost the same as in Japan.

4: Ordinary production workers participate in maintenance to a lesser extent, and stoppage ratios are slightly higher than for plants assigned 5 points.

3: Some maintenance personnel are trained internally, and some have external experience. Ordinary production workers do not participate so actively in maintenance. Skills of maintenance personnel are not very high and support by Japanese expatriates is required.

2: Maintenance personnel are mainly recruited externally as experienced workers. Ordinary workers do not participate in maintenance; maintenance is led by engineers, including Japanese.

1: Maintenance personnel are solely recruited externally as experienced workers. Maintenance is carried out under the leadership of engineers.

⑨ **Quality control**

5: The plant emphasises 'building quality into the production process'. Production workers participate actively in quality control in various ways (attending to quality; referring to standard work procedures that specify items to check for quality; applying their ability to recognise defective products; and exercising authority to stop production lines, as well as participating in quality improvement activities, active QC and ZD movements). In-process defect ratios and product quality at the shipment stage are both almost equivalent to what is achieved at Japanese plants.

4: The plant emphasises building quality into the production process, but there are fewer concrete measures. In-process defect ratios are slightly higher than in Japan.

3: The plant tries to build quality into the production process but finds it difficult. Therefore, it assigns more QC personnel or inspectors, or it sets up more check points than in Japan, so as to secure product quality at the shipment stage.

2: Ordinary production workers seldom participate in quality control, and quality control or inspection specialists reject defective products after meticulous inspection at many stages in the production process.

1: The plant emphasises procedures to reject defective products during final product inspection.

⑩ **Process management**

5: Small-lot production on a diverse product line is carried out as smoothly as in Japan, and through the following practices and measures: a diverse model mix on the same production line; frequent product changes; die and jig changes on-the-fly; strict in-process inventory management; applying and achieving the same standard times as in Japan; co-ordination of line balances led by first-line supervisors; preventive maintenance; quick trouble response through close interdivisional coordination; and *kaizen* activities.

4: Small-lot production on a diverse product line is carried out, but to a lesser extent than above.

3: Ordinary operations go smoothly, but the support of Japanese expatriates is required to respond to trouble or to major operational changes such as the introduction of new models. A smaller number of models is produced.

2: Mainly engineers and Japanese expatriates should respond to trouble and to carry out operational changes. The number of models is not large. *Kaizen* activities on the shop floor are not expected. There are some problems with production efficiency.

1: Process management is mainly carried out by engineers, including Japanese expatriates, and not by shop-floor workers. The number of models produced is extremely small. There are major problems with production efficiency.

III PROCUREMENT

⑪ **Local content**

5: Less than 20 per cent of parts are produced and procured locally.

4: From 20 per cent to less than 40 per cent.

3: From 40 per cent to less than 60 per cent.

2: From 60 per cent to less than 80 per cent.

1: From 80 per cent to 100 per cent.

⑫ **Suppliers**

5: Parts and materials and are mainly procured from Japan, with remaining parts obtained from Japanese affiliated suppliers.

4: Key parts and materials are procured from Japan. A high proportion of components obtained in host or third countries are from Japanese affiliated suppliers, including sister plants.

3: Only some of the key parts and materials are procured from Japan. Among parts obtained in host or third countries, half are from Japanese affiliated suppliers and the other half is from non-Japanese affiliated companies.

2: Parts and materials are procured mainly from non-Japanese affiliated suppliers in host or third countries, the only exception being some of the key parts.

1: Almost all the parts and materials, including key ones, are procured from non-Japanese-affiliate suppliers in host or third countries.

⑬ **Procurement method**

5: Practices such as just-in-time, maintaining quality without inspecting at time of procurement, or technological assistance and co-operation (sometimes joint product development or design-in) are implemented through long-term transaction relationships with suppliers.

4: The practices mentioned above are only implemented with some suppliers.

3: Though it is impossible to implement practices such as just-in-time, or maintaining quality without inspecting at time of procurement, some arrangements are made to reduce parts inventory or to facilitate smooth plant operations. Technological assistance is attempted with local suppliers in order to improve quality, cost and punctual delivery.

2: Local suppliers are relied on to maintain quality standards and observe delivery times.

1: Transactions with local suppliers are characterised mainly by spot trading. Parts inventories are quite high in order to cope with defective parts and delayed delivery.

IV GROUP CONSCIOUSNESS

⑭ **Small-group activities**
5: Most of the workers participate voluntarily and actively in small-group activities. They suggest subjects for the activities and achieve a substantial impact with regard to quality, productivity and safety.
4: More than 50 per cent of workers participate voluntarily and actively in small group activities, which enhance workplace morale but have limited substantial effects. Or, most workers participate actively, although their participation is mandatory.
3: 20 per cent to 50 per cent of workers participate voluntarily, or most workers participate where such participation is mandatory. The activities are carried out but without much enthusiasm.
2: Less than 20 per cent of workers participate, or activities exist only in special model cases. Or arrangements such as a system for suggestions is made to improve the atmosphere at the workplace.
1: Neither small group activities nor suggestion systems exist.

⑮ **Information sharing**
5: The plant tries to communicate the intentions of management to employees, to perceive employees' opinions, and to facilitate communication within the company, through meetings and gatherings at all levels, through the disclosure of information from management, and through small-group activities. There are no significant linguistic communication gaps.
4: Various provisions for information-sharing exist, but to a lesser degree than in the case of five points.
3: Attempts are made at information-sharing through meetings and other means at each level of the company.
2: The only information sharing is at meetings before work begins.
1: There are no special provisions for information sharing.

⑯ **Sense of unity**
5: The following devices and practices are fully implemented to facilitate a sense of unity among employees: cafeterias open to all employees, uniforms, open-style offices, company-wide social events, morning ceremonies, open parking, company-owned recreational facilities, and so on.
4: Many of the devices and practices mentioned above are implemented but to a lesser extent.
3: Only some of the above are practised.
2: Only some social events are held.
1: There are no special practices.

V LABOUR RELATIONS

⑰ **Hiring method**
5: All applicants, including those for ordinary production jobs, are screened carefully (through paper examinations, interviews and multi-tiered selection). The plant can select employees from among many applicants. The plant

emphasises new graduates in the case of recruitment at a higher level of academic background. The company selected the site for the plant by taking characteristics of labour into consideration.

4: Applicants are carefully screened but to a lesser extent than above.

3: Applicants are screened, but there are restrictions stemming from less competition among applicants and a high mobility of labour.

2: Employees are hired only by a very simple test because there are not so many applicants or because the plant must hire frequently.

1: There is no special selection.

⑱ Long-term employment

5: The plant is explicit about its intention to avoid lay-offs on managerial grounds as much as possible and, in fact, the plant has never laid off employees. Provisions for long-term employment are implemented and employees stay with the company for a long time.

4: The situation is basically the same as above, but to a lesser extent with regard to vigorously expressing its intentions. Or the stability of the workforce is slightly less.

3: The plant does not adhere firmly to a policy of avoiding lay-offs (employees have been laid off in the past) although it is not desirable to lay off employees on managerial grounds. The plant hopes key personnel will stay with the company for a long time, but at best, the only measures to secure long-term employment are slightly higher wages. Employee mobility is equal to the local average.

2: Managers think that it is unavoidable to lay off employees on managerial grounds, and the plant has laid off workers several times. There are no special provisions for long-term employment. As employee mobility is high, the plant can adjust the number of employees without resorting to lay-offs.

1: Managers believe it is natural to lay off employees on managerial grounds and the plant has frequently laid off employees. Employee mobility is very high.

Note: Employee mobility was considered both as an absolute ratio and with respect to the local average.

⑲ Harmonious labour relations

5: The plant maintains harmonious relations with a labour union and attempts active communication with employees through practices such as a labour-management consultation system. Or the plant avoids hostile labour relations by not having a labour union, and takes particular care to maintain good relations with its employees.

4: The plant maintains harmonious relations with a labour union, or in the absence of a union with employees directly, and it implements measures to facilitate harmonious relations, but to a lesser extent than above.

3: The plant has no problems with a labour union or employees, but it does not have special provisions for maintaining harmonious labour relations.

2: The plant meets some opposition regarding wage or hiring conditions from a union, although it is not serious. As a result, the plant has experienced strikes occasionally

1: Hostile labour relations exist, and the plant has experienced strikes frequently.

⑳ Grievance procedure

5: The plant actively attempts to satisfy employee demands such as improved labour and workplace environments, and grievances are resolved mainly on the shop floor or through managerial channels.

4: The plant attempts to satisfy employee demands. In addition to the managerial channel, the Personnel Department intervenes in the process of resolving grievances (the 'open door' approach).

3: The plant appears to pay some attention to employee demands. Grievances are resolved both on the shop floor and by official grievance procedures through a union.

2: The plant does not put much effort into responding to employee demands or complaints. Grievances tend to be resolved through the labour union channel.

1: The plant pays almost no attention to employee demands. There are many grievances and they are resolved only through the labour union channel. There were cases where grievance procedures reached the stage of external arbitration.

VI PARENT-SUBSIDIARY RELATION

㉑ Ratio of Japanese expatriates

5: Ratio of Japanese expatriates is 4% or more.
4: 3 per cent – less than 4 per cent.
3: 2 per cent – less than 3 per cent.
2: 1 per cent – less than 2 per cent.
1: less than 1 per cent.
Note: For plants with fewer than 500 employees, one percentage point was added to each of the above ratios.

㉒ Delegation of authority

Regarding products, investment, market, local personnel, R&D, etc:

5: Parent company in Japan makes basically all plans and decisions.

4: Parent company in Japan makes decisions to a substantial degree, while subsidiary submits suggested plans.

3: The subsidiary submits plans and the parent company evaluates them, and gives or withholds approval.

2: The subsidiary makes substantial plans and decisions while sounding out the intention of the parent company.

1: The subsidiary basically makes all plans and decisions.

Note: The share of equity held by the Japanese company in a joint venture, as well as the characteristics of the local partner should be taken into consideration.

㉓ Position of local managers

5: The most important senior management positions, including president (top management), are all held by Japanese.

4: The president is Japanese and the majority of important positions are held by Japanese.

3: Japanese and local people share management and other important positions fairly equally.

2: The president is a local person and the majority of important positions are held by local people.

1: The most important senior management positions, including president, are held by local people.

Note: Even if the number of Japanese expatriates holding senior management positions is small, if they have strong authority, the application is higher. The working language used at meetings serves as a reference.

Notes

1. Piore and Sable (1984).
2. Ōno (1978).
3. Monden (1983).
4. Itami (1991).
5. This in-house qualification system is quite different from the American type of qualifications. See Aoki (1988).
6. The representative argument is Okumura(1984).
7. Womack *et al.* (1990), and Abo (1994a). We should notice that US companies are catching up rapidly with their Japanese competitors in terms of both quality and production efficiency. However, the information is considered to be evidence for the effectiveness of the Japanese production system, if the revitalisation of US manufacturing companies, including the Big Three, is attributed partly to efforts at assimilating practices of the Japanese system.
8. Totsuka and Hyodo (1991), Kumazawa (1989), and Kamata (1982). Nitta (1988) introduces different evaluation regarding regulating the power of Japanese labour unions.
9. Murakami and Rohlen (1992).
10. The Dichotomous approach itself is useful when comparing between different societies. If, however, one concept of dichotomy is considered, explicitly or implicitly, to be superior to the other, the comparisons lead inevitably to biased conclusions.
11. We should take into consideration that insufficient transplantation of Japanese methods is supplemented with procurement of equipment and components from Japan, and the existence of Japanese expatriates and temporarily dispatched Japanese employees in the United States. See Abo (1994) and Chapter 2 of this book. However, the bringing in of personnel and materials from Japan cannot sustain the good performance of Japanese affiliated plants in the United States without the introduction of Japanese methods.
12. J. and S. Fucini (1990).
13. White and Trevor (1986), and Kumagai (1994)
14. Hymer (1976), and Buckley and Casson (1985).
15. Poter (1992).
16. Murakami (1992).
17. From the strictly academic point of view, this understanding of application and adaptation may be criticised. We think, however, that this convenient method is inevitable for international comparison.
18. Asanuma (1990), and Miwa (1990).

2 General Characteristics of Hybrid Factories in East Asia

Hiroshi Itagaki

This chapter explores Japanese affiliated factories in Taiwan, Korea, Thailand, Malaysia and Singapore. Surveyed factories that are owned by local capital or by non-Japanese multinationals are not examined in this chapter, and Japanese affiliates located in Taiwan and Korea will be treated separately from those in the three surveyed ASEAN countries of Thailand, Malaysia and Singapore. In total, twenty-five Japanese affiliates were surveyed in Taiwan and Korea in 1992, and another thirty-five in the three ASEAN countries in 1993. The particular elements of the Japanese production system and the extent of their application at Japanese affiliated plants provide important clues for distinguishing the characteristics of those affiliated plants located in Taiwan and Korea from their counterparts in the United States. Similarly, affiliated plants in the three ASEAN countries will be examined by drawing particular attention to the differences between them and the affiliated plants in Taiwan and Korea.

I CHARACTERISTICS IN TAIWAN AND KOREA

Outline of the Surveyed Factories

Turning first to the twenty-five Japanese affiliated plants surveyed in Taiwan and Korea, it is evident from Table 2.1 that the five auto assembly plants, seven auto parts plants six electronics assembly plants, and seven electronics component plants, represent a well-balanced survey according to industry type. A shortcoming of this field study, however, is the fact that seventeen factories were surveyed in Taiwan, whereas only eight were surveyed in Korea.

More than two-thirds (eighteen out of twenty-five) of the surveyed factories were joint ventures with the participation of local capital. Of these joint ventures, just half (nine factories) involved majority ownership

Table 2.1   Surveyed Japanese plants in Taiwan and Korea

	Automobile assembly	Automobile components	Electronics assembly	Electronics components	Total
Number of plants	5	7	6	7	25
Ownership (%)					
90–100[1]	0	1	3	4	7
50–less than 90	0	3	2	3	9
less than 50	5	3	1	0	9
Nationality of the top manager					
Japanese	1	4	3	5	13
Local	4	3	3	2	12
Number of employees					
1– 499	0	5	1	0	6
500– 999	1	1	1	3	6
1 000–1 999	1	1	1	3	6
2 000–2 999	1	0	2	0	3
3 000–	2	0	1	1	4
Start of operation[2]					
In or before 1960s	0	0	3	2	5
1970s	1	4	2	4	11
1980–5	2	0	1	0	3
1986 onwards	2	3	0	1	6

Notes:
1. Including cases where Japanese parent companies own the majority and all other owners are Japanese trading companies or Japanese banks.
2. Year of acquisition or equity participation.

Data as at the day surveyed.

by the Japanese participant. Moreover, almost half the plants surveyed employ local people among their top executives, in contrast to the United States, where twenty-nine out of thirty-four Japanese affiliates have Japanese top executives, a fact that suggests that localisation of management at Japanese affiliates in Taiwan and Korea is more advanced than it is in the United States (see Tables 2.1 and 2.8). Also, according to data published by the Japanese Ministry of International Trade and Industry, wholly-owned subsidiaries of Japanese companies account for about 30 per cent of Japanese manufacturing investment in Asia, while the equivalent for such investment in North America is about 70 per cent.[1] The Japanese equity seen in the selection of factories included in this survey is therefore representative of general trends in Japanese foreign investment.

Other than in the auto parts industry, where most surveyed plants had fewer than 500 employees, plant scale is fairly evenly distributed, ranging from small plants with fewer than 500 employees to large-scale plants with more than 3000 employees. Another characteristic of surveyed Japanese affiliates in Taiwan and Korea is that older, experienced plants and newly-established plants coexist, as seen by the sixteen companies that started operations or included Japanese equity participation up to the 1970s, and the six companies that have begun operations since the latter half of the 1980s. In these respects, the situation in Taiwan and Korea differs from that in the United States, where eighteen plants had fewer than 1000 employees, and eighteen plants embarked on local production after the 1980s, accounting for the majority of surveyed plants in both cases.

In terms of a balanced distribution by industry type, plant scale, years of operation, and Japanese share of equity, the survey described in this book can therefore be considered a fair and adequate representation of the realities concerning Japanese affiliates in Taiwan and Korea.

Hybrid Configuration in Taiwan and Korea

Table 2.2 demonstrates that, with the exception of a few items that reveal notable differences between Taiwan and Korea, Japanese affiliates in these two countries show basically the same tendency in regard to application. This is indicated simply by the fact that, with the single exception of Group III Procurement, the average application ratings from Group I Work Organisation & Administration to Group VI Parent–Subsidiary Relations are almost same. For this reason, hybridisation features as they occur in both countries will be discussed together, and differences will be mentioned only with regard to particular items where wider gaps were discovered.

Before discussing individual items of the Hybrid Evaluation Model, it is helpful to glance at the overall hybrid configuration. First, it is notable that the average degree of application for twenty-three items in Taiwan and in Korea is 3.3 points, exactly the same as it is in the United States (on the occasion of the second field study).[2] Also, Taiwan and Korea received almost the same rating at 3.4 and 3.3 points, respectively. Moreover, Japanese affiliates surveyed during the first field study carried out by this group in the United States received almost the same average rating of 3.2 points. Of course, looking at particular groups or items, there is a considerable difference between the degree of application at Japanese affiliated plants in Taiwan and Korea, and those in the United States.

Table 2.2   Hybrid evaluation of Japanese affiliated plants abroad

	Average of East Asian countries	Taiwan and Korea			ASEAN countries				USA
		Average	Taiwan	Korea	Average	Malaysia	Thailand	Singapore	
I Work Organisation and Administration	3.5	3.7	3.7	3.6	3.3	3.2	3.3	3.1	2.9
① Job classification	4.7	4.9	4.9	4.9	4.5	4.3	4.9	3.8	3.7
② Multifunctional skills	2.7	2.9	3.1	2.5	2.6	2.6	2.6	2.5	2.6
③ Education and training	3.3	3.4	3.3	3.5	3.3	3.0	3.4	3.5	2.9
④ Wage system	3.5	3.9	3.9	3.9	3.1	3.1	3.1	2.8	2.4
⑤ Promotion	3.4	3.7	3.9	3.4	3.1	3.3	3.0	3.0	3.1
⑥ First-line supervisor	3.2	3.4	3.4	3.3	2.9	2.9	2.9	3.3	2.9
II Production Control	3.4	3.5	3.5	3.5	3.4	3.4	3.2	3.8	3.3
⑦ Equipment	3.7	3.5	3.5	3.6	4.0	4.1	3.7	4.8	4.3
⑧ Maintenance	3.2	3.3	3.4	3.1	3.0	2.9	3.0	3.5	2.6
⑨ Quality control	3.4	3.6	3.6	3.6	3.2	3.3	3.0	3.5	3.4
⑩ Process management	3.4	3.5	3.5	3.6	3.2	3.1	3.2	3.5	3.0
III Procurement	3.2	3.2	3.1	3.4	3.2	3.4	3.1	3.5	3.0
⑪ Local content	3.0	2.9	2.7	3.3	3.1	3.2	3.0	3.5	2.6
⑫ Suppliers	3.7	3.5	3.3	3.9	3.8	3.9	3.8	3.8	3.9
⑬ Procurement method	3.7	3.2	3.3	3.1	2.8	3.0	2.5	3.3	2.5
IV Group Consciousness	3.3	3.4	3.5	3.3	3.2	3.2	3.1	3.3	3.2
⑭ Small-group activities	3.0	3.2	3.3	3.0	2.9	2.9	2.8	3.0	2.5
⑮ Information sharing	3.4	3.5	3.5	3.4	3.3	3.4	3.3	3.3	3.5
⑯ Sense of unity	3.5	3.6	3.7	3.5	3.3	3.3	3.3	3.8	3.5

Table 2.2 (continued)

	Average of East Asian countries	Taiwan and Korea			ASEAN countries				USA
		Average	Taiwan	Korea	Average	Malaysia	Thailand	Singapore	
V Labour Relations	3.2	3.4	3.4	3.3	3.1	3.1	3.3	2.8	3.6
⑰ Hiring policy	3.0	3.0	3.0	3.1	3.1	2.9	3.3	2.5	3.4
⑱ Long-term employment	3.2	3.3	3.3	3.3	3.0	2.9	3.3	2.5	3.4
⑲ Harmonious labour relations	3.6	4.0	4.2	3.5	3.3	3.3	3.3	3.3	4.4
⑳ Grievance procedure	3.1	3.2	3.2	3.1	3.1	3.0	3.3	3.0	3.3
VI Parent–Subsidiary Relations	2.6	2.3	2.4	2.1	2.9	2.8	2.8	3.3	3.6
㉑ Ratio of Japanese expatriates	1.5	1.5	1.6	1.3	1.6	1.7	1.3	2.5	3.7
㉒ Delegation of authority	2.9	2.7	2.8	2.6	3.2	3.0	3.4	3.0	3.6
㉓ Position of local managers	3.3	2.7	2.9	2.4	3.8	3.7	3.8	4.3	3.6
Average of 23 items	**3.3**	**3.3**	**3.4**	**3.3**	**3.2**	**3.2**	**3.2**	**3.3**	**3.3**

Nevertheless, the average degree of application in each country converges around a rating of 3.3 points. This is an interesting observation that will be returned to in the final part of this chapter. For the moment, it will suffice to point out that the average degree of application in Taiwan and Korea is similar to that in the United States, at just over 3 points.

A characteristic of hybridisation in Taiwan and Korea, which contrasts with that in the United States, is the absence of major differences with regard to application among the four industries. For example, in Taiwan and Korea the electronics industry and the auto assembly industry received an equally high average rating for application. In the United States, however, the electronics industry received a considerably lower degree than the auto assembly industry. As will be discussed in detail in Chapter 4, electronics assembly and electronics component factories in Taiwan and Korea conduct their large-scale operations in such a way that some of them produce even more diversified products than in Japan (various products from separate plants in Japan are sometimes manufactured at one factory – for example, mini-Matsushita or mini-TDK factories), some have vertically integrated production systems, and others specialise in making products for export to industrialised countries. This makes the electronics industry as strongly application-orientated as the auto industry, and this fact seems to be reflected in the hybrid configuration.

A Striking Contrast between High Application for 'Human–Method' and Low Application for 'Human–Result'

The Four-Perspective Evaluation provides a clue to understanding the hybrid configuration in Taiwan and Korea, the most notable feature of which is the sharp contrast between application rating for 'human-method', which constitutes items regarding human management such as work organisation (Group I), devices to stimulate group consciousness (Group IV), and long-term employment and grievance procedures (part of Group V), and the application rating of 'human–result', which consists of the two items, 'ratio of Japanese expatriates' and 'position of local manager'. Table 2.2 and Figure 2.1 illustrate how the application rating of 'human–method' (3.5 points) clearly exceeds that of 'human–result' (2.1 points). This is the most conspicuous difference between the characteristics of the hybrid configuration of Taiwan and Korea, and that of the United States. In other words, Japanese methods of human management have penetrated Japanese affiliates in Taiwan and Korea deeply and there is less dependence on Japanese expatriates at the

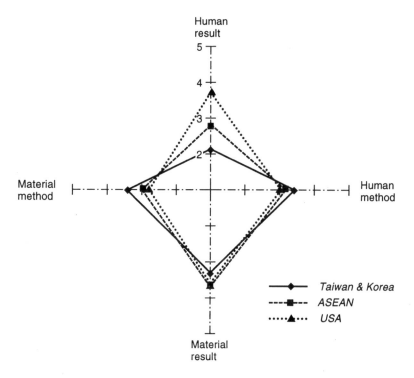

Figure 2.1   Four-perspective evaluation by country

management level. This will be examined more closely in accordance with the individual groups in the Hybrid Evaluation Model (below).

High application for Work Organisation and Administration   Among the elements in 'human-method,' it is noticeable that in Taiwan and Korea, the application for Work Organisation and Administration, which embraces core human factors of the Japanese production system, is higher than it is in the United States (Table 2.2, Figure 2.2). In particular, there is a large difference between application for the items Job classification and Wage system. Job classification evaluates the existence or strength of institutional barriers between job categories. A high 4.9 point application rating for this item (1.2 points higher than in the USA) implies that in Taiwan and Korea, as in Japan, divisions between job categories are weak and there is no rigid job demarcation. Rather than being introduced by Japanese affiliates, this common characteristic may actually stem from the fact that the 'job' concept itself was originally absent in all three countries.

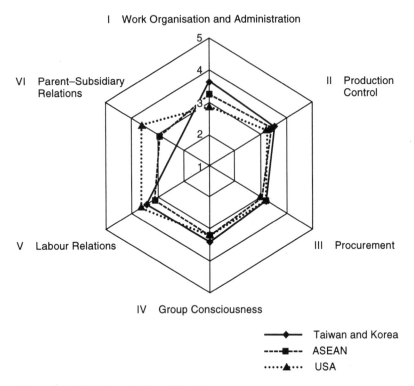

Figure 2.2   Hybrid evaluation of the six groups

In any case, the existence of feeble barriers between job categories is one of the crucial foundations for flexible work organisation. However, it is important to notice that, as mentioned in Chapter 1, Job classification is evaluated by considering institutional barriers between jobs rather than by inquiring whether actual operations, such as job rotation or reassignment of employees, are implemented as flexibly as they are in Japan.

The Wage system received a rating of 3.9 points, which is also much higher (1.5 points higher) than in the United States. This reflects the situation where most Japanese affiliates adopt the person-centred wage system based on a wage table similar to Japanese in-house qualifications made up of *kyū* (ranks) and *gō* (steps). This is unlike the traditional American job-centred system, where the wages of production workers are determined by job categories. Many Japanese affiliates in Taiwan and Korea also apply individual performance evaluations, the results of which are reflected in the wages of production workers. Apart from performance evaluations, which do seem to have been introduced from Japan, it may be one-sided to assert that the wage system based on a *kyū-gō* framework originates exclusively from Japan.[3] There are other large, local companies surveyed in Taiwan and Korea that have adopted a similar framework for their wage system. In any case, the person-centred wage system is another crucial part of the foundation for flexible work organisation and the formation of multifunctionally skilled workers.

Based on the foundation for implementing the Japanese production system provided by the job classification and wage system items, other items such as education and training, promotion, and first-line supervisors receive higher application ratings than Japanese affiliates in the United States. Japanese affiliates in Taiwan and Korea orientate themselves more strongly towards long-term and in-house skill formation with an emphasis on OJT and an internal promotion system, than do their counterparts in the United States. There is also a clear tendency for internally trained first-line supervisors to fill managerial roles governing work organisation at the shop-floor level and to take technical control of production processes, as well as to be responsible for labour management.

The difference between the application rating for work organisation found in Taiwan and Korea and that found in the United States may stem, first of all, from whether or not institutional obstacles to the introduction of Japanese methods exist. When Japanese companies embarked on local production in the United States, they had to cope with well-established production systems existing in an industrially advanced country. Typical examples are the traditions of Taylorism and job-control unionism. In Taylorism, each worker is assigned to a narrow and rigidly specified job. In job control unionism, the wages of production workers are determined exclusively by job categories (job-centred wage) and, as a rule, seniority (length of service) takes precedence over suitability or ability in deciding the order of moving up to higher wage ranks. It is obviously difficult to implement the flexible job assignment and work organisation characteristic of the Japanese production system under these circumstances. In order to increase the degree of application of the Japanese system at their plants in the USA, Japanese affiliates must replace the established systems with methods typical of the Japanese system. Since this is likely to create friction with the local environment, Japanese affiliates must be prepared to bear the burden of costs entailed in clearing such hurdles.

Japanese affiliates in Taiwan and Korea, on the other hand, do not face these entrenched obstacles, so they are able to introduce Japanese methods without great effort or serious friction. This accounts for their higher degree of application. It is also noteworthy that Japanese companies had an impact on the industrialisation of Taiwan and Korea. Furthermore, it is important to note that these host countries already had certain elements, such as job classification and wage systems, that resembled the Japanese system, at least in form. Although this is not the application of the Japanese system in a strict sense, as already mentioned, we consider it a form of application.

Discrepancy between formal systems and actual operations   Although much of the foregoing has been primarily concerned with the situation that obtains among Japanese affiliates operating in the United States, differences between conditions at Japanese affiliates in Taiwan and Korea and conditions at plants in Japan should not be overlooked. The wage system is a typical example. Many Japanese affiliates adopt a wage system that resembles the one in Japan in so far as it includes a wage table with *kyū* (ranks) and *gō* (steps), and the wages of production workers reflect individual performance evaluations. At the same time, however, there are appreciable differences between these and the typical Japanese system, one of which is performance evaluation. Some Japanese affiliates, although only a few, do not have performance evaluation for their production workers. Even in the factories where performance evaluations are implemented, local supervisors often hesitate to evaluate their subordinates strictly, or subordinates express open dissatisfaction with the evaluation. Generally speaking, therefore, the performance evaluation system does not work as well as it does in Japan. Many Japanese expatriates have ascribed these difficulties to differences in national character and cultures. However, it should also be taken into consideration that many factories have only recently introduced the performance evaluation system into environments where they are unfamiliar. Needless to say, trained, experienced and competent supervisors are indispensable for properly conducted evaluations, as is the appropriate mind-set among the workers for the acceptance of such evaluations, in order for such a system to function smoothly and efficiently.

Many plants invest a great deal of effort in education and training. While such training, with its emphasis upon OJT, essentially resembles the type of training that occurs in Japan, the lack of production experience, or the scale of operations at these Japanese affiliated plants often impede the progress of such a systematic training programme. In particular, newly-established plants are unable to afford the time required to foster the necessary personnel. In this case, Japanese affiliates often send a considerable number of their employees, including managers, engineers and key shop-floor personnel, to Japan for training, and also accept a number of Japanese trainers. In this way, insufficient application of 'method' is supplemented by a slightly different type of 'result'.

In many factories, first-line supervisors play almost the same role as they do in Japanese plants. However, not a few Japanese expatriates have pointed out that they are less capable than their counterparts in Japan, and that Japanese expatriates must often supplement their abilities. This shortcoming is primarily attributed to insufficient systematic training through OJT and a lack of experience. At the same time, it is noteworthy that there are those who believe it is difficult to foster supervisory personnel from the shop floor, and that even if such personnel were to be fostered successfully, it would not be a trivial task for them to bring their abilities into full play in a top-down orientated society, such as that of Korea.

Another notable difference is that the degree of application for Multifunctional Skills is a remarkably low 2.9 points, comparison with the average rating of 3.7 points for Group I as a whole.[4] This indicates that the penetration of Japanese practices that produce multifunctional skill formation and flexible work organisation lag behind the introduction of foundational or formal elements of the Japanese production system, such as job classification, wage systems and promotion. The low application for multifunctional skills illustrates the discrepancy between formal systems and actual operations. Of course, this varies a great deal from industry to industry; the auto assembly industry, where many plants report that 'planned job rotation is carried out', receives a rating of 3.8 points, which is almost same as the average of Group I (Table 2.3). In contrast, plants in other industries, and the electronics assembly and components industries in particular, have mentioned that 'Though multifunctional skill formation is desirable, it is difficult to implement because employees are unwilling', and these industries tend towards fixed job assignments. Differences between the industries are partly a function of their respective technological characteristics – namely, the extent to which multifunctional skills are required in shop-floor operations. For example, in the electronics assembly and component industries in Japan, the extent and significance of job rotation is not so high with regard to female employees who perform uncomplicated tasks. However, we cannot deny a difference between Japanese plants and their affiliates in Taiwan and Korea that attempt to create multifunctionally skilled workers. Generally, even at such plants, job rotation is basically implemented within work teams, and planned job rotation is seldom applied beyond the work team.

High mobility of employees between companies, or a high turnover

Table 2.3 Hybrid evaluation by industry

	Taiwan and Korea				Three ASEAN countries				United States			
	Auto assy	Auto parts	Elec. assy	Elec. parts	Auto assy	Auto parts	Elec. assy	Elec. parts	Auto assy	Auto parts	Comsm. elec.	Semi-cond.
I Work Organisation and Administration	3.9	3.7	3.8	3.6	3.4	3.3	3.2	3.2	3.3	3.1	2.4	2.9
① Job classification	5.0	4.8	4.8	5.0	4.8	4.7	4.2	4.6	4.8	4.2	2.8	2.7
② Multifunctional skills	3.8	3.3	2.5	2.4	3.1	2.5	2.5	2.3	3.2	2.7	2.1	2.6
③ Education and training	3.6	3.3	3.3	3.3	3.4	3.2	3.1	3.4	3.4	2.9	2.2	3.0
④ Wage system	4.4	3.7	4.0	3.9	3.1	3.2	2.8	3.2	2.1	2.6	2.0	3.1
⑤ Promotion	3.4	3.7	4.3	3.7	3.0	3.2	3.4	3.0	3.2	3.3	2.7	3.1
⑥ First-line supervisor	3.4	3.2	3.8	3.3	2.9	3.0	2.9	3.0	3.1	3.0	2.6	2.7
II Production Control	3.6	3.0	3.7	3.6	2.9	3.3	3.4	3.7	3.4	3.6	3.1	3.1
⑦ Equipment	3.6	3.0	3.2	4.1	3.0	4.2	3.8	4.7	3.9	4.8	4.0	4.6
⑧ Maintenance	3.2	3.2	3.8	3.1	2.8	2.8	3.2	3.2	2.9	2.8	2.1	2.6
⑨ Quality control	3.8	3.3	4.0	3.6	2.8	3.3	3.4	3.3	4.0	3.9	3.0	2.4
⑩ Process management	3.8	3.2	3.7	3.7	3.0	3.0	3.2	3.5	2.9	3.0	3.3	2.9
III Procurement	3.0	3.1	3.1	3.7	3.1	3.2	3.1	3.5	3.0	3.0	2.6	3.5
⑪ Local content	2.4	3.0	2.7	3.4	3.0	3.8	2.7	3.3	2.3	2.7	2.0	3.7
⑫ Suppliers	3.0	3.5	3.2	4.3	3.8	3.7	3.8	4.0	3.8	3.8	3.6	4.4
⑬ Procurement method	3.6	2.8	3.5	3.3	2.5	2.2	3.1	3.1	3.0	2.6	2.1	2.3
IV Group Consciousness	3.9	3.4	3.4	3.4	2.9	3.1	3.3	3.2	3.9	3.7	2.3	2.9
⑭ Small-group activities	4.0	3.3	2.8	3.1	2.9	2.7	3.0	2.8	2.7	2.8	2.2	2.4
⑮ Information sharing	3.8	3.2	3.7	3.6	3.3	3.2	3.5	3.3	4.4	3.9	2.4	3.3
⑯ Sense of unity	4.0	3.7	3.8	3.6	2.6	3.5	3.5	3.5	4.6	4.4	2.1	2.9

Table 2.3 (continued)

	Taiwan and Korea				Three ASEAN countries				United States			
	Auto assy	Auto parts	Elec. assy	Elec. parts	Auto assy	Auto parts	Elec. assy	Elec. parts	Auto assy	Auto parts	Comsm. elec.	Semi-cond.
V Labour Relations	3.6	3.0	3.8	3.4	3.2	3.0	3.1	3.2	4.2	4.1	2.7	3.5
⑰ Hiring policy	3.0	2.7	3.5	3.3	2.9	3.0	3.2	3.1	4.3	3.8	2.4	3.1
⑱ Long-term employment	3.6	3.0	3.7	3.3	3.1	2.8	3.0	3.1	4.9	3.8	2.2	2.3
⑲ Harmonious labour relations	4.2	3.5	4.5	4.0	3.9	3.0	3.0	3.4	4.2	5.0	3.4	5.0
⑳ Grievance procedure	3.4	2.8	3.5	3.1	3.0	3.0	3.0	3.3	3.2	3.9	2.8	3.6
VI Parent–Subsidiary Relations	2.2	2.4	2.1	2.6	2.4	2.7	3.0	3.2	3.5	4.2	3.0	3.9
㉑ Ratio of Japanese expatriates	1.6	2.0	1.2	1.3	1.3	1.7	1.6	1.6	1.8	4.6	2.6	3.9
㉒ Delegation of authority	2.4	2.5	2.8	3.3	2.8	2.7	3.2	3.7	3.3	4.0	3.2	4.0
㉓ Position of local managers	2.6	2.8	2.3	3.3	3.3	3.7	4.1	4.2	3.3	4.0	3.2	3.9
Average of 23 items	**3.5**	**3.2**	**3.4**	**3.4**	**3.0**	**3.1**	**3.2**	**3.3**	**3.5**	**3.6**	**2.7**	**3.2**

Table 2.4   Four-perspective evaluation by country

	Method		Result		Method/Result	
	Human	*Material*	*Human*	*Material*	*Human*	*Material*
Taiwan and Korea	3.5	3.4	2.1	3.3	1.7	1.0
Taiwan	3.6	3.4	2.2	3.2	1.6	1.1
Korea	3.4	3.3	1.8	3.6	1.9	0.9
ASEAN	3.2	3.0	2.8	3.6	1.1	0.8
Malaysia	3.2	3.1	2.8	3.7	1.1	0.8
Thailand	3.3	2.8	2.6	3.5	1.3	0.8
Singapore	3.1	3.4	3.4	3.9	0.9	0.9
USA	3.1	2.8	3.7	3.6	0.8	0.8

ratio, are major factors that restrict the formation of multifunctional skills. Interviews conducted with plant management indicated that the majority of affiliates experienced an average turnover ratio of 2–3 per cent per month, or 20–30 per cent per annum. Some factories even suffered a turnover ratio as high as 7–8 pe rcent per month. Moreover, these turnover ratios were relatively low because of the economic slump during the summer of 1992, when the field research was being conducted in Taiwan and Korea. During the preceding economic boom period, employee mobility was considerably higher, although turnover ratios varied from company to company and from area to area. The conscription system in the two countries also seems to accelerate employee mobility, since young employees who are conscripted often do not return to the company after being discharged from military service.

In Taiwan, an additional factor that contributes to a higher turnover ratio is an orientation towards independence as illustrated by the many cases of people who quit working for companies in order to establish their own businesses. Furthermore, this desire to become independent is often manifested among the most talented employees, including those at the shop floor level. This strong orientation towards independence is evidence of the entrepreneurship that prevails in Taiwanese society and that is a source of economic vitality sustained, in large part, by small and medium-sized businesses. However, unquestionably this restricts in-house skill formation through long-term employment.

Social differences stemming from a variety of sources including academic background also seem to be more of an impediment to internal promotion from the shop floor in Taiwan and Korea than in Japan.[5] This also weakens employees' incentives to remain in the employ of a company for a long time, to participate in plant operations, or to receive a good performance evaluation through the development of multifunctional skills.

In addition to such external, environmental factors, the attitudes of the Japanese affiliates themselves undoubtedly contribute to discrepancies between formal systems and actual operations. This is clearly demonstrated by the difference between application ratings for Education and Training (3.4 points) and for Multifunctional Skills (2.9 points). This can be explained as follows: Japanese affiliates certainly make an effort to train employees by emphasising OJT or by sending personnel to Japan for training. However, the level of training they pursue is limited and skills acquired are not as broad as in Japan. So long as employees are able partially to acquire the necessary skills, Japanese affiliates feel confident about compensating for a lack of flexibility in work organisation and the inefficient production of goods for export, through the advantages of a beneficial exchange rate between local currencies and the US dollar, and considerably lower wage levels than exist in Japan. In the case of products bound for the domestic market, Japanese affiliates are unenthusiastic about pursuing efficiency goals because of the limited size of the local market and the competitive edge incorporated within the products themselves.

Japanese affiliates will, however, not be able to maintain this type of approach towards plant operations because of the appreciation of local currencies against the US dollar, soaring wage levels, and intensified competition accompanying increased domestic employment income and the expansion of the domestic market since the end of the 1980s. Japanese affiliates are at a critical juncture and they must either take substantial steps to strengthen their production system by emphasising work organisation, or they must curtail local production. If they attempt the former, then they must inevitably implement Japanese methods in earnest. In fact, auto assembly plants in Taiwan did not actively implement multifunctional skill formation until competition became intense with the arrival of joint ventures with Japanese automobile makers in the passenger car market. Some Korean electronics plants have plans to begin actively implementing planned multifunctional skill formation.

Group Consciousness and Labour Relations: same application as in the USA The degree of application for items included under Group IV, Group Consciousness, particularly Information sharing and Sense of unity, is almost the same as that of Japanese affiliates in the United States. This may seem surprising in view of the fact that Taiwan and Korea share more cultural and behavioural characteristics with Japan than they do with the United States. It would seem, therefore, that these elements could be transferred more smoothly into host countries that demonstrate a similar type of social consciousness. An explanation for the similar degrees of application between plants in the USA and those in Taiwan and Korea may reflect the fact that some Japanese affiliates in the United States make strenuous efforts to introduce these elements, sometimes going to extremes in their attempt to care for local employees. In the United States, Japanese affiliates which are strongly inclined to apply the core of the production system receive high degrees of application for the subsystem. In fact, there is clearly a greater emphasis on the application of the subsystem than of the core system. This suggests that since Japanese affiliates in Taiwan and Korea face fewer obstacles to transplanting the core system, they therefore have less motivation to increase the degree of application of the subsystem. In short, Group Consciousness in Taiwan and Korea receives almost the same degree of application as in the United States, even though these affiliates make less of an effort to introduce those elements.

Elements subsumed under Group V, labour relations, such as Harmonious labour relations, are probably subject to similar conditions. In Taiwan, the labour union movement was stimulated, to some extent, by the repeal of martial law in 1987. In Korea, the labour movement was promoted energetically throughout the course of democratisation that took place during the same period. Nevertheless, particularly in Taiwan, fairly good labour relations were maintained without paying much attention to the labour union, unlike in the United States, where procedures for labour–management negotiations and problem-solving rules are firmly entrenched. Therefore the slightly lower degree of application for Harmonious labour relations in Taiwan than in the Unites States does not reflect poor labour relations but a lesser amount of care and attention regarding labour relations on the part of management. This is considered to be a negative factor according to the established criteria for application.

Nor are labour–management relations in Korea very poor at the present time. The difference in degree of application for harmonious labour relations between Taiwan (4.2 points) and Korea (3.5 points) reflects the labour disputes that existed in Korea in the latter half of 1980s. However, if severe labour disputes stem not only from low wage rates, especially the deterioration of real wages in the face of rapid inflation, but also from wide gaps in the corporate hierarchy and a promotion ceiling, then such disputes have deep roots that may have a considerable affect on future labour relations in Korea. However, Korean and Japanese managers at some Japanese affiliates stated that their labour disputes were not as severe as those that occurred in Korean companies in the same local areas.[6] If such relatively benign disputes were the result of egalitarian managerial practices of the Japanese affiliates, then, depending on the companies' policies and attitudes toward employees, the prospects for harmonious labour relations may be improved, despite the social origins of such problems.

Among Group Consciousness elements, only Small-group activities clearly receives a higher rating in Taiwan and Korea (3.2 points) than in the United States (2.5 points). In about ten of the factories surveyed it was reported that, in principle, all the workers participate in small-group activities. In practice, however, participation differed considerably from that in Japan. Even those factories that claimed full participation in principle in fact only achieved participation ratios of about 70 or 80 per cent. Most managers, local as well as Japanese expatriate, and in both Taiwan and Korea, stated that activities could only be carried out in a top-down framework where superiors ordered or set the theme of activities, and that the participants did not display much enthusiasm. In general, Japanese affiliates do not seek substantial results in terms of improved quality or efficiency through such activities. Rather, they seem to be looking for psychological effects such as higher employee morale.[7]

Differences between Japan and these two countries are reflected not only in the application of elements of the Japanese production system, but also in the different employee attitudes to participation. An important question is how differences in employee participation will influence the application of the core system, which is necessary for strengthening the local operation of Japanese affiliates. This will determine the future of the Japanese production system transplanted into these two countries. The present survey did not provide an adequate explanation for these different attitudes to participation. However, it is certain that the degree of tolerance by the employment system for the movement of employees from company to company, and the existence of promotion ceilings that vary in accordance with academic background, are relevant factors.

Low application for 'human–result'　In contrast to 'method', elements in 'human–result,' such as Ratio of Japanese expatriates and Position of local managers, received much lower ratings than in the United States. This reflects a lesser degree of reliance on Japanese expatriates, and a correspondingly greater amount of influence by local personnel in the upper ranks of the managerial hierarchy, respectively. Table 2.5 shows that fifteen out of twenty-five affiliates in Taiwan and Korea have less than 1 per cent Japanese expatriates, five plants between 1 and 2 per cent, and three plants between 2 and 3 per cent.[8] In contrast, in the United States,

Table 2.5   Ratios of Japanese expatriates to total employees in affiliated plants abroad

	Taiwan and Korea	Three ASEAN countries	USA
Less than 1 per cent	15	18	2
Less than 0.1 per cent	2	0	0
Less than 0.5 per cent	7	2	0
0.5 – less than 1 per cent	6	16	2
1 per cent – less than 2 per cent	5	13	5
2 per cent – less than 3 per cent	3	4	8
3 per cent – less than 4 per cent	1	0	2
4 per cent – less than 5 per cent	0	0	4
5 per cent – less than 6 per cent	1	0	2
6 per cent or more	0	0	11
6 per cent – less than 10 per cent	0	0	6
10 per cent or more	0	0	5
Total	**25**	**35**	**34**

thirteen of thirty-four plants have 5 per cent or more Japanese expatriates, among which five plants have more than 10 per cent, 14 have between 2 and 5 per cent and only two have ratios of less than 1 per cent. Furthermore, in Taiwan and Korea, almost half of the plants surveyed (twelve out of twenty-five) employ local personnel among their top executives, whereas in the United States, twenty-nine plants have Japanese top executives. This clearly illustrates that affiliates in the United States rely upon Japanese expatriates to a much greater extent than do the affiliates in Taiwan and Korea. It should be noted, however, that there are many small plants in the United States with only slight operating experience.[9]

The degree of application for the elements under Group VI, Parent–Subsidiary Relations, are strongly influenced by how long before operations were started up, percentage ownership in the joint venture, and the ratio of export to total production (Table 2.6). Not surprisingly, plants with a shorter operating history have a higher ratio of Japanese expatriates. Unexpectedly, however, the amount of Japanese equity is not clearly related to the ratio of Japanese expatriates. Furthermore, plants with higher export ratios have lower ratios of Japanese expatriates. On the other hand, as expected, those plants that have recently been established and have a high ratio Japanese equity and a high ratio of export to domestic production, receive a higher rating for degree of application for Position of

Table 2.6 The degree of application for the elements under Group IV in Taiwan and Korea

	Average	Start of operation		Percentage ownership			Export ratio	
		Until the end of the 70s	1980s or later	90% or more	50%–less than 90%	Less than 505	50% or more	Less than 50%
VI Parent–Subsidiary Relations	2.3	2.0	2.9	2.9	2.3	1.9	2.7	2.1
ⓐ Ratio of Japanese expatriates	1.5	1.1	2.1	1.4	1.6	1.4	1.3	1.6
ⓑ Delegation of authority	2.7	2.5	3.1	3.6	2.5	2.1	3.4	2.3
ⓒ Position of local managers	2.7	2.3	3.4	3.6	2.6	2.0	3.3	2.4

local managers, indicating that local managers wield relatively little authority.

One of the reasons Taiwan and Korea receive a lower degree of application for 'human–result' is that joint ventures with local capital account for the majority of Japanese affiliates in Taiwan and Korea. This is unlike the situation in the United States, where an overwhelming majority of surveyed factories are wholly owned by Japanese companies.[10] However, since, as mentioned above, plants with a smaller share of Japanese equity do not necessary have lower ratios of Japanese expatriates, the existence of joint ventures cannot fully explain the low application for 'human–result'.[11]

Rather, the low application of 'human–result' is attributed to the fact that Taiwanese and Korean managers have a thorough understanding of the Japanese system. This can be inferred from the way in which they replied to the survey questions generated by the detailed investigative format used to gather a wide variety of information regarding the twenty-three elements of the Hybrid Evaluation Model. They would have been unable to provide lucid and appropriate answers to the many questions without a through understanding of the Japanese system and how it was in fact being applied in plant management. Of course, Japanese affiliates cannot always employ local managers who have such a thorough understanding of the Japanese system. Even in those cases where they are fortunately able to recruit such individuals, their numbers may be limited. However, the interviews demonstrated repeatedly an impressive understanding that is clearly superior to that of managers in other areas. The ability of local managers to speak Japanese must also contribute to enhancing their perception of the Japanese system. This linguistic ability was evident in the fluent Japanese with which they replied to questions in the interview. Furthermore, not only top executives but also middle management can communicate in Japanese with headquarters or mother plants in Japan by telephone or facsimile. This also enables the operation of these Japanese affiliates with fewer Japanese expatriates, and it facilitates the penetration of the Japanese system into the local plants.

Personal contact and friendship among Japanese and local employees that arise on the occasion of education or training in Japan, or when assistance is provided by Japanese personnel in the host countries, also contribute to smoother telephone communications afterwards. This seems to be related in some way to a characteristic of the Japanese system, namely not to rely on descriptions in manuals, but rather to emphasise human networks and information that is picked up on the work site. It also illustrates that the effects of education and training are not confined to the immediate transfer of knowledge but are accumulated and diffused widely and deeply within a company as time passes.

Here again, it is important to be aware of the limitations. For example, in some companies, a few Japanese expatriates occupy the top management positions and hold strong managerial authority. This is reflected in application ratings for Position of local managers being higher than for Ratio of Japanese expatriates. Another limitation is that a top-down orientation of decision-making may prevail whether the plant is controlled by Japanese expatriates or by local managers. This top-down orientation illustrates that the number of local managers who have a good understanding of Japanese methods is limited, and that participatory and workplace-orientated management has not gained sufficient penetration.

Though a low degree of application in the 'human–result' category is common for Taiwan and Korea, it is notable that Korea receives a lower degree of application for ratio of Japanese expatriates and Position of local managers than does Taiwan (as mentioned, lower degree of application for position of local managers indicates that local managers occupy higher positions). This is partly because the fact that all the Korean partners are manufacturers and therefore strongly production orientated. The Taiwanese partners, on the other hand, are often non-manufacturers, such as distributors, and even when they are manufacturers they tend to assume the character of mercantile capitalists, seeking a quick return on their investment in the short term. In addition, it cannot be denied that the complex feelings that Japanese and Korean people often have for each other make it difficult for Japanese companies and expatriates to exert managerial authority, thus giving Korean partners a stronger voice. The difficulty that Japanese affiliates face in trying to run operations in Korea, which accounts for the smaller sample of Korean firms that were the subject of this survey,[12] means that in Korea, more than in other host countries, Japanese affiliates must employ talented local personnel who understand Japanese methods to act as their top executives, and then must not hesitate to delegate managerial authority to these local personnel. This is, in fact, precisely the way in which some electronics assembly plants manage to operate successfully.

Japanese affiliates in Taiwan and Korea have greater autonomy than affiliates in the United States. This means a lower degree of application for delegation of authority in Taiwan and Korea (2.7 points) than in the USA (3.6 points). This can be attributed to the fact that the majority of affiliated plants are joint ventures with local capital, as well as to the low degree of application for 'human–result'. However, it should also be noted that there are more than a few cases where the strong authority of Japanese expatriates enhances the independence of the affiliates from headquarters in Japan. Also, as was seen in the case of application for Position of local managers, those Japanese affiliates with a short local production history, those where the Japanese partners have a majority share of equity, and those which have a high export ratio (mainly to highly industrialised countries such as Japan and the United States), all receive a higher degree of application for delegation of authority (meaning that the Japanese side retains much decision-making authority – see Table 2.6). Many electronics parts plants are subject to these same conditions and therefore this industry receives a much higher application rating for Delegation of authority as well as for Position of local managers (3.3 points for both items), than the overall average rating for Taiwan and Korea (2.7 points).

Comparable Application for 'Material–Method' and 'Material–Result'

In the Four-Perspective Evaluation, the 'material–method' perspective refers to methods for the control of materials including production equipment, products, and components, and it consists of three items: maintenance, quality control, and procurement. The 'material–result' perspective refers to directly bringing in ready-made elements from Japan, and this subsumes equipment, local content, and suppliers. In the United States, and similar to the 'human' perspectives, 'material-result' clearly receives a higher application rating than 'material-method'. However, in Taiwan and Korea, the degree of application for the 'material–method' and the 'material–result' perspectives are very similar, at 3.4 and 3.3 points respectively (see Table 2.4). Compared with the United States, Japanese affiliates in Taiwan and Korea incline towards applying the 'material–method' aspect and rely less upon 'material–result'.

Application for 'Material–Method' and its limitation Among the elements in 'material–method', Maintenance and Procurement method clearly receive a higher application rating in Taiwan and Korea (3.3 points for Maintenance, 3.2 points for Procurement method) than in the United States (2.6 and 2.5 points, respectively). It is particularly notable that these elements are rated as high as the average application rating for all twenty-three items in Taiwan and Korea, while in the USA, they are among the elements that receive the lowest rating, along with Multifunctional skills, Wage system, and Small-group activities (see Table 2.2).

Again, there are important qualifications. The higher degree of application for Maintenance is not attributed to greater penetration of Japanese methods but to the internal fostering of maintenance technicians in Taiwan and Korea, unlike in the United States, where Japanese affiliates sometimes recruit experienced maintenance employees from the outside. In addition, there exists a rather large disparity between the maintenance capabilities of plants in Japan and of the affiliates in Taiwan and Korea, since the extent of equipment automation in Taiwan and Korea is generally not as high as in Japan. Also, parts procurement methods such as 'just-in-time' lag considerably behind those of their Japanese counterparts, although Japanese methods with regard to long-term trade relationships with and technological aids to suppliers have been introduced to a certain extent.

Under 'material–method', the degree of application for quality control at affiliates in Taiwan and Korea does not differ so much from that in the United States. In Taiwan and Korea, Japanese affiliates orientate themselves toward Japanese methods by which ordinary workers, at least formally, carry out quality checks during the production processes. This does not mean, however, that the resulting quality levels exceed those that are achieved in the United States. There are two ways of perceiving quality, one is that of actual product quality at the shipment stage, and the other is that which is expressed by in-process defect ratios. With regard to product quality at the shipment stage, there exists a considerable difference between Japanese affiliates in the United States, and those in Taiwan and Korea, who produce for local markets, especially in the case of the auto industry. Sales of Japanese products in the US market rely to a significant extent upon their reputation for reliability and high quality. Moreover, in case of the US auto market, cars produced locally sometimes compete with Japanese imports. This compels Japanese affiliates in the USA to secure an equivalent level of product quality to that of the imports, which they achieve partly by installing additional inspectors and inviting more Japanese expatriates, at considerable expense. On the other hand, in the domestic markets of Taiwan and Korea, the demand for quality is not as high because the markets in those countries are not as mature and because protective or prohibitive measures against competitive Japanese products are in place.[13] Therefore, Japanese methods of quality control are adopted only in a formal sense, and the actual situation of building quality into the production process reveals a considerable gap between what occurs in Japan and in Taiwan and Korea. The application for Quality control in Taiwan and Korea receives almost the same rating as in the United States. This is because the higher application of quality control methods in Taiwan and Korea is counterbalanced by the higher quality at the shipment stage in the United States.

Plants which manufacture for export markets also fail adequately to introduce the practices of building quality into the production process. This is readily demonstrated by in-process defect ratios. As will be examined in more detail under IV Plant Operating Performance, there are typically two to four times as many in-process defects in the affiliate companies in Taiwan and Korea as there are in Japan. However, some plants do exist, that have almost equivalent defect ratios or that achieve better performance because they manufacture mainly lower added value products. Poorer performance regarding in-process defect ratios does not only stem from lack of employees' attention to product quality. Some plants attributed it to unsatisfactory co-ordination between different sections, such as the front and rear production processes, or shop-floor and QC divisions, to lack of teamwork within a section, and to insufficient feedback of information. These deficiencies, along with the top-down style of decision-making already mentioned, seem to obstruct the implementation of Japanese methods of plant management. Export-orientated plants secure product quality at the shipment stage through various measures, such as stationing more inspectors or doubling quality checks by different employees. These measures are similar to those carried out at Japanese affiliates in the United States, but they can be implemented at a lower cost in Taiwan and Korea, because there is a smaller number of Japanese expatriates and because of the wage gap between skilled workers in the United States and those in Taiwan and Korea.

Those plants who mainly ship their products to the domestic market are obviously satisfied with mediocre quality. Plants that are export-orientated can save the time required to build quality into the production process, and also enjoy cost advantages by employing rigorous inspection systems to reject defective products. The Quality control element is thus another good example of the discrepancy between formal systems and actual operations.

Lower application for 'Material–Result' than in the United States   The degree of application for 'material–result', which demonstrates the extent to which production equipment and components are introduced from Japan, is lower in Taiwan and Korea than it is in the United States (see Tables 2.2 and 2.4). The lower application rating for Equipment (3.5 points versus 4.3 points in the USA) is attributed to the fact that in Taiwan and Korea, older, less-automated equipment is generally in use, unlike in the United States, where the newest production machinery is utilised, just like in Japan. The major reason for this is that in Taiwan and Korea the unit production per model is much smaller than in Japan or the United States. Japanese affiliates in Taiwan and Korea therefore restrict automation and use older machinery as long as possible to recover depreciation expenses. Some plants initially procure their machines from Japan, but then duplicate those machines themselves or procure similar machines from local vendors because manufacturing costs are considerably lower in Taiwan and Korea than in Japan.[14] It also demonstrates the strong capacity for absorbing technology.

With regard to parts procurement, the degree of application for Local content is somewhat higher (indicating lower ratios for local content) than in the United States. In contrast, the degree of application for Suppliers is clearly lower in Taiwan and Korea (3.5 points) than it is in the United States (3.9 points). This reflects a greater proportion of procurement from locally capitalised suppliers.

The opposing tendencies of application for Local content and for Suppliers in the United States and in Taiwan and Korea is explained by official and unofficial demands for higher local content. In the United States, where Japanese affiliates are compelled to increase their procurement of parts and materials from local sources, this results in a lower degree of application for Local content. On the other hand, since quality is an overriding concern in the US market, and since local content restrictions prevent the affiliates from procuring all of their components from Japan, they either manufacture parts internally, or turn inevitably to purchasing them from Japanese affiliated parts suppliers who have also established operations in the United States. If procurement from Japan or local vendors becomes too costly, the affiliates procure parts and materials from sister plants or other Japanese affiliated manufacturers in Mexico and Southeast Asian countries. These factors combine to result in a higher degree of application for Suppliers.

In Taiwan and Korea, demands for raising local content are not as strong as in the United States. Numerous locally-owned companies have received technological assistance from Japanese parts manufacturers and, particularly in Taiwan, a cluster of parts manufacturers has been formed. Furthermore, in the case of products for domestic consumption, quality standards are not as rigid. For these reasons, and in contrast to the hybrid configuration in the United States, the degree of application for local content in Taiwan and Korea is high (local content ratios are low) and the degree of application for Suppliers is relatively low (dependence on Japanese affiliated parts makers is low). These conditions of local content and suppliers, along with the matter of Japanese expatriate ratios, result in higher profitability of Japanese affiliates in Taiwan and Korea than those in the United States. These factors alone, however, do not fully account for this profitability gap.

In Taiwan and Korea, key components or materials that have a direct impact upon product function are also inevitably procured from Japan or from local Japanese affiliated parts makers. This is illustrated clearly by the conspicuously high degree of application for suppliers in the electronics parts industry (4.3 points) in comparison with that of other industries (see Table 2.3). Application for equipment in the electronics parts industry also receives a high 4.1 points, almost as high as the US average rating of 4.3 points. This reflects the export-orientated nature of the electronics parts industry, which manufactures products for direct export to Japan or for indirect export to Japan or the United States in the form of components that are incorporated into finished products for export. These kinds of products must meet rigid quality standards and, accordingly, plants that must achieve those higher quality standards inevitably procure their capital goods such as components and equipment from Japan: either directly, or indirectly via Japanese affiliated part suppliers. This situation is not limited to Japanese affiliates. Even Korean auto assembly companies procure much more from Japan in the case of autos produced for export than for the local market (see Chapter 4). The tendency for Japanese affiliates to supplement insufficient application of methods with a higher application of 'material–result' is common to all host countries, though the extent to which they do this varies from country to country.

It is notable that Japanese affiliates in Korea rely more on imports from Japan or procurement from Japanese affiliated suppliers than do affiliates in Taiwan. In other words, local content and suppliers receive a higher rating in Korea than in Taiwan. This reflects, first of all, the premature clustering of the component industry in Korea, as numerous researchers have observed.[15]

II CHARACTERISTICS IN THREE ASEAN COUNTRIES

Outline of the Surveyed Factories

Field studies were carried out in three ASEAN countries in 1993: namely, Thailand, Malaysia and Singapore. Table 2.7 describes the thirty-five Japanese affiliated plants surveyed, including eight auto assembly, six auto parts, ten electronics assembly, and eleven electronics parts plants. By country, fifteen surveyed factories are located in Thailand, sixteen in Malaysia, but only four in Singapore.

Regarding ownership, sixteen plants were categorised as Japanese

Table 2.7   Surveyed Japanese plants in three ASEAN countries

	Automobile assembly	Automobile components	Electronics assembly	Electronics components[1]	Total
Number of plants	8	6	10	11	35
Ownership (%)					
90–100[2]	2	1	3	10	16
50–less than 90	1	2	4	1	8
less than 50	5	3	3	0	11
Nationality of the top manager					
Japanese	5	6	10	11	32
Local	3	0	0	0	3
Number of employees					
1– 499	0	2	0	2	4
500– 999	3	2	3	1	9
1 000–1 999	1	1	5	4	11
2 000–2 999	1	0	2	2	5
3 000–	3	1	0	2	6
Start of operation[3]					
In or before 1960s	4	1	2	0	7
1970s	0	1	2	2	5
1980–5	3	2	1	1	7
1986 onwards	1	2	5	8	16

Notes:
1. Including semiconductors
2. Including cases where Japanese parent companies own the majority and all other owners are Japanese trading companies or Japanese banks.
3. Year of acquisition or equity participation.

Data as at the day surveyed.

wholly-owned (90 per cent or more of the equity is owned by Japanese companies), eight joint ventures had majority Japanese ownership of equity, and eleven joint ventures had minority Japanese ownership of equity. Although the ratio of Japanese wholly-owned plants to all plants surveyed was higher than in Taiwan and Korea, the number of joint ventures is larger than in the United Sates (see Tables 2.1, 2.7 and 2.8).

In notable contrast to Taiwan and Korea, almost all the surveyed plants are run by Japanese top executives. Only three plants employ local personnel among their top executives, one of which, moreover, is not a Japanese affiliate in the strict sense, in so far as it is an auto assembly company managed by a Malaysian public corporation and which has

Table 2.8   Surveyed Japanese plants in the USA

	Automobile assembly	Automobile components	Electronics assembly	Semi-conductors	Total
Number of plants	9	9	9	7	34
Ownership (%)					
90–100[1]	6	7	9	7	29
50–less than 90	3	2	0	0	5
less than 50	0	0	0	0	0
Nationality of the top manager					
Japanese	7	9	2	4	13
Local	2	0	2	1	5
Number of employees					
1– 499	0	7	2	4	13
500– 999	2	2	5	3	12
1 000–1 999	1	0	2	0	3
2 000–2 999	3	0	0	0	3
3 000–	3	0	0	0	3
Start of operation[2]					
In or before 1960s	0	0	0	0	0
1970s	0	0	6	3	9
1980–5	3	2	1	2	8
1986 onwards	6	7	2	2	17

Notes:
1. Including cases where Japanese parent companies own the majority and all other owners are Japanese trading companies or Japanese banks.
2. Year of acquisition or equity participation.

Data as at the day surveyed.

equity participation by Japanese companies. This suggests that most of the Japanese affiliates in ASEAN countries are managed under the leadership of Japanese expatriates. In each industry, plants range in size from those with few employees to those with 3000 or more employees, as is common in Taiwan and Korea. Of the surveyed plants, eleven have between 1000 and 2000 employees, and nine plants have between 500 and 1000.

Regarding the start of operations, twenty-five plants started up in the 1980s, accounting for the majority of plants surveyed. In particular, sixteen plants, almost half of those surveyed, were established in the latter half of 1980s and later. On the other hand, seven plants began to operate before the 1960s, and five in the 1970s. In Thailand and Malaysia, companies that started operations early are mainly engaged in supplying small quantities of a large variety of products to the local market. They comprise auto assembly plants with a diverse product line including models ranging in size, and mini-Matsushita-type electrical plants whose products range from miscellaneous appliances to colour television sets. These plants share characteristics with some of the Japanese affiliates in Taiwan. In contrast, almost all of the electronics assembly and parts plants that started operations in the 1980s are export-orientated. Particularly among the electronics assembly industry, the affiliated plants engage in the mass production of a few specific goods such as colour television sets, video-cassette decks or air conditioners. Japanese affiliates in ASEAN countries, then, are characteristically bipolarised into older, domestic-market-orientated and newer, export-orientated, plants.

Hybrid Configuration in Three ASEAN Countries

As Table 2.2 shows, with the exception of certain elements, the hybrid configurations for Thailand and Malaysia bear a close resemblance to each other, while that for Singapore has a very different configuration. However, four plants is too small a sample to conclude that this hybrid configuration is representative of the general situation among Japanese affiliates in Singapore. Therefore the following discussion will concentrate on hybridisation features in Thailand and Malaysia, and the characteristics of surveyed plants in Singapore will only be mentioned where it is deemed to be appropriate and necessary.

Unlike in the United States, where there are conspicuous differences between the four industries, in Thailand and Malaysia, the four industries reveal generally similar hybrid configurations (see Table 2.3), so they may be discussed together. There are, however relatively clear differences by industry in degree of application for Group II, production control and Group VI, parent–subsidiary relations. The auto industry, and particularly auto assembly, receives a lower application rating for these two groups, while the electronics industry, and particularly electronics assembly, receives a higher rating. In the case of production control, it is clear that there is a difference regarding equipment. While almost all the auto assembly plants use older, less automated machines, numerous electronics plants introduce new, highly automated equipment. Naturally, such electronics factories pay meticulous attention to machine maintenance and quality control. The high degree of application for parent–subsidiary relations in the electronics industry indicates that headquarters in Japan, or Japanese expatriates, exercise strong authority over plant operation. This contrasting hybrid configuration reflects the fact that the auto plants make products exclusively for the local market, while many electronics plants export their products to Japan or other highly industrialised countries such as the United States.

Interestingly, ASEAN countries receive an average rating of 3.2 points for all twenty-three elements, a rating that is almost the same as in Taiwan and Korea, or the United States (see Table 2.2). Moreover, not only Thailand and Malaysia but also Singapore receives an average rating of 3.3 points. This convergence will be considered in some more detail at the end of this chapter. Unlike Taiwan and Korea or the United States, the hybrid configuration for the three ASEAN countries surveyed is characterised by the fact that, with the exception of certain elements, the average ratings for the groups or elements in the Hybrid Evaluation Model are fairly consistent and converge around or a little higher than 3.0 points. The only elements that deviate conspicuously are Job classification, Equipment, and Position of local managers, which belong to the higher application group, and Multifunctional skills and Ratio of Japanese expatriates, which belong to the lower application group.

Limitations to 'Methods' Application

In examining the hybrid situation of Japanese affiliates in the ASEAN countries, the following two points, in addition to the social environment of each country, should be taken into consideration. How does 'late-comer' industrialisation – that is, later than that of Taiwan and Korea – influence the introduction of Japanese methods in Thailand and Malaysia? Do British colonial experiences or the influence of US corporations, which preceded Japanese companies, hinder the application of Japanese methods in Singapore and Malaysia?[16]

The fragility of horizontal barriers between jobs   The investigation of job classification systems is a first step in determining whether or not hindrances exist to the introduction of Japanese methods. Almost none of the Japanese affiliates surveyed have obvious institutional barriers between job categories. Even if plants have job grades for ordinary production workers, those grades are determined not by job category but by academic background and length of service. This is especially so in Thailand, which receives a high application rating of 4.9 points for Job classification, as high as the rating for Taiwan and Korea. In Singapore and Malaysia, however, a few plants exist that impose clear job demarcations, and set job grades corresponding to job categories. In Singapore (although the sample is small, as mentioned above) the influence of these plants reduce the rating for application for Job classification to 3.8 points, which is as low as in the United States. This seems to illustrate that the Western 'job' concept has penetrated these countries to some extent. However, since even in Malaysia and Singapore the majority of plants do not establish a rigid job classification system, it can be inferred that there do not exist any strong hindrances to the introduction of Japanese methods.

A person-centred, non-systematic wage system with wider gaps between ranks It follows from the situation regarding job classifications that only a few plants adopt a job-centred wage system as in the United States, where jobs determine wage rates. Most Japanese affiliates introduce a wage system which includes several ranks and where the specific rank at which a new employee starts out is determined by academic background. Even if an employee remains at the same rank, his or her wages increase every year. Wage rates therefore differ among employees at the same rank, in accordance with their age or length of service.

This is basically a 'person-centred' wage system and, in that sense, it is similar to the systems in Japanese affiliates in Taiwan and Korea. The wage systems of the surveyed plants in ASEAN countries, however, do not generally include systematic wage tables composed of *kyū* (ranks) and *go* (steps), and wage rates are determined by annually monitoring rank–wage trends at other companies in the same industry. Some Japanese affiliates do not introduce job ranks in the manner of Japanese in-house qualifications, but only create official positions such as supervisors and chief managers. At these plants, production workers' wages are determined either solely on the basis of length of service, or the basic wages of production workers are uniform.

Approximately two-thirds of the Japanese affiliates surveyed introduce individual performance evaluations for production workers, the results of which are reflected in wages. Performance evaluation systems can thus be considered to have penetrated ASEAN countries to a certain extent, although not to the extent that they have in Taiwan and Korea. Typically, performance evaluations influence the degree of the wage increases for individual employees. However, managers at many plants that introduce the performance evaluation system pointed out a difficulty in that evaluators are not accustomed to evaluating. Consequently, they often assign good grades to all their subordinates, or allow favouritism to influence their evaluation. This difficulty is also common to plants in Taiwan and Korea. Finally, most affiliates pay annual bonuses that are typically equivalent to two or three months' basic wage.

A notable characteristic of the wage systems at affiliated plants in ASEAN countries is the existence of considerably wider gaps between the wages paid at different ranks or positions than in Japan, and in Taiwan and Korea. A manager of an electronics assembly plant in Malaysia said 'Gaps between wage rates at different ranks or positions are wide and, moreover, the higher the ranks or positions, the wider the gaps. Section chiefs are paid more than ten times the amount paid to ordinary production workers, whereas in Japan they are paid three or four times as much.' In addition to the wage gaps between different ranks or positions, academic background sometimes affects wage rates so strongly that a certain employee's wage may never catch up with another who is stationed at the same position but has a higher level of education. In general, social gaps, especially those arising from academic background, are clear and wide among the ASEAN countries and this is reflected in the corporate hierarchy. In connection with gaps between positions, some plants have distinct payment systems, according to which ordinary production workers are paid daily wages and managerial staff are paid a salary.

Such wide social gaps are also reflected in the promotion system. At most of the Japanese affiliates, only employees with higher academic backgrounds are promoted to management-level positions, although at a few plants there is no ceiling for promotion from the shop floor. Of course, in a number of plants, production workers, including those with only an elementary school education, are promoted internally to the rank of supervisor. Compared with supervisors in Japan, however, their functions and capabilities are considerably limited.

In addition, in Thailand, where titles are an important source of prestige, it is very difficult to select and promote specific employees without demotivating workers who are passed over. However, taking advantage of this particular social characteristic, there is an interesting case where titles indicating the difficulty of jobs are utilised as a means of offering incentives.

Inclination towards fixed job assignment Despite fragile divisions between jobs, and the person-centred wage system, the formation of multifunctionally skilled workers remains limited. The degree of application for multifunctional skills is low, at 2.6, which is lower than the 2.9 point rating in Taiwan and Korea, and equivalent to the rating earned by affiliates in the United States. In twenty-one out of thirty-five plants, job assignments are fixed, or job reassignments are so restricted that changes only occur in the case of temporary assistance. Of course, some plants intend to implement job rotation in the future, even with a certain amount of expected resistance from the shop floor. Others, however, have no such plans, as they believe that job task assignments should be carried out accurately by confining workers to narrow job areas, and that, moreover, such an approach increases productivity.

Differences between industries should, of course, not be overlooked. Even in ASEAN countries, all auto assembly plants carry out job rotation within work teams. Moreover, some auto assembly plants implement a fairly long cycle time in that a specific worker would complete a large variety of different tasks within the specified time. Therefore, even if job rotation is limited, it can be considered that the formation of multifunctionally skilled workers takes place to a substantial extent. The auto assembly plants in ASEAN countries receive a rating of 3.1 points for application in multifunctional skills, slightly higher than the 2.9 point average rating among all four industries in Taiwan and Korea, though considerably lower than the 3.8 point rating for the average in the auto assembly industry in Taiwan (see Table 2.3).

Managers of Japanese affiliates in ASEAN countries cited the following impediments to job rotation: 'A high turnover ratio makes job rotation impossible' (electronics assembly plants in Malaysia); 'Employees are willing to do a fixed job, but unwilling to do more than one task if the wage is the same' (auto parts and electronics parts in Malaysia; electronics parts in Singapore); 'We want to implement job rotation, but it entails certain drawbacks. It hurts employees' pride as they think the jobs are being reassigned because they are incompetent' (auto assembly and electronics assembly in Thailand; auto parts in Malaysia); 'Employees are unwilling to move to a different workplace because of strong sense of companionship with their fellow workers' (auto parts in Malaysia); and 'Employees who have work experience at US affiliates have a strong desire to cling to their jobs' (electronics parts in Thailand).

Participation by ordinary production workers in maintenance operations is also considerably limited at many Japanese affiliates. Many plants deplored the low enthusiasm of ordinary workers for participating in preventive maintenance. In fact, some plants completely forbid ordinary workers to participate in maintenance operations. The tendency to separate ordinary production from product quality checking is more evident than in Japan, Taiwan or Korea. In general, operators do not participate very much in quality control, so plants must secure product quality by employing inspectors and other quality control personnel. There are, however, a few plants where methods of securing quality are almost the same as at mother plants in Japan. Thus narrow and fixed job assignments, and the separation of ordinary operations from trouble-shooting tasks, are the rule at affiliated plants in Singapore, Malaysia and Thailand.

Education and training   There are limitations to which Japanese affiliates are able to implement a training programme that emphasises OJT. This programme is supplemented by sending personnel to Japan for training, and inviting Japanese trainers to the local plants, just as in Taiwan and Korea. Newly-established, export-orientated plants in particular, or sometimes older plants that are attempting to renew and expand their facilities in order to cope with an expanding domestic market, devote themselves to education and training. Notably, some electronics plants in Singapore, along with or sometimes in place of their mother plants in Japan, function as training centres for their sister plants in other parts of Asia, including mainland China. This function of Japanese affiliates in Singapore stems from their high production control capability, the advantages of being a society where many languages, including Chinese, are spoken, and the commonality of their machines and equipment with those at their sister plants in the ASEAN countries and China, where production machines are less automated than in Japan.

Group Consciousness and labour relations   Application for Group consciousness is rated at 3.2 points, or almost the same as in Taiwan and Korea (3.4 points) and the United States (3.2 points). Small-group activities such as QC teamwork are carried out at twenty-eight Japanese affiliates, twelve of which have rules specifying that all workers should participate in such activities. The actual number of plants that implement small group activities is larger than in the United States, and their proportion to surveyed plants is as high as in Taiwan and Korea. However, enthusiasm, voluntariness and activity effectiveness are generally inferior to that seen at affiliates in Taiwan and Korea.

The majority of the plants adopt open-style offices, though the number of plants at which management-level employees have individual offices is greater than in Taiwan and Korea. Also, there are two auto assembly plants in Thailand that have separate dining halls for the managerial staff, a practice seldom found at Japanese affiliates in Taiwan, Korea or the United States. The plants seem to encounter some difficulty regarding a sense of unity among employees in Malaysia, which is a multi-ethnic and multireligious society, although there are no serious problems. As is well known, Japanese affiliates in Malaysia prepare meals for various ethnic groups at employee cafeterias, provide praying rooms for Muslims in factories, and extend the noon recess for praying on Friday.

The lower degree of application for Group V, labour relations, or for the element, Harmonious labour relations, does not indicate that labour relations in ASEAN countries are worse than in Taiwan and Korea or the United States (see Table 2.2). Indeed, there are few labour problems in Malaysia and Singapore, where labour movement is government-regulated. What it does reflect is that companies do not have to pay much attention to labour relations, unlike in the United States, where various bargaining rules have been formulated meticulously in the course of traditionally antagonistic labour relations.

'Material–method': maintenance, quality control and procurement The degree of application for maintenance receives a rating of 3.0 points, which is just between the average rating in Taiwan and Korea (3.3 points) and in the United States (2.6 points). It is higher than in the United States because this survey evaluated the hiring and development of inexperienced employees into shop-floor maintenance personnel as an example of application orientation. With respect to the maintenance capability itself, there are a number of plants where there are difficulties with preventive maintenance, where troubleshooting is not carried out quickly, and where, as a result, Japanese employees, including temporary visiting staff, must participate in maintenance operations.

Some plants try to build quality into the production process by using various practices such as establishing standard work procedures that specify particular items to check for quality. However, these attempts do not meet with substantial success, so the affiliates typically secure product quality at the shipment stage by stationing numerous personnel and adopting a double or triple checking system. In Malaysia and Thailand, the Japanese affiliates typically experience 'four times as many in-process defects as their Japanese mother plants' (auto assembly and electronics assembly in Thailand). Defects found during manufacturing are mainly the result of defective quality in externally procured components or parts that were damaged during transportation, or errors arising through manual operations such as improper insertion of parts. However, some managers maintained that in-process defect ratios at affiliates were lower than in Japan. Reasons they cited included the observation that their plants manufacture products with lower functionality than plants in Japan, or that their ordinary female production workers are young, whereas their counterparts in Japan are middle-aged part-timers. Some managers also recognised distinct advantages enjoyed by the local plants. In particular, they raised the point that since the manufacturing processes that are subcontracted out by Japan are completed in-house, this enables closer control over the process and facilitates feedback.

In not a few plants, Japanese employees must participate in solving quality problems, just as they do in the case of plant maintenance. Moreover, in Malaysia and Thailand, quality standards for products that target the local market are even lower than in Taiwan and Korea. This further decreases the application rating for quality control. The situation is much different in Singapore, however. An electronics parts plant manager there appraised the capability of his employees highly, saying, 'Our employees have the competence to properly carry out their duties, and are very capable of detecting quality problems or equipment malfunction.'

Regarding parts procurement, almost none of the Japanese affiliates have been able to implement just-in-time practices. Though there are a few plants which are reasonably satisfied with the quality and delivery of locally procured components, Japanese affiliates must nevertheless contend with greater and more frequent problems concerning quality, delivery times and missing items than do their counterparts in Taiwan or Korea. However, some plants, especially newly-established ones, are eager to provide technological assistance in the hopes of fostering the development of local suppliers.

Factors hindering method-type application

Although there are no clear institutional impediments to the introduction of Japanese production systems, method-type application is only achieved to a low extent. This is primarily attributed to a lack of motivation on the part of the Japanese affiliates themselves. In the case of products targeting the local market, various protective measures, such as high import tariffs, free the affiliates from having to secure product quality and production efficiency to an even greater extent than in Taiwan or Korea. A low wage rate is also an important factor, since export-orientated plants, which must secure a level of product quality at the shipment stage comparable to that achieved in Japan, station numerous inspectors at various stages of the manufacturing process to inspect quality rather than build it into the production process. The additional costs of the extra manpower are compensated by low wage rates. Finally, a crucial factor is the industrialisation of Thailand and Malaysia, which has a much shorter history than that in Taiwan and Korea. In general, these countries have not reached the stage where companies are able to introduce Japanese methods, such as job rotation. The challenge that the Japanese affiliates face now is to train their employees to work in modern factories and be able to carry out their assigned tasks properly. This is illustrated typically in the case of newly-established, export-orientated plants. Japanese affiliates of this type attempt to achieve production efficiency and product quality within a system based on the volume production of a limited variety of relatively low added-value products or models, and on work organisation that assigns individual workers to rigidly fixed job areas. This type of production system stands in sharp contrast to the small-lot, diverse-product system encountered in Japan, as it does to the traditional mass production system in the United States. As will be discussed in more detail later, the production system adopted by the newly-established plants in ASEAN countries is characterised by workplace-orientated management under the leadership of Japanese employees.

Regarding the social conditions of the host countries, it should first be recognised that the existence of a considerable disparity between upper and lower social strata makes it difficult for Japanese affiliates to implement Japanese practices. As noted upon in the section discussing the wage and promotion system, social gaps, as reflected in academic background, are introduced directly into the corporate hierarchy, and it is difficult for any given employee to catch up with another who has a higher level of education. These conditions would be expected to hinder participation in management on the part of a wide range of employees, as well as co-ordination among different sections on the principle of information sharing. However, according to a report by the World Bank, income gaps have narrowed and a middle class has been created in the ASEAN countries.[17] These changes may construct new circumstances that are more favorable to implementing Japanese methods. Second, it is unlikely that the Japanese system, which in its original form exists for a homogeneous group of employees, would function well in the multi-ethnic and multireligious societies of Malaysia and Singapore. Third, although turnover ratios differ remarkably from region to region, and company to company, another impediment is the high degree of employee mobility. Many factories located in large cities such as Bangkok, Kuala Lumpur and Singapore are concerned about high turnover ratios and employee recruitment. This also hinders the formation of multifunctional skills through long-term employment. Fourth, as examined in the section concerning multifunctional skill formation, it should also be remembered that people's differing behavioural patterns and sense of values pose yet another hindrance to the application of the Japanese production methods.

Where method-type application is insufficient, it is supplemented with result-type application, both in terms of human and material aspects.

Strong Reliance on 'Human-Result' and 'Material-Result'

Management under the leadership of Japanese expatriates   A notable difference between Japanese affiliates in Taiwan or Korea, and those in the ASEAN countries, is that Japanese expatriates in the ASEAN countries are clearly in control of management. As far as the actual ratio of Japanese expatriates to the total number of employees is concerned, there is little difference between the affiliates in Taiwan or Korea and those in the ASEAN countries. This is illustrated by the fact that eighteen out of thirty-five affiliates in ASEAN countries have a ratio of under 1 per cent; thirteen have between 1 and 2 per cent; and four have between 2 and 3 per cent (see Table 2.5). Nevertheless, there are salient differences between the roles of expatriates in these two regions. First, most of the plants in the ASEAN countries employ Japanese expatriates among their top executives. Second, Japanese expatriates also assume important executive, rather than advisory, positions in crucial divisions such as manufacturing, production engineering, production control, quality control, purchasing, accounting and finance, and marketing.[18]

The limited number of Japanese expatriates may be attributed to government policies of the host countries that restrict the number of work permits issued to Japanese nationals in order to promote a hasty transfer of technology. It is also the result of the corporate policy of the companies' Japanese headquarters that is aimed at curtailing personnel expenses. Some Japanese companies attempt to supplement the insufficient number of Japanese expatriates stationed at their ASEAN affiliates by dispatching many extra employees from Japan for short-term temporary assignments. As some managers of Japanese affiliates pointed out: 'The number of Japanese who are employed on short-term temporary assignments amounts to 2000 man-days annually' (auto assembly plant in Thailand); 'Now we have 150 man-day supporters from Japan each month' (electronics assembly plant in Thailand); 'There is no end to the number of temporary dispatched Japanese employees' (electronics parts plant in Singapore); 'Once work permits expire, other than for key positions authorised by the government, our plant cannot be operated without a number of Japanese employees who are temporarily brought in under the pretext of acting as trainers.' These temporary employees are indispensable, not only for newly established export-orientated plants, but also for old, experienced plants, that are renewing and enlarging production facilities in accordance with an expanding domestic market. They play various roles ranging from giving instructions on how to make production equipment in the host countries, to training local employees, providing assistance with the introduction of new production lines or new products, improving product quality, and giving instructions on how to increase local procurement.

Various factors underlie differences between affiliates in Taiwan or Korea and affiliates in the ASEAN countries regarding the application of the 'human–result' aspect of the Japanese production systems. Even in Singapore, a manager pointed out, 'Our local managers have not been trained to work in large corporations as well as those in the United States or European countries.' Moreover, it is hardly surprising that countries such as Thailand and Malaysia, where industrialisation has taken place only relatively recently, face a shortage of local managerial talent. There are also notable differences in the extent to which Japanese management and production methods are understood. Such differences stem from various elements, including a relative cultural dissimilarity to Japan (compared with Taiwan and Korea), a Western influence on people with higher academic backgrounds,[19] and linguistic communication difficulties. In addition, managers of many export-orientated factories mentioned, 'The presence of Japanese employees at the affiliates is indispensable for conducting business with Japan and other countries.' This need also stems from various factors including a shortage of experienced managerial talent, and a limited understanding of Japanese methods. At the same time, it should also be remembered that few Japanese companies maintain well-organised management systems for the control and co-ordination of their world-wide production and sales networks, and that, therefore, they rely strongly on the human factors of Japanese personnel.

Reliance on Japan for equipment and components   The higher degree of application for equipment at affiliates in ASEAN countries (4.0), compared with those in Taiwan or Korea (3.5) reflects the fact that most export-orientated plants in ASEAN countries procure their production equipment almost entirely from Japan. Of course, many affiliated plants are equipped with machines that are easier to operate and repair, since they are somewhat less automated than the machines installed at the mother plants in Japan. Some plants even utilise second-hand machines, partly on account of lower costs. Local content ratios are lower in the ASEAN countries than in Taiwan and Korea, since industries that can supply components have not developed to the extent that they have in Taiwan and Korea. For the same reason, functionally critical parts and materials are procured from plants in Japan or from local Japanese-affiliated suppliers. Export-orientated plants in particular display this tendency strongly. There is no doubt that reliance on Japan application in terms of 'material-result', that is, equipment and components, plays a crucial role in sustaining product quality of the Japanese affiliates.

Comparison Between Newer and Older Factories

As already mentioned, Japanese affiliates in the ASEAN countries can be divided into two groups. One group includes the older, domestic-market-orientated plants, which were established for the purpose of attempting to skirt around trade barriers such as high tariffs in the early days of Japanese foreign direct investment. Typical examples of this group are auto assembly factories and mini-Matsushita-type electrical plants. The other group consists of the newer, export-orientated plants, which started operations in the 1980s, and particularly in the second half of the 1980s, and which utilise new, automated equipment.

As shown in Table 2.9, comparison between these two groups reveals some interesting observations. The older plants receive higher application ratings for Multifunctional skills, and Small-group activities than do the newer affiliates. The older plants require more flexible work organisation, as they manufacture small quantities of a large variety of products. Also, Japanese methods seem to have penetrated the shop-floors spontaneously over the course of the long period of operation under the leadership of Japanese expatriates.

On the other hand, the newer plants receive higher ratings of application for Education and training, Equipment, Procurement methods, Hiring policy, and Delegation of authority. At the present stage, the newer factories attempt to achieve high product quality and high production efficiency by relying on new equipment from Japan, by assigning workers to more narrowly defined job areas, by specialising in the production of fewer products and models, and by engaging in mass production. At these plants, management places an important emphasis on the hiring of competent employees whom they train enthusiastically and sometimes send to Japan for additional training at the mother plants, in order to develop employees that have advanced skills for specialised tasks. Also, they are eager to foster the growth of local suppliers through the provision of technological assistance. In the future, the manufacture of additional products, as well as of products of higher added value, will be transferred to the affiliated plants, and therefore more flexible work organisation and more multiskilled workers will be required. Under such circumstances, efforts at education and training, hiring, and the fostering of local suppliers may lay the groundwork for raising the degree of method–aspect application.

Table 2.9 Comparison between older and newer plants in three ASEAN
countries

		Average	Older plants (before 1979)	Newer plants (after 1980)
I	Work Organisation and Administration	3.3	3.3	3.3
	① Job classification	4.5	4.6	4.5
	② Multifunctional skills	2.6	2.9	2.4
	③ Education and training	3.3	3.1	3.4
	④ Wage system	3.1	3.0	3.1
	⑤ Promotion	3.1	3.1	3.2
	⑥ First-line supervisor	2.9	2.9	3.0
II	Production Control	3.4	3.2	3.5
	⑦ Equipment	4.0	3.5	4.4
	⑧ Maintenance	3.0	3.1	3.0
	⑨ Quality control	3.2	3.1	3.3
	⑩ Process management	3.2	3.2	3.2
III	Procurement	3.2	3.2	3.4
	⑪ Local content	3.1	3.1	3.2
	⑫ Suppliers	3.8	3.8	3.9
	⑬ Procurement method	2.8	2.6	3.0
IV	Group Consciousness	3.2	3.2	3.1
	⑭ Small-group activities	2.9	3.1	2.7
	⑮ Information sharing	3.3	3.4	3.3
	⑯ Sense of unity	3.3	3.2	3.4
V	Labour Relations	3.1	3.1	3.2
	⑰ Hiring policy	3.1	2.9	3.2
	⑱ Long-term employment	3.0	3.1	3.0
	⑲ Harmonious labour relations	3.3	3.3	3.4
	⑳ Grievance procedure	3.1	3.1	3.2
VI	Parent–Subsidiary Relations	2.9	2.7	3.1
	㉑ Ratio of Japanese expatriates	1.6	1.5	1.7
	㉒ Delegation of authority	3.2	2.9	3.4
	㉓ Position of local managers	3.9	3.6	4.1
Average of 23 items		**3.2**	**3.1**	**3.2**

III   PLANT OPERATING PERFORMANCE

This section will deal with the performance of Japanese affiliates with regard to profitability, product quality and labour productivity. However, since the accuracy of the data obtained differs among the various plants that were surveyed, general performance trends will have to suffice.

Profitability

Japanese affiliates in East Asian countries are fairly profitable. In Taiwan and Korea, twenty-three out of twenty-five affiliates, and in ASEAN countries, thirty-two out of thirty-four plants surveyed (one plant in Thailand is excluded, because it started production just prior to our observations) were operating in the black (see Table 2.10). Furthermore, quite a few of these plants were profitable soon after the start of operations. In contrast, in the United States, many of the surveyed factories (including those which had been in operation for a long time) were not very profitable.

Data published by MITI, which targets a much broader sample of Japanese affiliates overseas, confirms the superior profitability of Japanese affiliates located in East Asian countries compared to their counterparts in the United States or Europe. Table 2.11 shows 1992 data for the electrical machinery and transportation equipment industries from MITI's data.[20] It clearly demonstrates the profitability of Japanese affiliates in the NIEs and ASEAN countries, in contrast to affiliates in the European Union (EU) countries, whose aggregate performance showed a deficit, or to affiliates in the United States, which were showing neither profit not loss.

However, it is clear that managerial conditions in the NIEs (including Taiwan and Korea) are becoming more severe. The manager of an electronics parts plant in Korea, for example, pointed out that his profit margin was becoming narrower. A survey conducted by the Japan Export and Import Bank has also shown that profitability self-evaluation by managers at Japanese affiliates in the NIEs deteriorated slightly between 1992 and 1994 because of slower economic growth rates in the NIEs as well as stagnating exports because of the economic slump in Japan.[21]

Our survey cannot fully explain the considerable difference between the profitability of Japanese affiliates in East Asia and in the United States. Profitability is determined not only by shop-floor operations but also by various other factors, such as overall managerial ability (including the function of the regional headquarters and the sales network); competitive conditions (influenced by the number of competitors, the existence of

Table 2.10   Plant operating performance in East Asia

	Taiwan and Korea			Three ASEAN countries			
	Total	Taiwan	Korea	Total	Thailand	Malaysia	Singapore
Profitability							
Black	22	15	7	32	14	15	3
Red	3	2	1	2	1	0	1
In-process defect ratios							
Superior to Japan	1	0	1	5	2	2	1
Equivalent to Japan	4	2	2	10	2	6	2
Inferior to Japan	20	16	4	20	12	7	1
Labour productivity							
Superior to Japan	0	0	0	2	1	1	0
Equivalent to Japan	6	2	4	10	1	5	4
Inferior to Japan	19	16	3	23	14	9	0

Table 2.11   Managerial performance of Japanese affiliated companies, by MITI data

	Asia	NIEs	ASEAN	USA	EC	World
Operating profit ratios to sales (%)						
Electrical machinery	5.2	7.0	2.9	0.0	−2.1	1.4
Transportation equipment	5.9	8.3	5.7	0.8	−5.0	0.3
Operating profit per company (millions yen)						
Electrical machinery	349	5.1	2.2	4	−277	126
Transportation equipment	528	913	445	195	−2 122	59
Sales per company (millions yen)						
Electrical machinery	7 346	8 528	6 853	13 481	13 283	9 543
Transportation equipment	12 570	16 228	12 171	35 750	50 688	25 832
Number of Japanese affiliated companies						
Electrical machinery	416	208	170	160	162	820
Transportation equipment	171	51	86	107	42	371

Source: MITI (1994a).

local rivals, and brand image and recognition); and the social environment (including government regulations such as safety standards and local content ratios). Discrepancies among the profitability levels of different host countries were, however, relevant to the motivation of Japanese corporations when they embarked upon foreign production. Trade friction essentially compelled Japanese companies to establish local production in the United States, at least in the initial stage, whereas economically rational judgements were the more determining factors in the case of East Asian operations. This contrast is reflected in the following differences in plant operations.

First, there is a remarkable difference between the number of Japanese expatriates, or the ratio of Japanese expatriates to total employees, at Japanese affiliates, according to region. It is said that personnel expenses for expatriates are more than three times as high as in Japan, and affiliates in East Asian countries, which are managed by fewer expatriates and which enjoy lower labour costs for local employees, are therefore more favourable from this perspective. Furthermore, the necessity for many Japanese expatriates is the result of inefficient plant operations, and so, in addition to the direct costs of higher personnel expenses, there are also other, invisible costs. In the United States, Japanese-style management at affiliates is implemented through the existence of many Japanese expatriates stationed at strategic points throughout the corporate organisation although, formally, they are often called 'co-ordinators' or 'advisers'.[22]

The second point concerns product quality resulting from competitive conditions. In general, the East Asian local markets are not as competitive as those in the United States. This eases the burden of having to secure high product quality at the shipment stage, and contributes to the good profitability seen among the affiliates in East Asia. In the United States, Japanese affiliates are compelled to secure an equivalent level of product quality to that in Japan, even though it is difficult to build quality into the production process. To achieve such quality standards, many Japanese affiliates in the USA have a ratio of inspectors or QC employees to ordinary production workers that is two to four times as high as in Japan. Moreover, wage rates of skilled workers such as QC personnel are higher than of ordinary workers, since US plants, unlike most of their counterparts in East Asia, adopt a wage system in which rates are determined by job categories. The presence of a large number of Japanese expatriates, as mentioned above, is also directly and indirectly relevant to securing product quality in the United States.

Third, Japanese affiliates in the United States, who face official and unofficial demands for higher local content, are compelled to increase their procurement of parts and materials from local sources, and thus occasionally overlook quality and cost considerations, which consume profits. On the other hand, affiliates in East Asia have the freedom to accept or reject parts from local suppliers, as they see fit, although the demand for higher local content in East Asia cannot be entirely disregarded. Of course, this is also related to the level of product quality required in the respective local market.

Quality

Quality is evaluated in two ways: one is the level at the shipment stage, and the other is the level expressed by in-process defect ratios. With regard to the shipment stage, as mentioned earlier, the quality of products that affiliates in East Asia export to Japan or the United States is equivalent to the quality of products that are made in Japan, whereas the quality of products for the local market is lower. Particularly in the auto assembly and auto parts industries, there is a wide gap between the quality achieved in Japan and that of East Asian countries. This is a result of low import competition, since Taiwan and Korea prohibit almost entirely the import of completely assembled cars from Japan, and because the ASEAN countries impose remarkably high import tariffs on motor vehicles. However, affiliates in East Asian countries will need gradually to improve product quality, as a growing local market and a certain amount of import liberalisation results in greater competition.

In-process defect ratios offer clues as to the performance of quality building into the production process. There are twenty-one affiliated plants in Taiwan and Korea and twenty in the ASEAN countries whose performance measured in terms of in-process defect ratios is lower than that of their respective mother plants in Japan (see Table 2.10). Among these plants, in-process defect ratios are typically two to four times as high as in Japan. Some managers remarked, self-deprecatorily, 'We actually face a heap of defective products.' These facts underscore the difficulty of building quality into the production process at affiliates located overseas.

At the same time, however, it should be noted that four plants in Taiwan and Korea have in-process defect ratios that are equivalent or even superior to those in Japan, and that another four factories outperform the best of their sister plants abroad, registering defect ratios that are just slightly lower than in Japan. Thus, eight out of twenty-five plants are able to achieve in-process defect ratios that are almost equivalent to their mother plants in Japan. This shows, therefore, that there are Japanese affiliates in Taiwan and Korea which are able to build quality into the production process that ranks among the best of their sister plants, even if slightly inferior to their mother plants in Japan.

Compared with the Japanese affiliates in Taiwan and Korea, an even higher proportion of affiliates in the ASEAN countries achieve a level of performance regarding in-process defect ratios that is equivalent to that of their mother plants in Japan. Five plants registered superior performance to their mother plants, and ten registered equivalent in-process defect ratios. Affiliates in Malaysia and Singapore registered the best performance, since more export-orientated plants are located there. Superior in-process defect ratios at export-orientated plants result mainly from fewer kinds of products being manufactured, each of which has a mechanism that is less complicated and is therefore more easily produced than those in Japan. Some affiliates attribute their good performance to their ability to monitor fully the entire production process and receive a large amount of feedback. Unlike Japan, where some of the manufacturing processes are undertaken by subcontractors, these affiliates carry out all the processes themselves.

Labour Productivity

Labour productivity was evaluated by comparing the 'standard time', that is, time allotted for the fulfillment of specific job tasks, and the 'achievement ratios', that is, the ratio of achieved tasks to specified tasks during the standard time. Even in such a simple comparison, it is clear that factories in Japan show high productivity, while labour productivity of the majority of the affiliates: nineteen plants in Taiwan and Korea and twenty-three in ASEAN countries, suffers in comparison to their mother plants in Japan (see Table 2.10). However, six plants in Taiwan and Korea and twelve in ASEAN countries register labour productivity that is equivalent to or higher than their mother plants. Although they are not in a majority, the existence of many plants with good labour productivity is a conspicuous characteristic of Japanese affiliates in East Asian countries (including the NIEs, ASEAN countries and China) which seems rarely to be observed in other host countries.

However, labour productivity in terms of standard time is only one aspect of actual production efficiency. A factory's production efficiency is determined by the overall strength of management and production, evaluated in terms of how flexibly and smoothly the plant can cope with the introduction of new products or equipment and change its model mix, how quickly it can resolve equipment or quality problems, how successfully it can take measures to prevent recurrence, and whether it can procure parts and materials with consistent quality and punctual delivery. Even affiliates in Taiwan and Korea lag far behind their mother plants in Japan when evaluated in these terms. At the present stage, affiliates in ASEAN countries are barely able to cope with these tasks, and without the assistance of their Japanese employees, would be even less so. Problems stem from the lack of adequately skilled personnel to assign to the tasks of securing quality, and maintaining and trouble-shooting equipment, and even more seriously, from the difficulty of achieving co-ordination and co-operation between different sections. Moreover, Japanese expatriates and local managers agree that it is difficult to develop *kaizen* activities through participation from the shop floor.

IV   CONVERGING AVERAGE DEGREE OF APPLICATION FOR TWENTY-THREE ITEMS

Finally, let us consider the implications of the fact that Taiwan and Korea, the ASEAN countries, and the United States all receive around 3.3 point application ratings for the twenty-three items in our Hybrid Evaluation Model, despite their distinct hybrid configurations (see Table 2.2).

The hybrid configurations of Taiwan and Korea are characterised by a much higher application rating for 'method'. This is attributed to the lack of clear institutional hindrances to implementing Japanese methods. Differences between Taiwan and Korea are reflected in Taiwan's higher application for 'human–method' and lower application for 'material–result', as opposed to Korea's lower application for 'human–result' and greater reliance upon 'material–result'.

ASEAN countries are similar to Taiwan and Korea inasmuch as they have no clear institutional obstacles to implementing Japanese methods, but nevertheless the affiliates in those countries failed to introduce Japanese methods adequately. This is because of policies on the part of the affiliates themselves and social conditions such as behavioural patterns and wider gaps between the different social strata. Strong leadership of a few Japanese expatriates and a reliance on 'material–result' compensates for insufficient methods. In the United States, where well-established production systems such as job control unionism often hinder the introduction of the Japanese system, there is a relatively low average degree of 'method' application, although its true extent varies from industry to industry according to the degree of necessity for implementing Japanese methods. In the USA, as in the ASEAN countries, insufficient application of 'method' is compensated by application of 'result', in terms of both human and material elements. In particular, high product quality and a certain degree of production efficiency at Japanese affiliates in the USA are undoubtedly sustained by numerous Japanese expatriates who are formally and informally stationed at strategic points within the organisation. Each host country (or region) is therefore characterised by its own distinctive hybrid configuration. In spite of these differences, however, the average degree of application for the twenty-three items in each country converges at around 3.3 points.

This can be explained as follows: elements that are relatively easily introduced into the host countries, and which are also strategically important for maintaining satisfactory managerial performance, may take precedence over those that are transplanted with more difficulty. Sometimes, affiliates may also have to implement certain Japanese methods, regardless of the accompanying tangible and intangible costs. In this case, affiliates can reduce tension or friction stemming from the application of such elements by means of adaptation, or lower application of other aspects. At the same time, limited managerial resources prevent affiliates from applying all the elements. The result of all of these factors is a 3.3 point rating, which represents a kind of balance between application and adaptation. Needless to say, the 3.3 point rating means the hybrid is positioned slightly closer to the Japanese model, which is one of the polar extremes in the hybrid model. It will be recalled that a rating of 5 points equates with a 100 per cent application of Japanese elements, and 1 point corresponds to the total absence of Japanese elements, and all with respect to the 'method', 'result', 'human', and 'material' aspects.

It is also notable that most of the factories that co-operated with the survey achieved acceptable performance in terms of production efficiency and product quality, although the extent varied from plant to plant. Therefore the 3.3 point rating must be interpreted as an average of plants which achieved a certain level of managerial performance. Also, the 3.3 point rating remains only an average, and individual plant deviations from that average should also be taken into consideration. Nevertheless, it seems clear that current attempts by the affiliates to apply Japanese systems result in an average 3.3 point rating, which represents a balance between aggressive application of elements necessary to maintain a certain level of managerial performance in an environment that differs from Japan, and adaptation to other elements necessary to avoid needless costs and tensions and thereby to stabilise plant operations.

Notes

1. Ministry of International Trade and Industry (1994a).
2. For the first field study in the United States see The Institute of Social Science, (University of Tokyo) (1990).
3. For example, one joint venture between a Japanese company and a Korean firm affiliated with one of big chebols introduced a similar framework for a wage system as a Korean firm. But it applied individual performance evaluations for production workers until one year before we visited. With regard to the Korean wage system, also see Kodama (1995).
4. The lower degree of application for Multifunctional skills in Korea is attributed mainly to the fact that there are no auto assembly plants in Japanese affiliates surveyed in Korea. In order to secure production efficiency and product quality, this industry relies on multifunctional skills of a wide rage of employees including ordinary production workers, to a larger degree than do other industries. Therefore, it receives a higher degree of application for Multifunctional skills than other industries.
5. Hattori (1988).
6. A view of Kumazawa (1989) on labour disputes at Japanese affiliates is entirely the opposite of these statements.
7. Even in Japan, of course, enthusiasm and the effects of small-group activities differ from company to company, or from plant to plant.
8. Though, exceptionally, one plant has between 3 and 4 per cent of Japanese expatriates and another between 5 and 6 per cent, these two plants have begun operating since the latter half of the 1980s.
9. For Japanese affiliated plants surveyed in the United States, see Abo (1994a), ch. 3.
10. Among thirty-four Japanese affiliated plants surveyed in the United States, there were only five joint ventures with the participation of local capital: Abo (1994a).
11. In three ASEAN countries, as will be mentioned later, more than half of Japanese affiliated plants surveyed were categorised as joint ventures with local capital. Nevertheless, almost all the plants are run by Japanese top executives.
12. At first, we planned to survey a similar number of Japanese affiliates in Korea as in Taiwan. However, we could visit only half of the plants targeted, first, because Japanese companies might feel some 'constraint' with Korean partners.
13. With regard to automobiles, import from Japan is prohibited almost entirely in both Taiwan and Korea. Regarding electronic and electrical products, the import of sixty-one items is prohibited in Korea, and VCRs have imposed tariffs of 22.5 to 27.5 per cent in Taiwan. MITI (1994b).
14. According to a manager of one electronics parts company, manufacturing costs are 40 per cent lower in Korea than in Japan.
15. Hattori (1987).
16. For the management of Japanese affiliates in ASEAN countries, see also Yamashita (1991).
17. The World Bank (1993).
18. See also Kumazawa (1989) and Kobayashi (1992).
19. Kawabe ((1991) stresses this point.
20. Ministry of International Trade and Industry (MITI) (1994a).
21. Tejima and Nakajima (1995).
22. Abo (1994a).

3 The Rapid Growth of the East Asian Economies and Japanese Foreign Direct Investment

The Asian Growth Triangle: Structure, Change and Perspective*

Jaw-Yann Twu

I INTRODUCTION

The Asian Growth Triangle discussed in this chapter refers, first, to the original USA–Japan–NIEs growth triangle (GT), which developed mainly between 1984 and 1987. It also refers to a new GT, the so-called 'compound GT', involving Japan–NIEs–China and USA–NIEs–China, which formed in the early 1990s and which has continued to develop gradually since then. This chapter will analyse the conditions underlying the rapid development of the original GT, and will review the process through which they evolved into the new compound GT, in order to illustrate the significance of their roles in East Asian economic development.

The main purpose of exploring the evolution and development of the Asian GT is to probe explain the factors behind the economic surge of East Asia (mainly the NIEs). Of course, there may be numerous aspects to each of the factors, and it may be difficult to distinguish internal from external causes. As is evident from various explanations in the literature for the industrialisation of the NIEs, as well as for East Asian economic development overall, a consensus has yet to be established.[1] This study is an attempt to provide a fresh analysis; an approach to understanding the East Asian development model from a new perspective.

II DEVELOPMENT OF THE ORIGINAL GT AND ITS ESTABLISHING CONDITIONS

Conventional GT Development

The rapid development of the original GT is evident from an analysis of the NIEs' import-dependence on Japan and export-dependence on the USA. As Table 3.1 indicates, NIEs exports to the USA and imports from Japan both peaked in 1986, at 37.2 per cent and 26.9 per cent, respectively. Exports to the US made up 31.2 per cent to 37.2 per cent of total exports between 1983 and 1988, while imports from Japan made up 25.0 per cent to 26.9 per cent between 1986 and 1988. Broadly speaking, 1983 to 1988 was the period of most rapid development for the US–Japan–NIEs GT.

What accounts for the rapid development of this GT during this period, and its subsequent decline thereafter? More importantly, did this original GT play an important role in promoting East Asian economic development? And what lessons does this provide for economic theory? This chapter will address these issues.

First, what are the reasons for the rapid development of the original GT during the period from 1984–8? Exports to the USA began notably to dominate exports from the NIEs in 1983–4, and imports from Japan, similarly, began to assume a pronounced lead among all NIEs imports in 1986–7. Theory provides a ready explanation for this trend: the existence of the US market was fertile soil for exports from the NIEs, and as the NIEs realised the necessity of importing equipment, spare parts and intermediate materials from Japan, these exports provided the means to pay for such imports. Naturally, a time lag occurred between the rise in exports to the USA and in imports from Japan. In any event, during the period of the original GT, the NIEs experienced a trade surplus with the USA and a trade deficit with Japan. These international economic relationships are important factors in the rapid economic take-off experienced by the NIEs.

From this perspective, the Asian NIEs enjoyed a special advantage, in contrast to other Third World developing countries. Although the reasons for this are worth pondering upon, it is first necessary to understand the contents and framework of the original GT.

Contents of the Original GT

The framework of the original GT is evident from Figure 3.1. The important features of the GT are summarised as follows:

1. A triaxial relationship constitutes the overall framework of the GT, with the USA as the main axis, Japan in the position of an intermediary, medium axis, and the NIEs at the outer edge, in the position of the smallest axis. This differs from the general accepted view, which regards the USA as an absorber (for providing the market) and Japan as a supplier (for providing machinery, equipment and intermediate materials). The absorber–supplier doctrine[2] only considers general factors of marketing supply and demand, and does not take into account the GT framework that arises from these relationships. This framework, however, is precisely the item we wish to emphasise.

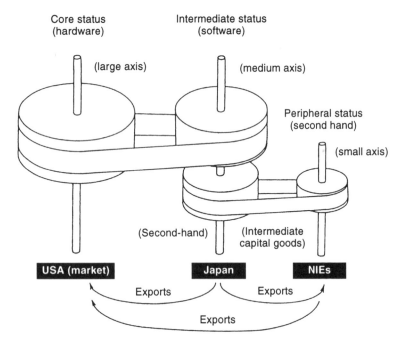

Note: *Core status*: opening up of domestic market, development of basic technology, providing of means of settlement (finance). overseas investment, acceptance of foreign labour, etc.

Intermediate status: opening up of domestic market, introduction of technology (second-hand), economic (second-hand), overseas investment, etc.

Peripheral status: export dependence, introduction of technology (second-hand), economic development (development dictatorship), introduction of foreign capital (foreign exchange system reform, land reform), etc.

Figure 3.1   The flow of technology

Table 3.1 Market sharing structure of NIEs' exports and imports, 1980–94, US$ million, %

Year	Total amount		USA (%)		Japan (%)		EU–4 (%)		NIEs (%)		ASEAN–4 (%)	
	Exports	Imports	Exports	Imports	Exports	Imports	Exports	Imports	Exports	Imports	Exports	Imports
1980	76 421	88 437	24.8	17.6	10.1	23.4	12.5	7.9	8.3	7.2	10.7	11.0
1981	86 640	99 668	26.2	16.9	10.5	23.3	10.5	7.5	8.9	7.7	10.6	9.8
1982	85 823	94 843	27.6	17.6	10.5	21.4	9.8	8.3	8.0	7.3	13.0	11.4
1983	93 365	98 653	32.8	18.1	9.5	22.7	9.2	7.9	7.5	7.1	13.0	11.2
1984	112 094	109 822	35.4	17.5	10.1	23.7	8.4	7.7	7.8	7.9	9.4	10.3
1985	114 001	107 222	34.8	16.8	10.0	22.8	8.0	8.5	7.7	8.2	7.6	9.6
1986	132 517	116 644	37.2	16.1	10.2	26.9	9.2	9.0	7.7	8.8	6.5	8.2
1987	178 054	156 956	35.1	16.1	11.5	26.4	10.4	9.5	8.4	9.5	6.4	8.1
1988	223 818	209 234	31.2	18.1	12.4	25.0	10.5	9.1	9.7	10.3	6.7	8.0
1989	246 498	235 555	29.8	18.0	12.5	23.8	10.3	9.0	10.1	10.5	7.7	7.3
1990	266 900	267 618	27.6	17.3	11.4	22.7	11.2	9.5	10.4	10.4	8.6	7.9
1991	305 570	310 733	24.5	16.4	10.5	22.7	11.1	8.9	10.9	10.7	9.2	8.4
1992	340 477	349 649	24.3	15.7	9.3	22.3	10.3	9.0	11.5	11.2	8.6	8.8
1993	376 432	384 737	23.2	15.3	8.8	21.1	9.7	9.0	11.6	11.3	8.7	8.8
1994	436 472	457 140	21.6	14.3	8.7	20.9	8.8	8.9	11.5	11.0	10.8	9.4

Note: EU–4 refers to four European countries: Britain, Germany, France and Italy.
Source: Economic Planning Agency of Japan, Statistics on the Overseas Economy, January 1996, pp. 93–8.

2. Simply speaking, the dominant characteristic of the GT's framework was the large disparity between the economic achievements of its members: on the basis of GNP, the USA was at the top, Japan in the middle, and the NIEs, as a group, at the bottom. In 1987, for example, the gross national product (GNP) of the USA amounted to US$4539.9 billion, of Japan US$2436 billion, and of the NIEs US$30 billion (data for Hong Kong were gross domestic product (GDP)). Comparative economic indices derived from these data put the NIEs at 100, Japan at 812, and the USA at 1514. If these indices are illustrated in the form of an expanded reproduction model with wheel-style circulation and each economy directly driven by the performance of the economy at the centre (that is, the USA) then it shows that if the US economy turns over once, the Japanese economy may turn over twice, while that of the NIEs turns over fifteen times. By the same token, based on their individual values for GDP, South Korea would have to turn over thirty-five times, Taiwan forty-four times, Hong Kong ninety-six times, and Singapore 221 times. In such a circulation system, the NIEs would be unable to remain upright because the centrifugal force would overwhelm the centripetal force within the system, implying disintegration of the NIE's economies. These conditions underscore the importance of Japans role as intermediary economy in adjusting the huge gap in economic development between the USA and the NIEs. There is no doubt that Japan can perform such a function. Through technology transfer, Japan adopted advanced US technology for itself and allowed the NIEs to take over the manufacture of secondary products suitable to their level of technology, thus mitigating the effects of technological shock. This is an undeniably important factor in promoting the economic development of the NIEs.

3. Needless to say, the source of the GT's technological progress was the USA. American technology benefited significantly from investment aimed at the development of military capabilities, the purpose of which was to defeat the former USSR (now Russia), and maintain the Pax Americana world system. On the other hand, it cannot be ignored that, as a core country, the USA provided the export market for the NIEs. The USA continued to maintain an open market in spite of its already huge trade deficit. This policy was due to the special advantage of the US dollar in international markets: namely, its position as key currency in the International Monetary Fund (IMF). This advantage provided the leverage to maintain a trade deficit without the necessity of tightening budgets and limiting imports. As a

result, the USA remains a major economic power today, even though the trade surpluses it enjoyed in the 1950s have long since been replaced by enormous trade deficits, and its currency has suffered radical depreciation.

4.   At least two conditions were necessary for the NIEs to enter the GT framework and experience the rapid development of their economies: (a) land and foreign exchange reforms that established a solid base for export-orientated industrialisation; and (b) the existence of a 'development dictatorship' that enforced the low-wage system and ignored environmental pollution. Land reform, in this context, means the replacement of a tenant-farmer system of land ownership with an owner-farmer system. It should also be pointed out that the agricultural surplus was not allowed to remain with the farmers for their own consumption but was allocated to export industries to earn foreign exchange (US dollars) for the state. In other words, land reforms did not only raise agricultural productivity, they also converted savings into investments. In Taiwan, the collection of the agricultural surplus by the central government was carried out through the barter of fertiliser for rice and through forced rice taxation (converting rice into cash for taxation).[3] In South Korea, in addition to forced rice taxation, the government enforced the collection of the agricultural surplus by decreasing the price of agricultural products and controlling the inflation of non-agricultural products.[4] Thus, both Taiwan and South Korea promoted land reforms by sacrificed the interests of the farmers and extracting the agricultural surplus for the governments revenue.

Foreign exchange reform means deregulating foreign currency exchange transactions and stabilising the exchange rate (especially against the US dollar). However huge trade deficits made this difficult to achieve. Taiwan was forced to implement reforms from 1957 to 1960, and South Korea from 1965 to 1966, but since the USA reduced its economic support during those periods, it was necessary for Taiwan and South Korea to earn foreign currency by themselves. In Taiwan's case, its domestic market was saturated and the country needed to export in order to overcome its industrial recession. Although US economic support was reduced, it should nevertheless be pointed out that substantial support remained, without which foreign exchange reforms would not have been possible.

Furthermore, under the 'development dictatorship' described above, trade unions were unable to organise labour for the purpose of increasing wages, and the populace as a whole had no way of combating environmental pollution. This resulted in low wages (relative to the labour productivity) and an expansion of highly-polluting enterprises. These conditions provided opportunities for a rapid expansion of activities by multinational corporations. Therefore, in the initial stage of export-dependent industrialisation, the policy of attracting foreign capital was set up quickly and carried out smoothly.

The two conditions mentioned above depended on the special circumstances of the Cold War. Without the politics of 'anti-Communism' these conditions would not have been fulfilled. From this point of view, the 'anti-Communist' ideology that was supported by most NIEs and the export liberalism advocated by the IMF and the General Agreement on Tariffs and Trade (GATT) both provided good opportunities for the NIEs to achieve rapid industrialisation.

Not all developing countries possessed the international and national conditions described above; in fact, these were found only in East Asia. According to the 1986 Japanese MITI Annual White Paper,[5] the success of the Asian NIEs could be attributed to three conditions. First, their foreign exchange rates were linked with the US dollar and therefore depreciated against the yen. Second, their open-door policy led to an inflow of foreign capital and technology, which contributed greatly to their economic development. And third, they enjoyed preferential tariff treatment by developed countries such as Japan and the USA. This explanation, however, is less than convincing, since these same three advantages were also enjoyed by a number of other Third-World countries. For this reason, it is necessary to explore the special conditions for the NIE's success.

III   FORMATION OF A NEW COMPOUND GT

Paralysis of the Original GT

Unfortunately, the function of the original GT did not last. After peaking in 1986, the original GT started to decline. As Table 3.1 indicated, the NIEs' share of exports to the USA, which was 37.2 per cent in 1986, fell rapidly to 29.8 per cent in 1989 and continued to erode to less than a quarter of all exports, or 21.6 per cent, by 1994. Showing a similar trend, the share of imports from Japan fell from its peak of 26.9 per cent in 1986 to 20.9 per cent in 1994, which was a 6.0 point, or

28.7 per cent decrease. Consequently, the original GT became slack or paralysed.

Why did this happen? Under the impact of its domestic economic recession, the USA was unable to continue playing its role as a core country in the original GT. It is well known that the US average annual balance of payments deficit has exceeded $100 billion since 1984 and that its total debt had risen to $770.5 billion in the period between 1984 and 1989. As a result, the USA, once a great creditor nation, has become a great debtor nation since 1987 by book value, or since 1988 by the market price. Based on market price, its net debt amounted to $611.5 billion in 1992. Naturally, this restricted the degree of openness of the US market towards exports from the NIEs. As an example, in January 1989 the NIEs 'graduated' from the general system of preference (GSP) and were no longer provided the tariff preference they had enjoyed for the ten years since 1976. Moreover, in order to weaken the NIEs' competitiveness and reduce their exports to the American market, the USA applied pressure on the NIEs to appreciate their currency. Furthermore, in 1988, the USA adopted the Omnibus Trade and Competitiveness Act to resist unfair business practices and to force the NIEs to open their markets and increase imports from the USA. Since then, the USA has shunned free trade (open markets) and replaced it with managed trade.

Although total exports from the NIEs to the USA increased from US$49.3 billion in 1986 to US$82.6 billion in 1992 (US$33.3 billion net increase), the proportion fell from 37.2 per cent in 1986 to 24.3 per cent in 1992, (a 12.9 per centage point, or 55 per cent decrease). As indicated in Table 3.1, the channel for NIEs' export to the USA tended towards paralysis and even collapse. This implied that the NIEs' economic growth had to change from export-dependence on the USA to expanding export markets outside the USA. With the US core status weakened, the function of the original GT became paralysed. One might even go so far as to say that, by 1990, the original GT had completed its historical mission.

Another factor in the decline of the original GT function is changes in economic conditions within the NIEs themselves. During the later stage of the original GT, two fundamental internal conditions for the economic development of the NIEs, namely the low-wage system and development dictatorship, as described above, changed and slowly disappeared. For example, in South Korea, Chun Doo-Hwan's military regime was replaced by Roh Tae-Woo's democratic system in 1987; in Taiwan, martial law was lifted in 1987, after thirty-eight years, and Lee Teng-Hui's democratic political system was established. Under these new political systems, the low-wage system collapsed and a large-scale labour movement was launched. In South Korea, wages rose by double-digit percentage points for two consecutive years. In 1991, the index of industrial wages reached 233.6 (taking the index base in 1985 as 100), in other words, it more than doubled within the six-year period 1985 to 1991. In the same period, Taiwan's industrial wages nearly doubled to 193.7 per cent of their 1985 level. The NIEs even began to introduce cheaper foreign labour to compensate for these higher costs. The export advantages that the NIEs had previously enjoyed were gradually lost.

At the June 1988 Toronto Summit, the term NICs (newly industrialising countries), which had been used since 1979, was replaced by NIEs (newly industrialising economies). Although this change was mainly the result of political considerations, it is worth exploring the economic implications. The NIC syndrome merits particular attention. This syndrome refers to problems that resulted from the development dictatorship, such as a growing disparity between industry and agriculture because of the reliance on exports for economic growth, labour problems, serious environmental pollution, asset-inflation, and rampant money worship. In short, prosperity and decay existed simultaneously in the NIC syndrome. Such unprecedented economic change disrupted the old political and economic framework and required a complete reconstruction of the system. The collapse of the development dictatorship symbolised the end of the old framework and the start of a more open and democratic system. Undoubtedly, this was a new challenge for the NIEs.

Formation of the Compound GT

As the original GT experienced paralysis and even collapse, a new compound GT gradually formed in its place. Its framework is illustrated in Figure 3.2 and its features can be summarised as follows.

1. As its name implies, the compound GT is composed of three layers: a base triangle; a middle triangle; and an upper triangle.
2. The base triangle is composed of two channels: Japan–Hong Kong/ Taiwan–China, and the USA–Hong Kong/Taiwan–China. From China's perspective, the former is an import channel and the latter an export channel. These two channels are linked and should be discussed together.
3. The middle triangle consists of multiple layers. On the upper layer there is a large GT including the USA–Japan–China and, on the bottom layer, the two channels mentioned above. Between these two layers there is a multiple triangle with the NIEs at the centre, and with

(A) China

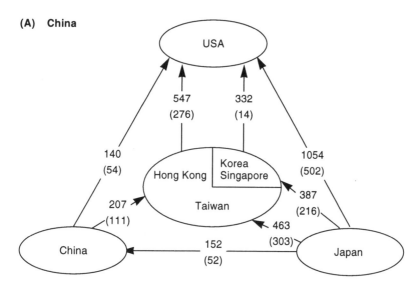

(B) ASEAN countries

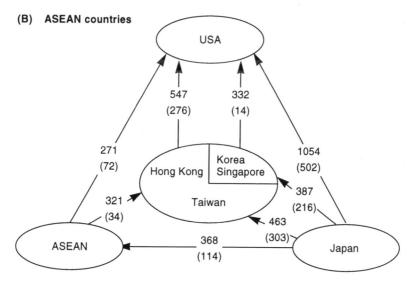

Notes:
1. Sign indicates the export direction, figure in ( ) indicates trade surplus.
2. Japan–NIEs–USA figures indicate total trade of NIEs.
3. Trade from NIEs, ASEAN and China is indicated.
4. Chinese export via Hong Kong marks 61.2 billion.
Source: Economic Planning Agency, *Overseas Economic Data*, July 1995, pp. 88–100.

Figure 3.2   Multi-structure on triangle trade, 1993, US$ billion, %

Hong Kong/Taiwan between China and the USA, South Korea between Japan and the USA, and Singapore among the USA, Japan and the ASEAN. In a framework of 'from each according to its ability and to each according to its needs', the members supplement one another well. As Table 3.1 indicated, mutual trade among the NIEs has expanded quickly and flourished. Furthermore, the growth of imports among the NIEs has depended mainly on Hong Kong's increasing imports from other NIEs, and on the opening of the Chinese market.

4. The upper triangle was discussed above. In addition, among China, the USA and Japan, China has only been integrated into this GT for a short time and its export scale is still small. However, if China continues to open and expand its economy, the value of its exports will easily exceed US$200 billion and perhaps even reach US$250 billion by the end of this century. In this case, it is predictable that the upper GT involving these three big countries will experience rapid development.

The formation of the above compound GT depended mainly on the progress in opening up the Chinese economy, foreign capital investment, and export expansion in the ASEAN. We shall analyse the third factor first.

ASEAN Regional Co-operation[6]

The Association of South East Asian Nations (ASEAN) was created in 1967. While it is commendable that ASEAN has been sustained for such a long period, it may be appropriate to observe that it has achieved good regional political co-operation, but no similar economic co-operation. Its performance was particularly poor in the mid-1980s when the Japanese yen appreciated and the US dollar depreciated, a period in which some ASEAN economies stagnated and exports were reduced. The data show that, although ASEAN advocated export expansion, total exports in 1986 fell to US$42.5 billion, which was the lowest level in the 1980s, a 7.2 per cent decrease compared with 1985. After that period, another surge of foreign investment from the NIEs (notably South Korea and Taiwan), which resulted from their own currency appreciation, rising wages and worsening internal investment environment, produced a significantly improved international environment for ASEAN's development.

ASEAN regional co-operation is mainly focused on political activities, with economic co-operation relegated to a secondary role. The Vietnam

War and Kampuchean civil war provided opportunities for ASEAN political co-operation, while economic co-operation, in contrast, was relatively weak. Economic co-operation began with the convening of the 1976 ASEAN Summit in Manila. Some agreements were reached for basic commodity (food and oil) production and industrial co-operation, such as ASEAN Industrial Projects (AIPs) and ASEAN Industrial Joint Ventures (AIJVs), for co-operation in trade (Preferential Trade Agreement), and joint approaches in external relations. However, the proportion of regional trade did not rise at all. Therefore, economic co-operation between 1976 and 1990 was only nominal, or well started and poorly finished. This may, in fact, be attributed to the appearance of a new opportunity for political co-operation. With the internationalisation of the Kampuchean problem after December 1978, ASEAN presented a proposal for supporting Democratic Kampuchea (a regime involving the Sihanouk Norodom and Son Sann cliques). Because of their focus on such political affairs, ASEAN was not much interested in economic co-operation.

However, after the Paris International Peace Agreement for Kampuchea in October 1991, ASEAN lost an international platform for its political efforts. Thereafter, its attention was redirected to economic co-operation, and the regional market was expanded again. The forth ASEAN Summit decided to put AFTA (ASEAN Free Trade Area) into effect from January 1993 (in fact it delayed to January 1994) and to reduce the CEPT (Common Effective Preferential Tariff) to near zero within fifteen years.[7] The main purpose of realising such regional integration was to increase ASEAN's external bargaining power.

Of course, ASEAN's tendency to put a higher priority on political than on economic co-operation enabled it to avoid falling into the protectionism trap, and allowed all of East Asia to maintain free trade to certain extent. If ASEAN had erected tariff barriers as other areas did, East Asia would have changed its character and might have followed the EU or NAFTA (North America Free Trade Agreement) models. Therefore, the greatest contribution of ASEAN to East Asia is that it prevented East Asia from falling into the protectionism trap. However, this was not anticipated by ASEAN.

There were also some impressive achievements by ASEAN in absorbing foreign capital and promoting economic growth. According to a recent White Paper published by the Japan External Trade Organisation (JETRO), one of the elements that encouraged the flow of direct investment towards Asia was the softening of regulations imposed upon foreign capital as well as changes in the official policy of the recipient countries. Since the latter half of the 1980s, the ASEAN countries have eschewed an attachment to national capital and come to appreciate the role of foreign capital in industrial development. They have actively invited foreign capital through easier regulations and measures to promote a more hospitable environment for foreign investment (JETRO Direct Foreign Investment by Japan and the World (1995) p. 25). For example, in 1992, Thailand permitted majority foreign participation in joint ventures capitalised at greater than one billion baht, and in the same year, Indonesia permitted 100 per cent foreign participation in enterprises capitalised at a minimum of US$250 thousand, down from US$1 million, and eliminated areas from which foreign investment had been forbidden.

Notable also was the decision reached at the third ASEAN Summit in December 1987, related to the rate of participation for foreign capital in AIJVs. Namely, the upper limit on foreign capital participation, which previously stood at 49 per cent, was raised to 60 per cent, on condition that each ASEAN member country's capital participation equalled at least 5 per cent of the investment. This decision symbolised a turning point in ASEAN policy towards foreign investment.[8]

The high tariff policy of the ASEAN countries was also extremely attractive to investors such as Japan and the NIEs as a means of protecting their share of the ASEAN regional market.

Thereafter, ASEAN moved quickly to welcome foreign capital. For example, Indonesia, Malaysia, the Philippines and Thailand absorbed foreign investment valued at about US$11.81 billion in 1988 and US$30.36 billion in 1990 (in contrast to as little as around US$1.6 billion in 1985).[9] ASEAN exports increased rapidly as a result. After 1986 they increased at a rate of more than US$10.0 billion a year, exceeding US$100 billion in 1991, and rising to US$151.8 billion in 1994.

Turning to regional shares of exports and imports, Table 3.2 shows that NIEs' exports dominated, at 26.1 per cent in 1994. Exports to the NIEs have surpassed those to the USA since 1990, and to Japan since 1991. In 1994, Malaysia led the group, with exports to the NIEs amounting to US$18.9 billion, followed by Indonesia and Thailand, each with US$9.3 billion. This represented an increase in exports for these countries ranging from 2.9 times for Malaysia to 3.8 times for Thailand between 1988 and 1994. It is also notable that, unlike the decreasing trend for exports to the USA, the share of exports to the EU rose after the late 1980s, reaching a peak in 1991.

Concerning imports, Japan remained the leader with 26.9 per cent of imports by ASEAN countries sourced from Japan in 1993, followed by the NIEs at 20.6 per cent, and the USA with only 14.5 per cent. Between 1988 and 1993, the ASEAN import market increased by US$78.9 billion (130

Table 3.2 Market sharing structure of ASEAN–4s' exports and imports, 1980–94, US$ million, %

Year	Total amount Exports	Total amount Imports	USA (%) Exports	USA (%) Imports	Japan (%) Exports	Japan (%) Imports	EU–4 (%) Exports	EU–4 (%) Imports	NIEs (%) Exports	NIEs (%) Imports	ASEAN–4 (%) Exports	ASEAN–4 (%) Imports
1980	47 157	39 157	19.1	16.1	34.5	24.2	7.1	11.1	18.0	13.6	3.4	4.0
1981	48 331	43 282	17.7	15.5	33.4	25.0	5.7	11.5	18.3	14.1	3.7	4.1
1982	46 328	46 063	16.0	16.5	24.0	24.0	5.7	11.0	21.2	17.2	4.2	4.3
1983	46 574	47 738	19.1	16.3	30.9	23.7	6.2	10.8	21.1	19.4	4.5	4.4
1984	51 201	44 614	19.6	17.9	31.5	23.9	6.0	10.6	19.5	16.6	4.4	5.1
1985	45 742	37 187	19.7	16.1	31.1	23.3	6.4	11.5	20.0	16.5	4.9	6.0
1986	42 457	35 929	20.1	17.0	28.3	24.1	8.8	12.1	19.2	17.3	4.1	4.9
1987	52 384	45 491	20.1	15.3	26.0	23.9	8.9	11.7	20.8	18.2	4.2	4.9
1988	63 462	58 804	19.7	15.7	24.6	24.2	9.5	11.9	21.1	18.6	4.1	4.4
1989	74 801	75 531	20.7	14.6	24.2	25.4	9.3	10.9	20.3	19.2	4.6	4.5
1990	86 453	96 381	19.2	14.1	24.3	26.2	10.2	12.2	21.6	19.3	4.4	3.9
1991	101 034	113 082	18.4	13.8	22.9	26.1	10.6	11.3	23.1	21.1	4.3	3.9
1992	117 080	122 489	19.8	14.3	20.1	25.6	10.5	11.7	23.6	21.2	4.7	4.5
1993	132 469	137 788	20.5	14.4	19.2	26.7	10.1	11.1	24.2	20.9	4.6	4.4
1994	151 827	166 652	20.2	14.0	18.6	27.8	10.3	11.6	26.0	21.2	5.5	5.0

Note: As Table 3.1.
Source: Economic Planning Agency of Japan, *Statistics on the Overseas Economy*, January 1996, pp. 99–104.

per cent), from US\$58.8 billion in 1988 to US\$137.7 billion in 1993. Of this, imports from Japan were valued at US\$22.5 billion and from the NIEs at US\$17.7 billion, representing 28.6 per cent and 22.5 per cent of that increase, respectively. It is notable that the combined percentage increase of imports from these two sources accounted for more than half (51.1 per cent) of the entire increase. A brisk influx of foreign investment from Japan and the NIEs was undoubtedly partly accountable for the large increase in imports from these origins. By the same token, the increase in ASEAN exports described above was also partly the result of the export-orientated production built through foreign investment from Japan and the NIEs. In this sense, the new compound GT can be considered to comprise mainly of Japan–NIEs–ASEAN/China. The role played by the USA was not so large because its trade share was less than a fifth and tended to be declining. This analysis therefore confirms that ASEAN and China have played an important part in the new compound GT.

Growth of the Chinese Economy

The growth of the Chinese economy has led to the integration of this giant nation into the compound GT. As explained above, China is involved in two channels: an export channel, made up of China–Hong Kong–USA; and an import channel through Japan–Taiwan/Hong Kong–China.

In 1992, 44.1 per cent of Chinese exports were made to Hong Kong (US\$37.5 billion), of which 34.7 per cent was re-exported (by Hong

Table 3.3   Market share of China's exports, 1992, US\$ million, %

Total exports	Direct exports			Share of exports via Hong Kong[b]	Total share
	Destination	Share	Amount		
84 998	Hong Kong	44.1	37 512		
	Japan	13.8	11 699	8.6	22.4
	USA	10.1	8 594	15.3	25.4
	EU–4[a]	6.2	5 230	2.7	8.7

Notes: a   EU–4 refers to four European countries: Britain, Germany, France and Italy.
     b   The share of redistribution of the exports to Hong Kong (HK\$403 782 million): the USA, 34.1% (HK\$139 977 million); EU–4, 19.6% (HK\$79 202 million); Japan 7.6% (HK\$30 707 million); and Canada, 2.6% (HK\$10 019 million).
Sources: Economic Planning Agency of Japan, *Statistics on the Overseas Economy*, January 1994, pp. 102–4; Census and Statistics Department, Hong Kong, *Annual Review of Hong Kong External Trade*, 1992.

Kong) to the USA; 25.4 per cent of exports was made to the USA (15.3 per cent via Hong Kong); and 22.4 per cent to Japan (see Table 3.3). Clearly, most Chinese exports were to Hong Kong or via Hong Kong to the USA and Japan. As a result, a strong China–Hong Kong–USA/Japan export channel was formed. It is also significant that the USA granted most favoured nation treatment (MFNT) status to China.

Through the import channel, in 1992, China's imports from Hong Kong made up 25.5 per cent of its total imports, which, though less than the export share, still came to a third after adding the 7.9 per cent from Taiwan, and 17 per cent of its total imports came from Japan. This means that over half of Chinese imports (50.4 per cent) came from Hong Kong, Taiwan and Japan. In terms of point of origin of products imported from Hong Kong, those made in Japan accounted for 26.2 per cent, and from Taiwan, 23.1 per cent (see Table 3.4). This implies that nearly half (49.3 per cent) of the goods imported from Hong Kong are Japanese or Taiwanese products. It is also notable that about 30.1 per cent of Taiwan's imports (US$21.8 billion) were from Japan. Clearly, Japan, and not the USA, was the largest indirect supplier of products to China.

Regarding the composition of Chinese imports, it will be seen that the largest proportion of products imported from Japan and Taiwan comprised textile yarn, fabrics and related articles (valued at HK$16.9 and accounting for 34.4 per cent of total imports from Taiwan). The second largest proportion was accounted for by electrical machinery, apparatus and appliances, and electronic parts (valued at HK$9.5 billion and accounting for 11.2 per cent of total imports from Japan and 6.7 per cent

Table 3.4   Market share of China's imports, 1992, US$ million, %

Total imports	Direct imports			Share of imports via Hong Kong[b]	Total share
	From	Share	Amount		
80 610	Hong Kong	25.5	20 538		
	Japan	17.0	13 681	6.7	23.7
	USA	11.0	8 900	2.2	13.2
	EU–4[a]	10.3	8 281	1.6	11.9
	Taiwan	7.9	6 370	5.9	13.8

Notes: a   EU–4 refers to four European countries: Britain, Germany, France and Italy.
 b   The share of imports from the original country via Hong Kong (HK$212 105 million): Japan, 26.2% (HK$55 565 million); Taiwan, 23.1% (HK$49 046 million); China, 9.5% (HK$20 205 million);; USA, 8.6% (HK$18 183 million); South Korea, 6.8% (HK$14 340 million); and EU–4, 6.3% (HK$13 446 million).
Source: As Table 3.3.

from Taiwan). The third largest proportion of imported goods was specialised machinery for particular industries (HK$8.7 billion, and accounting for 8.5 per cent of total imports from Japan and 8.1 per cent from Taiwan).[10]

In comparison, Taiwan's imports from Japan were made up largely of machinery and electronic parts (US$10.5 billion in 1992, and 48.2 per cent of total imports from Japan); followed by base metals and articles (US$2.55 billion, or 11.7 per cent of total imports); then transportation equipment (US$2.2 billion, or 10.1 per cent of total imports); and, finally, chemicals (US$2.1 billion, or 9.4 per cent of total imports).[11] As supplementary information, Figure 3.3 shows that a large part of Japanese exports to the NIEs comprises electronic and machinery products. Obviously, importing and using the technology from Japan was an important reason for Taiwan to be able to provide China with production equipment. It is through such commodity trade between Japan–Taiwan (Hong Kong)–China that advanced technology flowed from the upper level (Japan) to lower levels (Taiwan and China). The general outline of

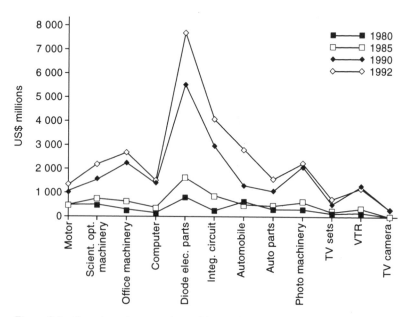

Figure 3.3   Japan's main export items (electronic parts and machinery) to NIEs, 1980–92).

Source: *Annual Report 1993*, Customs and Tariff Bureau, Ministry of Finance, Japan, pp. 470–87.

this technology flow shows that Japan basically improved technology that it received from the USA, and then transferred it to Taiwan (Hong Kong), which retained the high (capital-intensive) technology and transferred the low (labour-intensive) technology to mainland China.

Hong Kong and Taiwan made huge investments in mainland China in order to accomplish this technology transfer. In 1992, they signed investment contracts for about US$45.6 billion, or 78.4 per cent of total foreign capital contracted in China. Joint ventures with direct participation by Hong Kong accounted for half of all foreign joint ventures in China, and adding the 22.6 per cent share of joint-management enterprises, Hong Kong investment contracts comprised 72.4 per cent of total foreign capital contracts in China. Technology transfer and direct foreign investment, the two wheels of a cart, played indispensable roles in the Japan–Hong Kong (Taiwan)–China GT.

This triangular relationship is apparent from Figure 3.2. For example, in 1993, Hong Kong and Taiwan had large trade deficits with Japan, totalling US$30.3 billion, and in the same year, they greatly increased their exports to China to HK$63.4 billion, in the case of Hong Kong, and to US$14.0 in the case of Taiwan. This triangular relationship between Japan, Taiwan and China (via Hong Kong) was a new phenomenon in the 1990s.

Changes in international relationships have had an important bearing upon China's integration into the Asian GT and on the formation of the compound GT. If diplomatic relations between China and the USA had not been established, China would never have achieved the accomplishments described above, not even through its policies of opening its economy and introducing foreign capital. Without the US market, Chinese exports would not have expanded so well, and China would not have been able to absorb so much foreign investment. A stable and growing relationship between China and the USA is therefore a determining factor in the future development of the compound GT.

IV   CONCLUSION: SOME REMARKS AND PROSPECTS

East Asia has achieved export-orientated industrialisation and rapid economic growth by relying upon both the original and compound GTs. As Table 3.5 indicates, the NIEs exports amounted to US$436 billion in 1994, thus surpassing those of Japan (US$395 billion) by about 10.4 per cent. Total exports from East Asia (the NIEs, ASEAN, China and Japan) amounted to US$1104 billion, thus surpassing those from the USA (US$512 billion) by about 115.6 per cent, and EU external exports

Table 3.5   East Asia's exports and comparing indices, 1994, US$ billion, %

Country Region	Export Amount	Index (Japan as 100)	Index (US as 100)	Index (EU as 100)
Japan	395	100.0	77.1	62.0
NIEs	436	110.4	85.2	68.4
ASEAN–4	152	38.5	29.7	23.9
China	121	30.6	23.6	19.0
Total (East Asia)	1104		215.6	173.3
East Asia (except Japan)	(709)	(179.5)	138.5)	(111.3)
USA	512	129.6	100.0	80.4
EU (external trade)	637	161,3	124.4	100.0

Notes: EU exports refers to the external trade only; East Asia: NIEs, ASEAN and China, except Japan.

Source: Economic Planning Agency of Japan, *Statistics on the Overseas Economy*, January 1996, pp. 143.

(US$637 billion) by 73.3 per cent. In this sense, East Asia can be described as the largest export zone in the world, and in achieving this stature it has set a record in the history of capitalist development. It is therefore, worth examining closely this major historical change closely.

Taking a long-term view, there does not seem to be any possibility for an original GT, not to mention a compound GT, to be established in Europe and the USA. As early as 1956, Kaname Akamatsu proposed a 'Flying Geese Pattern of Development' as a basis for describing the Japanese development model.[12] Later, in consideration of the fact that Japanese development was largely based on the NIEs long-term trade deficit with Japan, Kim Yung-Hoo amended the 'Flying Geese Pattern of Development' and came up with the 'Cormorant Fishing Pattern', alluding to the method by which a fisherman uses a cormorant to catch his fish. Accordingly, the NIEs (the cormorants), could not consume their own exports (the fish) but had to yield them to Japan (the fisherman). It is interesting to observe that the Japanese applied Western economic theory to create the 'Flying Geese Pattern of Development,' and that the Japanese goose then metamorphosed into the NIEs' cormorant.[13]

Although the 'Cormorant Fishing Pattern' has merits, some points are debatable. First, this pattern may have limited applicability, in so far as it describes export-orientated industrialisation which only suits East Asian countries (regions), and particularly the NIEs; it seems unsuitable as a model for describing the economic development of Latin American and African countries. Second, it does not provide an objective assessment of

Japans intermediary function. To put it briefly, without Japan playing the role of intermediary, the emergence of the NIEs, not to mention the 'Cormorant Fishing Pattern', would not have been possible. At this point, the 'Cormorant Fishing Pattern' contains something of the chicken and the egg paradox.

The use of Western economics, based mainly on the analysis of Western society and to economy, to analyse economic development in East Asia has serious shortcomings. Although it searches for common historical features, it contains a Eurocentric or Western bias[14] and national consciousness which renders it of limited value in exploring the East Asia boom. The discovery of such limitations may be regarded as one of the outcomes of the present study.

But what of the future? In order to sustain and promote the development of the compound GT, certain conditions such as mitigation of the conflict between Japan and the USA, active opening of the Japanese market, and the promotion of political and economic efficiency and technological progress in China are required. There are other points which must also be emphasised. First, in order to strengthen the compound GT's development mechanism and to guarantee its growth and smooth functioning, the NIEs, acting as intermediary, should create more development opportunities. Second, all countries included in the compound GT should promote and deepen their mutual dependence, understanding, trust and support, and thus create a favourable international interdependent relationship. Such a world outlook and ethics are required for East Asia to hold a leading position in the world economy. It should be pointed out that there have been insufficient opportunities for East Asia to experience such international interdependence. Therefore, this is a matter of pressing importance. From this perspective, a great deal of hope and expectation is placed upon contributions from the East Asian countries concerned in the near future.

Notes

* I am very grateful to Dr Liqun Jia (the JSPS foreign research fellow at the School of Economics, Nagoya University) for her kind help in preparing this paper. The responsibility for the opinions expressed in this paper is mine alone.

1. For a literature survey or systematic discussions see, for example, Islam (1992) pp. 69–105; The World Bank (1993) pp. 79–104; and Hirakawa (1992).
2. See Watanabe (1990).
3. For an earlier study, see Twu (1967) pp. 1–22.
4. See the latest analysis of Kwon (1994) pp. 188–207.
5. MITI (1986) pp. 275–81. For critical comments, see my paper; Muraoka (1991) pp. 154–72.

6. For more details see Muraoka (1986) p. 64.
7. See Imada and Naya (1992) p. 142.
8. See Joint Press Statement Meeting of the ASEAN Heads of Government, Manila, 14–15 December 1987, Item 30(b), Meeting of the ASEAN Heads of Government, December 1987, published by the ASEAN Secretariat, 1988, p. 50.
9. See Economic Planning Agency of Japan (1994) p. 103; also Institute of Southeast Asian Studies (1993) pp. 43–5.
10. Census and Statistics Department of Hong Kong (1992) pp. 107–9.
11. Council for Economic Planning and Development of Republic of China (1993) p. 225.
12. Akamatsu (1956).
13. Kim (1994) pp. 130–40.
14. Hodgkin (1975) pp. 114–15.

Foreign Direct Investment by Japanese Manufacturing Companies in East Asia

Nobuo Kawabe

I INTRODUCTION

After the appreciation of the yen triggered by the Plaza Accord of September 1985, Japanese companies stepped up investment in the ASEAN countries, accelerating the industrialisation of those countries based on exporting. While the Japanese companies that rushed into East Asia, particularly the ASEAN region, developed local production and sales networks for purchasing and marketing materials and products in the host countries, they also developed networks of head offices and factories in Japan. In this way, the Japanese companies created an international division of labour that produced and marketed high value-added products locally in the NIEs, and set up parts and component procurement centres and operational headquarters there.

Japan helped to make up for the lack of the industrial structure in East Asia by supplying machinery, equipment, parts and components. At the same time, Japan itself became more important as a market for the products and parts produced in East Asia. Foreign direct investment (FDI) by Japanese companies, exports of machinery and equipment, and imports of products and parts, all combined to transfer Japanese corporate dynamism to East Asia.

In addition, after the second appreciation of the year, which started around February 1993, Japanese companies began transferring their production to China as well as to the ASEAN region. Expanding Japanese investment strengthened ties between Japan, the NIEs, and ASEAN, and reinforced production and sales networks in Japan and the region, including China .[1]

II TRENDS IN FOREIGN DIRECT INVESTMENT BY JAPANESE COMPANIES IN EAST ASIA

The Globalisation of Japanese Companies

Although postwar Japanese FDI first began in 1959, as shown in Figure 3.4, Japanese investments increased dramatically after 1985. In the 1960s, Japanese investment mostly sought to establish sales bases supporting the development and export–import of natural resources. Asia was the recipient of most investment in natural resource development; the developed countries were selected mainly for trade and service sector-related investment by Japanese trading and banking corporations.

In the 1970s, labour shortages and wage increases in Japan stimulated Japanese FDI. Manufacturers, especially, embraced FDI as a solution to these problems, and investments by small and medium-sized businesses (SMBs) began to take off, especially in Asia. Also, in this period, Japanese electrical appliance makers began to produce colour televisions in the United States to avoid trade conflicts with that country.

In the 1980s, Japanese FDI matured and new characteristics began to appear because of changes in industry and geographical areas. The share of natural-resource-related and labour-intensive product investment, which accounted for most of the investment in the 1970s, decreased. Accordingly, the weight of investment in the developing countries where labour-intensive investment was concentrated, fell. On the other hand, the

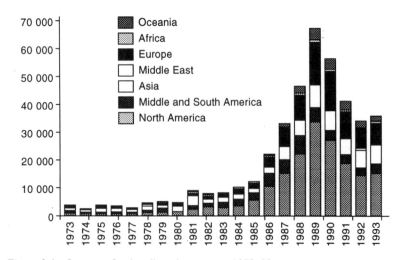

Figure 3.4   Japanese foreign direct investment, 1973–93

share of investments in the developed world increased steadily because of more investment in non-manufacturing areas and in technology-intensive areas such as electrical machinery, transportation equipment and other machinery. While Asia accounted for about 30 per cent of Japan's investment in the 1970s, in the 1980s this fell to less than 20 per cent. North American investment, on the other hand, grew from less than 20 per cent, to more than 40 per cent. Europe's share of Japanese investment also rose from less than 10 per cent, to more than 20 per cent[2] (see Figure 3.4, Tables 3.6 and 3.7).

While investment in the United States and Europe forged ahead, investment in developing countries dwindled, for several reasons. First was the cumulative debt problems of Central and South America and Africa; second, the completion of the first stage of import substitution investment; third, low demand and low market prices for primary resources; and fourth, a decrease in the large-scale industrial projects and natural resource development projects of the 1970s.[3]

On the other hand, the share of overseas non-manufacturing investment rose. While the manufacturing sector accounted for 53 per cent of Japan's accumulated investment value between 1951 and 1983, this increased to 70 per cent in the 1980s. The growth of non-manufacturing investment was supported by factors such as the deregulation of financial and insurance sectors in host countries, a highly valued yen and the emergence of a bubble economy in Japan, and the growth of the service sectors in the developed countries. In the manufacturing sector, investment by electrical and electronics, transportation equipment, and chemical companies grew, replacing resource-related investments.

In assembly areas such as electricals, electronics, and transportation equipment, Japanese production systems, including the *keiretsu* system, created competitive advantages. Because of this competitive edge, such companies tended to be involved in trade conflicts and so invested in their overseas markets.

SMBs played a very active role in overseas investment, accounting for 20 – 25 per cent of the total number of investments. One of the reasons SMBs were so active was the contribution of their subcontracting companies following the parent companies overseas. Japanese foreign investment leapt in the second half of the 1980s. Between 1985 and 1989, the value of investment increased by 500 per cent, from $1.2 billion to $6.8 billion. However, after peaking in 1989, investment by value dropped to $3.4 million, almost half of its peak value. In 1993, investment recovered a little, and began increasing again in 1994.

After the 1985 yen appreciation, Japanese investment in Asia increased

Table 3.6 Japanese foreign direct investment by region, $ millions, %

	N. America		S. America		Asia		Middle East		Europe		Africa		Oceania		Total	
1973	913	26.1	822	23.5	998	28.6	110	3.1	337	9.6	106	6.0	208	3.0	3 494	100.0
1974	550	23.0	699	29.2	731	30.5	64	2.7	189	7.9	55	2.3	108	4.5	2 396	100.0
1975	905	27.6	371	11.3	1 101	33.6	196	6.0	333	10.2	192	5.9	182	5.5	3 280	100.0
1976	749	21.6	420	12.2	1 245	36.0	278	8.0	337	9.7	272	7.9	162	4.7	3 463	100.0
1977	735	26.2	456	16.3	865	30.8	225	8.0	220	7.8	140	5.0	165	5.9	2 806	100.0
1978	1 364	29.7	616	13.4	1 340	29.1	492	10.7	323	7.0	225	4.9	239	5.2	4 599	100.0
1979	1 438	28.8	1 207	24.2	976	19.5	130	2.6	495	9.9	168	3.4	582	11.6	4 996	100.0
1980	1 596	34.0	588	12.5	1 186	25.3	158	3.4	578	12.3	139	3.0	448	9.5	4 693	100.0
1981	2 522	28.2	1 181	13.2	3 338	37.4	96	1.1	798	8.9	573	6.4	424	4.7	8 932	100.0
1982	2 905	37.7	1 503	19.5	1 384	18.0	124	1.6	876	11.4	489	6.3	421	5.5	7 702	100.0
1983	2 701	33.2	1 878	23.1	1 847	22.7	175	2.1	990	12.2	364	4.5	191	2.3	8 146	100.0
1984	3 544	34.9	2 290	22.6	1 628	16.0	273	2.7	1 937	19.1	326	3.2	157	1.5	10 155	100.0
1985	5 495	45.0	2 616	21.4	1 435	11.7	45	0.4	1 930	15.8	172	1.4	525	4.3	12 218	100.0
1986	10 441	46.8	4 737	21.2	2 327	10.4	44	0.2	3 469	15.5	309	1.4	992	4.4	22 319	100.0
1987	15 357	46.0	4 816	14.4	4 868	14.6	62	0.2	6 576	19.7	272	0.8	1 413	4.2	33 364	100.0
1988	22 328	47.5	6 428	13.7	5 569	11.8	259	0.6	9 116	19.4	653	1.4	2 669	5.7	47 022	100.0
1989	33 902	50.2	5 238	7.8	8 238	12.2	66	0.1	14 808	21.9	671	1.0	4 618	6.8	67 541	100.0
1990	27 192	47.8	3 628	6.4	7 054	12.4	27	0.0	14 294	25.1	551	1.0	4 166	7.3	56 912	100.0
1991	18 823	45.3	3 337	8.0	5 936	14.3	90	0.2	9 371	22.5	748	1.8	3 278	7.9	41 583	100.0
1992	14 572	42.7	2 726	8.0	6 425	18.8	709	2.1	7 061	20.7	238	0.7	2 406	7.0	34 137	100.0
1993	15 287	42.2	3 370	9.4	6 637	18.4	217	0.6	7 940	22.0	539	1.5	2 035	5.6	36 025	100.0

Source: Bureau of International Finance, Ministry of Finance, *Annual Reports*.

Table 3.7 Japanese investments in East Asia, $ millions, %

	Indonesia	%	Thailand	%	Malaysia	%	Singapore	%	Hong Kong	%	Korea	%	China	%	Taiwan	%	Total	%
1983	178 012	24.0	37 626	5.1	111 293	15.0	267 789	36.1	11 876	1.6	31 028	4.2	1 592	0.2	103 000	13.9	742 216	100.0
1984	90 955	18.6	79 435	16.3	114 071	23.4	74 641	15.3	5 669	1.2	37 492	7.7	20 666	4.2	65 000	13.3	487 929	100.0
1985	66 050	16.4	25 324	6.3	32 790	8.1	92 315	22.9	14 046	3.5	36 921	9.2	21 997	5.5	114 000	28.3	403 443	100.0
1986	26 481	3.3	87 293	11.0	64 568	8.2	104 493	13.2	52 433	6.6	142 563	18.0	22 838	2.9	291 000	36.8	791 669	100.0
1987	294 918	17.2	210 198	12.3	147 796	8.6	268 126	15.6	108 014	6.3	247 239	14.4	70 136	4.1	367 000	21.4	1 713 427	100.0
1988	297 851	12.6	626 115	26.6	346 202	14.7	173 223	7.3	84 797	3.6	253 935	10.8	202 679	8.6	372 000	15.8	2 356 802	100.0
1989	165 839	5.2	789 095	24.9	470 586	14.8	677 594	21.4	116 269	3.7	250 654	7.9	206 268	6.5	494 000	15.6	3 170 305	100.0
1990	535 847	18.0	714 297	24.1	582 257	19.6	269 717	9.1	113 524	3.8	146 864	4.9	160 976	5.4	446 000	15.0	2 969 482	100.0
1991	578 534	19.6	594 815	20.1	612 720	20.7	176 852	6.0	120 596	4.1	157 310	5.3	308 778	10.5	405 000	13.7	2 954 605	100.0
1992	941 262	31.8	297 242	10.0	465 403	15.7	136 917	4.6	85 342	2.9	90 612	3.1	649 725	22.0	292 000	9.9	2 958 503	100.0

Source: Bureau of International Finance, Ministry of Finance, *Annual Reports.*

dramatically. The high-valued yen hurt companies that relied on exporting, and the cost merits of overseas production were suddenly clear. While the United States attracted still more investment in terms of value, numbers of investments in Asia surpassed those in the United States, accounting for 47.1 per cent of Japan's total overseas investments. However, the average value per investment was only $1.7 million in Asia, compared with $5.8 million in North America.

Let us look at the characteristics of Japanese investment in Asia during the 1980s. First, investments were weighted heavily toward manufacturing, with investment in the electrical appliance and electronics industries particularly high. Second, numbers of investments by SMBs were large. While investment by SMBs in ASEAN and China grew, SMB investment in NIEs such as Korea and Taiwan fell.[4]

After the yen appreciation of September 1985, Japanese companies quickly shifted their export production bases from the NIEs to ASEAN countries (see Table 3.7), and investments in assembling industries such as electronics in the ASEAN region increased. The ASEAN countries were now positioned as supply bases for parts and components and for low-priced goods, particularly electrical goods. Investment in the warehousing and transport industries, which support manufacturing, also increased.[5]

Japanese overseas investment, which experienced double-digit growth during the 1980s, fell from 1989, when it reached its peak by value. In 1992 Japanese investment decreased to about half of its 1989 level. Japanese investment in almost all areas except China ebbed, and investments in the electrical and chemical industries generally declined. Investment in the automobile industry did not fall so much because investment in North America and Europe rose.

Several factors contributed to the slowdown in Japanese foreign investment after 1989. First, large-scale projects were generally completed. Second, the economies of the developed nations stagnated and Japanese foreign subsidiaries experienced financial problems because of dull property markets. Third, manufacturing investment collapsed with the bursting of Japan's economic 'bubble'; and, fourth, banking institutions recorded poor financial performances. Japanese subsidiaries in the United States were particularly hard hit. The average current profit–sales ratio there fell from 2.9 per cent in 1988, to 1.8 per cent in 1990, while Japanese subsidiaries in Asia and Europe were averaging 5.0 per cent and 3.2 per cent, respectively.

Investments in the electrical appliance industry fell, for several reasons. First was the slowdown in demand for electronics products in the United States and Europe. Second was the worsening financial performance of

Japanese electronics makers and their subsidiaries in the United States and Europe. The third factor was the advance of localisation, including R&D, and increased local procurement ratios were urgently needed because of expanded local production.[6]

However, Japanese investment began increasing again in 1993 and 1994. In 1994, investments by manufacturing companies in Asia increased with further appreciation of the yen, which reached ¥100 to the dollar. Investments in China now showed a particular increase. Although Japanese investments had been concentrated mainly in labour-intensive industries such as textiles, light industrial products and electronics parts, after 1994 investment widened to mass-produced audio-visual equipment and facsimiles. Assembler–makers expanded their overseas investments, followed by manufacturers of materials and parts. In addition to investment to establish local Japanese export bases, investment was also seen in consumer products such as beer, mayonnaise, and fats and oils, for the expanding Chinese market.[7]

III FACTORS PROMOTING JAPANESE INVESTMENT IN EAST ASIA

Factors Encouraging Japanese Investment

In the late 1980s Japanese FDI increased, particularly in East Asia, pushed by factors from the Japanese side and pulled by factors from the host country side. First, let us analyse the push factors.

As we have already seen, mutual investment between developed countries was increasing, and Japanese companies invested aggressively in the United States and Europe. While the Japanese stepped up investment in the developed countries, they also expanded their investments in Asia. Particularly after 1989 when Japanese overseas investment peaked and then started declining, Asia enjoyed a very large share of Japanese investment compared with the developed countries.[8]

What were the factors favouring Japanese investment in Asia? First, Japanese companies were rich in management resources such as capital, technology and sales networks, and were thus positioned to become players on the global scene. This meant becoming local producers as well as merely exporters. A particular advantage was the establishment of Japanese brand names in Asia. However, after the jump in the value of the yen brought about by the Plaza Accord of 1985, Japanese exporters lost their competitive advantage. Further rationalisation was not enough to remedy the situation for many and they were forced to shift production overseas. The Asian countries offered cost advantages with low wages conjunction with high-quality labour. At the same time, the infrastructure in Asia was superior to that of developing countries.

The Japanese companies that started producing in developed countries after the yen appreciation produced only for the local market. However, those that shifted production bases to Asia needed not only to supply the local market but also to establish bases for export to the United States, Europe and Japan.

The trend to establish offshore production bases began after 1985 and accelerated after 1993, when the yen became still stronger. After 1993, automobile and electrical appliance assemblers and parts makers, and chemical companies in ASEAN, China and the NIEs increased exports of locally-produced products, particularly to Japan. While auto makers tended to increase production capacity in ASEAN, the electrical appliance companies reorganised and integrated their existing production bases, and embraced new investment in China.[9]

Pull Factors in East Asia

The surge of Japanese FDI into East Asia also reflected pull factors in the host countries. The two major pulls were deregulation or liberalisation of investment by foreign companies, and the expansion of local markets as a result of rapid economic growth.

When the Asian countries that expanded in the 1960s began slowing down in the mid-1980s, their governments began to liberalise foreign capital investment in an effort to stimulate growth. For example, in 1984 the South Korean government revised its Foreign Capital Introduction Law, which changed lists of industries that could not be introduced into lists of industries that were welcome. The Korean government also liberalised its policy on remitting profits to foreign countries. In 1985, the Korean government decreased the number of industries closed to overseas capital investment. In 1988, Korea was rescheduled as an IMF Article 8 country, and soon afterwards announced the Liberalisation of Capital Plan promoting deregulation. In Taiwan, where protection against overseas investment was relatively weak in manufacturing, the government liberalised foreign investment regulations in sensitive manufacturing fields, insurance, finance and distribution. In 1986, the Taiwanese government amended the Alien Investment Decree to deregulate overseas investment in the finance and service industries. By 1988, direct investments by foreigners were almost completely liberalised.

The ASEAN countries, which understood the importance of foreign enterprise in industrial development, actively sought out foreign capital by deregulating and expanding incentives. In Thailand in 1980, the government approved full foreign ownership of export-orientated companies. The Thai government in 1986 lowered the minimum value of investment in export industries by foreign companies, and liberalised foreign currency control by shifting to IMF Article 8. In 1992, Thailand deregulated the foreign capital investment ratio, approving 51 per cent foreign ownership for investments of more than 1 trillion baht, in both primary and tertiary industries. In Malaysia, the government enacted the Promotion of Investment Act, which approved 100 per cent ownership by foreign companies with high export ratios.[10]

In China, where reform and liberalisation policies were promoted from 1979, foreign capital and technology were welcomed. These policies were accelerated by the four Special Economic Zones set up in 1980, the enforcement of the Joint Venture Ordinance in 1983; the liberalisation of fourteen Coastal Port Cities in 1984; the Coastal Area Development Strategies proposed by Secretary General Chao Xi-Yang; and the establishment of Hainan Island as a Special Economic Zone.

In response to these policies, Japanese investment in China surged somewhat but then withdrew rapidly after the Tian'anmen Square Incident. However, after Deng Xiao-Ping's 'Lecturing Travel in the South Area', China strengthened its reform and liberalisation policies, and adopted a rapid growth policy. As a result, prospects for the future improved and Japanese investment in China increased again.

Furthermore, in Vietnam and India, regulations shutting out foreign companies were softened, and Japanese investment in those countries climbed. In 1986, Vietnam introduced its *dōimōi* (reform) policy, which promoted the introduction of market mechanisms aggressively. In 1988, Vietnam enacted its Foreign Investments Law and accelerated liberalisation as if to demonstrate its commitment to *dōimōi*. In response, the IMF and World Bank began lending to Vietnam again and this, in turn, attracted foreign investment to Vietnam from 1988. In 1994, Japanese investment in Vietnam surged as the cement and auto industries decided to follow the lead of their audio-visual equipment counterparts and invest in Vietnam.[11]

India's economic policy also shifted, from relying on public corporations to utilising the vitality of private enterprise, including foreign capital. India began to develop aggressive policies to bring in foreign investment. Although Japanese investment in India is still limited, there are some success stories in the transportation equipment industry.[12]

In addition to deregulation of foreign investment, the other pull factor was the expansion of the domestic market of the host country and the increased demand for infrastructure. Consumer markets in East Asia expanded in the 1980s because of increased national incomes brought about by high economic growth. The NIEs, as well as Japan, began to play an important role in the Asian consumer market. The rise of the middle class in Malaysia and Thailand also led to a steady consumption boom. Expanding consumer demand prompted existing companies to expand production facilities and sales networks, and to introduce new products. By per capita income, Singapore and Hong Kong reached the level of some lower-league developed countries, passing the $10 000 mark in 1989, and $17 000 in 1993. Taiwan's per capita income reached $9 942 in 1992, and $10 000 in 1993. Korea reached $6 899 in 1992, and $8 500 in 1993. Among the ASEAN countries, Malaysia attained $1 700 in 1991 and $3 200 in 1993, and Thailand $1 700 in 1991 and $2 000 in 1992.

In Indonesia, the Philippines and China, per capita income is still less than $1 000, but real consumer demand in the cities cannot be measured by these statistics. For example, in cities such as Shanghai and Kasha, expensive durable goods such as air conditioners, karaoke sets and motorcycles are strong sellers, and famous brands of cosmetics and shampoo are quite popular. In addition to the development of the consumer market, the need for infrastructure also creates markets. Unless the Asian countries build communications infrastructure, electric power stations, roads, sea ports and airports, railways, industrial estates, and water supply and sewerage systems, they cannot achieve high economic growth. According to the Asian Development Bank, the total demand for infrastructure in the NIEs, ASEAN, and China will be $1 trillion by the year 2000.

Japanese businesses see this infrastructure development as a business opportunity. To best utilise foreign capital, the East Asian countries introduced a Build–Operate–Transfer (BOT) system. Japanese companies are actively taking advantage of the BOT system by seeking orders for projects, machinery, equipment and plant.[13]

IV   FOREIGN DIRECT INVESTMENT BY SMBS

Trends in SMB Investment

Compared to US and European investment, one of the characteristics of Japanese foreign direct investment is the prevalence of SMBs. Investments by Japanese SMBs grew from the late 1960s to the beginning of the 1970s, mainly in Asia. However, after the first oil crisis, investments by SMBs slowed until the late 1970s as worldwide recession bit and companies reduced the size of management. In the 1980s, particularly after 1983, SMB investment started growing again, particularly in the developed countries. This was because of a recovery in business capacity, the increased value of the yen, and a general predilection toward foreign direct investment. In 1982, SMB investment accounted for 35.6 per cent of all Japanese investment by total value, and 38.5 per cent by numbers of investments. In 1985, these ratios grew 38.5 per cent and 15.3 per cent, respectively. By 1988, SMB investment accounted for 59.6 per cent of all Japanese investment by total numbers of investments.

However, after 1988, when investment by Japanese SMBs peaked, the ratio of SMB investment fell from 53.8 per cent the following year, to 39.8 per cent in 1991. Investment in the United States decreased dramatically, and Japanese investment in Europe and Asia also fell. In 1992, Japanese investment dipped slightly from the previous year. On the other hand, SMB investment in China continued to increase, offsetting the decline in the NIEs and ASEAN countries.

Let us look at some reasons for the decrease in SMB investment. First, from late 1990, SMBs experienced a deterioration in business conditions, and their financial situation worsened. Second, interest rates went up and credit was tightened. In contrast to big businesses, SMBs cannot easily raise funds on the stock market and so tend to rely on financial institutions for loans. Since overseas investment fixes capital, it is important to obtain capital at a low rate of interest. The average interest rates for new loans were 4.218 per cent in 1987, and 4.296 per cent in 1988, rising to 5.810 per cent in 1989, 8.126 per cent in 1990, and 6.877 per cent in 1991 because of increases in the official discount rate. As a result, it became difficult for SMBs to raise capital for overseas projects. In addition, the decrease in the value of land used for collateral brought serious problems to loan-dependent SMBs.[14]

One of the characteristics of investments by SMBs is a high ratio of investment in manufacturing. In the manufacturing sector, developing countries' (including Asia) share of investments by number of investments fell. While Asia's share was 54.4 per cent in 1975 and 55.0 per cent in 1984, this fell to 45.6 per cent by 1985. The share of SMB investment by number of investments in North America increased to 44.3 per cent over the same period. In 1987, the number of investments in Asia was 474 (44.6 per cent), and in North America, 455 (42.8 per cent). In the second half of the 1980s, when Japanese overseas investment increased dramatically, Asia's share by number of investments also increased. In 1989, SMB investment in Asia's manufacturing sector accounted for 64.7 per cent of all Japanese overseas investment by number of investments, while investment in North America accounted for 24.3 per cent, and Europe 9.0 per cent.[15]

After the yen appreciation of 1985, investments by SMBs in East Asia increased, because Asian countries became attractive as production and export bases. By 1987, investments by number in NIEs were large, and Korea and Taiwan alone accounted for 40 per cent of the total SMB investment in the manufacturing sector by numbers of investments. However, in 1988 investment in Thailand increased, and the share of Malaysia and the Philippines also grew at the expense of the share of the NIEs. This was caused by changing competitive conditions in the NIEs, including increasing wages, labour shortages, the development of a labour movement, unfavourable currency exchange rates, abolition of preferential duties by the United States, and aggressive courting of foreign investors by the ASEAN countries using various incentives and deregulation.[16]

Investments in China by SMBs also increased. In particular, investments in textiles moved to China, and machinery, including electrical appliances and electronics parts, foods, lumber, chemicals and miscellaneous goods followed. In 1993, textile investments peaked, accounting for 45.4 per cent of all manufacturing sector investment. By number of investments, some 178 investments or 90.8 per cent of Japan's total overseas textile investment was concentrated in China.[17]

The manufacturing sector accounts for more than 30 per cent of investments by number. In the manufacturing sector, machinery and miscellaneous goods account for 43.1 per cent and 22.0 per cent respectively. In 1984, the non-manufacturing sector accounted for 65.1 per cent, and the commerce and service industries have been increasing steadily since.

Some factors that boosted investment by Japanese SMBs were their accumulated organisational capabilities, including management, technology and investment capital (particularly among venture-type and high-technology SMBs); the narrowing difference in wages between Japan and host countries; the increasing need to develop foreign production; and the growth in investment by subcontractors following their parent companies.[18]

Overseas SMB ventures were twice as likely to be joint ventures than wholly-owned companies. The predominance of joint ventures was particularly high in Asia. Generally speaking, joint ventures have the following merits. First, they offer very easy access to local markets because the investor can use their production bases and sales networks. Second, business resources such as sales networks, brand names, technology and management expertise can be shared. Third, joint ventures reduce the amount of capital and risk. Fourth, local partners play an important role in negotiating with the local government, in securing local employees, and in minimising dissatisfaction among local workers. Fifth, the subcontractors that follow parent companies cannot depend wholly on their main client. Some minimise risk through joint ventures of their own with local companies, which gives them access to local production facilities.[19]

While some SMBs supply local markets, others choose to export. Many SMBs were set up overseas with the primary purpose of re-exporting to Japan, and many export to Europe and the United States as well. Thus the importance of Asia as an export base is growing as many companies transfer production offshore in an effort to recover export competitiveness that has been lost because of the higher yen. Some SMBs export all their locally made product to Europe, the United States, and Southeast Asia. Many host countries welcome Japanese SMB investors, wishing to use Japanese SMB expertise to boost their economic development. In many cases, Japanese SMB technology is mid-level technology, both labour-intensive and capital intensive. This level of technology is both applicable and transferable to developing countries.[20]

In the case of South Korea, despite an increase in exports after 1986, the country found itself still reliant on imports of vital parts and machinery. The Korean government recognised the need to develop machinery and supporting industries, and looked to Japanese SMBs to transfer their technologies through investment. In 1994, in Thailand, the government introduced such incentives as tax exemptions to companies investing in the development of parts and tools for machinery and supporting industries. Taiwan and Malaysia are now using overseas investment to build up their industrial infrastructure.[21]

V   FORMATION OF A GLOBAL MANAGEMENT SYSTEM

Introduction of Multi Head Offices

Since the yen's appreciation, Japanese corporations have been rapidly reforming their global management systems to cope with the ever-advancing globalisation of their business resources, including goods, human capital, financial capital and technology. As a part of this process,

Japanese companies have been reviewing strategies of purchasing parts from the optimum supplier, producing at the optimum site, and marketing products in optimum markets. Japanese companies have also been conducting R&D in overseas markets from a long-term, global perspective, and directing their investment at seamlessly linking and combining these strategies.

The introduction of the multi head office system is a first move in this direction. Multi head offices reflect the division of global markets into different regions and the allocation of independent head office functions to these regions. Underlying this system is the growing complexity of the activities of multinationals attempting to keep up with a globalising world economy. Multi head offices also reflect the need to evaluate unique local markets on an individual basis to enable management to keep up with changes in each market. Moreover, conflicts of interest between the head office and local subsidiaries in overseas markets cannot be dealt with by the vertical management structures represented by traditional overseas divisions or product divisions.

In 1988, under the slogan 'First year of the internationalisation era', Matsushita Electric introduced a new management system consisting of individual 'activity' headquarters for four different regions. This new approach established a matrix of management between regional activity headquarters and existing product divisions. The establishment of overseas production sites in the electronic component and parts markets could provide an opportunity to strengthen intersecting functions. Further examples might be Sony Corporation and Kyocera, both of which established regional activity headquarters in Asia, Europe and North America. Honda, Asahi Glass and other corporations also divided their markets into a North American and a European area and subsequently established regional headquarters there.

In response to increased competition in Asia, Lion Corporation divided the region into three subregions and plans to shift head office responsibilities to these locations. Another example is provided by Fujikura Cable, which has been expanding rapidly in Asia, especially Thailand. Fujikura Cable used the operational headquarters (OHQ) system in Singapore when it set up a subsidiary there. Fujikura next transferred responsibility from its head office in Japan to the Singaporean subsidiary, which is now responsible for the co-ordination and management of all branches and subsidiaries in the region. Other Japanese corporations, too, have made use of the OHQ system in Singapore: namely Sony Corporation and Toshiba.

Reports indicate that others such as Kao, Uniden and Nomura Securities are also planning to introduce a multi head office system, following in the footsteps of Sony Corporation, Honda, Yamaha, Hoya, Tateishi Electric, and others. By June 1993, Japanese electronics makers alone had established 103 regional co-ordination and management subsidiaries, mainly in Europe and North America.[22]

International Specialisation

The development of the multi head office system is being further accelerated by the evolution of a horizontal division of corporate functions. This horizontal division combines systematically various regional activity bases across national borders. Horizontal division encourages optimal choices in each overseas production base in the interests of that base, minimises production costs, and facilitates the mutual provision of parts and products within the corporation worldwide. Japanese corporations are becoming increasingly active beyond national borders as they attempt to respond to the changing economic environment. In Southeast Asia, Japanese corporations make use of differences in income, wages, industrial development and technology between the countries of the region, developing cross-border strategies based on import, export, manufacturing under agreement, domestic production, and local production. As a consequence, the degree of international specialisation within corporations has increased rapidly. Along with the increase in the number of overseas production sites and parts procurement bases, Japanese corporations now consciously consider global markets in terms of location, production, marketing, and finance from the outset. This tendency can be described as globalisation in terms of the optimum distribution of managerial resources on a world-wide scale.[23]

Generally speaking, direct investment by Japanese manufacturers differs from region to region. Whereas direct investment in Europe and North America usually focuses on sales within those markets, direct investment in Asia is not only aimed at sales within the country of location but also at exports to third countries, including Japan itself. This leads to increased international specialisation. Direct investment also reflects corporations' desire to transfer production to their own production bases in Southeast Asia, whose international competitiveness has declined because of the rapid rise of personnel expenses and distribution costs in Japan. Domestic manufacturing bases, which have seen their traditional products being transferred to Southeast Asia, have moved on to high-value-added products, further strengthening the division of tasks between Japan and Asia. This was made possible by two main factors. First, Southeast Asian countries now have local parts manufacturers thanks to the expansion of Japanese parts manufacturers into the region and the nurturing of locally managed ventures through technology transfers. This has strengthened the industrial foundation of Japanese manufacturing companies in Asia and has also considerably improved Asia as a consumer market.[24]

As demonstrated by the remarkable appetite for investment by Japanese manufacturers, including SMBs, the rise of the yen brought about a re-evaluation of the advantages of Asia as a manufacturing base. Within the global strategies of Japanese corporations, Asia established itself as a base for world-wide exports of semi-finished products and parts. Even before the rise of the yen, though, there were examples of international specialisation in products and production processes in industries such as textiles, metals and machine manufacturing. However, it was only after the yen appreciation that the manufacture of standard audio products, electric fans and other home appliances began to be transferred abroad on a large scale, and these products began to be exported on to third countries or to Japan. Japanese companies will certainly continue shifting no-longer-competitive products and processes offshore, manufacturing more high-value-added products in Japan, and performing R&D and design in Japan.

In addition, systems that facilitate this international specialisation and task division are also emerging in countries where Japanese corporations are located, especially the ASEAN countries. For example, on 18 October 1988, the ASEAN Conference of Finance Ministers signed the cumbersomely named Memorandum on the Plan for Mutual Supplementation of Parts for the Automobile Industry. This memorandum stipulated a 50 per cent tariff reduction on automobile parts, and equal treatment of products imported from the signatory countries and domestically manufactured products. In this way, the memorandum provided a framework for further facilitation of the division of tasks in terms of various production processes. For export-orientated industries, this agreement provided further benefits, such as exemption from tariffs, and can be taken as further encouragement of international division and specialisation within corporations.

Another step towards international specialisation can be seen in the growing trend of establishing bases overseas for the supply of parts. A number of cases have been reported where Japanese corporations established international purchasing offices (IPO), mainly in Singapore, for the procurement of parts in the region. This suggests that the key to enhancing a company's international competitiveness nowadays is reducing parts procurement costs.[25]

Asia, as a whole, is now in the process of establishing a system of interregional specialisation whereby Asian countries are roughly divided into levels of economic development. Whereas the ASEAN economies can be classified as predominantly labour-intensive, the NIEs are generally technology-intensive. This Asian order of interregional specialisation and division of tasks sees Japan as its industrial centre.[26] The rise in investment by Japanese corporations in ASEAN countries can be traced to two main reasons. The first is the deterioration in the investment climate in the NIEs brought about by such factors as rising labour costs, currency fluctuations and a rise in labour–management disputes, which cause Japanese corporations to look to the ASEAN countries for cheaper, more reliable labour. The second reason for increased Japanese investment in ASEAN is the overall growth of direct investment by Japanese SMBs. Furthermore, the ASEAN countries appeared more attractive to Japanese companies when they began to seek foreign investment for their own export development. (Fostering export-orientated industries would facilitate their industrial development.)

Because of the strong economic growth in East Asia, the Asian NIEs are backing away from traditional labour-intensive industries and are increasingly embracing technology-intensive industries. Against this background, Japanese corporations are currently expanding their investments into the Asian NIEs to utilise them as bases for the manufacture and export of high-technology products.[27]

Amid these developments, the auto and electronics industries in particular are making significant progress in international specialisation and the division of tasks. The global viewpoint adopted by auto and electronics makers inside their companies has improved international co-operation and division of tasks between Japanese and foreign players in those industries. Honda's technology tie-up and capital investment in Sang-Yang Industries of Taiwan, and Mitsubishi Motors Corporation's investment in Taiwan's Zhomg-Hua Automobile Industries are examples of this trend. In 1985, Taiwan introduced the 'New Automobile Industry Development Strategy Act' with the aim of transforming the region into a world-class supply base for motor vehicles and automotive parts. In South Korea, international specialisation and division of tasks did not stop with Japanese–Korean co-operation (including Japanese auto makers Mitsubishi Motors Corporation and Mazda, and Japanese auto parts manufacturers), but went on to include supplementation projects between Korean and American car parts manufacturers. This led to specialisation and the three-way division of tasks between Korea, Japan and the United States. The case of MMC Sitti Pol, Mitsubishi Motors' joint venture in Thailand launched in 1988 to produce cars for the

Canadian market, is a good example of this kind of international specialisation.

In the electrical and electronics industry, Japanese corporations are in the mid-1990s working towards restructuring their manufacturing bases within Asia. This restructuring is based on global corporate strategies premised on specialisation and division of tasks within individual corporations and industries. Japanese companies frequently embrace international specialisation and division of tasks by transferring the production of 'mature technology' products such as radio-cassette recorders to Asia, and manufacturing high-technology products at home. Even within the NIEs region, Japanese companies are shifting these mature technology products to countries with cheaper production costs. For example, the Victor Company of Japan shifted production of its radio-cassette recorders for the Japanese home market from Singapore to South Korea for labour cost and currency reasons, while Hitachi transferred its production of exports for the European market from Taiwan to Singapore for currency-related reasons. Moreover, to staunch the decline in profits caused by the rise of the yen, Matsushita Electric started manufacturing the main components for its air conditioners, such as rotary compressors and fan motors, at its production base in Malaysia. As a result of this shift, Matsushita's Malaysian factory has developed into the world's largest export base for window air conditioners, and functions as a leading supply base for components and parts.[28]

Not only the big Japanese players but also SMBs have been promoting specialisation and division. The number of globally-minded SMBs seeking to export from third-country production bases in Asia, Europe or North America is growing. There has been a constant rise in the number of companies that differentiate between domestic and overseas production locations, allocating the 'low-end' mass-production goods to their overseas factories while producing prestigious or high-technology products that require extremely precise or small-lot production at home, as well as products that must be delivered swiftly after ordering.[29]

The establishment of a system of specialisation and division of tasks by Japanese set makers, especially in the electronics industry, is also being accelerated by direct investment (in terms of the number of cases) in Asia by the Japanese mechanical engineering industry, which consists mostly of SMBs. Japanese electronic component makers own 332 local production subsidiaries in Asia, far more than their American and European rivals, which have only seventy-three and fifty-nine Asian subsidiaries, respectively. Furthermore, the Japanese electronic components industry is developing Asia into the leading producer of electronic parts and components ranging from resistors, ICs, and electronic motors to magnetic heads.

Parts used by the local subsidiaries of small and medium-sized Japanese manufacturers are being purchased from Japan, local producers, other Japanese manufacturers located in the region, or from NIEs and ASEAN countries. The development of networks for purchasing parts and components and trading finished products has further promoted specialisation and division in manufacturing. This in turn is playing an important role in linking the Asian economies with each other.[30]

In the spring of 1993, the Japanese currency started to rise again. As a result, profits from domestic exports have been declining since, and pressure to utilise overseas manufacturing bases as export bases has been mounting. For example, in the United States, where price competition is very severe, Japanese electrical appliance companies concentrate on producing large televisions while importing small and medium-sized ones from Asian production bases. This reflects an effort to improve cost competitiveness through production specialisation. Concentrating production in a single plant with the capacity to meet not only the entire domestic demand of a certain product, but the entire regional demand as well, achieves economies of scale and more efficient use of management resources.[31]

Such networks further promote world-wide specialisation and division of tasks. The growth in imports from overseas Japanese production bases plays a particular role in this. The rise of overseas Japanese factories is caused only by the competitive advantage of imported products in the wake of the steep rise of the yen, but also by the improvement of manufacturing facilities in these locations. These imports of overseas Japanese-made products amounted to 6.9 per cent of Japan's total imports in 1991, or 13.2 per cent of the total imports of manufactured goods, and ranged from products as diverse as cars, electrical appliances, machinery, electronic parts and components, textile fibres, and foodstuffs.[32]

Since 1985, the Japanese manufacturing industry has undergone a process of rapid globalisation. Rather than worrying about their domestic production bases being undermined, Japanese companies again went on actively to broaden their manufacturing bases in the ASEAN and NIEs countries, along with the renewed rise of the yen in 1993. In the future, Japanese companies will continue to work towards the establishment of a large-scale system of specialisation and division of tasks, this time including regions and countries such as China, Indonesia and Southwest Asia.[33]

Notes

1. JETRO (1995) p. 23.
2. JETRO (1990) pp. 18, 23–4.
3. JETRO (1986) p. 23.
4. JETRO (1992) p. 40.
5. JETRO (1990) p. 28.
6. JETRO (1993) pp. 61–2, 68.
7. JETRO (1995) pp. 41–2, 47, 48–9.
8. JETRO (1985) pp. 13–14.
9. For a study of Japanese investment in the ASEAN countries after 1985, see Yamashita (1991), and for a recent study of Japanese investments in East Asia, see Ono and Okamoto (1995) especially ch. 3; JETRO (1993) pp. 64–5.
10. JETRO (1995) p. 25–6.
11. Ibid., pp. 43–4.
12. Ibid., pp. 44–5.
13. JETRO (1994) p. 28.
14. For the development of investments by SMBs after 1985, see the Small and Medium Enterprises Agency (1995). JETRO (1993) p. 47.
15. JETRO (1991) p.57.
16. JETRO (1990) p. 29.
17. JETRO (1994) pp. 41–2 and JETRO (1995) pp. 4.
18. JETRO (1989b) p. 33.
19. JETRO (1991) pp. 58–9.
20. JETRO (1989b) pp. 34–5, JETRO (1985) pp. 18–19; and JETRO (1986) p. 20.
21. JETRO (1987) p. 28. Among the many studies of the relationship between Japanese SMB investments and the development of supporting industries in the East Asian countries are Mukaiyama (1993), Takeuchi (1996), and Kawabe (1995).
22. JETRO (1989b) p. 40.
23. JETRO (1988) pp. 40–1. For the international division of tasks by Japanese companies and the role of East Asia, see Aoki (1993).
24. JETRO (1989b) p. 31 and JETRO (1993) pp. 87, 89.
25. JETRO (1989b) pp. 38–9.
26. JETRO (1988) p. 17.
27. JETRO (1988) pp. 17–19.
28. JETRO (1999) p. 22 and JETRO (1989b), p. 3.
29. JETRO (1991) p. 59.
30. JETRO (1992) p. 42.
31. JETRO (1995) pp. 57–8.
32. JETRO (1994) pp. 53–4, 56–7.
33. JETRO (1995), pp. 53–9.

4 Characteristics of the Four Industries Targeted in Our Field Study

The Automotive Assembly Industry

Hiroshi Kumon

I PROFILE OF THE AUTOMOTIVE ASSEMBLY PLANTS SURVEYED

Analysis was undertaken of specific features of the automobile industry in East Asian countries (Taiwan, Thailand, Malaysia) taking into account the following factors: the influential presence of Japanese automobile firms; the inability of these firms to gain the benefits of economies of scale; a protection-orientated market that is changing towards an open-door policy; and the special nature of the Korean automobile industry.

The strong presence of Japanese firms in East Asian countries has been achieved by Japanese automobile companies entering this region through joint ventures or technical tie-ups to a greater extent than US or European companies. The Japanese presence in the form of joint ventures and technical tie-ups is as follows. In Taiwan, of the eleven local automotive firms, Japanese companies have equity holdings in five companies and technical tie-ups with two others. In Thailand, Japanese firms have ten subsidiaries that participate in joint ventures. In Malaysia, Japanese firms hold equity in six operations and have technical tie-ups with eleven companies. Since Japanese subsidiaries have high market shares in these ventures, Japanese automobiles have an overwhelming presence. Japanese firms are also planning to make inroads in Vietnam and the People's Republic of China, where markets are beginning to open.

In general, developing countries or newly-industrialised countries begin automobile production through a form of semi-knocked down (SKD) or completely knocked down (CKD) manufacturing. East Asian countries changed their policy from importing products to domestic assembly in the

135

late 1950s and early 1960s. Local production commenced with either SKD or CKD manufacturing. Japanese automobile firms have co-operated with these ventures since the early production stages of SKD or CKD, in the form of technical tie-ups and joint ventures.

Local plants are small to medium-sized, and equipment is less automated. An annual capacity of 200 000 units with two shifts is regarded as the standard scale under which facilities can be operated effectively without idle periods. Japanese automobile firms operate similar-sized plants in the United States. If a firm is not able to sell 200 000 units, it usually enters a joint venture with a US or Japanese company to secure full production capacity by selling the automobiles through the two companies. In East Asia, however, only Korea has plants with an annual capacity of more than 200 000 units. All the plants in other East Asian countries have smaller capacities, ranging from a medium size of 100 000 units to a small size of approximately 40 000 units annually. Some plants did not even employ a conveyor belt line, or did not maintain a rigid cycle-time system. These plants started their production in the form of SKD or CKD.

Another common characteristic of these plants is that they sell products mainly for the domestic market. Although the electronics industry in East Asia has plants producing solely for export, the automotive plants produce vehicles mainly for the domestic market. Some automotive plants export some of their products or have future export plans. With the recently industrialised East Asian nations, there are a number of problems regarding production: one is introducing and mastering the management system concerning both manufacturing and production control within plants; and the other is the cost and quality of parts and materials. The automobile industry needs many kinds of parts and materials, so cost and quality of the parts and materials are crucial for the assembly industry to compete with overseas companies. These plants also rely on imports of key parts from Japan. Although East Asian automotive plants are at the stage where they can raise local content levels past CKD standards, their finished automobiles are mainly for the domestic market.

The most urgent issue for East Asian manufacturers is competing with automobile imports. Recently, East Asian nations have begun to change their policy, from protectionism by import prohibition or customs duties, to import liberalisation.

Though East Asian countries commonly aim to increase competitiveness with foreign investment and manufacturing techniques, there are two different types of policy. One is the open-market policy to stimulate the establishment of new assembly companies through joint ventures with foreign capital. The other is the national car project that gives preferential treatment to a designated company. Taiwan and Thailand are moving towards an open-market policy, while Malaysia is embracing the national car project. Needless to say, both policies cannot be defined in the simple terms whereby the former allows setting up joint ventures freely and the latter does not permit the establishment of non-national car plants. Nevertheless, it is possible to describe two distinct types. The automobile industry is more suited to large operations and requires supporting industries. Governments need to develop the industry while taking into consideration the limited plant scale resulting from the size of the domestic market, and fostering the expansion of supporting industries. Accordingly, liberalisation policies and national car projects stand in striking contrast to each other. Each policy has its respective merits and demerits. Through free competition, liberalisation policies may raise competitiveness in terms of cost and quality. Ultimately, however, companies may not be able to attain adequate economies of scale because they are established within relatively small local markets. A national car policy may make it possible to attain some degree of economy of scale because governments provide tax concessions for automotive companies. Such measures, however, do not boost competitiveness in local markets and may compromise product variety in order to attain economies of scale.

The Korean automobile industry is in a special position among East Asian automobile industries as it started from a national car project and developed into an export industry. Resulting from centralised government policy in the 1970s, the Korean automobile industry formed an industrial organisation consisting of the big three automobile makers. These automobile makers constructed American-style volume production plants in the 1980s, and developed an export industry. They have also attained strong R&D capabilities as well as gaining high local content rates, even though they received foreign assistance. Although Korean manufacturers have close relations with foreign companies in the form of technical tie-ups and equity holdings, they control management policy. Japanese makers have equity holdings, but have never participated in the management process. The Korean automobile industry is the single example in East Asia of local makers holding sole management rights. The Korean manufacturers entered international markets by constructing volume production plants in the 1980s, but their competitive edge was weakened because of quality problems. In the 1990s, they began to introduce the Japanese production system to increase quality and efficiency.

Analysis here is focused on Taiwan, Thailand and Malaysia. Though the

Table 4.1   Profile of automotive assembly plants surveyed in Taiwan

Plant	AGTw	AFTw	AETw	ACTw	AATw
Start of operation	1984	1956	1973	1969	1989
Entry mode	JV 49%	JV 25%	JV 25%	JV 13.5%	JV 45%
Number of employees	1 867	3 549	2 009	4 380	538
Number of Japanese	34 1.8%	14 0.4%	2 0.001%	2 0.001%	11 2.0%
Products	Pass, Car 1 Com. Vcl. 4	Pass. Car 5 Com. Vcl. 4	Com. Vcl. 5 Pass. Car 1	Pass. Car 2 Motorcycles	Pass. Car 2 Com. Vcl. 1
Annual capacity	45 000	132 000	87 000	40 000	42 000
Current shift	2	1	2	1	1
Production volume	45 399	67 724	73 108	49 000	22 217

Notes: Interviews undertaken in 1992.
    Pass. Car = passenger car; Com. Vcl. = commercial vehicle.

study group also visited Korea and Singapore, the Korean case is covered later as there are no Japanese automobile makers that participate in management decisions there. There is also a lack of information about Korea. Singapore has been omitted as it does not have any automobile makers (see Tables 4.1 and 4.2).

To gain entry into these markets, Japanese automobile firms participate in joint ventures. Although one Japanese truck manufacturer operates a wholly-owned subsidiary and has equity in other subsidiary, this is exceptional. All other examples are of joint ventures with local partners. The most critical problem for a joint venture is determining which partner controls the management. Of course, there are examples where management is controlled by local partners, and examples of it being influenced by the Japanese side. In Taiwan, the majority of joint ventures are managed by local partners. On the other hand, in the main Japanese companies hold management control in Thai plants. In Malaysia, local partners manage all joint ventures. In Taiwan, local partners hold the management initiative in three cases and Japanese companies maintain it in two, where they have an equity holding over 45 per cent. In Thailand, a 48 per cent stake provides the Japanese side with management control of a joint venture, resulting in five Japanese-managed plants and one locally-managed plant. In Malaysia, an equity holding of 30 per cent is the determinant for management control under the *Bumiputera* policy (the

Table 4.2 Profile of automotive assembly plants surveyed in ASEAN

Plant	AGTh	AFTh	AETh	ACTh	ADTh	ABTh	AGM	AEM
Location	Thailand	Thailand	Thailand	Thailand	Thailand	Thailand	Malaysia	Malaysia
Start of operation	1964	1962	1962	1993	1963	1964	1968	1985
Entry mode	JV 60%	JV 25%	JV 48%	JV 94%	JV 47.9%	JPN 100%	JV 28%	JV 19.8%
Number of employees	3 400	3 328 (200)	2 123 (621)	526 (66)	2 050 (750)	657 (161)	600	3 737
Number of Japanese	23 0.7%	5 0.02%	29 1.4%	5 1.0%	16 0.8%	9 1.4%	3 0.5%	24 0.7%
Products	Pass. Car 2 Com. Vcl. 1	Pass. Car 4 Com. Vcl. 1	Pass. Car 2 Com. Vcl. 3	Pass. Car 2	Com. Vcl. Bus	Com. Vcl. Bus	Pass. Car 3 Com. Vcl. 18	Pass. Car 2
Annual capacity	107 000	96 000	126 000	30 000	100 000	9 960	18 000	100 000
Current shift	2			1		1	1	2
Production volume	85 000	67 000	46 324	8 500	76 000	8 800	16 000	99 000

Notes: Interviews undertaken in 1993.
Pass. Car = passenger car; Com. Vcl. = commercial vehicle.
Temporary staff shown in parentheses.

Pro-Malay policy). One so-called national car plant is controlled by the government, and the Japanese side is quite influential in the one private company.

Of the plants studied, all were classed as medium or small in size. Annual capacities for plants operating two shifts ranged from 30 000 to 130 000 units, with 70 000 to 80 000 as the average. The limiting factor for production is determined by the capacity of the painting equipment, which cannot easily be increased. For production, a shift system and an operation rate are chosen according to prevailing market conditions. The production volume is variable, with a shift system of one or two shifts together with the setting of operation rates for equipment. There are two typical sizes of plant capacity that operate two shifts: one produces 40 000 units and the other 100 000 units.

Plants began to adopt the Japanese production system around 1986. Two reasons encouraged the introduction of this system: government policy changes and higher domestic demand for automobiles stemming from increased motorisation. The policy change from protectionism to an open market occurred in the following way. Japanese automobile makers provided the design specifications as well as production techniques to the local plants through technical tie-ups and equity participation . Each local plant, however, could only produce cars at a cost and with a level of quality that could compete in a domestic market protected from international competition via import quotas or high import duties. During the early stages, even though there were several Japanese-affiliated plants, competition was weak and local plants were able to profit from a monopoly enterprise within a protected market. Under such protection, local plants did not require the high quality or low costs that the Japanese production system could offer. Accordingly, Japanese expatriates only partially implemented the Japanese system at that time. In the mid-1980s, local plants began to introduce the system only after they found that they had to compete with imported cars following changes in government policy. In Taiwan, the turning point was in 1985, when the government implemented a policy to scale down the high rate of custom duties by 5 per cent per year. The Taiwanese duty on imported cars at the time of writing is 30 per cent, though imports of Japanese cars are still prohibited. In Thailand, the government decreased customs duties from 300–400 per cent, to 68.5 per cent for passenger cars with less than a 2.4-litre capacity, 42 per cent for capacity of more than one litre, and 60 per cent for commercial vehicles. Also, tariffs on CKD parts were decreased, from 112 per cent on passenger cars and 60 per cent on commercial vehicles, to 20 per cent for all types. To protect its domestic automobiles, only the

Malaysian government maintains duties of 140–300 per cent for passenger cars.

II HYBRID EVALUATION IN THE AUTOMOTIVE ASSEMBLY INDUSTRY

Six-Group Evaluation

The following discussion on application levels relates to Table 4.3. The application ratio of the automotive assembly industry in East Asia was 3.2 points, slightly less than the East Asian industry total of 3.3 points. In addition, the application ratio for each group of elements was just over three points, even though these show an application orientation. Comparing average points for each industry, automotive assembly scored less than electronics assembly (3.3 points) and electronics parts (3.4 points), but exceeded automotive parts (3.1 points). There is a significant difference in the application ratio among industries when the same ratios are compared to North American industries. The North American automobile industry recorded high application points: automotive parts was 3.6 points, with automotive assembly 3.5 points. On the other hand, the electronics industry had a low ratio of 2.7 points. Accordingly, automotive assembly was classified as the application type and electronics assembly classified as the adaptation type. The application ratio of electronics assembly and parts manufacturers exceeds the ratio of automotive assembly and parts manufacturers in East Asia. This difference stems from the strategies of automotive manufacturers operating in East Asian countries. The automotive assembly plants produce cars mainly for the domestic market. Electronics assembly, in contrast, has two types of plant: one for special export products and the other dedicated to domestic products. Automotive assembly plants have few exports, generally competing with foreign cars in the domestic market. At export-orientated electronics plants, the management standards for quality and cost are designed to meet international criteria. For these reasons, the East Asian electronics industry shows a rather high rate of application.

The six-group evaluation of the application ratio of the automotive assembly industry follows. The application orientation groups that recorded more than 3 points were: Work organisation (3.6 points), Production control (3.2 points), Parts procurement (3.1 points), Group consciousness (3.3 points), and Labour relations (3.3 points).

Table 4.3   Application ratio of the automotive assembly industry

	Asian average	S	Taiwan	ASEAN	Malaysia	Thailand	USA
I Work Organisation and Administration	3.6	0.4	3.9	3.4	3.3	3.4	3.3
① Job classification	4.8	0.5	5.0	4.8	4.0	5.0	4.8
② Multifunctional skills	3.4	0.5	3.8	3.1	3.0	3.2	3.2
③ Education and training	3.5	0.5	3.6	3.4	3.5	3.3	3.4
④ Wage system	3.6	0.9	4.4	3.1	3.0	3.2	2.1
⑤ Promotion	3.2	0.5	3.4	3.0	3.5	2.8	3.2
⑥ First-line supervisor	3.1	0.5	3.4	2.9	2.5	3.0	3.1
II Production Control	3.2	0.5	3.6	2.9	2.8	2.9	3.4
⑦ Equipment	3.2	1.0	3.6	3.0	3.0	3.0	3.9
⑧ Maintenance	2.9	0.6	3.2	2.8	2.5	2.8	2.9
⑨ Quality control	3.2	0.7	3.8	2.8	3.0	2.7	4.0
⑩ Process management	3.3	0.7	3.8	3.0	2.5	3.2	2.9
III Procurement	3.1	0.3	3.0	3.1	3.0	3.1	3.0
⑪ Local content	2.8	0.6	2.4	3.0	3.0	3.0	2.3
⑫ Suppliers	3.5	0.6	3.0	3.8	3.5	3.8	3.8
⑬ Procurement method	2.9	0.7	3.6	2.5	2.5	2.5	3.0
IV Group Consciousness	3.3	0.6	3.9	2.9	3.0	2.9	3.9
⑭ Small-group activities	3.3	0.6	4.0	2.9	3.0	2.8	2.7
⑮ Information sharing	3.5	0.6	3.8	3.3	3.5	3.2	4.4
⑯ Sense of unity	3.2	0.9	4.0	2.6	2.5	2.7	4.6

Table 4.3 (continued)

	Asian average	S	Taiwan	ASEAN	Malaysia	Thailand	USA
V Labour Relations	3.3	0.5	3.6	3.2	3.3	3.2	4.2
⑰ Hiring policy	2.9	0.5	3.0	2.9	2.5	3.0	4.3
⑱ Long-term employment	3.3	0.8	3.6	3.1	3.0	3.2	4.9
⑲ Harmonious labour relations	4.0	0.7	4.2	3.9	4.5	3.7	4.2
⑳ Grievance procedure	3.2	0.5	3.4	3.0	3.0	3.0	3.2
VI Parent–Subsidiary Relations	2.3	0.9	2.2	2.4	1.7	2.7	3.5
㉑ Ratio of Japanese expatriates	1.4	0.6	1.6	1.3	1.0	1.3	3.8
㉒ Delegation of authority	2.6	1.1	2.4	2.8	2.0	3.0	3.3
㉓ Position of local managers	3.0	1.4	2.6	3.3	2.0	3.7	3.3
Average of 23 items	**3.2**	**0.3**	**3.5**	**3.0**	**2.9**	**3.1**	**3.5**

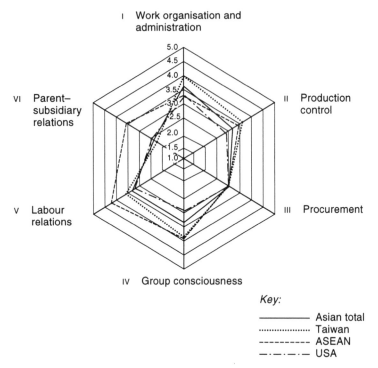

Figure 4.1   Automotive assembly (six groups)

Parent–subsidiary relations scored an adaptation orientation of 2.3 points (see Figures 4.1 and 4.2).

Comparing the automotive assembly industry with the average points for the East Asian total, the automotive industry only exceeds the East Asian average by 0.1 points in Work organisation and Labour relations. Group consciousness was the same, and both Production control and Procurement were less than the East Asian average by 0.2 and 0.1 points, respectively. The higher points of the East Asian average in Production control and Procurement reflect the influence of the electronics industry, which has plants specialising in exports, depends greatly on Japan for equipment and parts, and needs to introduce the Japanese system. Concerning Parent–subsidiary relations, the automotive assembly recorded 0.3 points lower than the East Asian average of 2.6 points. This score appears to reflect the strategy of the electronics industry with its export-orientated plants. Generally speaking, the number of Japanese expatriates is fewer per plant than in North America, because East Asian governments

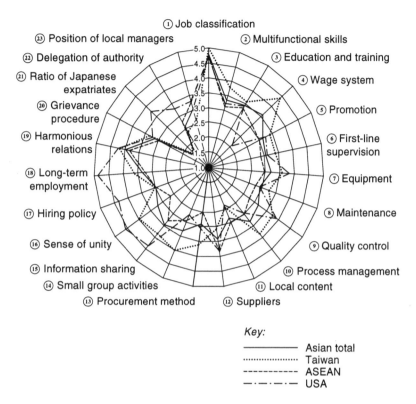

① Job classification
㉓ Position of local managers   ② Multifunctional skills
㉒ Delegation of authority   ③ Education and training
㉑ Ratio of Japanese expatriates   ④ Wage system
⑳ Grievance procedure   ⑤ Promotion
⑲ Harmonious relations   ⑥ First-line supervision
⑱ Long-term employment   ⑦ Equipment
⑰ Hiring policy   ⑧ Maintenance
⑯ Sense of unity   ⑨ Quality control
⑮ Information sharing   ⑩ Process management
⑭ Small group activities   ⑪ Local content
⑬ Procurement method   ⑫ Suppliers

Key:
——————— Asian total
·················· Taiwan
----------- ASEAN
—·—·—·— USA

Figure 4.2   Automotive assembly (23 items)

restrict foreign expatriates by rarely issuing work permits. Greater numbers of Japanese expatriates are stationed at export-orientated electronics plants because local governments and Japanese companies put greater importance on these.

The North American average for the six-group evaluation for application ratio was 3.5 points, compared with East Asia's 3.2 points. The plants in North America scored more than 3 points in all six groups, but, East Asian automotive assembly plants achieved slightly more than two points for Parent–subsidiary relations and scored more than three points in all other groups except Work organisation. Overall, the East Asian averages are less than North America's. North American plants achieved high levels of application for Labour relations (4.2 points), Group consciousness (3.9 points), and Parent–subsidiary relations. Excluding the East Asian core groups, the peripheral groups scored lower points than North America. East Asian plants gained fewer than 0.5 points compared with North American plants in Group consciousness (−0.6 points), Labour relations (−0.9 points), and Parent–subsidiary relations (−1.2 points). In North America, Japanese automotive plants had to raise the application ratio in those peripheral groups to implement Japanese-style work organisation and production control on the shop floor. This was because the existing mass production system, or Fordism, differed from the Japanese system. East Asia, however, has no established production system, so it is not necessary to raise the application ratio of the framing groups.

Special consideration needs to be paid to the difference in the application ratio between Taiwan and the ASEAN countries. Taiwan achieved substantially higher points than the ASEAN average. Even though these differences exist in other industries, they are greater in the automotive industry. Taiwan's average was 3.5, whereas ASEAN countries scored 3.0. There are no such substantial differences in other industries. Application points for Taiwanese plants exceed ASEAN countries in the following four groups: Work organisation (+0.5), Production control (+0.7), Group consciousness (+1.0) and Labour relations (+0.4). In Group consciousness, Taiwan's score exceeds the ASEAN countries' by one point. Taiwan also scored higher on Production control (+0.7) and Work organisation (+0.5). Conversely, Taiwan rated lower than ASEAN countries in Parts procurement (−0.1) and Parent–subsidiary relations (−0.2).

Four-Perspective Evaluation

The Four-Perspective Evaluation (see Table 4.3 and Figure 4.3) describes the specific features of the East Asian automotive industry. The Four-Perspective Evaluation for the automotive industry reveals contrasting application points between Human–Method and Human–Result. The level of application of Human–Method was high at 3.5 points, but application of Human–Result was extremely low at 2.2 points. On the other hand, the application of Material–Method ranked in the middle at 3.0 points, and Material–Result showed a strong application orientation at 3.2 points. Thus the human elements show a contrasting pattern; high orientation to application for methods and high orientation to adaptation for results. With materials, however, though both methods and results scored close to three points, results exceeded methods. Accordingly, the ratio was 100 for results and 118 for methods, regarding the Results–Method ratio. Comparing this ratio with the East Asian average for all industries, the

Table 4.4   Four-Perspective evaluation for the automotive assembly industry

Region		Asia total	Taiwan	ASEAN	USA
Method	Human	3.5	3.9	3.2	3.5
	Material	3.0	3.5	2.7	3.3
Result	Human	2.2	2.1	2.3	3.6
	Material	3.2	3.0	3.3	3.3

application point of Human–Method for the automotive industry was slightly higher than the East Asian total by 0.1 point, but achieved a lower rating for the other three aspects. The application ratio of Human–Method was 3.5, but for the other aspects, the automotive industry recorded 0.2 points lower than the East Asian total – 0.2 points less for both Human–Result and Material–Method, and 0.3 points lower for Material–Result. As noted above, the average application ratio for the automotive industry was 3.2, 0.1 points lower than the East Asian total. By breaking it down into the Four-Perspective Evaluation, the automotive industry achieved similar points as the East Asian total only in Human–Method, and scored fewer points in the other three aspects. The East Asian total achieved a general application ratio higher than the automotive industry through gaining higher points than the other three aspects. These relatively high scores reflect the application ratio in the electronics assembly and parts industries.

In a comparison of the East Asian automotive industry with the North American automotive industry using the Four-Perspective Evaluation, the North American application ratio exceeded 3 points in all four aspects, achieving higher points than the East Asian automotive industry in all aspects. Points for the North American automotive industry were: Human–Method and Human–Result, 3.6; and Material–Method and Material–Result, 3.3. All four aspects recorded more than 3 points and there was no difference in application points between methods and results for the categories of Human–Result and Material–Result. Comparison with the East Asian automotive industry reveals the application of the East Asian industry to be lower in all four aspects, with Human–Result recording 1.4 points fewer than the North American automotive industry. In the other three aspects, the East Asian automotive industry recorded 0.3 points fewer than the American automotive industry for Material–Method; 0.2 points for Human–Method; and 0.1 points for Material–Result.

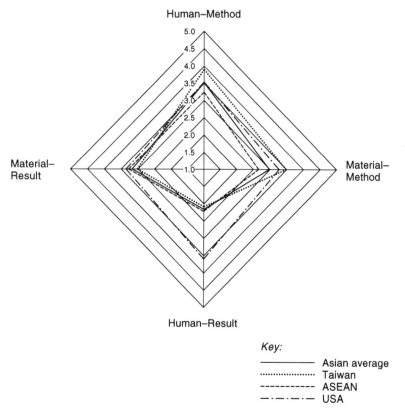

Figure 4.3   Automotive assembly (four-perspective evaluation)

The Four-Perspective Evaluation also exposed differences in points
between Taiwan and the ASEAN nations. As stated earlier, there was a
difference of 0.5 points in average application between Taiwan and
ASEAN countries. It is interesting to note how this difference affects the
Four-Perspective Evaluation. Taiwan recorded higher points for both
Human–Method and Material–Method, and achieved slightly lower points
for Human–Result and Material–Result. Taiwan exceeded ASEAN
countries by 0.7 points in Human–Method and by 0.8 points in
Material–Method. Conversely, Taiwan recorded 0.2 fewer for
Human–Result and 0.3 points fewer for Material–Result. A breakdown of
the application points for Taiwan and ASEAN countries follows. Taiwan
scored highly for Human–Method (3.9) and for Material–Method (3.5). In
contrast to this, Human–Result was 2.1 points and Material–Result 3.0

points. For ASEAN countries, Human–Method was 3.2 points and Material–Method 2.7 points, indicating an adaptation orientation. Human–Result was 2.3 points and Material–Result 3.3 points. Therefore the Taiwanese application ratio for methods exceeded those of ASEAN countries but, conversely, was lower than the ASEAN countries' level for application of results. For the Results–Method ratio, methods achieved a higher application orientation in Taiwan: 100 for results versus 146 for methods. Contrary to this, both results and methods achieved a close ratio in ASEAN countries: 100 for results versus 107 for methods. A clearer understanding of the differences in application ratio between Taiwan and ASEAN countries is obtainable though looking at each element. Taiwan exceeded the ASEAN countries by more than 0.5 points in the elements of Multifunctional skills, Wage system, First-line supervisor, Quality control, Process management, Procurement method, Small-group activities, Information sharing, Sense of unity, and Long-term employment: all elements that relate to methods. In contrast to this, the ASEAN nations exceeded Taiwan by more than 0.5 points in Local content, Supplier's and Position of local managers. These three elements belong to the Results group. It can be said that the application ratio in Taiwan considerably surpassed that of the ASEAN countries for such items as Work organisation, Production control and Procurement – elements that are related to plant operations.

A specific feature of the Taiwanese auto industry is the high rate of application in methods-related elements; whereas a high rate of application in results, especially Material–Result, is a distinguishing feature of ASEAN countries. Because ASEAN countries are not as industrialised as Taiwan, the high rate of application in Material–Result for ASEAN countries stems from a strong dependency on materials from Japan – a necessary condition for plant operation.

Japanese firms can easily transfer human-related Japanese systems within East Asia without major difficulty because there are some cultural similarities. In East Asia, human-related systems are not based on the job classification system as in the USA and Europe. Familiarity with the Japanese system brought about a high rate of application in human-related elements in Taiwan and also led to a score of more than three points for ASEAN countries. There are no job categories in East Asian countries that determine employees' duties and wages and include a career progression as in North America. But Malaysia, a former colony of Britain, has a job-based wage system. Although some Japanese firms depend on this system, reform is possible. This does not mean, however, that transferring the Japanese system to East Asia is a simple process.

Regarding Material–Method, Taiwan achieved a high rate of application at 3.5 points, whereas ASEAN countries scored only 2.7 points. Because of the later industrialisation of ASEAN countries, the application ratio for method, which is difficult to transfer from Japan, is relatively lower than that of Taiwan.

III   APPLICATION SITUATION OF THE JAPANESE PRODUCTION SYSTEM

Work Organisation

This section begins with an outline of the main points regarding work organisation (see Table 4.3). The application rating as an items group was 3.6. All six items exceeded three points: job classification (4.8); multifunctional skills (3.4); education and training (3.5; wage system (3.6); promotion (3.2); and first-line supervisor (3.1). This figure is 0.1 higher than the East Asian total of 3.5 points. On an item-by-item breakdown, only the rating of multifunctional skills in automotive assembly exceeded the East Asian total substantially; all other items showed few differences. Compared with the rating of automotive assembly in North America, only the ratings of Wage system in East Asia substantially exceeded those of North America.

The 4.8 application rating for job classification was similar to the figure for Japan. Because neither Taiwan nor Thailand have Western-style job classification systems, Japanese companies do not need to change the system there. However, one automotive assembly plant in Malaysia scored less than the others, preventing the application rating of this item from reaching 5.0 points. In Malaysia, where British influence still exists, Japanese companies do not hold the management initiative in joint ventures, the labour union is organised at the industry level and the wage system is determined by job base. However, the Malaysian wage system and labour unions are not based on the so-called job control unionism, which follows the tradition of skilled trade unions in Europe, so the job categories transcend the company level and are similar throughout society. The one plant that received a lower rating in this item had many wage grades determining wages within the company. Its job categories were not recognised outside the company.

The rating of wage system, relating to job classification, was 3.6, indicating application orientation. East Asian automotive plants have a range of ratings for this item. In the United States, Japanese automotive plants followed the local wage system, even though the number of job classifications were simplified into two or three categories. Wage rates, following this system, are determined by the simplified job classifications, and there is no performance evaluation for individual workers. Basically, there are two job categories: production and maintenance. The wage rates are identical within the same job, so the rating for wages was very low in the United States. Contrary to this, a basic wage based on the employee's school background is popular in East Asia. Wages are determined by the employee's attributes, and not by the job. But there are large gaps between different school backgrounds, especially between shop-floor workers and administrative employees. Most plants adopted performance evaluation for all employees as a determinant of wage, except for one plant in Malaysia. Even though most plants have performance evaluation as a system, there is scepticism about the workings of the system; mainly whether performance evaluation is carried out objectively and wheter it did, in fact, determine wages.

There is a difference in the rating of wage system between Taiwan and the ASEAN countries. Taiwan was 4.4, while the ASEAN countries scored 3.1. This difference is based on three reasons: wage differences relating to school background in ASEAN countries are greater than in Taiwan; the performance evaluation system for shop-floor workers does not work well in some Thai plants, even though the Japanese side holds management power in the joint venture; and the performance evaluation system is not adopted at one Malaysian plant because of opposition from a labour union.

Some interesting cases relating to evaluation for shop-floor workers follow. In Taiwan, it was reported that a first-line supervisor responsible for performance evaluation tended to evaluate workers under him by making no distinctions between workers, to avoid protests from the workers that the evaluations were unfair. Employees may complain to supervisors directly about their lower wages after finding out the salaries of co-workers. To combat this problem, one Japanese manager said that they have set a distribution ratio of evaluation to determine differences. Namely, the company decided the distribution ratio of evaluations as follows: 5 per cent to receive an A ranking; 25 per cent a B; 40 per cent a C; 25 per cent a D; and 5 per cent a rank of E. Managers guide supervisors to evaluate workers using this distribution. Managers examine the results of performance evaluations at the section level, and finally senior managers adjust the results to follow the distribution ratio. As managers maintain the fairness of the system through readjusting the evaluation, they say the performance evaluation system works well, and once the difference is made between workers, it is very difficult to narrow.

In Thailand, managers try to maintain fairness of performance evaluations by setting a distribution ratio. For example, one company in Thailand decided that an ability wage, constituting half of the full wage, is determined by performance evaluation. There are three grades of evaluation, A, B and C, each rank being multiplied by a coefficient. There is a case that while the Japanese side controls management in a Thai joint venture, in reality the Japanese managers could not grasp how wages were determined. Wages are, in fact, determined by such items as school background, length of service and performance evaluation. The evaluation system was supposed to be divided into five grades from administrative to shop-floor workers, but it was difficult to assess that the system was working fairly. Japanese managers responded that favouritism is spreading throughout the plant and that complaining, self-assertive types tend to get a high evaluation. Assuming that this is a normal practice in Thailand, it is quite difficult for such a system to work well. In a plant that commenced operations recently, the Japanese management set six grades for the evaluation process. The first-line supervisor and the section manager make an evaluation together for each worker, after this, the department manager adjusts the results in order to maintain fairness. On the question of Thais disliking their achievements being evaluated and employees being different from each other, the managers answered that 'Wages tend to be determined by emotional judgement, and emotional factors affect as much as 50 per cent of judgement.' They added, 'We'd like to reduce the emotional factor in evaluation to only 10 per cent within three or five years. Therefore, we try to maintain fairness by focusing on ability-based judgement and on administration by target. We are considering combining the administration by target with performance evaluation. Each worker is given a target to achieve. For example, he can obtain an A evaluation the next time by reducing his defects score by half, or by cutting his absences from three days to one day for a set period of time. In this way, we intend to mix performance evaluation with administration by target. Thais have the potential to be competitive, so it is important to create an environment where competition can be stimulated.'

There is a split in Malaysia regarding the adoption of performance evaluation because workers are not accustomed to it, and the labour unions, following the British tradition, are opposed to it. One plant adopted it, but the other did not. At the plant where the system is not adopted, Japanese managers responded that, 'Wages are determined by length of service, they rise automatically, and we cannot make exceptions for labour union members. The labour union opposes the system, demanding equal treatment. This is an obstacle preventing the introduction of the Japanese system on the shop floor.'

The application rating for promotion was 3.2 points. This rating exceeded three points because most plants adopted a company qualification system where employees get a higher position within a series of company qualifications though accumulating performance evaluation points and recommendations from their supervisors. But the rating is confined to slightly above three points because some plants did not adopt the company qualification system and some introduced restricted qualifications, which separated administrative employees from shop-floor workers in the qualifications. In addition, performance evaluations did not work well in the plants stated above. The Japanese-style promotion system, where employees get a higher position within a series of company qualifications as well as a higher status employment position by improving skills and administrative ability, is difficult to establish smoothly without appropriate measures. Therefore, it is necessary to establish such systems as company qualifications, unlimited promotion and fair performance evaluation in order to overcome discriminatory promotion based on school background, or unfair promotion founded on such questionable standards as those existing in local firms.

All Taiwanese plants have introduced the qualification system and there are no upper limits on promotion. Recommendation by a supervisor is a necessary condition for promotion. Employees get higher positions depending on company qualifications and job status. Only one plant, where the local partner controlled management, separated administrative employees from shop-floor workers for qualifications and provided no qualification steps for shop-floor workers. However, ordinary workers are able to move from the shop floor to administrative positions by exhibiting above average ability and accumulating good evaluations.

Among the six automotive assembly plants visited in Thailand, three plants had the company qualification system but one did not adopt it. Among the plants with the company qualification system, two had introduced almost the same system as its Japanese parent company, and one plant followed the system for Thai government officers. In the plant without a company qualification system, the Japanese managers understood the necessity of introducing it but were sceptical as to whether Thais would value company qualifications that were not recognised outside the company. Promotion only followed along job position lines. On this point, a Japanese manager elaborated, 'We should increase job positions to give senior employees better treatment as long as the existing system is retained. The level of job position is understood by people outside the company. But we are sceptical about introducing a company qualification system. None the less, we must adopt it in the future.' This quote refers directly to the meaningless increase of administrative positions resulting from promotion by length of service. At the same time, the managers also stressed the importance of introducing a company qualification system as well as having work performance evaluations.

The situation in Malaysia differs slightly from that in Thailand. There are earnings differentials based on disparity of jobs among races, and British systems also remain. At one plant, Japanese managers mentioned that promotions were carried out within the company, and recommendations by the supervisor were necessary, the same as within Japan. But they added that, unlike in Japan, there was no company qualification system. The class system, established during British colonialism, still remains, so employees are separated into the categories of 'exempt' and 'non-exempt'. There are office workers as well as shop-floor workers who cannot move up to administrative positions. At another plant, Japanese managers reported that they were trying to introduce a Japanese-style promotion system, which allowed promotion to shop manager or middle manager from the shop floor. Such promotions may appear three or five years down the road. The plant in question produces so-called national cars. It hires Malays as the first preference in accordance with the *Bumiputera* policy. As a national car company, it promotes Malays on the shop floor to administrative positions.

The automotive industry's rating for multifunctional skills was 3.4, exceeding the 2.7 points of the East Asian total by 0.7 points. This is a result of automotive assembly plants implementing programmes to raise worker skills. This item, with a score of 3.4, is characteristic of the automotive industry. The evaluation standard for this item was based on the development level of multiskilled workers through job rotation within teams. As the cycle time is longer and the scope of duties is greater than in Japan, it is possible to assess that by mastering only his own job, a worker has reached the initial stage of multifunctional skills. Large differences exist between Taiwan and ASEAN countries regarding this item. Taiwan is rated highly, with 3.8 points, whereas the ASEAN countries achieved 3.1. The factors hindering the development of multifunctional skills in East Asia is different from North America and Europe where fixed job allocation based on segmented job classifications and job control unionism by industry-wide labour unions are a major barrier. This development also depends on a sense of work and wages on the part of East Asian workers. Some workers do not like to teach their mastered skills to other employees, to protect their favourable position – a sense of the ownership of skill. They also do not like to work longer hours for the same wages, which is a concept of wages based on job. In addition, some plants claimed that an inadequate number of employees was preventing them from implementing job rotation because of a high turnover rate. In Taiwan, plants have tried to overcome beliefs by employees that hinder the implementation of raising multifunctional skills by combining education and training with performance evaluation. They have gradually produced multiskilled workers together with lower turnover rates because of stable employment conditions. Nowadays, job rotation within a team is implemented frequently. Japanese managers however, claimed that, 'They should teach others their skills more freely. Even though they rotate their jobs, it is very difficult to ask them to increase productivity.' In Thailand, automotive assembly plants also have tried to carry out job rotation and gained a certain level of positive results, but the extent of rotation is limited to that within a team. In Malaysia, two plants have implemented job rotation. At one plant, although the union did not permit performance evaluations, it was not against job rotation to raise worker skill levels. Managers at another plant felt that employees frequently undertake job rotation without understanding the importance of mastering the skills required.

The rating for first-line supervisor was 3.1, the lowest in the Work Organisation group. Taiwan exceeded the ASEAN countries in this item: Taiwan was 3.4 and ASEAN countries 2.9. Generally speaking, there is a lack of adequately trained foremen in East Asia because of the recent introduction of industrialisation. Managers therefore put great importance on fostering the development of first-line supervisors through education and training. Supervisors are promoted within the company and are expected to carry out the role that supervisors do in Japan. Whereas supervisors in North American plants are not expected to make performance evaluations, because of a different system, in East Asia they are expected to undertake this role. At a plant in Taiwan, where the Japanese side controls management policy, managers explained that supervisors undertake both production control and worker management but are not as proficient at process control as are Japanese supervisors. On the other hand, Thai supervisors are expected to play the same role as in Japan, but they are not skilled at planning. A Japanese manager, commenting on the differences between Japanese and Thai supervisors, answered, 'There is no way to compare them. First-line supervisors are more competent than ordinary workers, but I do not set them very high targets.' In one Malaysian plant, a Japanese manager answered,

'Supervisors lack clout, because managers are active, even on the shop floor.' From these comments it is possible to conclude that first-line supervisors have not yet been trained sufficiently in East Asia.

Production Control and Procurement

This section begins with the analysis of Production control and Procurement. Production control was placed in the core group with Work Organisation, and Procurement in the quasi-core group. Items in the two groups belong to Material in the Four-Perspective Evaluation. These two groups indicate the level of application of plant operations from the materials perspective. As stated above, the East Asian automotive industry has stepped up its production capabilities from simple CKD to raising its local content rates in products that are mainly for the domestic market. Automotive assembly plants must not only put a great many parts together, but parts suppliers must deliver quality products in accordance with assembly makers' specifications. The automotive assembly industry needs to develop the manufacturing industry systematically, from materials to parts, but the East Asian countries have depended on Japan for the supply of important materials and key components. In addition, the plants are small to medium-sized, supplying exclusively the domestic market. This recent development of automobile assembly: high dependency for materials and parts on Japan; small and medium-sized plants; and primarily supplying the domestic market, seem to have a negative effect on the application of the Japanese system but result in a dependency on Japan for materials. In fact, the application rating in production control was 3.2, and procurement was 3.1, which tend slightly towards application. Although there are no major differences between the North American automotive industry's and the East Asian total, the East Asian automotive assembly level of application is slightly lower than that of the USA. The rating of production control is lower than both by 0.2 points. The rating of local content is lower than the East Asian total by 0.1 points, and the same as North America. This means that the East Asian automotive assembly industry applies methods less than the others from a materials point of view. Each item consisting of two groups achieved a lower score than the East Asian total and that of North American plants. The rating for Equipment was lower than North America by 0.7 points, and also lower than the East Asian total by 0.5 points. The rating of quality control was lower than North America, by 0.8 points. By classifying items of the two groups into methods and results of the Four-Perspective Evaluation, the material–method was 3.0 and material–result was 3.2. Whereas material–result recorded higher points than methods even for the East Asian total, the rating of the automotive assembly industry is lower than the East Asian total by 0.2 points in material–method and by 0.3 points in material–result. Also the rating of the East Asian automotive assembly industry is lower than North America by 0.3 points in material–method and by 0.1 points in material–result.

There is also a distinct difference between Taiwan and the ASEAN countries for these groups. Particularly in relation to the Four-Perspective Evaluation, points for material–method and material–result reveal a higher capability for automobile production in Taiwan than in ASEAN countries. In Taiwan, material–method as 3.5 points, and material–result as 3.0 points, indicate a high rate of application in methods and a moderate dependency in material–result. In contrast to this, in ASEAN countries, material–method was 2.7 points, and material–result as 3.3 points, which means adaptation orientation in methods and dependency in material–result – the opposite combination from Taiwan.

On an item-by-item basis, equipment was rated at 3.2, substantially lower than the scores for North America and East Asia. Contrary to the general impression arising from the late industrialisation of East Asian countries, this rating is low, at slightly over 3.0 points. This is assuming that these countries import much more equipment from Japan, which is not in fact correct. The rating exceeded 3.0 points for the following reasons: even in the case of new plants, automotive assembly plants did not necessarily provide the same equipment as the Japanese parent company did in Japan; and local partners tended to buy Western-made equipment. Although automotive assembly plants generally involve the four processes of stamping, welding, painting and assembly, East Asian automotive assembly plants do not necessarily have the stamping process because they started as CKD operations, and still exhibit some earlier characteristics. In addition, if a plant has a stamping process, it does not produce all the stamped parts, but relies on Japanese imports and local suppliers as well. Because welding and painting processes are less automated, manual labour is used extensively. The most expensive equipment is painting machines followed by stamping machines. These machines came not only from Japan but also from other countries. There is a difference in rating for this item between Taiwan and ASEAN countries; Taiwan was 3.6 and ASEAN countries 3.0. This is because plants in Taiwan are mainly equipped with Japanese stamping machines, and are also provided with Japanese-made painting equipment. On the other hand, in Thailand, many plants were not equipped with stamping machines and did not import painting machines from Japan. In Malaysia, the national car plant imported its main equipment from Japan, but other CKD plants did not necessarily buy key machines from there. Management at a truck plant in Thailand with a long history reported, 'We bought the main equipment locally. If we buy machines from Japan, we will have trouble with maintenance because of differences in machine size. To avoid maintenance trouble, it is easy to buy machines in Thailand. There are many machine manufacturing companies that have technical tie-ups with Western or Japanese firms.'

The rating for maintenance was 2.9. Generally speaking, the ASEAN countries are poor at training proficient maintenance workers, so the rating of this item was low. Each plant sends maintenance workers to Japan, and Japanese specialists also come to train local workers. Even though local plants did not depend much on maintenance workers because there is less automated equipment, the lack of maintenance is a hindrance to plant operations. Regarding the hiring and training of maintenance workers, many plants hire general workers without selection for maintenance skills, and subsequently select some of these workers to train as maintenance specialists. But, in Malaysia, two plants responded that they hired maintenance workers separately and trained them with on-the-job training within the plant or in Japan. In Taiwan, most plants have stamping machines. They have a lot of trouble with adjustment and repair of dies, so Japanese expatriates were in charge of die adjustment in one plant. On this topic, a Japanese manager remarked, 'Even though local workers go to Japan to master die adjustment skills, after coming back to Taiwan, they do not willingly teach these skills to co-workers, or they sometimes resign from the company.' The quality control application rating was 3.2, 0.8 points lower than North America. This is because even though East Asian automotive plants are adopting the idea of an incremental build-up of quality by paying attention to it in each manufacturing process, they do not implement the system fully, and therefore do not achieve international quality levels in some cases. There is also a large difference in the application rating between Taiwan and the ASEAN nations. Taiwan scored 3.8 points and ASEAN 2.8 points. In East Asia, the so-called five Ss (*seiri* (arranging); *seiton* (order); *seiso* (cleaning); *seiketsu* (cleanliness); and *shitsuke* (discipline) appear to be a precondition for quality control activities. Plants place great importance on the five Ss in Taiwan and ASEAN countries. The reason for the difference of rating between Taiwan and the ASEAN countries stems from the level of implementation of the Japanese-style quality control method as well as quality standards achieved, but it also depends on the way companies respond to new government policy concerning imported automobiles. In Taiwan, the government has lowered customs duties on automobiles gradually since adopting a liberalisation policy in 1985. Such duties now stand at 30 per cent. Each plant has raised the quality of each manufacturing process gradually to compete with imported cars. The Japanese parent companies maintain international quality standards, so local plants have tried to boost quality levels to match them. An interesting transformation from the US quality control method to the Japanese system occurred at one plant where the local partner had management power. It had originally adopted US-style quality control, checking quality at the final inspection stage, but it changed to the Japanese system after the introduction of the liberalisation policy. Local partners invited Japanese specialists to advise on quality control on the shop floor. The method of quality checks is the same as in the parent company in Japan: that is, both the departments of quality control and manufacturing send quality specialists to monitor the manufacturing process. On the shop floor, each worker writes the results of quality checks on the 'quality improvement sheet'. If there is no problem, it is marked in blue and if there is a problem, it is marked in red. In the case of a red mark, the foreman writes down on the confirmation sheet the type of problem and the final result. Managers gather in the audit room to examine the results of the quality check every morning and then provide feedback to the shop floor. In this way, quality is raised on two fronts. One relays the inspection results from the audit room to the shop floor, and the other improves work standards on the shop floor. But at times, the system is not implemented thoroughly, and in this case quality is guaranteed through inspections at the final stage.

Both Thailand and Malaysia are more protectionist against automobile imports than is Taiwan. Thailand has lowered customs duties to some degree, and the Malaysian national car plant is raising quality to be able to export its products. They have made an effort to build quality within the manufacturing process, but have not yet achieved satisfactory results. Accordingly, some plants place larger numbers of inspectors at the final stage. One plant in Thailand guaranteed quality by using a different system from the parent company in Japan. It stationed inspectors in the manufacturing process, because the Japanese system did not work well there. None the less, the defect rate on the assembly line was four times the Japanese average and double at the shipping stage. The most frequently detected defect at the shipping stage was missing parts. This stems from simple causes: workers forgot to attach a part correctly to the body; required parts were not sent to the local plant from Japan; and parts were not delivered to the plant from local suppliers. A graph depicting quality levels of overseas subsidiaries of the Japanese parent company placed the plant in question at the very bottom. Because Thai consumers value exterior appearance and colour, the company tries to maintain a high level of quality at the shipping stage.

The rating of process control was 3.3 points. Generally, East Asian automotive plants (excluding the national car plant in Malaysia) produce various models. Although annual production capacity is between 40 000 and 100 000 units, welding and assembly comprise multiple lines, producing several models. With complex lines, there are four or five assembly lines, each producing a different model. Therefore the cycle time is very long. One plant, whose parent company in Japan has a cycle time of one minute, has set it at four to five minutes in Taiwan. The cycle time in one of the lines of the same plant is extremely long at fifteen minutes. The arrangement plan of the machines or lines is complicated because many plants have engine assembly processes related to the necessity of increasing local content levels. Therefore, process control is not easy, even for small or middle-sized plants. In addition, supervisors are not able to perform their role of process control and work control efficiently. Accordingly, the rating of process control is not very high. Despite this situation, one plant in Taiwan implements small-lot production with mixed model assembly similar to Japan. This plant also carries out rational production control by providing a production control board that shows the flow of each body in the line, enabling control room employees to monitor shop-floor operations. Generally speaking, Taiwanese plants are superior in production control to ASEAN plants.

For procurement, the rating for local content was 2.8, higher than North America by 0.5 points. Even though East Asian countries claim to be raising local content levels, they can not fully produce materials and parts, and therefore depend on Japan for supplies of these. Taiwan rated at 2.4, 0.6 less than the ASEAN countries, indicating higher local content levels. In Taiwan, local content levels are rising as local parts suppliers improve production capabilities, quality and cost performance, though key parts still come from Japan. Assembly plants have stamping machines within the plant or nearby, so they are self-sufficient for such parts. Also, engines are assembled within the plants. In Malaysia, engines are assembled within plants to raise local content levels. Even though local plants import materials and parts from Japan, if they process and assemble them into products, these products are regarded as being 'locally manufactured'. Therefore, ascertaining actual local content levels is difficult. In ASEAN countries especially, their limited ability to produce materials locally means that true local content levels are less than the levels claimed. For example, automotive assembly plants in ASEAN countries install engine assembly lines to follow the local content rule for engines, but some lines are too short to assemble the necessary parts fully. Such lines would be defined as a subline of a main automotive assembly line in Japan. It seems that they are trying to raise local content levels for the sake of following rules, rather than for improving production.

The rating for suppliers was 3.5, indicating a high dependency on Japanese or Japanese-affiliated suppliers. Taiwan recorded 3.0 and ASEAN countries scored 3.8 points. ASEAN countries depend on both Japanese imports and purchases from local Japanese affiliates.

Procurement method for East Asian countries was 2.9 points, showing a degree of adaptation orientation. There were differences in rating between Taiwan and ASEAN countries for this item: Taiwan was rated at 3.6, with ASEAN countries at 2.5 points. Taiwan's higher score reflects an improvement in quality, cost and delivery on the part of local suppliers, guided by assembly makers following the liberalisation of car imports. In fact, assembly makers organise Japanese-style *kyōryokukai* (collaborative organisations of assembly makers and parts suppliers) in Taiwan. Assembly makers provide guidance regarding the quality of parts to local suppliers. As a result, just-in-time delivery with partial use of the *kanban* system was adopted. Parts inspection, however, is carried out at random, and some parts are inspected completely, which does not occur in Japan. In ASEAN countries, though the assembly makers organise *kyōryokukai*, they do not systematically guide parts suppliers on quality, cost or delivery. They send engineers to suppliers when problems are detected. Most assembly plants carry out inspections at random or at full scale. One plant inspects all parts. Although full-scale inspections consume much time and effort, they do reduce expenses ultimately by preventing line stoppages caused by missing parts. One plant responded that the delivery rate within a designated day two years previously was 88 per cent but has now reached 95–98 per cent. Delivery rates have improved, but assembly line stoppages still occur because of missing parts. One assembly plant in Malaysia had a delivery rate of 60–70 per cent, so this maker had to stock many parts within its plants.

Group Consciousness and Labour Relations

The ratings for the two groups group consciousness and labour relations were 3.3, showing an application orientation, but lower than the North American automotive industry – by 0.6 points for group consciousness and 0.9 points for labour relations. These two groups are formed as peripheral groups to allow core groups to function smoothly. In North

America, Japanese-affiliated automotive plants showed a high rate of application in these peripheral groups for transfer of the Japanese production system, even though it was different from the traditional local system. In East Asia, however, the two groups did not record such a high ratio, with work organisation a relatively low 3.6. It is possible to assume that it is not necessary to transfer the Japanese system within these peripheral groups to East Asia to ensure the core groups function well, because there is no established production system, such as Fordism, and there are also institutional similarities with Japan. The difference in application ratings between Taiwan and the ASEAN countries is clear: for group consciousness–Taiwan was 3.9, and ASEAN 2.9; and for labour relations–Taiwan was 3.6 and ASEAN scored 3.2 points.

For small-group activities, the application rating was 3.3, exceeding North America's 2.7. The 3.3 rating was influenced strongly by Taiwan's score of 4.0 points. ASEAN countries scored 2.9 points. While all plants have in East Asia small- group activities, there are differences regarding participation rate and activity content between Taiwan and the ASEAN countries. The rate of participation reached somewhere between 75 per cent to 90 per cent in Taiwan, whether the activities were implemented in company time or outside it. Each plant taught the basics of small-group activities within the general education and training programme. Participating in such education was a prerequisite for promotion. On this subject, one plant manager commented, 'There are 141 groups and the rate of participation is 90 per cent of employees under the rank of supervisor officially. In reality, active groups number 120 and the rate of participation is approximately 85 per cent. Each group arranges a certain time for group activities. Activity time takes place during working hours.' At another plant, activities are carried out once every Saturday for 50 minutes, by stopping the line during company time. A plant that achieved a 100 per cent participation rate even outside company hours reported that the activities were serious, and that *kaizen* (continuous improvement) was being undertaken. Therefore, it can be said that small-group activities are being implemented in a proper manner. But, in ASEAN countries, the situation is different and the participation rate extremely low. A manager at one plant whose Taiwanese sister plant realised 100 per cent voluntary participation declared the situation to be less than encouraging: 'Our policy states that all employees must participate, but it is very difficult to secure time for activities because many employees come to work by bus.' Poor commuting conditions in Bangkok appeared to be a major disincentive. It was a similar situation for most plants. Typical comments were, 'There are only seven QC circles but they are not active'. and 'At first there were twenty groups but now only eight groups are active.' Only one plant implemented small-group activities in company time. A Japanese manager from this plant remarked, 'There are about a hundred circles. Activities are conducted for thirty minutes every Thursday from 2:30 in the afternoon. Elite groups were sent to Japan to participate in a company-wide QC meeting. QC activities provide opportunities to visit Japan, so enthusiasm is high.' Overall, however, small-group activities did not appear to be functioning well in Thailand.

In Malaysia, the national car plant commenced small-group activities with the inauguration of the plant. The line is stopped once a month during company time to gain full employee participation. Another CKD plant conducted these activities on a voluntary basis for one hour a week without payment, but only seventeen groups were organised. In East Asia, only one plant in Taiwan realised a high level of small-group activities with full participation on a voluntary basis, as in Japan, but other plants in Taiwan also gained a high rate of participation, voluntarily or not. In contrast to this, in ASEAN countries the participation rate is limited unless it is conducted by means of stopping the line in company time.

Regarding information sharing and sense of unity, the ratings point to an application orientation in general, but lower than in North America. There was a large gap in ratings between Taiwan and ASEAN countries. Whereas the application rating for information sharing was 3.8, and sense of unity 4.0 in Taiwan, ASEAN countries scored much lower, with information sharing and sense of unity at 3.3 and 2.6, respectively. The 2.6 score is a feature of ASEAN countries. Some reasons are: social distinctions based on school background or jobs in ASEAN countries are more pronounced than in Taiwan; distinctions between shop-floor employees and office administrative employees are present in wages and promotion as well as in the company cafeteria; high turnover rates of staff prevent the building of unity; and local managers who do not like to lose privileges tend to retain such barriers within the company. If a company qualification system which ties both classes equally resulting in dissolving such divisions, managers often will not intend to put the system into practice. Such distinctions were present in Taiwan, but, managers took action to reduce class differences and achieved positive results. It is interesting to note that the difference between the two regions for this item stems from dissimilarities regarding the stage of economic development and the social and cultural base.

The application rating as a group for labour relations was 3.3, which is almost the same as the East Asian total for all industries, and lower than North America by 0.9 points. This group shows an application orientation, and the Taiwanese rating was higher than in ASEAN countries. But the difference in points was smaller than for Group consciousness.

The application rating for hiring policy was 2.9, tending slightly towards adaptation. Taiwan was 3.0 and ASEAN countries 2.9. There was a certain amount of adaptation involved with the selection of location as a first stage for hiring policy because joint ventures either had no chance to select a location or choose a government-developed industrial complex. Hiring policy also adapted to local customs. Both in Taiwan and the ASEAN countries, automotive assembly plants combine both regular and irregular hiring of employees. In Thailand, many plants hire temporary workers sent from an employment agency, amounting to approximately 10 per cent of all employees. From this group, some full-time workers are also selected.

The application rating for long-term employment was 3.3: Taiwan being 3.6 and ASEAN countries 3.1. This indicates an application orientation. Taiwan accomplished greater long-term employment for employees than did ASEAN countries. Japanese subsidiaries attach great importance to long-term employment, as do East Asian companies, but East Asian labour markets have a higher rate of turnover compared to Japan. In Taiwan automotive assembly plants succeeded in encouraging employees to stay in the company in order to implement job rotation and create multifunctional skills, but many plants were worried about the high rate of turnover. In addition, some plants in Thailand and Malaysia resorted to lay-off when there was a shift system change from two shifts to one because of business fluctuations. This lowered the rating of this item.

The application rating for labour relations was extremely high, at 4.0, with Taiwan being 4.2 and ASEAN countries 3.9 points. Most automotive assembly plants have labour unions, except for one plant in both Taiwan and Thailand. Labour unions are organised within the company in both Taiwan and Thailand. Although labour unions are generally organised on an industry-wide level in Malaysia, two Japanese-affiliated plants altered the labour unions to Japanese-style company-wide organisations. In general, labour relations are cooperative. They have a labour management consultation system to discuss periodically management situations, as well as a collective bargaining system that allows wage negotiations.

Parent–Subsidiary Relations

This group clearly indicates an adaptation orientation. The application ratio is low at 2.3, lower than the East Asian total by 0.3 points. Compared with North America's 3.5, the application ratio of the automotive assembly industry is extraordinarily low. Furthermore, Taiwan and the ASEAN countries recorded almost the same points: the former was 2.2 and the latter 2.4. Both items reveal an adaptation orientation. Although ratio of Japanese expatriates was 1.4 and delegation of authority 2.6, indicating localisation of management, position of local managers was 3.0. There is a difference in the application rating of the last item between Taiwan and ASEAN countries; Taiwan tends towards adaptation, at 2.6, and ASEAN countries indicated a level of application at 3.3 points. In Taiwan, the ratio of Japanese expatriates to employees is low, local plants are relatively independent of the Japanese parent company, and indigenous managers control management–all indications that Taiwan has a high localisation of management. The situation is slightly different in ASEAN countries. Particularly in Thailand, it is difficult to gain an image of management being localised. Local plants are dependent on Japanese expatriates, who are temporarily dispatched at a higher than nominal ratio for Japanese expatriates. On this subject a Japanese manager remarked, 'We bring in Japanese expatriates to Thailand for short periods as though they are on business trips, tending not to station employees permanently because of high income tax and the limited number of work permits issued by the government.'

Two opposite styles coexist in Taiwan concerning management power. Local partners control management at three plants and the Japanese side maintains it at two plants. In the former plants, the Japanese partner holds less than a 25 per cent equity share, and the ratio of Japanese expatriates to local employees is less than 1 per cent. Both the chairman and president are Taiwanese, and Japanese expatriates mainly act as advisers or at best in vice-presidential or board of director positions. In short, the Japanese did not occupy positions of high authority. In this case, as the Japanese system was introduced with the initiative of the Taiwanese managers, a key point for adoption of the system depends on how they recognised its necessity. On the contrary, in assembly plants where the Japanese side controls management, it has more than a 45 per cent equity holding, the ratio of Japanese expatriates is approximately 2 per cent, and they filled the main management positions, such as president and senior managers, and, in one case, even down to department managers. In other words, the Japanese occupied the positions of authority within the company.

In Thailand, the Japanese side controls management at five plants and the local partner controls it at one. In plants where Japanese managers dominate, the Japanese companies had more than a 48 per cent equity stake, and the Japanese expatriates filled the president's position as well as those for vice-president and senior managers. In the Thai-controlled plant, the Japanese company holds 25 per cent of the equity, the ratio of Japanese expatriates to local employees is less than 1 per cent, and Japanese occupy the vice-president and senior manager positions. As the Thai government does not readily issue work permits, the ratio of Japanese expatriates remains somewhere between 0.7 per cent and 1.4 per cent, or about 1 per cent on average. As stated above, some of the plants depend on Japanese employees coming on a short-term basis. Those plants depend much more on Japanese expatriates than do other plants. Therefore, the Japanese have more influence on plant operations than previous statistics might suggest.

In Malaysia, the *Bumiputera* policy has a strong influence on the management of automotive assembly plants. At the national car plant, the president was a Malay who received guidance from a Japanese adviser in the initial stages, then because of the recession in the Malaysian economy a Japanese took over as president at the request of the prime minister. After boosting the plant's performance successfully, control was returned to a Malay, with a Japanese playing an advisory role. The Japanese side holds less than a 20 per cent equity share. In another CKD plant, the Japanese side holds 28 per cent of the equity, lower than the 30 per cent maximum permitted for foreign companies. The Japanese influence management decisions by having a management committee that is organised by four managers, including two Japanese. In spite of the effective influence on decision-making, only three Japanese expatriates are not able to fully implement the Japanese system on the shop floor.

IV   THE AUTOMOTIVE ASSEMBLY INDUSTRY IN KOREA

The Korean automotive industry is worth commenting on. Three assembly plants were visited, to conduct interviews with managers and receive plant tours. The interviews were not adequate because of a lack of prior communication. This incomplete communication with Korea reflects a high intention to be independent of Japanese automotive companies. The Korean and Japanese sides did not negotiate management policy even if they had substantial equity holdings. Therefore, the Korean case is separated from the main part of the application situation for Japanese-affiliated plants.

The Korean automotive industry develops export markets, performs research and development, and produces parts independently at much higher levels than other East Asian countries, excluding Japan. The government introduced a policy to concentrate various types of CKD operations into three companies, bringing about the birth of Korea's big three automobile makers. This policy succeeded in securing economies of scale for the industry. During the 1980s, the Korean Big Three built high-volume production plants with annual capacities over 200 000 units. They also succeeded in exporting their products.

The Korean Big Three firmly maintain management power locally, even though they have received capital and formed technical tie-ups with foreign companies, including Japanese automobile makers. These Japanese companies did not participate in management decisions. The success of the Korean automobile industry stems from their own efforts. So what is this industry's relationship to the Japanese production system? It was learnt that Japanese expatriates used to be dispatched to Korean plants, but two Japanese makers with equity holdings in two Korean companies no longer station their staff there. Historically, Korea imported manufacturing techniques from foreign makers, especially Japan. They introduced operation techniques and management methods for human resources from companies in Japan, the United States and Europe. It is possible to assume that the major makers have created a Korean-style system by mixing the three methods.

Specific features of the Korean hybrid system are analysed by using the Four-Perspective Evaluation. The specific feature of the Korean hybrid is application-orientation in Human–Method of 3.2 points, even though there is no Japanese involvement in the plants now. This is probably because of the country's institutional similarities with Japan, a phenomenon also seen in Taiwan. The application rating for Human–Result is the lowest, at 1.0, because only Koreans engage in plant operation. There is a large discrepancy between the 3.2 points for Human–Method, with 1.0 point for Human–Result. But there is scepticism about the actual functioning of the Japanese elements with regard to Human–Method. In Korea, performance evaluation as a determinant of wages, multifunctional skills and the function of first-line supervisors, are all different from Japan. For material elements, both methods and results show adaptation orientation: Material–Method was 2.6, and Material–Result 2.2 points. For example, Korean plants do not use the Japanese system for quality control, but secure quality at the final inspection process, as is done in the United States. This low rate of application in Material–Method indicates that the US system, having been imported with volume production-type assembly plants during the 1980s, is still alive.

The Korean automobile industry has achieved the highest performance in East Asia outside of Japan. It has succeeded in creating its own methods by combining foreign techniques, and has benefited substantially from achieving large economies of scale. The Korean automobile industry, however, has suffered a lowering of its competitive edge in world markets because of quality problems. Labour relations have been unstable since the labour unions were liberated. Korean managers have begun to adopt the Japanese production system on the shop floor in the 1990s. Implementing the Japanese production system is the main issue dividing managers and labour unions in Korea. The way in which the system will be introduced is providing great interest to industry watchers.

V   CONCLUSION

To summarise this chapter: first, the application rating of automotive assembly plants in East Asian countries was 3.2, which is slightly lower than the East Asian total. Electronics assembly and electronics parts industries exceed automotive assembly in this area. This is because automotive assembly plants mainly produce cars for domestic markets, but the products of the electronics assembly plants are sold in the domestic market and abroad. There are export-specific plants in the electronics assembly industry. On the other hand, automotive assembly plants only export a small portion of total output. The plants have reached the stage where they can compete with imported cars in the domestic market.

Second, Taiwan exceeds ASEAN countries substantially in terms of application rating. This is an important factor in the East Asian automotive assembly industry because, while other industries have shown similar trends, the automotive assembly industry has large differences. The average points were 3.5 in Taiwan and 3.0 in ASEAN countries. Taiwan outperformed ASEAN countries in the next four item groups: Work organisation (+0.5); Production control (+0.7); Group consciousness (+1.0); and Labour relations (+0.4). Taiwan especially outranks ASEAN countries in Group consciousness. In contrast to this, Taiwan was lower than ASEAN countries in two groups: Procurement (−0.1) and Parent–subsidiary relations (−0.2).

Third, the Four-Perspective Evaluation of the East Asian automotive assembly industry revealed that Human–Method and Human–Result contrasted. Human–Method was high, whereas Human–Result tended towards adaptation. On the other hand, Material–Method was in the middle at 3.0 points, and Material–Result was 3.2 points, indicating a slight application orientation. Regarding human elements, methods show a high application orientation and results indicates high adaptation.

Regarding material elements, both methods and materials were close to three points.

Fourth, Taiwan and the ASEAN countries differ in the points for the Four-Perspective Evaluation. Taiwan greatly exceeds the ASEAN countries in methods for both human and materials aspects and lower than ASEAN countries for results. Actually, Taiwan surpasses ASEAN by 0.7 points in Human–Method and by 0.8 points in Material–Method. But Taiwan trails ASEAN countries by 0.2 points for Human–Result, and by 0.3 points for Material-Result.

Therefore, high application of methods is specific to Taiwan, and high application of results, especially Material–Result, is specific to ASEAN countries. The high application rating of Material–Result in ASEAN countries is because they depend heavily on Japan for materials. This high dependence on materials from Japan is a necessary condition to operate automotive assembly plants because of their more recent industrialisation compared with Taiwan. In contrast, there are similarities with Japan in human-related institutions in East Asia, so the Japanese system is transferable without radical reformation of the local system. In East Asia, human-related systems are not based on jobs, as in the West. Accordingly, the application rating of Human–Method is extremely high at 3.9 points in Taiwan and 3.2 points in the ASEAN countries. But Malaysia, once a colony of Britain, has a job-based wage system and some Japanese-affiliated plants follow this. Reformation of the traditional systems seems likely. In spite of this, Material–Method of the Japanese system has not transferred smoothly. The rating for ASEAN countries was a low 2.7 points. The reason for the low application rating of Material–Method is the same as the reason for the high points of Material–Result: ASEAN countries have a lower level of industrialisation compared with Taiwan and therefore rely to a greater extent on Japanese imports.

The Auto Parts Industry

Nobuo Kawabe (Sections I and II) and Kunio Kamiyama (Sections III and IV)

I   INTRODUCTION

Relationship with US Survey

Our earlier research, in 1989, analysed the application and adaptation of the Japanese production system in North America. This was based on visits to ten automotive components factories in Canada and the USA. At that time, Japanese auto assemblers and parts manufacturers had only recently set up full-scale production in the United States.[1]

This survey, however, focuses on Taiwan, Korea, Thailand and Malaysia, where Japanese auto components manufacturers started production rather earlier. Moves into the region were triggered by the yen appreciation following the Plaza Accord in 1985. For this research, fourteen factories were visited: five in Taiwan, two in Korea, three in Thailand, and four in Malaysia. Because one Korean factory produced not auto parts but metal moulds it was excluded from this study, though this factory is mentioned occasionally.

Characteristics of the Auto Parts Industry

The auto parts industry consists of peripheral companies that provide assemblers with processing services and a large number of components. The production processes of the machinery and metal industries which underpin the automobile industry can be classified into materials production and processing, assembly and finishing. With such an industry configuration, production systems based on vertical divisions of labour are economic and efficient.[2]

It is difficult to identify the overall characteristics of the auto parts industry. The production items within each factory are varied, and the production processes in each factory are different. The factories selected for this survey between them produce a wide variety of products and components. In Taiwan, AHTw produces engine parts, steering power trains, and transmission parts; BATw, car air conditioners and car coolers;

BDTw, radiators, blowers, starter motors and alternators; BFTw, resins for interior and exterior application, and urethane parts; and BGTw makes wire harnesses. In Korea, BGTw makes wire harnesses. In Korea, BDK manufactures auto instruments, while BBK produces metal moulds and press moulds. In Thailand, BGTh manufactures wire harnesses and air conditioners for buses; BDTh produces alternators, starter motors and air conditioners; and BETh makes seats, interior parts and leaf springs. In Malaysia, BAM assembles radiators; BCM produces shock absorbers; and BDM makes alternators, regulators, starter motors and wiper motors.

In the production of such a wide variety of items, economies of scale based on high production volume are vital. Because the parts or components define the safety and performance of the vehicle, it is very important for assembler–makers to obtain parts and components that are not only inexpensive but also offer high quality and meet exacting specifications. As recent gains in the value added to automobiles depend mainly on improvements in the functioning of parts, the importance of parts production within the auto industry is increasing. The auto parts industry now drives the development of the auto industry as a whole.[3] More than ever before, assembler–makers must now emphasise the importance of economy, quality, cost and delivery when procuring parts and components.

Auto maker–assemblers procure their parts or components in one of two ways: they themselves may produce the components, or they may procure them from outside makers (the market). Each method offers advantages and disadvantages. Manufacturing one's own components reduces transaction costs but raises management cost. In procuring components from outside makers or subcontractors, stability of supply and quality may be problem but management cost are reduced. Because of this dilemma, Japanese auto assembler–makers use the *keiretsu* (enterprise grouping) system. This is an intermediate form of procurement – a compromise between producing one's own goods and simply buying them in the market. While assemblers and parts manufacturers linked in the *keiretsu* system are legally independent, they usually work together to co-ordinate product supply and quality, solving the inherent problems of trading within a closed hierarchy and in an open market. It is often noted that *keiretsu* links among Japanese auto parts makers give the Japanese auto industries competitive advantages over the auto industry in the United States and Europe.[4] Every Japanese auto parts factory maintains a close relationship with a particular assembler–maker, providing that assembler–maker with parts and components. Accordingly, Japanese auto parts makers, whether they are independent or part of a *keiretsu* system,

Table 4.5 Profile of Japanese-owned auto parts plants visited in Taiwan, Korea, Thailand and Malaysia

		Taiwan			
Factory	AHTw	BATw	BDTw	BFTw	BGTw
Location	Taoyuan	Guanyin	Taoyuan	Xinzhu	Pingdong
Start of operation	1976.10	1987.7	1988.5	1988.3	1971.2
Ownership	Joint venture (parent company in Japan 30%, 40 local businessmen 70%)	Joint venture (parent company in Japan 33%, Taiwan enterprise 60%, employees 20%) 20%)	Joint venture (parent company in Japan 80%, Taiwan enterprises 20%)	Joint venture (parent company in Japan 75%, Taiwan enterprise 10%, 3%, Local businessmen 10%)	Wholly owned by parent company in Japan
Employees (Japanese)	382 (4)	260 (2)	193 (10)	133 (4)	1 750 (10)
Sales	780 000 000 NT	1 200 000 000 NT	2 515 000 NT	368 000 000 NT	1 899 199 000 NT
Affiliation	AF	AF	AG	AG	Independent
Main supplier	AFTw (40%) others	AFTw AKTw others	AGTw (40%) ACTw (15%)	AGTw (95.4%) others	2 American enterprises (85%)
Main products	Engine parts, stairing power train, transmission parts	Air conditioners (for car)	Radiators, heater blowers, starters, alternators, air conditioners (for buses)	Resin (for car decoration), urethane foam parts, instrument panels, others	Wire harnesses (for car)

Table 4.5   (continued)

Factory	Korea		Thailand		
	BDK	BBK	BGTh	BDTh	BE
Location	Ch'angwon	Kyonggido	Phitsanulok	Samut Prakan	Samut Prakan
Start of operation	1977.8	1987.10	1992.7	1973.10	1963
Ownership	Joint venture (parent company in Japan 50%, Korean enterprise 50%)	Joint venture (parent company in Japan 35%, general merchant ing Japan 10%, Korean enterprise 55%)	Joint venture (parent company in Japan 90%, Local enterprise 10%)	Joint venture (parent company 36%, Thai Toyota 8 %, Japanese Thai 12%, Thai enterprise 44%)	Joint venture (parent company 70%, Nissho Iwai 15%, HHT 7%, Thai Farmers Bank 3%, others 5%)
Employees (Japanese)	838 (3)	109 (2)	3 38 (6)	905	1 267 (7)
Sales	W43.8b	W5.3b	BT2.6b	3 117 000 000 BT	2 322 000 000 BT
Affiliation	R	Independent	Independent	AG	AG
Main supplier	3 Korean assemblers	3 Korean assemblers others	Japanese makers except Fuji juko	Japanese and European companies	Toyota (25%) Isuzu, Honda, Hino, others
Main products	Instruments (for car)	Mould presses, mould, mould base (electronics)	Wire harnesses	Alternators 65.5%, air conditioners 17.9%, others 17.4%	Seat 43%, trim 28%, vacuum forming 3% leaf springs 18%, stabilisers 3%, spiral springs 2%, precious springs 3%

Table 4.5   (continued)

Malaysia

Factory	BDM	BDM	BAM	BCM
Location	Banggi	Banggi	Shah Alam	Kuala Langat
Start of operation	1983.4	1983.11	1970.2 (1983)	1983.10
Ownership	Joint venture (parent company 40%, TTMSB 30%, HICOM 30%)	Joint venture (BDM 40%, parent company 27%, HICOM 23%, TTMSB 10%)	Joint venture (BA 20%, Local enterprises)	Joint venture (parent company 25%, UMW 25%, others 50%)
Employees (Japanese)	338 (8)	293 (3)	110 (2)	302 (4)
Sales	97 000 000 M$	117 000 000 M$	32 000 000 M$	63 000 000 M$
Affiliation	AG	AG	AF	AG
Main supplier	Proton, Toyota, Ford, Mercedes Benz, others	Proton, Toyota, Ford, Honda, Volvo, others	Proton (33%)	Toyota, Volvo, Proton
Main products	Alternators, regulators, wiper motors, radiators	Air conditioners for cars, buses	Air conditioners, condensers, evaporators	Shock absorbers

share certain common characteristics which reflect assembler–makers' needs for a style of production management that can secure high product quality and meet delivery schedules.

While Japanese auto parts makers in general share these characteristics, the next section discusses only the specific characteristics of the auto parts factories covered by this survey (see Table 4.5).

II   AN OVERVIEW OF THE FACTORIES SURVEYED

Overview of Japanese Auto Parts Manufacturers in Asia

As of 1994, members of the Japan Automobile Parts Manufacturers Association had invested in forty-one overseas manufacturing subsidiaries in Korea, seventy-seven in Taiwan, ninety-four in Thailand, and thirty-one in Malaysia (see Table 4.6). By country, the number of subsidiaries and affiliates varied considerable. The number of Japanese auto parts factories in Korea was less than half of that in Taiwan, though both are NIEs. Two factors explain this difference. First, in an effort to encourage their own local companies, the Koreans regulate foreign capital very strictly, compared with the Taiwanese. Second, Korean auto assembler–makers belong to chebol behemoths that produce parts and components themselves, whereas in Taiwan independent auto parts makers often set up joint manufacturing ventures with foreign corporations, many of which are Japanese auto parts makers.

Thailand and Malaysia also differ, though both countries belong to the ASEAN community. In Thailand, the number of investments by Japanese auto parts makers is more than three times that in Malaysia. Japanese investors are attracted by Thailand's relatively larger market and by the absence of a national car assembler–maker such as Malaysia's Proton. This explains why there are more Japanese auto assemblers and parts makers in Thailand.

The fourteen factories in the survey echo the general trend of Japanese auto parts makers' overseas investments in Taiwan, Korea, Thailand and Malaysia over the past thirty years, particularly in the timing of investment and in plant operation. To better understand the fourteen factories, let us focus on the larger picture of Japanese investment in Taiwan, Korea, Thailand and Malaysia from the mid-1960s.

Table 4.6   Japanese-owned auto parts makers in Korea, Taiwan, Thailand and Malaysia

Year	Korea	Taiwan	Thailand	Malaysia
1954		1		
1955				
1956				
1957				
1958				
1959				
1960				
1961			1	
1962		1		
1963			3	
1964				
1965			1	
1966	1	4	1	
1967		1	1	
1968		5		
1969		4	2	
1970		1	1	1
1971	2			
1972	1		1	1
1973			6	1
1974	1	1	3	
1975		1	1	
1976	1	1	2	1
1977	2	1		
1978		4		1
1979		3	2	1
1980	1		1	1
1981		1	2	
1982	1			1
1983		3	1	8
1984	1	2	1	1
1985	2	2		
1986		4	2	4
1987	15	23	8	
1988	6	5	10	3
1989	2	1	7	1
1990	2	4	8	5
1991	2	1	7	
1992	1	2	7	
1993			7	1
1994			8	

Source: Japan   Auto   Parts   Manufacturers   Association,   *Kaigai Jigyō Chōsa* (Survey of Overseas Activities) 1994.

Commencement of Operations

Among the factories included in this research, Thailand's BETh, which started operations in 1964, has the longest history. The next oldest, Taiwan's BDTw, started producing wire harnesses in 1971. Both BDTh and BGTh started operations in Thailand in the 1970s. In 1976, AHTw started producing engine parts in Taiwan. Korea's BDK which began making auto instruments in 1977, also has a long history. Most of the other factories were set up after the sharp appreciation of the yen in 1978 and 1988. The investment situation in Asia clearly differs from that in the United States, where Japanese auto makers established operations after 1983. Table 4.6 shows trends in investments by Japanese automotive parts makers in Taiwan, Korea, Thailand and Malaysia. (While some motorcycle parts makers have been included, their impact is negligible.)

Most Japanese auto parts makers moved overseas after the mid-1980s, although some began their investment activities from the 1960s and 1970s. The companies that invested during the 1960s and 1970s targeted the small replacement parts markets in Asian countries. The wave of investment in the mid-1980s reflected growing demand caused by rapid motorisation. Local governments removed various regulations restricting foreign auto assemblers and parts makers, and began welcoming overseas corporate investors. Japanese auto parts makers sought to take advantage of this liberalisation, and by the mid-1980s it had become clear that the Japanese automobile and parts makers had a competitive advantage over other foreign companies in terms of quality and cost. This helped Japanese companies to play a very important role in the development of local auto parts makers, which were necessary for the development of a local automobile industry.[5]

In Taiwan, two large waves of investment by Japanese auto parts makers have occurred since the 1960s. The first wave started around 1965 and continued until the early 1970s. In particular, four companies in 1966 and five in 1968 stand out. The second wave came in 1985, after the yen appreciation and the establishment of Taiwan's New Automobile Industry Development Law.

The first wave of investment by Japanese auto parts makers in Taiwan occurred during a period in which the Taiwanese government introduced aggressive economic development measures. Foreign auto parts makers were expected to introduce new technologies into Taiwan.[6] Between 1966 and 1970 the monopoly held by Yue-Loong was broken, and Sanfu, Sang-Yang and Lio-Ho entered the automobile industry through individual technical tie-ups with Fuji Heavy Industries Ltd, Mitsubishi Motors

Corporation, and Toyota Motor Corporation (Lio-Ho later changed its name to Ford, after Ford held the majority of its stocks). In 1976, Yu-Tyan Machinery Co entered the automobile industry through a technical tie-up with Peugeot. In 1972, Taiwan enacted its cumbersomely named Localisation Act for the Machinery and Electric Machinery Industries. This legislation sought to increase the level of localisation to 70 per cent for automobiles under 3.5 tons. In 1973, the importation of completely assembled cars was prohibited. However, it was impossible to attain significant localisation during the 1980s because of such intractable problems as parts quality and cost.[7] Accordingly, in 1979, the Taiwanese government passed the Automobile Industry Development Law. In 1983, this was followed by the Centre–Satellite Factories Development Promotion Law, which sought to develop a *keiretsu* of parts makers. However, since the auto parts industry as a whole was weak, this was not realistic. Instead, a system evolved in which assembler-makers procured parts and components from the same established parts makers.[8]

The second Japanese advance into Taiwan occurred after the yen appreciation and the enactment of Taiwan's New Automobile Industry Development Law in 1985. This law, which enabled the Taiwanese government to abolish existing protectionist policies, sought to encourage competition in the auto parts industry. The law lowered local content in automobiles from 70 per cent to 50 per cent over three years, and was applied equally to both local and joint ventures without limiting export ratios. The government encouraged powerful foreign auto assemblers and parts makers to co-operate with local companies and to bring their advanced technologies to Taiwan. All the leading Taiwanese parts makers signed up with foreign counterparts and developed licensing production arrangements. As a result of this climate, between 1986 and 1988 Japanese auto parts makers invested vigorously in Taiwan. In 1987, some nineteen Japanese parts makers – and in 1988, a further six – invested in Taiwan.[9]

Whereas the Japanese auto industry showed no great interest in Taiwan in the 1970s, some Japanese auto parts makers began investing in Korea from that time. After the Plaza Accord of 1985, however, investment by Japanese parts makers began to surge. In 1987, fifteen Japanese companies invested in Korea, and a further six followed in 1988. Korea had announced a new automobile development policy in 1970. Its main objective was to attain 100 per cent local production and develop a national car. The policy also sought to lower costs by mass producing core parts such as engines and bodies. In 1974, with the mass production of a 100 per cent Korean-made car in mind, the Long-Term Automobile Industry Development Plan was announced. Its four objectives were as follows. First, to attain over 95 per cent of localisation by the end of 1975. Second, to separate assembler–makers and parts makers to develop the parts industry and achieve a horizontal division of labour in which a single factory produced a single part (excluding core parts, such as engines and bodies) Third, to encouraged the introduction of foreign capital and technologies; and fourth, to focus on new factories in the Chang Won Machinery Industrial Estate. As a result of this government-devised development plan, auto parts makers appeared in rapid succession. By 1975, the number of parts manufacturers had reached 200. The ratio of localisation increased from 21 per cent, to 66 per cent in 1972, and reached 85 per cent by 1976.

However, these government-led policies failed because of the 1970s oil crises. In addition, as the Japan–US automobile trade conflict worsened, Japanese auto assemblers and parts makers began to consider investing in Korea. In 1981, Korea announced rationalisation measures for its automobile industry, announced a machinery industry development plan, and a Ten-Year Plan for the Development of Small and Medium-Sized Companies. In 1983, the specified Manufacturing Field System was abolished, and responsibility for developing auto parts makers was transferred from the government to the assembler–makers themselves. Individual assemblers set up 'co-operation groups' and advised parts makers on quality and process management, cost and delivery, and provided parts makers with financial as well as training and educational support. For example, both Kia Motors and Hyundai Motors developed their own parts makers with co-operation from Mazda and Mitsubishi affiliated parts makers.[10] Thus Korean localisation reached 98 per cent by the mid-80s, and many Korean-made auto parts began to be exported. However, important parts and components such as injectors, drive shafts, power steering pumps and switches were imported from Japan, with an attendant serious loss of trading opportunities for Korea.[11]

Thailand saw some investment by Japanese auto parts makers in the 1960s and early 1970s. However, the main focus of investment was between 1987 and 1990. Out of four factories surveyed, three began production before the 1970s or during that decade. These were BE in 1964, and BD in the 1970s. The fourth factory, BG Phisanolok factory, began production in July 1992.

In Thailand, measures to develop an indigenous automobile assembly industry began in 1962 with the Industrial Investment Promotion Law, which led to the establishment of ten assembler–makers. The main objective of the law was to promote the growth of the automobile assembly and parts industries by cutting back the importation of completely assembled automobiles. By 1978, the importation of fully assembled passenger cars was completely prohibited, and a new domestic production plan was announced. However, when the localisation allowance reached 45 per cent, a recession occurred and the domestic production plan was frozen.

In 1986, exports of light industrial products and processed agricultural and marine products increased rapidly. The Thai government, encouraged by the export success of Korean- and Malaysian-made automobiles, now tried to promote domestic automobile production and exports of assembled cars and parts. With economic growth of around 10 per cent for the three years from 1987, the domestic Thai automobile market grew rapidly. A more favourable climate for exporting encouraged by a highly valued yen made it possible to gain economies of scale for some parts manufacturers through investment in production equipment.

In July 1991, the Thai government slashed import duties on assembled cars, parts and components. Domestic auto parts makers consequently demanded lower duties for imports of raw materials to compete with the lower tariffs on imported parts and components, and the Thai government acquiesced.[12]

In Malaysia, investment by Japanese auto parts makers began in earnest when production plans for a national car, the Proton Saga, got under way in 1983. Among the factories surveyed, BDM began its operations in July 1983, and BCM in October 1983. While BAM started operations in 1970, BA came to be involved in BAM in 1983 through a technological joint agreement that saw BA acquiring a 20 per cent share of BAM. In this way, the 1983 birth of Malaysia's national car played an important role in promoting investment by Japanese auto parts makers. As in other Asian countries, Malaysian investment by Japanese auto parts makers became particularly active after 1986.

In 1983, the Mahathir administration established Perushaan Automobile National Sdn. Bhd. (Proton) as a joint venture between Mitsubishi Motors, Mitsubishi Corporation, and Hicom, a government enterprise. In July 1985, the new company began producing the Proton Saga. After Malaysia banned imports of fully assembled automobiles, ten manufacturers had to be content with knockdown production of some twenty-six Japanese and European auto makers' models. However, these producers could not attain sufficient economies of scale.

The establishment of Proton was essential for the localisation of parts and components. The government hoped to develop a Japanese pyramid-type auto parts subcontracting system with a parent assembler–maker presiding over primary, secondary and tertiary subcontracting makers. As a basic principle, the Malaysian government stipulated that Hicom, Proton and a joint venture combining these two would carry out direct production of basic parts and components such as transmissions, chassis, and related parts. In 1989, the Malaysian government established a special fund for the development of auto-related industries, in particular providing low-interest capital for *Bumiputra* companies (those owned by native Malays) starting production of parts for Proton. Between 1985 and 1989, the number of domestic vendors increased from twenty-seven to sixty-six. Most of these were joint ventures or technological tie-ups with Japanese companies.[13]

In Malaysia, Thailand and other ASEAN countries, the situation surrounding Japanese automobile companies was very different from that in the United States and Europe. In the West, Japanese auto companies started local production on a scale that made them internationally competitive right from the start and the Japanese enjoyed organic links between different production bases from the beginning. This, however, was not the case in Asia.[14]

In the ASEAN countries, including Thailand and Malaysia, the automotive components market of each country was too small to support a full-scale automotive industry encompassing materials manufacturing to parts production and on to assembly. In order to solve this difficulty, in October 1988 the ASEAN Brand-to-Brand Complementation Programme (BBC Programme) was introduced. This programme can be traced back to the policy of division of labour for automobile parts decided at the ASEAN Economic Ministerial Conference in 1980. But because each country had its own plans for domestic automobile production, ASEAN plans for division of labour in parts production were thwarted.

The BBC Programme was created to promote automotive industries on a non-governmental level. Participating countries with local content policies automatically treated BBC parts as domestic parts and thus lowered import duties for these items to the minimum of 50 per cent. If the localisation of these target items exceeded 50 per cent and two or more countries participated in their manufacture, the products were recognised as local and granted a reduction in duties. Then, the right was granted to choose parts suppliers on a free commercial basis. In future, this is expected to have positive results, such as encouraging the division of labour for auto part production in the ASEAN region, allowing auto makers and parts manufacturers to avoid overlapping investments in the area, improving production and quality, lowering costs because of mass production and tax breaks, and strengthening export competitiveness. Mitsubishi, Toyota, Mercedes-Benz, and Volvo are among those which have already put forward plans under the BBC Programme and been accepted.

Toyota's plan is based on mass production systems that concentrate production of diesel engines in Thailand, gasoline engines in Indonesia, steering parts in Malaysia, and transmissions in the Philippines. Under the BBC Programme, Mitsubishi Motors imports transmissions from the Philippines and pressed body parts from Malaysia, while it exports Thai-made automobiles to Canada, improving the balance of foreign currency reserves. In November 1991, Nissan initiated a mutual supply of electric parts and tools between Thailand and Malaysia, and now sends 100 diesel engines for commercial vehicles from Thailand to the Philippines every month. Mazda and Honda are also moving in the same direction.[15]

Motivation for Investing Abroad, *Keiretsu* Relations

Japanese auto parts makers invested in Taiwan, Korea, Thailand and Malaysia in response to the developing automobile and auto parts industries in those countries. Investment was also clearly influenced by the governments' policies towards foreign investment. On the other hand, Japanese companies also had their own reasons for investing in East Asia. Generally, four such motivations can be discerned: (i) to supply spare parts; (ii) to respond to assemblers moving offshore; (iii) to secure the export market; and (iv) to establish a sales base in the local market. In this way, the motivation for Japanese auto parts makers to invest in East Asia are very different from their motivation to invest in the United States. Japanese companies invested in the United States to avoid the effect of the yen appreciation in the late 1970s and, after 1985, to mitigate trade friction between Japan and the United States.

By the mid-1980s, all four countries had introduced very strict polices on foreign direct investment. For example, in 1971, BGTw, a Taiwan-based electric wiring maker that supplied automotive assemblers, was permitted to operate with full financing on condition that it exported its output. Up to 1986, its sales in Taiwan had been limited to a maximum of 10 per cent of total sales. As a result, while BGTw is usually thought of as an AG *keiretsu* company, as Table 4.5 shows, it sold to companies other than AG. Today, the company runs ahead of government regulations, and its independence is increasing. Many auto parts makers tend to follow the assembler–makers they supply in investing overseas. In contrast to electric parts makers, auto parts manufacturers generally follow assembler–makers because of high transportation costs if they do not. Looking at individual factories' customers, auto parts makers clearly invested in Asia to supply their assembler–makers. For example, AHTw and BATw depend heavily on AF-related AFTw, while BDTw and BFTw rely on AG-related AGTw. However, reliance on a particular assembler is in decline. Whereas AFTw once made up some 90 per cent of AHTw's total sales, today this ratio has fallen to 40 per cent because of the intensification of competition and globalisation in assembler–makers' business activities.

However, individual companies' reasons for moving offshore are quite complicated. BBK, a subsidiary of BB, which produces all car doors for AZ in Japan, was established for two reasons. First, to export to Japan cheap moulds produced in Korea because supply in Japan could not keep up with demand at that time (1987). The second reason was to establish a business base in Korea. However, the first reason for establishing BBK–to export cheap moulds to Japan–was not fulfilled: BBK insisted that it exported only a very small quantity of its moulds to Japan, and its real purpose for exporting to Japan was to show the locals the high quality standards required by Japan. BBK's second reason for its establishment – to establish a local business base – was realised to some extent, although there still remain some problems in supplying moulds to local companies. BDK, a subsidiary of BF, which is an AG-related automotive instruments company, was established for more complicated reasons. Because AG was planning to invest in Korea, BF established BDK as a joint venture with a local partner. However, AG withdrew from Korea because it was concerned about relations between Japan and China in the wake of the announcement of the Four Principles of Trade with China. (These stated that companies that operated in Korea or Taiwan were not permitted to operate in China.) So, BDK and the AG-related company supplied instruments to various local assembler–makers. In Korea, because supporting industries were lagging significantly behind assembler–makers in their development, companies such as BDK could deal with various local assembler–makers as an independent entity.

In the case of Thailand, motivation for investment by Japanese companies differed according to the timing of the investment. BETh, established in 1963 and operating since 1964, has a long history in Thailand. It sought to meet the automobile development polices of the Thai government by supplying replacement parts and duly began supplying Japanese assembler-makers when they set up in Thailand. Other parts makers, such as BD and BG, which started their operations in the 1970s, began doing the same thing. BG's Phisanolok factory started operating in 1992 to meet the spiralling demand caused by rapid motorisation in Thailand, and in particular, to meet increasing orders from AGTh.

Incentives for auto parts makers to invest also affect their relations with assembler–makers. Despite the fact that the Thai market is still small, many assemblers have invested there. Both BD and BE – both AG-affiliated companies – supply various Thai assemblers; BGTh delivers to all Japanese assemblers except one; while BETh supplies 25 per cent of its total sales to AG, its largest customer, using a just-in-time delivery system. The company also supplies AC, AF, AB, AD, and other Japanese and non-Japanese assembler–makers.

In Malaysia, the major motivation for Japanese investment was the launch of the Proton Saga in 1983. This national car project also reflected the Malaysian government's local parts policy. BAM, established by an American company in 1970 to manufacture spare parts, was typical of companies responding to this incentive. BA, which realised the importance of the Proton Project, linked up with BAM in 1983 and by 1986 owned 20 per cent of its stocks. In 1983, BDM and BCM both started their operations in response to the Proton Project. Moreover, these companies had further reasons to get involved. First, they wished to secure a new market, and second, they wanted to supply Japanese assembler–makers. Malaysia provided incentives to those seeking to secure a new market. If a foreign company could meet certain conditions (gain an 80 per cent market share, supply cheaper spare parts for repairs, and command 50 per cent of the market within five years), CKD makers would be prohibited to import. BDM, an AG-related company, had a particular reason for wishing to supply a local joint venture, United Motor Works (UMW). BD aimed to head off AF – AG's arch rival in Malaysia as well as in Japan.

In Malaysia, it was essential for auto parts makers to deal with Proton, which controlled more than 70 per cent of the domestic market. The market share of other assembler–makers was very small. As Japanese auto parts makers' connections with Japanese *keiretsu* assembler–makers were very slight, BDM, BCM and BAM supplied both Japanese and European assembler–makers in an effort to attain economies of scale.

Forms of Ownership

Interestingly, the strategies of the auto parts makers are reflected in their ownership. In Asia, joint ventures between Japanese and local companies proliferate. In the United States, by contrast, out of ten factories selected for the survey, all but three were 100 per cent Japanese owned. Although three were joint ventures, two of them were ventures with subsidiaries of Japanese companies or Japanese trading or banking corporations.

In Taiwan, in contrast, joint ventures are common, but the ratio of ownership differs depending on the *keiretsu*. For example in AF-*keiretsu*, AH owns 30 per cent of AHTw, while BA has 33 per cent of BATw. In AG-*keiretsu*, BD owns 80 per cent of BDTw, and BF 75 per cent of BFTw. It is easy to see the difference in ownership strategies between the AF company and AG. In Korea, the government's preference for local capital is clearly reflected in ownership: the Japanese side owns 35 per cent of BBK and 50 per cent of BDK.

In both Thailand and Malaysia, Japanese companies invest through joint ventures. However, in these two countries, larger numbers of investing parties are involved in joint ventures. Moreover, the ratio between Japanese and local ownership varies depending on the time when the joint ventures were established. Before the mid 1980s, local companies owned the majority stake with minority ownership by Japanese compose. After that, Japanese companies owned the majority, with minority ownership by local companies, and the ratio of local capital continued to plummet.

In Thailand, Japanese interests own 85 per cent of BETh, which started operations in 1964. BE owns 70 per cent and Nissho Iwai Corporation, 15 per cent. Hong Hen Thai, an agent for Taiwanese spare parts, owns a further 7 per cent, Thai Farmers Bank 3 per cent, and others the remaining 5 per cent. These joint ventures are examples of a typical configuration of makers, trading companies and local partners seen in the early years of Japanese foreign investment. In the case of BDTh, which started operations in 1973, Japanese interests own 56 per cent. Of this, BD owns 36 per cent, AGTh 8 per cent, and Japan-related Thai capital the remaining 12 per cent. However, in the case of the BGTh's Phisanolok factory, which started operations in 1992, BG and a local Chinese businessman own 90 per cent and 10 per cent, respectively.

The same phenomenon is evident in Malaysia, where the ratio of Japanese ownership is low. The Japanese own 20 per cent of BAM, which began operations in 1970, and 40 per cent of BDM, which started operations in 1983. However, the Japanese side, including the parent company and its local subsidiary, own a relatively high 67 per cent of BDM. In the case of BAM, BA owns 20 per cent, Malaysian Complex Kewangan Industry controls 58 per cent, and Wang Sdn. Bhd. and others 20 per cent. The Japanese parent company and UMW each own a 25 per cent stake in BCM.

Keeping in mind the above characteristics of the auto and parts industries, and investment by Japanese auto parts makers, next we shall analyse the application and adaptation of the Japanese-style production system in overseas Japanese auto parts factories in Taiwan, Korea, Thailand and Malaysia.

III APPLICATION OF THE JAPANESE SYSTEM.

USA Scores Higher, Variation Among Plants

The operating style of automotive parts factories is generally defined by the assembly plants they supply. The auto parts supplier must meet conditions such as quality, cost and delivery, laid down by the auto assembler–maker. Most of the leading Japanese parts makers gradually developed delivery systems known as just-in-time (JIT) systems for assemblers employing Japanese-style business practices. The JIT delivery system complements a production style orientated to the high quality and low costs required by auto assemblers.

The system used by Japanese firms for production is known as the Japanese-style production system. Historically, this was influenced by the auto assembly industry's postwar production methods. By the late 1960s, Toyota had almost completed its unique Toyota production system, though Nippondenso, Japan's largest auto parts maker, did not introduce this until after the rapid appreciation of the yen resulting from the freeing of the US dollar exchange rate in 1971. With the success of Toyota's system, during the 1970s, the Japanese-style production system was established at the centre of the Japanese auto industry. In the 1980s, the steep rise of the yen in the wake of the Plaza Accord gave a powerful impetus to the expansion of the offshore auto parts industry, which had hitherto been mainly confined to Japan. Against this background, this chapter will focus on the management and operation of Japanese auto parts makers. Particular attention will be paid to the application of Japanese-style production systems in overseas factories and adaptation to the local environment.

First, we shall compare the application of the Japanese-style system in Japanese auto parts factories in Asia with its application in Japanese auto parts factories in the United States. The United States study took place in 1989 as against 1992 for the NIEs plants (in Taiwan and Korea), and 1993 for the ASEAN plants (in Thailand and Malaysia). (In all cases, all plant inspections were carried out at the same time of the year – August/September.) Thus the possibility exists that the Asian plants benefited from an additional three years of experience over the US plants, and changed their management style accordingly. Nevertheless, the survey remains effective in representing the overall characteristics of both sides.

The most striking feature of the Japanese auto parts industry in the United States is a strong tendency to apply Japanese-style management and production systems. This tendency is stronger than that seen in other industries and is particularly noticeable in the 'Human' and 'Material'

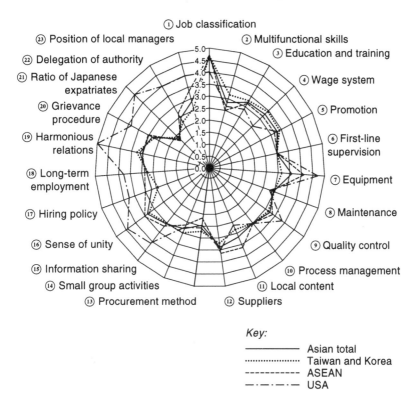

Figure 4.4   Hybrid evaluation (23 items) of auto parts industry

results aspects. The efforts of the local plants played a significant role in the high rate of application of Japanese systems within Japanese auto parts plants in the United States. In spite of small plant sizes, production systems similar to those in Japan were pursued. This enabled the Japanese subsidiaries to supply both local Japanese assembler–makers and the local Big Three. Consequently, Japanese auto parts plants in the United States show a high average application score (3.6) (see Table 4.7).

In contrast, the average degree of application in Asia was only 3.2 in Taiwan and Korea, and 3.1 in Thailand and Malaysia. Furthermore, in a study comparing the application of the Japanese production system by industry, the US auto parts industry scored the highest, Taiwan and Korea scored lowest, with Thailand and Malaysia between the two. (The lowest scores were seen in the auto assembly industry.)

Judging by these scores, auto parts plants in Asia clearly trail their US

Table 4.7   Hybrid evaluation in the auto parts industry

	Taiwan and Korea (A)	Malaysia and Thailand			United States of America	(A) − (B)
		(B)	Malaysia	Thailand		
I Work Organisation and Administration	3.7	3.3	3.2	3.4	3.1	0.4
① Job classification	4.8	4.7	4.3	5.0	4.2	0.1
② Multifunctional skills	3.3	2.5	2.7	2.3	2.7	0.8
③ Education and training	3.3	3.2	2.7	3.7	2.9	0.1
④ Wage system	3.7	3.2	3.3	3.0	2.6	0.5
⑤ Promotion	3.7	3.2	3.0	3.3	3.3	0.5
⑥ First-line supervisor	3.2	3.0	3.0	3.0	3.0	0.2
II Production Control	3.2	3.3	3.2	3.5	3.6	−0.1
⑦ Equipment	3.0	4.2	4.3	4.0	4.8	−0.8
⑧ Maintenance	3.2	2.8	2.7	3.0	2.8	0.4
⑨ Quality control	3.3	3.3	3.3	3.3	3.9	0.0
⑩ Process management	3.2	3.0	2.3	3.7	3.0	0.2
III Procurement	3.1	3.2	3.2	3.2	3.0	−0.1
⑪ Local content	3.0	3.8	4.0	3.7	2.7	−0.8
⑫ Suppliers	3.5	3.7	3.7	3.7	3.7	−0.2
⑬ Procurement method	2.8	2.2	2.0	2.3	2.6	0.6
IV Group Consciousness	3.4	3.1	2.8	3.4	3.8	0.3
⑭ Small-group activities	3.3	2.7	2.0	3.3	2.9	0.5
⑮ Information sharing	3.2	3.2	3.0	3.3	4.1	0.0
⑯ Sense of unity	3.7	3.5	3.3	3.7	4.4	0.2

Table 4.7 (continued)

	Taiwan and Korea (A)	Malaysia and Thailand			United States of America	(A) − (B)
		(B)	Malaysia	Thailand		
V Labour Relations	3.0	3.0	2.7	3.3	4.1	0.0
⑰ Hiring policy	2.7	3.0	2.7	3.3	3.8	−0.3
⑱ Long-term employment	3.0	2.8	2.7	3.0	3.8	0.2
⑲ Harmonious labour relations	3.5	3.0	2.7	3.3	5.0	0.3
⑳ Grievance procedure	2.8	3.0	2.7	3.3	3.9	−0.2
VI Parent–Subsidiary Relations	2.4	2.7	2.4	2.9	4.2	−0.3
㉑ Ratio of Japanese expatriates	2.0	1.7	2.0	1.3	4.6	0.3
㉒ Delegation of authority	2.5	2.7	1.7	3.7	4.0	−0.2
㉓ Position of local managers	2.8	3.7	3.7	3.7	4.0	−0.9
Average of 23 items	**3.2**	**3.1**	**2.9**	**3.3**	**3.6**	**0.1**

counterparts in implementing the Japanese production system in local plants. While it is difficult to identify reasons, Asian assembler–makers' requirements appear to be less strict than those of US assemblers, making it unnecessary to implement the Japanese system rigidly in Asia. In the United States, where auto assemblers are supplied by local Japanese parts makers as well as US parts makers, Japanese assemblers face strict competition from the Big Three. The Japanese offshore companies in Asia, on the other hand, continue to use the knockdown production system. Furthermore, the Asian countries selected for the survey employ protectionist policies, making them less competitive and influencing the degree of application. If Asian auto parts makers produced for developed export markets, there would probably be a stronger tendency towards implementing Japanese-style production systems.

Although the number of factories in the survey was limited, application scores by country were as follows: ASEAN countries as a whole scored 3.1, though Thailand returned a score of 3.3, and Malaysia 2.9. One reason for the discrepancy in scores is that in the ASEAN region, all six plants were joint ventures, whereas in the three plants in Thailand, the Japanese were the majority equity holders. In Malaysia's case, two companies had minority holdings, while the remaining one was majority funded by a combination of the Japanese parent and the local Japanese subsidiary (a joint venture with a local company). This difference in application scores within the same region was also repeated in plants in Taiwan and Korea, which scored 2.2 and 4.0, respectively. This indicates that the motivation to apply the Japanese system varies greatly from company to company.

High Scores for Factory Work Organisation

As noted previously, average application scores in Asian auto parts plants are lower than those of their US counterparts. However, it is interesting to note that Group I, which represents the core of the Japanese production system, recorded higher scores than the United States. In Group I, the Japanese plants in Taiwan and Korea had an especially high average score of 3.7, while Japanese plants in the ASEAN countries returned an average of 3.3, against 3.1 for their US counterparts. The high application scores for Group I are reflected in other industries as well. In the United States, the traditional labour practices tend to impede the adoption of the Japanese system, as is shown in items such as wage system or job classification. In Asia, on the other hand, there are fewer obstacles to hinder application. This partially explains the high degree of application for Group I. Setting this aside for a short while, this section will investigate the reasons for different application scores among ASEAN subsidiaries on the one hand, and Taiwanese and Korean subsidiaries on the other, and will compare auto parts to other industries.

First, we shall analyse the disparity in the application scores for ASEAN countries (3.3) and Taiwan and Korea (3.7). The largest difference, 1.0, was found in the job rotation item, compared to 0.5 in Job training. In the other three items, differences were all below 0.2, but in all six items, Taiwanese and Korean subsidiaries scored higher than ASEAN ones. Taiwan and Korea also scored above the US plants in every item, as a result of high application scores for the core system. On the other hand, in the ASEAN countries, scores for job rotation and promotion were below the scores of the United States for those items, while First-line supervisors in ASEAN countries scored in line with their US counterparts. Below, we shall examine each item individually in an effort to highlight the characteristics of the auto parts industry in Asia.

In contrast to the American system, which is based on very clear job demarcation and strict job classification, Asia (like Japan) does not have a clear job classification system and lacks clear demarcation between jobs. This led to high scores for job classification.

This way of working would make it easier for Japanese companies to develop multiskilled workers through job rotation. However, there is a large gap in job rotation application scores between the ASEAN countries on the one hand, and Taiwan and Korea on the other. In Taiwan and Korea, some factories seek to apply a job rotation system. A certain Taiwanese plant requires certain tasks, such as assembling starters or alternators, to be done by the same line. This is not possible in Japan because these parts are made in different plants. In ASEAN plants, jobs are not rotated systematically. Many of the workers there prefer not to rotate jobs, and where Job rotation does occur, workers may demand wage increases.

These circumstances explain the gap in job rotation application scores between Taiwan and Korea, and the ASEAN countries. However, some factories in Taiwan and Korea also neglect job rotation (which can develop multiskilled labour) for the same reasons that job rotation is not popular in ASEAN countries. Possibly, differences in management style in areas such as personnel management and training contribute to the different application scores between the plants. However, even in cases where scores are similar, such as in Malaysia and Thailand, management style differs. In Thailand, the plants of two Japanese firms were planning to introduce a job rotation system and another firm, although it had not yet introduced job rotation into any of its three plants in Thailand, had already introduced multiskilling into two of the plants. In Malaysia, however, factories seemed less enthusiastic, perhaps because of some residual British influence.

The differences in attitude towards job rotation are revealed in the scores for education and training. Here, Taiwan and Korea scored 3.3, and the ASEAN countries 3.2. The United States and Malaysia scored a low 2.9 and 2.7 respectively. Thailand, however, achieved a remarkable 3.7. This high score was due mainly to a high-scoring wire harness plant, which implemented an extensive job training course. Under this programme, 240–250 people were sent to Japan each year on a six-month training programme. Annual schedules were also used at each level of training. After one week of off-the-job training, newly-hired employees participated in a one-week, one-to-one OJT programme, supervised by a production line leader.

Job rotation scores in Japan's Asian plants are higher than in Japan's US plants, though the reasons differ between Taiwan, Korea and Thailand. In the first two countries, multiskilling is fostered more aggressively than in the United States. In Taiwan and Korea, despite the large deviation between plants, operators receive general OJT training designed to make them competent in at least three or four jobs. In Thailand, although the rotation system is not practised everywhere, training employees in Japan has raised Job rotation scores.

Scores for wage system and promotion were 3.7 for Taiwan and Korea, and 3.2 for the ASEAN countries. In the United States, the wage system category returned an especially low 2.6, whereas promotion achieved 3.3, lower than for plants in Taiwan and Korea but higher than for plants in ASEAN countries.

The high application scores for the wage system category in Taiwanese and Korean plants reflects the usage of wage tables based on job capability to decide the basic wage. In Taiwan, this basic wage makes up 70–80 per cent of the total wage. This system is similar to Japan's. The United States, however, employs a different wage system. In the case of blue-collar workers, where payment according to job is standard, performance evaluation was very difficult, even discounting the intervention of the UAW. The discrepancies between US and Japanese wage systems led to the low application scores here.

Thus Taiwanese and Korean wage systems resemble the Japanese system. However, factors such as those discussed below have contributed to the lower application scores of Asian plants. Korea's performance evaluation system did not function efficiently because of the influences of disputes between labour and management during the late 1980s. In

Taiwan, superiors hesitate to evaluate subordinates. Moreover, bonuses range from two to four months' salary, lower than the Japanese average. In ASEAN countries, some plants decide wages under three-year labour agreements, while in other plants, ordinary workers (those below supervisor) are not evaluated. For these reasons, the ASEAN plants scored below Taiwan and Korea. In contrast to Taiwan and Korea, in some of the ASEAN plants, the wage system tended to be controlled by the labour unions. (In ASEAN countries, all six plants were unionised, as compared to five out of six in both Taiwan and Korea.) However, many of the ASEAN plants execute performance evaluation of ordinary workers in contrast to US labour union regulations covering wage systems of almost every plant.

Unlike Wage system, ASEAN application scores for promotion were slightly below those of the United States. In Taiwan and Korea, an internal promotion system is favoured at the supervisory or team leader level. Unlike the situation in the United States, there are no seniority regulations, and consequently application scores were high. In ASEAN countries, there is no special status system for promotion as in Japan. Furthermore, some factories are required to hire from outside. In Malaysia, ability to perform is not the basis for promotion. On occasion, selection is race-related; one reason for the low application scores. Throughout Asia as a whole, performance evaluation seems to function poorly, unlike in Japan. In Taiwan and Korea, there are cases of promotion being determined by seniority, with almost complete disregard for performance. In two particular plants, only staff with a certain level of experience are eligible to sit the promotion test and, of those candidates, only half pass. The situation is quite different in Japan where a recommendation from a supervisor is often enough to ensure the promotion.

The application score for first-line supervisors was 3.0 in both ASEAN countries and the United States, and 3.2 in Taiwan and Korea. In Asia, first-line supervisors are promoted from within the factory. While their production, safety and quality assurance duties are similar to those of their counterparts in Japan, their attitude towards performance evaluation shows signs of weak labour management. In some plants in Taiwan and Korea, first-line supervisors are responsible for daily production line balances. However, these supervisors lack the IE ability seen in Japanese plants, which explains the lower application scores.

In conclusion, Asia as a whole, unlike the United States, has no traditional regulations for labour practices and their administration by labour-management. Within Asian region, Taiwan and Korea on the one hand, and ASEAN countries on the other, recorded quite different application scores. However, this does not mean that the plants in Thailand and Malaysia necessarily recorded low scores, but that variation can be seen from factory to factory. Indeed, some factories tended to achieve high scores, suggesting that in the future, as the importance of the automobile industry grows in the ASEAN countries, so will the application of Japanese practices.

Lower Group Consciousness in Asia

As stated above, auto parts plants in the United States as a whole show a strong tendency to apply Japanese systems. Yet in Group I, the core of the Japanese-style production system, the score was a relatively low 3.1. Therefore, in order to strengthen application, Group IV (Group Consciousness) was introduced as a subsystem of Group I. This boosted the score to a high 3.8. In Taiwan and Korea, the average score for Group IV was 3.4, and in ASEAN countries, 3.1. Both scores are below the average for US plants. Analysing by item, scores for Information sharing and Sense of unity were also well below US scores. ASEAN's low degree of application was accounted for largely by Malaysia's low scores, as Thailand's scores were similar to Taiwan's and Korea's.

In plants in Taiwan, Korea and Thailand, small-group activities achieved a common score of 3.3, 0.4 points above the average score for this item in the United States. Many of the plants in the United States are looking to establish a voluntary small-group activities system as seen in Japan, but face many difficulties. In the United States, the number of plants carrying out small-group activities with full member participation is quite limited. This is not so in Asia, where small-group activities with full participation are quite common, even though they are an integral part of the job. The disparity in group consciousness scores between the plants in the United States and Asian countries can be attributed to this factor.

The difference in application scores may also be attributed to the difference in time span over which the survey was taken: 1989 for the United States as against 1991–92 for Asia. Gaining from the experience of these extra two or three years, offshore Japanese auto parts makers were able to make several adjustments. For example, they exchanged the voluntary participation system for small-group activities for a 'total participation' style. In Taiwan, a plant running voluntary small-group activities eventually had to discontinue the programme after it failed, and in 1989 introduced a total participation programme.

Whereas Taiwan and Korea implemented small-group activities in all plants, Malaysia organised QC circles only in one of the three plants there.

The Malaysian plant achieved good results organising the 32-circles in which so-called seven tools for quality control (including control chart, cause and effect diagram, Pareto distribution, and so on) are used. No such circles operate in the other two Malaysian plants, however. One of these, a 20 per cent Japanese minority joint venture set up in 1986, was considering the introduction of small-group activities. The other plant had previously used the system but abandoned it, and had no intention of restoring it as it was unpopular with employees. Accordingly, Group consciousness scores in Malaysian plants are relatively low.

The score for small-group activities in Asian plants (excluding Malaysia) surpassed the US scores. On the other hand, scores for information sharing and sense of unity in Taiwan, Korea and in ASEAN countries were less than for US plants, despite the expectation that Asian plants would score highly on these items if a strong inclination to raise the application score exists. Some plants in Asia have been as enthusiastic as US plants in implementing a Japanese-style system. For example, they have adopted such strategies as open-plan offices, company sports days, company trips, cafeterias where management and workers dine together, and meetings for people on a similar level. One factory in Taiwan, despite confining small-group activities to model circles, has introduced activities such as monthly workshop meetings, weekly shop-floor meetings, quarterly private meetings by (accounting) management for all employees, interviews for all employees after a thirty-day trial period, and Monday morning gatherings. A certain plant in Thailand holds sports events, end-of-year parties, annual policy speeches by the president, monthly managers' meetings, monthly conferences with the labour union, monthly quality meetings, monthly meetings to discuss cutting costs, and quality assurance meetings. In addition, this Thai plant creates daily production schedules and operate committees such as a Five S system, QC, safety, improvement planning, TPM (total productive maintenance), and supplier meetings.

Unlike the factories in the United States, where all the Japanese expatriates can speak a fair amount of English, in Asia only a limited number of Japanese employees can speak the local languages. In addition to this, the predominance of joint ventures in Asia brings application scores there down below those of plants in the United States.

Application scores in Asia for long-term employment and grievance procedures are below the scores of US plants. Long-term employment scored 3.8 in the United States, 3.0 in Taiwan and Korea, and 2.8 in ASEAN countries. For grievance procedures, the United States scored 3.9, Taiwan and Korea 2.8, and ASEAN countries 3.0. In Asia, the application

Table 4.8   Four-perspective evaluation of auto parts industry

	Method		Result		Method/Result	
	Human	*Material*	*Human*	*Material*	*Human*	*Material*
Taiwan and Korea	3.5	3.1	2.4	3.2	1.5	1.0
ASEAN	3.2	2.8	2.7	3.9	1.2	0.7
Malaysia	3.0	2.7	2.8	4.0	1.1	0.7
Thailand	3.4	2.9	2.5	3.8	1.4	0.8
USA	3.4	3.1	4.3	3.7	0.8	0.8

of the core system, Group I, scores above the United States, but, as seen in Table 4.8 and Figure 4.5, the application of Human–Methods aspects is 3.5 in Taiwan and Korea, just 0.1 points above the United States, and 3.2 in ASEAN countries, 0.2 points below the United States' score of 3.4. In Asia, although there are fewer restraints to hinder application of the Human–Methods aspects of the Japanese system, there is less of a tendency to implement these aspects than in the United States.

Limits Reached in Material–Methods Aspects

In the Asian auto parts industry, compared with the United States, the characteristics revealed in Human–Methods scores are further amplified in Material–Methods scores. Material–Methods characteristics proved to be difficult even for enthusiastic American plants to adopt. Asian plants found even more difficulty, however (scores were especially low in the ASEAN countries). Plants in the United States, Taiwan and Korea all scored 3.1, while ASEAN countries scored 2.8. A comparison of all three items shows an interesting trend.

Quality control in the US plants received the highest score, 3.9, while both Taiwan and Korea on the one hand, and the ASEAN countries on the other, scored 3.3. Auto assemblers in the United States have advanced hugely, and quality standards are just as high there as in Japan. In Asia, assemblers' requirements for quality may at times be lower than in the United States. Whatever programmes the management introduces to improve quality control in Asian plants, without the commitment of the employees themselves, high quality tends to be elusive. A Japanese factory manager in Malaysia admitted that there is less building-in during processing and, even with triple checking, some inferior products get

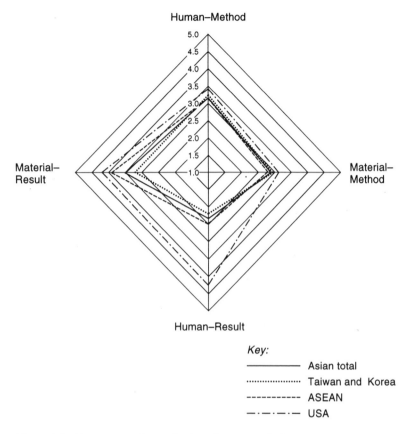

Figure 4.5   Four-perspective evaluation of auto parts industry

through. One factory in Taiwan, however, requires workers on the production line to use a QC checksheet. This is an impressive example of strict quality control in a foreign subsidiary.

In contrast to quality control, when it came to maintenance, the US and ASEAN plants scored below Taiwan and Korea – 2.8 compared to 3.2. Taiwan's and Korea's high score can be attributed to internally-trained personnel and commitment to daily checks by ordinary shop-floor workers. However, even in Taiwan and Korea, it is not always possible to have internally-trained maintenance staff, and at times, hiring experienced workers from outside is unavoidable. Finding qualified maintenance personnel from outside, though, is not always easy. This contrasts with Japan, where preventative maintenance is highly advanced, and maintenance employees are internally trained and treated in the same way as other operations staff in the plant. Has it not been for this difference, the Taiwanese and Korean plants could have scored even higher than 3.2.

With an average score of 2.8, the plants in ASEAN countries had even more problems with maintenance than the plants in Taiwan and Korea. In ASEAN countries, the participation of ordinary shop-floor workers in maintenance is limited to such things as cleaning and lubricating. Operators have scant knowledge of their machines and are consequently unable to detect mechanical problems. As a result, the ASEAN factories need to rely on expert maintenance personnel, which are hard to hire. Consequently, the overall application scores for maintenance in ASEAN countries are low. There is, however, an exception – the Thai wire harness factory. This wire harness factory sends technician-level staff to Japan for six months to be trained as maintenance personnel. However, even where staff are sent to Japan for training, the factory still places considerable emphasis on the training of maintenance personnel within the company.

Procurement received a score of 2.8 in Taiwan and Korea, 3.0 in the United States, and 2.2 in ASEAN countries. These low scores indicate that the Japanese-style procurement system, typified by the 'just-in-time' delivery system, is encountering application problems in other countries. In particular, the introduction of the *kanban* system appears to be less than successful. One company that is famous for implementing this system in Japan has not secceeded in introducing it in Taiwan between the subsidiary plant and local suppliers, which include Japanese-owned parts makers. Moreover, some plants still insist on inspecting all parts from outside suppliers. Although they have a long way to go, plants in Taiwan and Korea are making efforts to improve the quality of parts from local suppliers, and also delivery times. These efforts are reflected in higher application scores for Asia than for the United States.

On the other hand, in Malaysia and Thailand the plants enjoy far less support from related industries, resulting in lower application scores. As locally procured parts are still subject to quality problems, vital parts must be imported from Japan.

In conclusion, the establishment of a Japanese-style parts procurement system remains a long way off. However, while locally produced parts may be lower in quality, they are still considerably cheaper than Japanese parts. A Japanese manager of a Malaysian plant commented that locally procured parts are 50 per cent cheaper, and if quality is improved, they will be exported to Japan in the future. If the Asian automobile industry builds on its experience and if higher levels of production become possible, Japan may be able to develop a strong division of labour system within Asia in the near future.

Finally, Material–Methods aspects are difficult to apply, both in the United States and in Asian countries (especially in ASEAN countries), and thus application scores remain quite low.

Results Scores Differ between ASEAN Countries and NIEs

In applying Japanese production techniques, differences in Methods led to differences in Results. For the United States, the average score for applying the Japanese production system in Human–Results areas was 4.3, whereas Taiwan and Korea managed only 2.4, and ASEAN countries 2.7. Interestingly, in Results, Taiwan and Korea scored below ASEAN countries. On the other hand, Methods scores in Taiwan and Korea were higher than in ASEAN countries. This is further reinforced in Material–Results areas. That is, scores for Material–Results were 3.7 in the United States, 3.2 in Taiwan and Korea, and 3.9 in ASEAN countries. As a result, ASEAN countries, which cannot apply Methods aspects of the Japanese system to the same extent as Taiwan and Korea, tends to rely on directly imported parts and equipment from Japan.

The differences in Results reflect the Human–Results areas, where Taiwan and ASEAN countries scored below the plants in the United States. The lower Human–Results scores in Asian plants compared to US plants is caused by the low ratio of Japanese expatriates to total employees. Although one plant in Taiwan has ten Japanese expatriates out of a total of 193 employees, there are few cases of a such a high ratio of Japanese expatriates in other countries.

Several reasons can be suggested for the low number of Japanese expatriates. First, the percentage of joint ventures in Asia is high compared to the United States. Second, unlike the United States, there is less inclination in Asian countries to establish production systems similar to Japan's. There are several reasons for this. For example, in addition to the high number of joint ventures in Asia, the average wage level is also lower in Asia, and requirements by assembler–makers more lax. Third, plants in Asia have longer operational experience than plants in the United States. Fourth, local governments have sometimes intervened to restrict the number of Japanese expatriates in Asian plants. Finally, because plants in Asia tend to be more labour-intensive than plants in the United States, these plants naturally have a lower ratio of expatriates to total employees. But this does not mean that Japanese employees at Asian plants have less to do. In fact, because of their small number, a greater burden of responsibility tends to be placed on them.

Unlike Human–Results, Material–Results scores for plants in Taiwan and Korea differ considerably from scores for ASEAN plants. The main reason for the low degree of application in plants in Taiwan and Korea is because of low scores for Production equipment. At 3.0, these are 1.8 points below the average scores in the United States. In the case of Group III, Procurement, scores for Local content at plants in Taiwan and Korea surpassed scores at plants in the United States by 0.3 points. Scores for Suppliers at plants in Taiwan and Korea were 0.2 points below the average scores for plants in the United States, reflecting the low level of Japanese supporting industries in Taiwan and Korea. While in the United States, production equipment is almost all Japanese, on a dollar basis, about half the production equipment used in plants in Taiwan and Korea is locally procured. It is cheaper to produce the equipment locally using Japanese blueprints than to import the equipment from Japan. In one Korean plant, only 10 per cent of the total equipment is Japanese made. For example, after one machine was imported from a Japanese parent company, the same kinds of machine were constructed in the Korean plant. And the same company purchased blueprints for speedometers and tachometers from its parent company in Japan after they had undergone a complete model change in 1992. At that time, local engineers were dispatched to Japan to master the manufacturing techniques, and the equipment was produced in Korea.

Scores for application of the Japanese system in Material–Results areas were 3.9 for plants in ASEAN countries, 3.7 for plants in the United States, and 3.2 for plants in Taiwan and Korea. The Material–Results aspect was the only one in the Four-Perspective Evaluation categories in which ASEAN countries scored higher than the United States. Although the score for suppliers (3.7) was the same as for plants in the United States, the score for local content was 3.8, well above the score achieved by US plants (2.7). The direct importation of Japanese parts and components played a vital role in raising that score. In the category of Production equipment, although ASEAN countries scores were higher than for plants in Taiwan and Korea (3.0), their score of 4.2 was below that of plants in the United States (4.8).

Some plants in ASEAN countries are still using old-fashioned Japanese production equipment, which explains why scores are lower than in the United States. However, at least half of the factories employ the same types of equipment currently used in Japanese factories, boosting scores above those at plants in Taiwan and Korea. Recently, some of the plants in

ASEAN countries have begun to increase the amount of locally made equipment, which is one third the cost of Japanese imported machinery. But the low level of the development of supporting industries makes ASEAN plants dependent on Japanese equipment. This dependency is reflected in the low scores for Methods categories.

This phenomenon is even clearer in procurement. In Thailand and Malaysia, local content still remains at 25 per cent to 50 per cent in spite of government regulations. One reason for the low rate of local content is that, except in the case of Korea, local auto parts makers cannot achieve economies of scale because local automobile production is limited. This makes local parts more expensive than imported parts. However, a more valid reason for low local content is the poor quality of local parts and the unavailability of sophisticated parts. Compared to Taiwan and Korea, supporting industries are relatively undeveloped and Japanese parts makers are few. Both these factors contribute to the low scores for local procurement in the ASEAN subsidiaries. However, some Japanese parts makers give occasional technical assistance to local vendors and this may raise levels of local content in the future.

Because of the above factors, Material–Results scores (that is, the application of the Japanese production system in the Material–Results aspects of the various categories) differ greatly between NIEs and ASEAN plants. In the area of equipment in particular, NIEs plants use a high percentage of locally procured equipment compared to ASEAN plants, which rely on directly imported machines from Japan and enjoy almost the same production systems as in Japan. The ASEAN plants, which scored lower in the Methods aspects, also relied heavily on imported parts and components from Japan.

Low Scores for Asian Labour Relations

This final section discusses the category of labour relations. Whereas plants in Asia scored poorly in labour relations (3.0), plants in the United States scored a high 4.1 in this category, despite fears of UAW intervention. Success in obtaining good Japanese-style labour relations in the US context can be attributed to several factors. These include cautious hiring policies; a long-term employment policy emphasising the characteristics of 'Japanese-style management'; and an enterprising grievance procedure adapted to American conditions. On the other hand, the plants in Asia trailed US plants in all four items of the Labour relations group. The biggest difference, however, was in harmonious labour–management relations. This was the category where disparities in scores between the plants in ASEAN countries on the one hand, and Taiwan and Korea on the other, were largest. Japanese auto parts companies that set up in the United States were careful to take measures to stabilise labour relations to avoid conflict with the UAW. As a result, no unions were formed, and co-operative labour relations were achieved. This was reflected in a perfect score of 5.0 for Harmonious labour–management relations. However, the plants in Taiwan and Korea achieved no more than 3.5, and ASEAN plants averaged 3.0.

In the six factories surveyed in Taiwan and Korea, five plants were unionised, and labour relations were basically co-operative. However, several incidents and factors drastically lowered scores for the plants in Taiwan and Korea. These included the 1987 abolition of martial law in Taiwan, the widespread conflict between workers and employees that swept Korea in the 1980s, and strikes at two factories. But the ASEAN plants scored even lower than plants in Taiwan and Korea. All six ASEAN factories in the survey were unionised and many of them enjoyed stable relationships with the unions. However, some of them had heavy-handed industrial union committees that had 'a strong position', troubling the government with their 'aggressive style'.

For the long-term employment category, Taiwanese and Korean plants scored 3.0, while ASEAN plants averaged 2.8. Both scores were well below the 3.8 of the US plants, where Japanese auto parts subsidiaries emphasise a 'no lay-offs' policy in their local production. In Taiwan, some factories stress a 'compassionate attitude' towards employees. These factories try to encourage long-term employment by providing a bonus for long service. This, however, is not typical in Asia. Other factories in Taiwan and Korea, and in ASEAN countries as well, do not support 'no lay-offs' and some have laid off workers or put voluntary resignation into operation at various times, resulting in a low score for this category.

Scores for the hiring policy and grievance procedures categories in Asian auto parts plants were also below scores at US plants. The high hiring policy score of 3.8 achieved at US plants is a result of a thorough selection process. Once plant locations have been selected through exhaustive feasibility studies, employees are rigorously selected from long lists of applicants. As plants in Asia have no such system, their scores in this category were lower. In Taiwan, the difficulty of finding suitable workers is a common complaint, but elsewhere in Asia, especially Thailand, the high wages offered by the industry makes hiring workers relatively easy. In the ASEAN countries, however, it is difficult to find experienced technicians and engineers. Low hiring policy scores of 2.7 in

Taiwan and Korea, and 3.0 in ASEAN countries can easily be understood against this background.

For Grievance procedures, US plants achieved a high 3.9. Plants in Taiwan and Korea, however, scored only 2.8, and ASEAN plants, 3.0. In the United States, auto parts plants not organised by unions are seeking to adopt an effective procedure for redressing grievances. In Asia (including Japan), as no established system for settling grievances exists, companies lack positive grievance reconciliation measures. In Asia there are few plants with the 'open door' policy found in the United States; instead, labour–management councils address grievances, or grievances are heard through unions.

IV CONCLUSION

This section summarises the management and operational style of auto parts factories in Asia. The overall average score for Taiwanese and Korean plants was 3.2, and 3.1 for ASEAN plants. Both of these were below the 3.6 averaged by the US plants. In the Work Organisation and Administration categories (Group I) – the core group of the twenty-three-item, six-group evaluation, Asian plants bettered the 3.1 scored by US plants; Taiwanese and Korean plants scored 3.7, and ASEAN plants, 3.3. However, while US plants exhibited an overall strong tendency towards the application of a Japanese system of production, there was no such clear tendency in Asia. This is because Asia lacks an institutional or environmental framework on which to hang the Japanese production system.

In the Human–Methods areas, which include the six items of Group I, Taiwan and Korea scored 3.5, 0.1 points above the United States, while ASEAN countries scored 3.2. This indicates that the favourable conditions that exist in Asia for the application of the Japanese production system are not being used to their fullest extent. As mentioned in the Material–Methods discussion, Taiwan and Korea, and the United States all achieved a score of 3.1, while ASEAN countries scored only 2.8. This low score reflects difficulties in application and little enthusiasm in Asian countries for Methods aspects. Scores for Methods and Results differed between ASEAN countries on the one hand, and Taiwan and Korea on the other. Taiwan and Korea scored higher than ASEAN plants for Methods, but lower than ASEAN plants for Results. In Human–Results, ASEAN countries gained 2.7, whereas Taiwan and Korea scored 2.4. In Material-Results, ASEAN countries scored 3.9, and Taiwan and Korea 3.2. Taiwan and Korea had practically the same score as America for Methods, while ASEAN countries' low score in Methods was partially offset by a high score in Results.

The Japanese auto parts industry in Asia has now reached a turning point. The Asian automobile industry is undergoing rapid growth and change, with the government of each country pushing for deregulation and liberalisation. This will force auto assembler–makers to review purchasing policy and Japanese parent companies to retool management strategies. Such changes will influence the managerial and operational position of local factories.

In Korea, although some of the auto assembler–makers are minority partners in joint ventures with Japanese companies, they use local management methods. The same applies in Malaysia, where about 70 per cent of the domestic market share is dominated by Proton. In Taiwan and Thailand, operational styles are very Japanese-influenced, though not all auto assemblers are majority-owned by Japanese corporations. Changes in the auto assembly industry are affecting the operational style of auto parts makers. Japanese auto assembler-makers, especially those in Taiwan and Thailand, have been increasing production volume with the intention of realising true large-scale mass production in the future. This will give greater momentum to the auto parts makers and encourage them to construct more effective production systems. The move towards an interlocking parts and components supply system within Asia, especially in ASEAN countries, will also help accelerate the development of an effective auto parts and components production system. However, in ASEAN countries, where the Big Three makers, European makers and Korean makers plan to enter the market, severe competition will be unavoidable. The fortunes of these assemblers will directly affect the fortunes of the parts makers. In Korea and Malaysia, the rising competition within the auto assembly industry is forcing auto parts makers to respond.

Finally, factories producing for export through labour-intensive production, such as the wire harness plants in Taiwan and Thailand that are exporting to North America and Europe, will spread from the NIEs area to the ASEAN countries, and on into China. Moreover, auto parts makers in Asia will begin to export to Japan, as Asian electronics makers have done. Advantages such as low wages and suitable local technical skills will be the crucial factors in determining location in the future.

Notes

1. Abo (1994a), esp. ch. 5; and. Sumiya et al. (1992)
2. Adachi (1993).
3. Hayashi (1989) pp. 53–4.
4. On this point, see Chūshō Kigyō Chōsakai (1992).
5. JETRO (1986) and JETRO (1992), particularly the parts relating to Korea.
6. Chi (1990) pp. 28, 100. On the development of industries and foreign investment policies, see Sumiya et al. (1992), ch. 2.
7. Asamoto (1992a) pp. 153–6.
8. Kojō (1991) pp. 118–19.
9. Sei (1989) pp. 39, 41–2, 53; and Kojō (1991) pp. 105–7. For Taiwanese auto parts makers, see Asamoto (1992b) pp. 74–7, 87.
10. Sei (1987) pp. 59–7.
11. Yanagimachi (1994) pp. 143–4, 145, 146. On the Korean automobile and auto parts industries, see Mizukawa (1993). For *keiretsu* in the Korean automobile and auto parts industries, see Mizuno (1993).
12. Adachi (1993) pp. 39–45.
13. Horii (1991) see ch. 5.
14. Kobayashi and Hayashi (1993) p. 29. Also, Adachi (1993) p. 46; and Kojō (1994) pp. 55–68.
15. Interview with Mr Chūji Yukawa, Manager of the International Division, Japan Auto Parts Manufacturers Association, 4 August, 1993.

The Electronics Assembly Industry*

Tetsuo Abo

I ELECTRONICS ASSEMBLY IN EAST ASIA: AN OVERVIEW

The Japanese electronics assembly industry in East Asia has several special features.

1. In the late 50s and early 60s, in the first wave of serious overseas production activities, Japanese electronics manufacturers began to set up significant numbers of local plants in East Asian countries such as Taiwan, Thailand, Malaysia and Korea. From the second half of the 1960s and into the 1970s, the industry expanded to Central and South America, Oceania, Africa, and finally to North America and Europe.

   The two main operation models employed were the export-orientated free trade zone (FTZ) type, and the 'mini-Matsushita' ('mini-M') type. The 'mini-M' model replicated, for each closed local market, a complete set of the parent Matsushita's electrical and electronic product lines, from fans and VCRs to audio products, office automation equipment and electronic components. As its name implies, the 'mini-M' type was essentially for low-volume production.

2. During the rapid yen appreciation following the 'Plaza Accord' of 1985, the electronics assembly industry led a second wave of Japanese manufacturers into East Asia. Now the 'mini-M' type began to be replaced by the 'new-Matsushita ('new-M') export-based type, which used highly automated state-of-the-art plant and equipment to gain a competitive edge in mainly world markets (see the case study in Chapter 5 below).

3. The electronics assembly industry is in many ways the most representative of Japan's manufacturing industries in the East Asian region. With almost the whole spectrum of electrical and electronic product lines, diverse technology ranging from low- to high-tech, all kinds of production approaches from low-volume, high-variety, to mass production and large-scale deployment of logistics for parts and material procurement, the industry has been leading the development of the East Asian region as a hub of world economic growth. The impressive sequential or stepped development taking place in East

Asia in the 1990s has been dubbed a 'flying geese' pattern of development.[1]

4. Since the latter half of the 80s, East Asian economic development and interregional relations have been in a transitional phase. As Taiwan and Korea have reached a new, maturing, stage in their development, they have been looking for new direction (see Ernst (1994)). The two recognise the necessity of upgrading their technologies toward specialised product lines and new higher value-added products. They are also taking an interest in local R&D activities, including supporting local production in the ASEAN countries and in mainland China. Production approaches in the ASEAN countries are changing from the 'mini-M' type to a mixture of 'mini-M' and 'new-M'.

II PROFILE OF SURVEYED PLANTS

Table 4.9 shows the profiles of sixteen Japanese electronics assembly plants in newly industrialising economies (NIEs) and the ASEAN region. Four of these plants are in Taiwan, two in Korea, six in Malaysia, three in Thailand and one in Singapore. An outline of the sixteen plants follows.

1. The earliest Japanese electronics overseas ventures were CCTh, a typical 'mini-M' venture started in Thailand in 1961, and CETw, established in 1964 in Taiwan. In the latter half of the 60s, similar CEM plants were set up in Malaysia, CCTw (the biggest 'mini-M') and CATw were opened in Taiwan, and CATh in Thailand. (Some of these, including CEM and CATh, began exporting a limited range of their products.) Next, in the early 70s, CGK and CFK, typical FTZ models, were established in Korea. After the late 80s, a large number of 'new-M' export plants appeared, mostly in Malaysia. These included CCM, a typical 'new-M' plant, and CGM, CBM, CFM1, which in fact began in 1981 as a kind of FTZ venture (the second and third 'new-M' plants were set up in the late 80s), and CFM2. Some 'new-M' plants were also set up in Thailand (CDTh for example), and some, including CHS, in Singapore. (In 1988, CHS set up another large VCR plant, a joint venture with a European manufacturer.)
2. Almost 70 per cent of the plants surveyed (eleven of the sixteen) are variations of joint ventures with local firms. This is one of the most significant features of Japanese overseas plants in the Asian region.
3. Although numbers of employees at the sixteen plants surveyed vary widely from 309 (for the colour television (CTV) and video-cassette

Table 4.9   Profile of Japanese-affiliated electronics assembly plants surveyed

			ASEAN		
Plant	CBM	CFM	CFM1	CFM2	CGM
Location	Malaysia	Malaysia	Malaysia	Malaysia	Malaysia
Start of operation	Apr. 1989	Jul. 1967	Sep. 1981	Jun. 1990	May 1988
Form of establishment	Greenfield	Greenfield	Greenfield	Greenfield	Greenfield
Entry mode	JV	JV	JV	JV	WO
Equity share of Japan (%)	50	35	50	70	100
Capital	70 mRM	41.9 mRM	1760 mYen	2600 mYen	30 mRM
No. of employees	2631	600	1893	1235	1800
No. of Japanese expatriates	21	6	15	9	19
Products	VCRs, VCR kits, PCBs	Fans, electric rice cookers, motors, air-conditioners, refrigerators	CTV, display monitors, VCRs, chassis	VCRs	CTVs, deflection yokes, flyback transformers, tuners
Production volume (000s units/yr)	VCRs and VCR kits; 2250	CTVs; 2000 chassis; 850?	VCRs; 1500 ('93 plan)	CTVs; 1600	CTVs; 1100
Export ratio (%)	100	95	(n.a.)	100	100
Foreign versus domestic market	New M	Mini-M	New M	New M	New M

209

Table 4.9 (continued)

		ASEAN			
Plant	CCM	CDTh	CCTh	CATh	CHS
Location	Malaysia	Thailand	Thailand	Thailand	Singapore
Start of operation	Apr. 1989	Jul. 1990	Dec. 1961	Nov. 1970	Feb. 1979
Form of establishment	Greenfield	Greenfield	Greenfield	Greenfield	Greenfield
Entry mode	WO	JV	JV	JV	WO
Equity share of Japan (%)	100	70	48.65	49	100
Capital	120 mRM	100 000 mB	100 mB	105mB	6.6mS$
No. of employees	1289	640	2239	1550	840
No. of Japanese expatriates	32	7	6	14	8
Products	CTVs,	Room air-conditioners, packaged air-conditioners	CTVs, audio equipment, fans batteries	Refrigerators, washing machines, CTVs, electric rice cookers, fans, pumps	CTVs
Production volume (000s units/yr)	CTVs; 1100	Room air-conditioners, 146	CTVs; 300	Refrigerators; 200	CTVs, 1100
Export ratio (%)	100	75	(n.a.)	36	97
Foreign versus domestic market	New M	New M	Mini-M	Mini-M	New M

Table 4.9 (continued)

	NIEs					
Plant	CETw	CGTw	CCTw	CATw	CFK	CGK
Location	Taiwan	Taiwan	Taiwan	Taiwan	Korea	Korea
Start of operation	Jan. 1964	Sep. 1984	1969	Dec. 1969	Jun. 1973	Oct. 1972
Form of establishment	Greenfield	Greenfield	Greenfield	Greenfield	Greenfield	Greenfield
Entry mode	JV	WO	JV	WO	JV	WO
Equity share of Japan (%)	49	100	56	100		100
Capital	11 500 mYen	1158 mYen	2.2 mNY$	300 mNT$		4100 mWon
No. of employees	2086	420	5922	758	1194	2812
No. of Japanese expatriates	5	5	50	9	3	1
Products	CTVs, VCRs, refrigerators, air-conditioners, washing machines, Telecommunications equipment	VCRs	CTVs, VCRs	CTVs, character displays, audio equipment	Calculators, electronic typewriters, audio equipment, telephones, cash registers	Audio equipment MDDs, headphones, optical pickups, VCR motors, video heads
Production volume (000s units/yr)	CTVs; 50 VCRs; 50 refrigerators; 70	VCRs; 350	CTVs; 120 VCRs; 120	CTVs; 12/m Ch. displays;13/m	(n.a.)	Audio equip.; 140/m MDDs; 300–3500/m
Export ratio (%)	Modest	60	(n.a.)	99	(n.a.)	(n.a.)
Foreign versus domestic market	Mini-M	New M	Mini-M	New M	New M	New M

Note: 'Mini-M' = the affiliates whose marketing is aimed at local market; 'New M' = those mainly exporting abroad, including Japan.; JV = Joint venture; WO = Wholly owned.

recorder (VCR) division at CCTw, which employs a total of 5922), to 2812 (at CGK), the average of 1,394 is almost double that of the nine Japanese consumer electronics plants in the United States (averaging 749 employees each) (see Abo, 1994a, Table 6.5, p. 152). This statistic highlights the significance of the electronics assembly industry in terms of plant size in East Asia. In terms of the ratio of Japanese expatriates to total employees, the difference between East Asia and the United States is even clearer: 0.73 per cent compared to 1.99 per cent.

4. The variety of product lines at East Asian plants is much higher than at similar plants in the United States, where, typically, only a couple of models of CTVs or perhaps microwave ovens are produced. An East Asian venture may produce office information and communications equipment, electronic components, CTVs, VCRs and a plethora of other home appliances such as fans, washing machines, refrigerators, air conditioners and stereos. The size of production in terms of unit volume is also generally larger in Asia than in similar ventures in the United States. For example, many plants in East Asia, especially in Malaysia, produce CTVs and VCRs in unit lots of one to two thousand, whereas only the two largest plants in the United States produce CTVs in lots of around a thousand.

III   EVALUATION OF SIX GROUPS AND TWENTY-THREE ITEMS

Using the Hybrid Evaluation model (see Chapter 1 of this book and Abo, 1994a, chs 1 and 2), we shall first analyse the Japanese electronics assembly plants in the East Asian region in terms of application and adaptation. After averaging the twenty-three items for an overall score, we shall evaluate the six groups, then the individual items.

Average overall scores

As shown in Table 4.10, the 16 Japanese electronics assembly plants in East Asia return an overall average score of 3.3, far higher than the 2.7 scored by plants in the United States. This score is higher than the overall average score of 3.2 achieved by the four industries in East Asia (as against 3.3 in the USA), revealing the strategic importance of the electronics industry in this region. For the electronics industry, the difference in the scores between the NIEs and the ASEAN countries (3.4 as against 3.2, respectively) is very narrow compared with the difference

Table 4.10 Hybrid evaluation in electronic assembly plants

	Tw	K	NIEs	M	Th	S'pore	ASEAN	Asia	USA
I Work Organisation and Administration	3.6	4.2	3.8	3.2	3.2	3.0	3.2	3.2	2.4
① Job classification	4.8	5.0	4.8	4.2	4.7	3	4.2	4.2	2.8
② Multifunctional skills	2.3	3.0	2.5	2.5	2.7	2	2.5	2.4	2.1
③ Education and training	3.0	4.0	3.3	3.0	3.0	4	3.1	3.0	2.2
④ Wage system	3.8	4.5	4.0	2.8	2.7	3	2.8	3.1	2.0
⑤ Promotion	4.3	4.5	4.3	3.5	3.3	3	3.4	3.6	2.7
⑥ First-line supervisor	3.8	4.0	3.8	3.0	2.7	3	2.9	3.1	2.6
II Production Control	3.6	3.9	3.7	3.5	3.1	3.5	3.4	3.3	3.1
⑦ Equipment	3.3	3.0	3.2	3.8	3.7	4	3.8	3.4	4.0
⑧ Maintenance	3.8	4.0	3.8	3.2	3.3	3	3.2	3.3	2.1
⑨ Quality control	3.8	4.5	4.0	3.5	3.0	4	3.4	3.4	3.0
⑩ Process management	3.5	4.0	3.7	3.7	2.3	3	3.2	3.2	3.3
III Procurement	3.3	2.7	3.1	3.4	2.8	3.3	3.2	3.0	2.6
⑪ Local content	3.3	1.5	2.7	2.8	2.3	3	2.7	2.6	2.0
⑫ Suppliers	3.3	3.0	3.2	4.0	3.3	4	3.8	3.4	3.6
⑬ Procurement method	3.5	3.5	3.5	3.3	2.7	3	3.1	3.1	2.1
IV Group Consciousness	3.2	4.0	3.4	3.4	3.1	3.3	3.3	3.2	2.3
⑭ Small-group activities	2.5	3.5	2.8	3.0	3.0	3	3.0	2.8	2.2
⑮ Information sharing	3.3	4.5	3.7	3.7	3.0	4	3.5	3.4	2.4
⑯ Sense of unity	3.8	4.0	3.8	3.7	3.3	3	3.5	3.4	2.1

Table 4.10   (continued)

	Tw	K	NIEs	M	Th	S'pore	ASEAN	Asia	USA
V Labour Relations	3.6	4.1	3.8	3.0	3.3	2.5	3.1	3.2	2.7
⑰ Hiring policy	3.3	4.0	3.5	3.2	3.7	2	3.2	3.2	2.4
⑱ Long-term employment	3.5	4.0	3.7	3.0	3.3	2	3.0	3.1	2.2
⑲ Harmonious labour relations	4.5	4.5	4.5	3.0	3.0	3	3.0	3.4	3.4
⑳ Grievance procedure	3.3	4.0	3.5	3.0	3.3	3	3.1	3.2	2.8
VI Parent–Subsidiary Relations	2.5	1.3	2.1	3.1	2.7	3.0	3.0	2.5	3.0
㉑ Ratio of Japanese expatriates	1.3	1.0	1.2	1.7	1.3	2	1.6	1.4	2.6
㉒ Delegation of authority	3.3	2.0	2.8	3.3	3.0	3	3.2	2.9	3.2
㉓ Position of local managers	3.0	1.0	2.3	4.3	3.7	4	4.1	3.3	3.2
Average of 23 items	**3.4**	**3.5**	**3.4**	**3.3**	**3.1**	**3.1**	**3.2**	**3.1**	**2.7**

between the two regions for the auto assembly industry (3.5 as against 3.0, respectively).

There are several reasons for the difference between the electronics and auto assembly industries. On the supply side, the human resource environment in east Asia plays a crucial role, not only in terms of relatively low labour costs, but also in the qualitative nature of East Asian workers and managers. As described in the previous chapters, East Asians are generally familiar with the human-related work practices of Japanese companies and share the Japanese work ethic. Workers are diligent, patient and co-operative, making them suitable for meticulous, flexible-type assembly of tiny chips and components in a group-orientated assembly and administrative environment. On the demand side, local and world market conditions play an even more important role, especially in the electronics industry. With both domestic and export markets expanding rapidly in East Asia, it would seem natural to choose direct foreign investment and set up large-scale production bases within East Asia's protected economies. Until recent times, however, the automobile assembly industry did not find any markets in East Asia that could compare with the United States in terms of return on investment and spacious sites for plants.

The overall score is simply the result of averaging the differences among the scores of groups, items and regions. Let us now investigate the meanings and implications behind the differences.

Evaluation of the Six Groups (Groups I–VI)

In the Figure 4.6, the differences in the application degrees (scores) by groups among the three regions are clearly drawn.

1. Except for Group VI (Parent–Subsidiary Relations), the scores of the six groups are in descending order of NIEs, the ASEAN countries and the United States. It appears that the NIEs offer a much more desirable profile than do the ASEAN countries or the United States, since, with far smaller direct commitment by the parent companies, the Japanese electronics assembly plants in the NIEs realised higher application scores for Groups I to V. In particular, the conspicuously high scores of Group I (Work Organisation and Administration) (3.8), and Group V (Labour Relations) (3.8) suggest that the human-related work environment and ancillary conditions of the NIEs strongly support the 'mini-M' or 'FTZ' types of electronics assembly.

2. The generally higher application scores in the ASEAN region

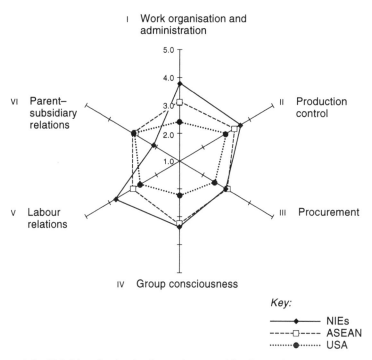

Figure 4.6   Hybrid evaluation in electronics assembly plants: six groups

compared with the United States suggest that it is easier for Japanese electronics firms to assemble their products in ASEAN subsidiaries than in the USA. The shape of the ASEAN hexagon, however, is similar to the US hexagon. In Group vi, ASEAN subsidiaries achieve the same application score (3.0) as US subsidiaries, far higher than their NIEs counterparts (2.1). Judging from the above, the ASEAN subsidiaries perform somewhere between NIEs and US hybrids, though apparently closer to the US subsidiaries (in particular, the Japanese parents show a deeper commitment to their ASEAN offspring than to their US ones). (But this assessment includes an important difference in the evaluation of items between ASEAN and US subsidiaries – see the next section

3. The application scores of NIEs and ASEAN subsidiaries are almost the same in Group ii (Production Control), Group iii (Procurement), and Group iv (Group Consciousness), although the similarity between some scores simply results from some items within the groups offsetting others (see next section). So far as it is possible to make

evaluations at a group level, the Group II (Production Control) scores are relatively high and consistent for all regions (including the United States), and for all industries. This might be expected, as all plants in the regions are in a competitive situation (see Figure 2.1 in Chapter 2 of this book). Second, in Group III (Procurement), the application scores of NIEs and ASEAN electronics assembly subsidiaries are not only close but much higher than the scores of their US counterparts. This reflects the technological weakness of local ASEAN and NIEs suppliers and the lower local content requirements in Asia (see also Chapter 2 above). Third, the difference in Group IV (Group Consciousness) scores between East Asia and the United States simply reflects the more patient and co-operative attitude of local people in East Asia, and the relative lack of enthusiasm and commitment of Japanese electronics parent companies towards their US offspring discussed in the previous paragraph.

Evaluation of Twenty-three Items

Having formed an overall picture of the hybrid plants of the Japanese electronics industry in East Asia, we should now include an item-level analysis to illuminate more complex aspects. Quite different item-level scores can offset each other to create similar scores at group level.

As shown in Table 4.10 and Figure 4.7, the scores of the NIEs, ASEAN countries and the United States for the twenty-three items generally reflects the scores of the six groups (Group I to Group IV). (NIEs subsidiaries scored the highest, US subsidiaries the lowest.) However, focusing on the specific scores of the items reveals several essential differences from the six-group evaluation. These differences would affect the transfer of systems or technology.

1. In two core groups, Group I (Human-related) and Group II (Materials-related), the application scores of individual items, such as ② Multi-functional skills, ⑦ Equipment, and ⑩ Manufacturing process management, are notably different from the general trend of the six groups described above, according to whether the subsidiaries are NIEs, ASEAN, or US subsidiaries.

    In the area of multi-skills – the core of the flexible Japanese system – the application scores for all three regions are extremely low. Clearly, it is difficult to train Japanese style multi-skilled workers anywhere. It is especially important to point out here that at Japanese electronics assembly plants in East Asia, and in the NIEs in particular,

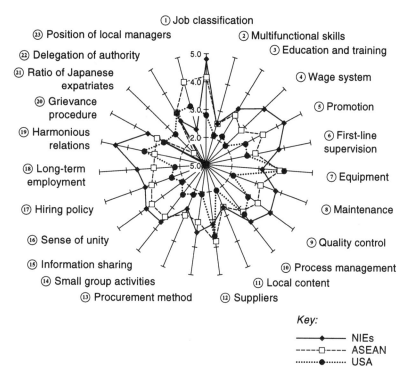

Figure 4.7 Hybrid evaluation in electronics assembly plants: 23 elements

the application scores for ancillary systems for multi-skill training such as ① Job classification, ④ Wage system, and ⑤ Promotion are quite high. Clearly, a formal system is one thing, but to have the system working properly is quite another.

Interestingly, the application scores for equipment, in contrast to many other items, is totally reversed in descending order of the United States, the ASEAN countries and the NIEs. The Japanese plants in the United States and ASEAN countries that import Japanese-made machinery and equipment generally seek to cover the inadequacies of the transferred Japanese systems. On the other hand, at the Japanese plants in Taiwan and Korea (and to some extent, at the 'mini-M' plants in ASEAN countries), standardised equipment, measuring instruments, conveyers, and even some automation machinery can be procured locally or made in-house (for example, by CCTw, CGTw, CETw, CFK and CGK). This is in addition to second-hand machinery and equipment imported from Japanese parent companies.

2. In the subcore group, Group III (Procurement), the NIEs and ASEAN
    score of 2.7 for Item ⑪ Local content is much higher than in the
    United States (2.0). This indicates that the technology levels of
    suppliers in the NIEs and ASEAN countries are lower than levels in
    the United States. However, this does not necessarily mean that
    Japanese electronics assemblers in the United States favour local
    procurement far more than do Japanese assemblers in the NIEs.
    Rather, judging from the reversal of application scores in Item ⑫
    suppliers between the United States (3.6) and the NIEs (3.2), clearly
    many local suppliers in the United States (and in Maquiladora,
    Mexico) (see Choi and Kenney 1995; and Kamiyama 1992) are
    Japanese-affiliated in terms of 'country of origin'. These would
    include subsidiaries, joint ventures and technological joint ventures. It
    is also significant that the NIEs and ASEAN scores for ⑬
    Procurement Methods (3.5 and 3.1, respectively) are far higher than
    the US score (2.1). This would suggest that the lower local content in
    US subsidiaries would have been more or less inevitable had
    sufficient technology not been transferred from Japan.

3. For almost all of the items within subsystem-related Group IV (Group
    Consciousness), and human-related Group V (Labour Relations), NIEs
    and ASEAN plants score far higher than US plants. We need not
    concern ourselves with each item to point out how much easier it is in
    Asia than in the United States to implement the practices surrounding
    the core systems. This contrasts with the automobile assembly
    industry. Application scores for these items in Japanese-operated US
    auto plants generally match those for Japanese electronics assembly
    plants in Asia, although the Japanese auto firms operating in the
    United States must have attained the high application levels indicated
    by the scores at great cost to themselves (see Chapter 4).

4. The most characteristic difference in terms of items, as well as of
    groups, among the three regions appears in the items of Group VI.
    First, the reversal of scores for Item ㉑ Ratio of Japanese expatriates
    between East Asia and the United States is particularly noticeable.
    The very low scores for NIEs (1.2) and ASEAN (1.6) compared with
    the score of 2.6 for the United States are most exceptional. There are
    also a few similar cases, such as for ⑦ Equipment and ⑫ Suppliers,
    mentioned above. It should be noted, however, that even the large
    difference (1.4) between NIEs, ASEAN plants and US plants is much
    smaller than in the case of auto assembly (2.2), auto components
    (2.6), and electronic components (2.6). This is mainly because, in the
    United States, the 2.6 scored by the electronics assembly for ㉑ Ratio

of Japanese expatriates is far lower than the 3.8 scored for the auto assembly industry, the 4.6 scored for the auto components industry, and the 3.9 for semiconductor plants. This also reflects the somewhat haphazard nature of electronics assembly in the United States. It goes without saying that the ratio of Japanese Expatriates is not simply a product of the amount of investment or size of plant, but largely depends on the degree of applicability of the human-centred Japanese system. In the case of the US auto assembly plants, the ratio of Japanese expatriates is far higher than in East Asia, because of higher investment and numbers of employees (see Chapter 4). Second, the scores for ㉓ Position of local managers among the three regions are interestingly different from Items ㉑ Ratio of Japanese expatriates and ㉒ Delegation of authority. While the scores for Item ㉒ are not so different, ㉓ Position of local managers for ASEAN, at 4.1, is far higher than for both the NIEs (2.3) and the United States (3.2). This means that in the ASEAN region, a very small number of Japanese expatriates (almost the same level as in the NIEs) occupy important managerial positions. These expatriates compensate in some way for the poorer understanding of Japanese practices by local managers. Conversely, in the NIEs, local managers in relatively elevated positions support a low number of Japanese expatriates. In the United States, the relatively elevated position of American managers is probably for reasons of diplomacy: quite a large number of Japanese managers play an important role behind the scenes. This situation is also commonly seen in the other industries, but the gap (1.8) between the position of local managers in ASEAN countries and the NIEs is especially large in electronics assembly. For the other industries, the gap is less than 0.9 (see Table 2.3 in Chapter 2 above).

IV FOUR-PERSPECTIVE EVALUATION

As we have seen, although the item and group scores for the Asian plants are generally higher than those for US plants, between NIEs, ASEAN countries and US electronics assembly plants set up by the Japanese, one or two scores are conspicuously reversed. The implications of this irregularity, in terms of the transfer of technology, can be better analysed through the Four-Perspective Evaluation system (4-PE), the other aspect of our methodology explained above in Chapter 2. The 4-PE system is based on the four perspectives of Human–Methods, Material–Methods, Human–Results, and Material–Results.

It is significant that methods tend to be clearly ascendant over results for the East Asian region compared with the United States.

1. The simplest indicators are the methods/results ratios in Table 4.11. These are 149.8 per cent, 99.5 per cent, and 77.9 per cent for electronics assembly plants in the NIEs, ASEAN countries and the United States, respectively. The contrast among the regions is revealed starkly in electronics assembly (see Table 2.4 in Chapter 2 above for the average scores).

2. In Figure 4.8, the descending order in the application scores in NIEs, ASEAN, and the USA for both Human–Methods and Material–Methods are regularly spaced. The differences among the three regions in the ease of transferring Japanese-style plant operation methods and the stress laid on the strategic importance of those methods are clear.

3. Turning to results, the reversal of Human–Results scores between the NIEs (1.8) on the one hand, and the United States and ASEAN countries (2.9) on the other, is particularly noticeable. As mentioned above (and as shown in Figure 4.7), the identical score for Human–Results for the United States and ASEAN countries is simply the result of averaging the reversed scores of Item ㉑ Ratio of Japanese expatriates and Item ㉓ Position of local managers. In anycase, it is impressive that Japanese electronics assembly plants in the NIEs require far fewer Japanese expatriates and in lower positions (and roles) to realise very high application levels in Material–Methods and Human–Methods.

4. In the electronics assembly industry, the Material–Results scores for the three regions, in contrast with the remaining perspectives, are very close, at 3.0, 3.2 and 3.4 for the NIEs, United States, and ASEAN countries, respectively. This order, however, reflects a reversal of the scores for Item ⑦ Equipment and Item ⑫ Suppliers, between NIEs (lower) and the USA and ASEAN countries (higher) (see Figure 4.7). Everywhere, productivity and quality have to be ensured by company-specific hardware-orientated technologies, even at the plants in the United States that may simply implement the final production processes for CTVs or microwave ovens.

5. In this Four-Perspective Analysis, two points stand out. First, the NIEs' electronics assembly plants are the most receptive towards Japanese production systems. The extended tetragon formed by the NIEs' scores in Figure 4.8 (the highest application scores for Human–Methods/Material–Methods and the lowest for Human–

Table 4.11 Four-perspective evaluation of electronics assembly by country and region

	Methods			Results			Method/Results
	Human (A)	Material (B)	Total (C)	Human (A')	Material (B')	Total (C')	(C)/(C')(%)
NIEs	3.7	3.8	3.7	1.8	3.0	2.5	149.8
Taiwan	3.5	3.7	3.5	2.1	3.3	2.8	125.0
Korea	4.1	4.0	4.1	1	2.5	1.9	215.8
ASEAN	3.2	3.2	3.2	2.9	3.4	3.2	99.5
Malaysia	3.2	3.3	3.2	3.0	3.6	3.3	97.0
Thailand	3.2	3.0	3.1	2.5	3.1	2.9	106.9
Singapore	3.0	3.3	3.1	3.0	3.7	3.4	91.2
USA	2.4	2.4	2.4	2.9	3.2	3.1	77.9

Note: (c) = The average of total value of the Methods as a whole, namely (Methods' total value)/14 (items).
(c') = The average of total value of the Results as a whole, namely (Results' total value)/5 (items).

Results/Materials–Results) is probably the most desirable shape, as the higher methods scores were realised with far fewer Japanese staff (compared to local managers), and with relatively little machinery and equipment made in Japan.

Second, the shape of the tetragon for the ASEAN countries is similar to the same four-sided figure for the United States. This suggests that the managerial and socio-cultural conditions prevailing in the ASEAN region are closer to conditions in the United States than to conditions in the NIEs. Certainly in terms of the difficulty of substituting Japanese expatriates for local managers, the ASEAN countries resembles the United States more than they do the NIEs. However, the essential difference between the ASEAN countries and the United States is that, in the former, there are far fewer Japanese staff to offset the weakness of the position and influence of local managers. So far we cannot discover any exact reasons for this except to suggest that Japanese managers may find ASEAN workers and managers (particularly overseas Chinese) easier to delegate to as they are not so culturally dissimilar.

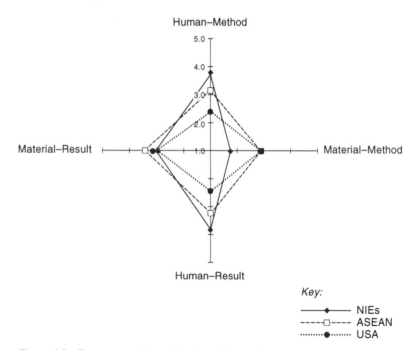

Figure 4.8   Four-perspective evaluation of electronic assembly plants

V   EAST ASIAN HYBRID ELECTRONICS ASSEMBLY FACTORIES

From the above evaluation and analysis, it is clear that Japan's 'hybrid' electronics assembly plants in East Asia represent the Japanese hybrid factories in the region, which is the industry's world production centre. The following explains the types of 'hybrid plants' and their characteristic features.

East Asian Types

NIEs

From the FTZ and 'mini-M' type to specialised and higher added-value products for both export and local markets

1. Progressing from the FTZ model to export bases for higher added-value and intermediate-class products

    The role of FTZs in Taiwan and Korea is diminishing because of rapidly increasing wages, the high exchange rates of the Taiwan and Korean currencies, and trade friction between these countries and the United States. As a result, some Japanese electronics assembly plants have moved away from lower added-value and lower-priced products, to higher added-value and intermediate-class finished products and components. Although FTZ regulations on domestic sales have been relaxed gradually, more than 90 per cent of the items produced in the hybrid factories in East Asia are exported. In that sense, CGK and CFK are typical, and CATw to a lesser extent. CGK and CFK are both headed by Korean CEOs, which is reflected in the very low Human–Results score. However, CGK and CFK still show exceptionally high scores for Human–Methods and Material–Methods. This strength enables the plants to implement a surprisingly large variety of low-volume production ('flexible mass-production'). CGK produces radio-cassettes, microdynamic drivers, headphones, optical pick-ups, motors for VCRs, video heads, and many other items. CFK produces electronics products such as typewriters, calculators, audio products, cash registers, and telephones. (For more about CGK, see the case study in Chapter 5 of this book).

    CATw is another example of flexible production in Taiwan. CATw is also an interesting example of a typical 'phased technology transfer'. On the one hand, CATw has upgraded its Taiwan product lines to intermediate-class items such as displays, stereo sets, CD players, and CTVs, some of which have begun to be exported to Japan. At the same time, CATw transferred the production of its lower-priced products to its ASEAN plants. For example, CATw's Malaysian plant now produces CTVs and has taken over from the Taiwan plant in exporting CTVs to the US market via the Mexican Maquiladora plant. CATw's Malaysian plant also exports audio products to Singapore and elsewhere.

2. From 'mini-M' to specialisation of product lines and regional division of labour in East Asia.

'Mini-M' electronics plants have faced increasing challenges from competitors in ASEAN countries and China as wages have risen, currencies have appreciated and trade policies have been liberalised. In response, these 'mini-M' plants are struggling to reform their styles and profiles. Generally, the NIEs' 'mini-M' plants, located mainly in Taiwan, are seeking to become production bases for intermediate-class product lines, and to shift lower added-value products to the ASEAN region. In this 'phased transfer' of production technologies, a complementary and interdependent network of production is emerging in the East Asian region, including Japan.

CCTw is a typical case (see Chapter 5 below). CETw is a little smaller, but similar (see Abo, 1994b). Since the latter half of the 1980s, such export-orientated products as CTVs, VCRs, air conditioners, refrigerators and washing machines have been transferred to plants in the ASEAN region. In the 1990s, discontinued audio product lines were shifted to Malaysia. While CETw, like CCTw, imports some higher-level products from Japan, it is now surviving with a very low level of results, and with correspondingly low costs. CGTw, a relatively new plant (opened 1984) that specialised in intermediate-class VCRs and imported larger and more sophisticated products from Japan, has recently begun to export more than half of its products to North America (see Chapter 5 below). We have already described the case of CATw in some detail.

ASEAN: From 'Mini-M' to 'New M', or Both?

1. 'New-M' type.

A very interesting and rather unusual change has appeared in the ASEAN region. While the conventional 'mini-M' model plants are somehow surviving, a quite distinct type of plant, the 'new M', has emerged alongside, or is perhaps replacing, the 'mini-M' model. C company operates a 'new M' plant as an export base in Malaysia alongside its 'mini-M' plant. That is, both types of plant are being operated by the same company in the same country. 'New M' plants were set up primarily in Malaysia as export bases to supply the world market in CTVs, VCRs and other consumer electronics. They were designed to take advantage of tax incentives and lower wage costs, similar to the advantages offered in FTZs, in response to the appreciation of the yen in the late 1980s (for CCM, see Chapter 5 below). The significant feature of the 'new M' plants is that their technology has leapfrogged one or two stages over the 'mini-M' plants. The 'new M' plants are highly automated and use almost state-of-the-art machinery that measures up well even against Japanese parent plants.

However, controversy has arisen over whether such a quick fix can work in the long run (see 4.9, Conclusion, below). In Figure 4.9, it is clear that, compared with their 'mini-M' predecessors, 'new M' plants gain higher scores for Material–Results and Human–Results-related items such as equipment, local content, and suppliers, as well as for Group VI (Parent–Subsidiary Relations) items. Conversely, the 'new M' plants also show lower scores for Human–Methods- and Material–Methods-related elements such as job class, multi-skills, wage system and maintenance, and for most of the human- and labour-related groups.

As Table 4.9 shows, CCM is the most representative 'new M' CTV plant. It was established in 1988, adding later a VCR plant (1990) and several other important C company component and consumer electronics plants. CCM makes an interesting comparison with C's 'mini-M' plants, which have been operating since 1965, also in Malaysia (see Chapter 5 below). How can both 'new M' and 'mini-M' electronics consumer goods plants belonging to the same company operate alongside each other in the same country?

Let us look at the background to the plants. The following plants, CGM (established 1988), CBM (established 1989; became a joint venture in 1991), CFM1 (established 1981; gained a new high-speed line in 1991), and CFM2 (established 1990), were all set up or reorganised as 'new M's by mainly newcomers to the ASEAN countries. CGM is the first large-scale CTV plant operated by G company in Asia, and has one of the highest application scores along with CCM. Although G pioneered overseas electronics assembly in the United States and Europe (Abo 1987), it was a latecomer to East Asia (apart from Korea, as mentioned above) and is now vigorously catching up in this region (see Chapter 5 below). CBM, one of the

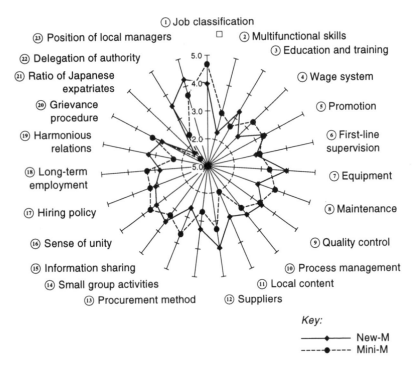

Figure 4.9   Hybrid evaluation of the 'New-M' versus 'Mini-M' in ASEAN: 23 elements

biggest VCR plants but still among the lower-scoring (both for results and methods, so that 'smart' type) electronics assembly plants in ASEAN, was established in 1989 and reorganised in 1991 as a joint venture with a large European electronics company. This was mainly to realise economies of production scale as well as to enjoy technological co-operation from both sides. However, very stiff competition among Japanese and European companies prevails. For example, after company B established a joint venture with a large European company at its Berlin VCR plant, in 1982, the European partner made a joint venture production agreement of its own with H in Singapore. (We could not visit the plant at this time.) CFM1 (CTVs) and CFM2 (VCRs) are similar plants to CBM in terms of 'smart' production. We can include CHS (CTVs), a twin plant of the above VCR joint venture in Singapore, and CDTh (air conditioners) in the 'new M' category, but these are rather loose examples in the sense of 'easy-going' types. Their Human–Results and Material–Results (parts procurement) scores are high in the lowest total application group only.

2. ASEAN 'mini-Ms' type.

The features of ASEAN 'mini-M' plants (Figure 4.9), in contrast to ASEAN's 'new M' plants, are very clear. Scores for most methods-related items are rather higher, while scores for all results-related items are much lower. 'Mini-M' plants in ASEAN countries are 'natural hybrids', in the sense that results-related equipment procurement, as well as parts and employees, reflect local adaptation or orientation (lower application scores). On the other hand, most methods-related items achieved moderate scores, with the important exceptions of education and training, parts procurement, and harmonious labour relations. On the whole, the ASEAN 'mini-M' plants seem to be low-cost ASEAN-type transplants of Japanese production methods. The problem is, however, how 'mini-M' plants can compete with the 'new M' plants, including those in the Japanese domestic market?

CONCLUSION

East Asian Patterns in Hybrid Factories

In all of the above analyses, the most salient feature of the so-called hybrid factories is their ability, with a smaller number of local Japanese managers they have (more local managers), typically to achieve high scores for core human and material items (Groups I and II), subcore items (Group III), and human-related subsystems and conditions (Groups IV and V). If we can call the pattern of high methods but low Human–Results scores the 'East Asian pattern', such a pattern seems to happen almost naturally in the electronics assembly industry in the Asian region. The pattern is perhaps evidence of the greater cultural applicability of Japanese human-related systems to Asia. A high methods (both human and results) ratio can be seen even in the United States, for example in the case of auto makers, though much higher costs are incurred because of the need to maintain a large number of Japanese expatriates (higher Human–Results), large-scale training facilities, supplier systems, and other factors.

The difference between the NIEs and ASEAN countries, however, should not be underestimated.

In the NIEs (Taiwan and Korea), as we have already seen time and again, the typical 'Asian pattern' is very clear, though the performance results of this hybrid pattern do not always meet expectations. Performance in productivity, quality, functions of products, and profitability in local plants is affected by the scale and scope of production, costs of inputs, and so on. This is the result of strategic decision-making by the parent company, and is also influenced by the developmental stage of the region where the plant is located. Japanese electronics assembly bases in the NIEs – Taiwan in particular – are now in transitional phases. The local-orientated 'mini-M' plants need to be upgraded, as mentioned above.

While in the degree of their 'hybridisation', the ASEAN electronics assembly plants lie somewhere between the NIEs and US hybrids, the ASEAN plants have now begun to take a new direction. They are progressing towards the 'new M' type, with special emphasis on Material–Results and, to some extent, Human–Results. As pointed out earlier, this raises the interesting question of whether is it possible for the ASEAN plants to become a new export base for the world market by leapfrogging some steps in the methods-orientated transfer of Japanese techniques, and 'fast-forwarding' to a new stage of highly automated, expatriate manager-led technology.

An optimist could point to exceptionally high scores in such items as education and training, and parts procurement methods, and argue that the ASEAN plants could, in the future, bridge the technological gap. In fact, some Japanese electronics companies in ASEAN countries are trying vigorously to do this, as is a Japanese semiconductor plant in the United States (Abo, 1997). A pessimist, on the other hand, could argue that, because of the lack of a deep-rooted technological base in ASEAN countries, current progress could be undone in the future when Japanese expatriates leave. So far, no obvious conclusions have emerged in either theory or practice.

The topic of ASEAN's ability to adopt Japanese practices is arousing increasing interest and discussion.[2] So far, however, no definite answers have appeared. P. Krugman's recent argument may be related to this question (Krugman, 1994). The ASEAN countries must find some way to bridge the gap created by a results-led technology transfer, which leapfrogged the methods-perspectives of Japanese systems. Later, they must in some way transfer what they missed in methods to their plants. As Krugman pointed out, failure to do this could limit technological development. The competitive edge attained by the leapfrogging may be too superficial, and not adequately connected to ASEAN societies. However, it is probable that the ASEAN plants will try to make up for their weakness in methods by stressing, perhaps to the same level as the

NIEs plants, critical elements such as education and training, including intensive training courses for local employees (as we have seen with CCM), parts procurement methods, and harmonious labour relations (see Figure 4.9).

Let us look at some evidence for this. Recently, the patterns of the hybrid Japanese auto and electronics plants, especially the semiconductor plants in the United States, have begun changing away from the relatively result-orientated patterns of 1989 (see also Abo, 1997) to a methods-orientated pattern. Second, even in Japan, there are now many cases where plants are changing from highly automated, long, straight assembly lines, popular at the peak of the 'bubble economy' in the very early 1990s, to divided, shorter lines supported by higher-multi-skilled operators: for example, the factories of NEC Saitama (mobile telephones), Toshiba Fuchu (PCB and Plant systems), Matsushita Kofu (compressors), Toyota Kyushu and Motomachi, and Honda Sayama.[3]

Future Prospects

Looking at the Japanese electronics assembly industry, it is difficult to say whether Krugman's evaluation of the potential of technological development in East Asia is entirely accurate. His evaluations are based principally on analytical factors such as total factor productivity, an American or Western concept.[4] We can safely point out, however, that the methods-orientated aspects – in particular, the emphasis on training – of the Japanese (corporate) system would produce a subtly different course of industrial development from that in Russia or other non-Asian developing regions on which Krugman's argument depends. The fact that the societies of East Asia resemble Japan's in some ways should be conducive to producing a similar economic model. Although it is still not easy to predict the future of the two hybrid alternatives, the 'mini-M' and the 'new M', it would seem that the 'new M' model, with its strong emphasis on making up for the lack of methods perspectives (caused by emphasising results at the expense of methods to accelerate development) will become a mainstream model in the East Asian region. Factors favouring the 'new M' model include the necessity to build a new world export base outside Japan, the sociocultural affinity between Japan and East Asia, and the suitability of the electronics assembly industry to such a cultural environment.

The result of the 'hollowing-out' of the electronics assembly industry in Japan as a massive amount of production facilities are transferred offshore remains unclear. At any rate, continuous large-scale changes in the whole structure of the industry are inevitable. But will these changes be limited to the assembly of standardised products where the cost of labour and land are the crucial factors? Or will the industry transfer more sophisticated and high value-added products and R&D activities overseas as well? 'New M' plants and the shift of some R&D activities to East Asia in the face of punishing yen fluctuations is an example of progress in the latter direction. If essential technologies also move offshore, the 'phased technology transfer' otherwise known as the 'flying geese' pattern of transfer may not continue, no matter how desirable the broad diffusion of technology may be from the viewpoint of regional economic development in Asia.

During this large structural change, there has also been a systematic division of labour between Japan and East Asia across the whole front of electronics assembly and sales activities in the region (including mainland China), from parts, components and materials, to differentiated products. Throughout East Asia, the electronics assembly industry is developing a region-wide vertical and horizontal division of labour embracing both developed and developing countries. The industry profile is not yet perfectly self-complementary, however. Export markets of finished products are still largely dependent on the United States and Europe. Perhaps the industry will reach out to embrace West Asia or Oceania. Whatever happens, the industry is already undertaking a fascinating experiment never before seen in an industry or region in history.

Notes

* Miss Kim Yanhee, graduate student, University of Tokyo, contributed greatly to the preparation of tables and figures in this section. For the analysis of the Japanese electronics assembly plants in NIEs, see also Chapter 5 in Itagaki (1996).
1. For the discussions related to the stepped development and 'flying geese pattern' in Asian region, see Akamatsu (1956), Kojima (1978), Ozawa (1995), and Cho (1994).
2. One of the few interesting discussions regarding the recent 'new M'-type practices of the Japanese plants in ASEAN countries is that of a 'black box', suggested by Professor S. Yamashita (1994).
3. See, *Nihon Keizai Shinbun* (in Japanese), 4 and 6 January 1996 and 6–8 February 1996; and *The Nikkei Weekly*, 31 October, 1994.
4. In the use of total factor productivity a quantitative evaluation of labour and capital is done. But all other factors which cannot be explicitly explained are included in the 'residual'. According to our model of the Japanese management and production system, the qualitative aspects of labour and capital such as less-demarcation and work-site-orientated flexible ways of work and management are significant factors in deciding competitive advantage of Japanese production technology. These very important factors are relegated to the 'residual' by total factor productivity methods.

Electrical Component Factories

Du-Sop Cho

I INTRODUCTION

A continuation of the previous chapter, this chapter uses the results of field interviews to ascertain the extent to which 'Japanese-style' manufacturing systems are applied in Japanese-affiliated electrical component companies in Asia. Section I introduces the structure of the chapter.

Section II of this chapter briefly describes the distinguishing characteristics of the electronic components industry, including the features that set electronic component plants apart from auto or electrical assembly plants. Today, the Japanese electronic components industry supplies the world. To reach this point, a system able to mass produce items in billions of units while keeping quality at a level measurable in parts per million (ppm) has been needed. Managerial excellence was an essential ingredient in the relentless battle to miniaturise components and expand functionality. Section II examines five characteristics of the electronics component industry.

Focusing on the eighteen companies that were the subject of this study, Section III focuses briefly on Japan's motivation for entry into offshore electronics assembly in Asia, the nature of its entry, and basic business indices. With 300 Japanese-affiliated electronic components manufacturers already in Asia, and numbers still growing because of the strength of the yen, this eighteen-company sample may appear to be too narrow. However, in terms of technological capability, corporate size, dynamic overseas development, methods of overseas management, and other qualitative factors, these firms are clearly representative of Japan's electronic components industry, and are sufficient for observing criteria relating to the application of Japanese-style manufacturing systems.

Section IV outlines of the results of the survey, based on the evaluation model for determining the degree of application. Focusing on the averages of the eighteen companies surveyed, this section shows the characteristics of the overseas subsidiaries and some of their problem areas. It shows how the 'results' and 'methods' of technology transfer differ according to the country chosen, while the Four-Perspective Evaluation illustrates the reasons for these differences.

Section V takes up some of the conclusions reached in Section IV on the characteristics of the electronic components industry, examines some major differences between Japanese parent plants and their overseas offspring, and looks at some of the reasons for these differences.

Tying together loose ends, Section VI compares the results of Asian factories with the conclusions of a report (Abo, 1994) on overseas factories in the USA in an effort to investigate the significance of the Japanese-style production system.

II CHARACTERISTICS OF THE ELECTRONIC COMPONENTS INDUSTRY

Focusing on the companies surveyed, this section raises some points that are unique to Japan's electronic components industry.

Electronic components manufacturing was Japan's first industry to establish overseas production bases. More than half of the companies surveyed in this study established their overseas bases from the latter half of the 1960s to the first half of the 1970s. In the high-growth 1960s, Japan's electronic components industry experienced a major bottleneck caused by a labour shortage and rapid wage rises.

In contrast to the electronic components industry of the 1990s, that of the 1960s and 1970s was labour intensive. The labour force demanded young female workers in large numbers. Then, unable to sustain this requirement, the industry simply abandoned female-based assembly. Japan simply could not support a large female labour force and eventually reached a crisis in terms of corporate growth. In order to deal with this problem, some managers went as far as to build hotel-like dormitories to lure workers from distant parts of the country, a strategy that was doomed to failure.

In the latter half of the 1960s, interest in cheap foreign labour grew, and the Newly Industrialising Economies (NIEs) such as Taiwan established free trade zones (FTZ) in an effort to attract multinationals. Since Japan needed a source of cheap labour, and overseas countries welcomed employment opportunities and industrial growth, Japanese electronic components producers shifted rapidly to offshore production, a trend that has continued into the 1990s. Until the 1970s, the Japanese factories in other Asian countries were mainly branches concentrating on assembly. Generally, they were export bases for shipping products back to Japan and to other developed countries. However, the emergence of local consumer electronics companies and the arrival of Japanese assembly companies began to create local markets. It is estimated that, in the 1990s 70 per cent of Asia's total production is sold to Asian consumers, including the Chinese. This reflects a major shift in overseas companies' strategic position since the 1970s; the trend to local sales indicates the emergence of an Asian economic sphere. National aspirations play an important role in this. Within Asia itself there is very little regional division of labour in the electronics component industry, a point that sets the industry apart from the auto assembly or auto parts industry.

In contrast to the auto parts industry, many electronic components companies are independent-minded, and their ties with the assembly companies are not necessarily permanent. Accordingly, few electronic components companies enter overseas markets together with an assembly company. Most elect to establish independent overseas electronic components assembly bases.

On the other hand, the Asian region has a truly competitive industrial structure, and inter-company rivalry, especially between Japanese-affiliated firms is growing. The competitive structure is heightened by trends among the assemblers' customers. During the recent yen appreciation, Japanese-affiliated firms in Asia stepped up efforts to source their materials, except for a few key parts, from local Asian suppliers. When the Japanese-affiliated Asian companies decide on a supplier, they do not base their decision on the procurement history of their Japanese company, but on the basis of cost, quality and delivery (CQD). Unlike auto parts, electronic components, whose specifications are often generic, can be marketed to a wide range of customers, provided they are not too bulky. For firms able to meet the needs of the assemblers, rapid growth is virtually assured. If a firm cannot meet these needs, however, it faces a dilemma. As long as the Asian market as a whole continues to expand, competition within the industry will not be too severe. In future, if China should become a major player, and if the market continues to grow steadily in the long term, it is likely that competition among individual companies will intensify. In that case, the success of overseas subsidiaries will depend on the extent to which they can apply Japanese-style manufacturing systems, and on their ability to perform *kaizen* activities. Companies that do not recognise this and simply pursue low labour costs will probably lose their competitiveness in the long term.

Compared with other industries, the electronic components industry is being 'hollowed out' on the labour and technology fronts.

Until the surge of the yen in 1985, Japan suffered very little 'technology drain.' Any production lost from Japan involved low-grade goods rather than strategic components or production expertise. Moreover, the domestic economy was booming and impervious to challenges from overseas production. Then, between the latter half of the 1980s and the first half of the 1990s, domestic demand waned, and increasingly production was transferred to overseas factories. As the production of strategic goods and accompanying manufacturing technology were transferred overseas, concerns arose that this could lead to the 'de-industrialisation' or 'hollowing out' of Japan's labour and technology. Although there is no evidence that any of the companies in this survey shed jobs because of overseas production, their satellite factories in Japan did experience employment losses. Some of the companies closed branch factories in regional areas, and began to consolidate production. In some instances, regional economies suffered, or the rate of technological improvement slowed (Seki, 1993).

Although it is difficult to imagine a technology drain in a country such as Japan, Japanese company headquarters, which are the main repositories of the company's design and innovation skills could decline in prestige if high-value-added jobs continue to be transferred overseas at the current rate and no new products or process technologies are created at home. The international strategy of DCTh (see Table 4.12), 85 per cent of whose production is now based offshore, is interesting in this regard. If offshore shift is interpreted as deindustrialisation, the company is the most deindustrialised company surveyed here. However, it has not reduced its domestic production, and neither has it shed any jobs. Rather, the company has simply expanded, on both the domestic and international fronts. The whole operation is still led by its Japanese parent, the source of its innovation which shows it how to capitalise on overseas production to expand business. The company chose a good time to begin overseas production and followed up with a series of innovations to avoid the effects of deindustrialisation.

Some new overseas factories have emerged in East Asia with the same level of production facilities as their Japanese parents. Although only a fraction of the surveyed firms were affected by this trend, it shows the need for a new approach to technology transfer and factory management systems. Until recently, labour-intensive production policies focusing on labour management and quality control were sufficient. Now, however, with local factories competing with plants in Japan in automation and equipment, new comparative advantages have to be sought, such as maintenance of machines and facilities. Sophisticated facilities and the automation or computerisation of inspection and adjustment processes improve product quality and shorten start-up times. However, servicing and maintaining these complex systems can present a major challenge. To

Table 4.12   Outline of the surveyed factories

Plant	DAK1	DAK2	DIK	DJK	DATw	DJTw
Location	Korea	Korea	Korea	Korea	Taiwan	Taiwan
Start of operation	1987.7	1970.8	1973.7	1973.12	1970.8	1968.8
Ownership	JV (95%)	JV (50%)	Wholly-owned	Wholly-owned	JV (50%)	JV (80%)
Paid-in Capital (¥)	10 bil	4.2 bil	846 mil	1.1 bil	2 bil	1.3 bil
No. of employees	802	3370	864	669	1274	1983
Japanese expats.	22	3	5	6	4	6
Japanese employees (%)	2.7	0.09	0.58	0.90	0.31	0.90
Main products	Micro printers, video heads, tuners, keyboards	Switches, video heads, hybrid IC, volume controls	Inductors, condensers, registers, hybrid IC	Ferrite cores, ceramic condensers, coils	Tuners, modulators, switches, keyboards	Soft ferrite, condensers, coils, magnetic products
Total production units	(n.a.)	530 mil	7.7 mil	(n.a.)	340 mil	6.3 bil
Sales (¥)	7.2 bil	30.1 bil	8.9 bil	6.7 bil	10 bil	21.1 bil
Export sales (%)	70	0.30	100	90	10	39
Main market	Japan	Korea, Japan	Korea, Japan	Japan, Taiwan	Taiwan, Japan	Japan, Hong Kong
Turnover rate (Mon.)	0.83	1.70	2.27	2.50	3.51	3.10
Direct:Indirect	74:26	75:25	65:35	71:29	57:43	77:23
Male:Female	34:66	32:68	53:47	40:60	36:64	30:70
Average age of employees	24	24.5	26.1	25.9	28	30.4

Table 4.12 (continued)

Plant	DKTw	DDS	DES	DGS	DBM	DFM
Location	Taiwan	Singapore	Singapore	Singapore	Malaysia	Malaysia
Start of operation	1968.8	1972.12	1976.8	1987.7	1989.1	1990.1
Ownership	Wholly-owned	Wholly-owned	Wholly-owned	Wholly-owned	Wholly-owned	JV (80%)
Paid-in Capital (¥)	1.2 bil	270 mil	(n.a.)	1.5 bil	5 bil	400 mil
No. of employees	1040	1170	650	1300	350	280
Japanese expats.	4	34	15	32	7	4
Japanese employees (%)	0.38	2.90	2.30	2.50	2	1.40
Main products	LC filters	Ceramic condensers	Semiconductors, ASIC	Optical pick-ups, drives	Semiconductors	Wire harnesses
Total production units	150 mil	(n.a.)	18 bil	(n.A.)	720 mil	240 mil
Sales (¥)	3.7 bil	24.1 bil	31.6 bil	33.5 bil	(n.a.)	1 bil
Export sales (%)	85	50	50	(n.a.)	100	20
Main market	Japan, Europe	Malaysia, Thailand USA		ASEAN	USA, Singapore	Singapore
Turnover rate (Mon.)	3	2	1		3	5
Direct:Indirect	79:21	59:41	80:20	(n.a.)	95:5	83:17
Male:Female	14:86	29:74	60:40	(n.a.)	45:55	12:88
Average age of employees	29.7	29	28	(n.a.)	25	26

Table 4.12 (continued)

Plant	DJM	DLM	DCTh	DDTh	DHTh	DLTh
Location	Malaysia	Malaysia	Thailand	Thailand	Thailand	Thailand
Start of operation	1989.1	1973.9	1980.8	1989.4	1988.5	1990.3
Ownership	Wholly-owned	Wholly-owned	JV (93.2%)	Wholly-owned	Wholly-owned	JV (93%)
Paid-in Capital (¥)	1.85 bil	360 mil	29.5 bil	1.8 bil	360 mil	10 bil
No. of employees	2000	1309	18 712	2750	1267	1950
Japanese expats.	29	8	167	31	9	18
Japanese employees (%)	1.45	0.60	0.90	1.10	0.70	0.90
Main products	Electronic components	Semiconductors	Miniature bearings, electronic components	Ceramic filters	Electronic components	Colour picture tubes
Total production units	(n.a.)	264 mil	(n.a.)	(n.a.)	2.1 mil	3.2 mil
Sales (¥)	10 bil	1.8 bil	4.8 bil	14 bil	4.8 bil	(n.a.)
Export sales (%)	40	100	(n.a.)	80	(n.a.)	100
Main market	Singapore, USA	Asia, USA	Japan, USA	Malaysia, Japan	Asia	Singapore, HK
Turnover rate (Mon.)	3	1	1	2–3	(n.a.)	2
Direct:Indirect	75:25	(n.a.)	70:30	85:15	80:20	87:13
Male:Female	20:80	(n.a.)	17:83	1:99	26:74	65:35
Average age of employees	22	22	24.5	19	21.4	(n.a.)

offset the enormous depreciation costs accompanying major capital investment in advanced systems, overseas factories must improve their operating rates and be better managed. Staff need to be trained to inspect, maintain and improve the equipment and machinery used for production. This takes time and money. In addition, the high labour turnover in the East Asian region can thwart a company's best intentions to improve its personnel line-up. If key persons can simply walk away after receiving advanced technical training, the plant can make little progress. With these factors to contend with, the operating rates of many factories established in the 1990s fell because of inadequate maintenance.

To upgrade their facilities successfully, the Japanese East Asian hybrids must revise their training from the ground up. While these companies relied on on-the-job technical training in the past, there is a limit to how successfully automation- and microcomputer-based technologies can be taught by senior staff in the workplace. It is now considered necessary to provide short-term 'off-the-job' training to staff responsible for maintenance, adjustment and inspection. However, as we shall see in Section V, this is not always being done.

When an electronic components firm establishes an overseas factory, it systematically applies the experience accumulated through existing subsidiaries. A new plant in Malaysia or Thailand for example is supported not only by a direct flow of resources from Japan, but also by the past experience and knowledge, products and production processes accumulated in markets such as South Korea, Taiwan, and Singapore. These are included in the same package as the resources from the Japanese parent company. While it is important to post personnel to oversee the production transfer between headquarters and the overseas plant, it is still more important to ensure that the overseas plant maximises the technology transfer. This is why managers talk of 'the art of technology transfer'. Japanese companies that have set up their second overseas plants in Malaysia and Thailand report that past business experience in the Asian NIEs speeded up the establishment of their plants. Companies without this past experience were forced to rely on trial and error. For example, Company 'DJM' which first entered the Far East Asian market in the latter half of the 1980s, was still suffering from inconsistent quality and poor operating rates in the early 1990s. In contrast, 'DJM's' main rivals who were other Japanese-affiliated firms had developed effective management systems backed by years of experience, expanded their product lines, and continued to upgrade their technology. According to a manager at 'DJM', his company tried to make up for lack of practical offshore experience and to catch up to more experienced competitors by 'compressed learning':

producing a wide range of products using the most advanced facilities. But while basic operating procedures may be comparatively easy to learn or transfer, the ability to respond to trouble and change is directly related to the length of operating experience at factory-floor level. Company 'DJM' demonstrated that this kind of ability cannot be acquired overnight.

III OUTLINE OF THE SURVEYED COMPANIES

Table 4.12 contains a brief outline of the eighteen overseas factories that were the subject of this study. Companies 'DAK1' to 'DKTw' in Korea and Taiwan received on-site visits in August 1992. Companies 'DDS' to 'DLTh' were visited in August 1993. The products produced by fourteen companies included ferrite cores, capacitors, tuners, and other electronic components. In addition, the study included three semiconductor plants, and one colour picture tube (CPT) plant. By the 1970s, some nine companies were producing overseas, and this doubled after 1980. Of the nine firms that set up overseas production in the 1980s, eight established operations when the Plaza Accord of 1985 began to propel the yen upwards. This was the beginning of the second wave of overseas production.

The countries targeted for overseas production included South Korea (four firms), Taiwan (three firms), Singapore (three firms), Malaysia (four firms), and Thailand (four firms). Thus, production bases were spread fairly evenly, making it meaningful to compare the subsidiaries in one country with those in another through the Four-Perspective Evaluation featured here.

Sixteen of the eighteen overseas production subsidiaries were wholly-owned companies. The two exceptions were both subsidiaries of Company 'A' ('A' is a parent company of DAK1, DAK2 and DATw) which has joint ventures with large local companies. In addition to a policy tendency to use joint ventures to enter foreign markets, 'A' subscribed to the historic view of Japanese firms contemplating overseas operations that their mission was to promote the local economy and facilitate technology transfer. Company 'A's' managers believed that instead of a go-it-alone policy, a joint venture was the most effective way to achieve those ends. The other sixteen joint ventures mainly employed silent local partners who played no real management role; restrictions on the percentage of ownership tend to encourage the establishment in Asia of joint ventures with locals. The companies in this study were all firmly under Japanese control, and Japanese business approaches and practices were therefore easily implemented. On the other hand, among overseas subsidiaries there have been many cases where management clashes have prevented the application of Japanese-style production methods.

Among the eighteen subsidiaries surveyed, wide disparities were noted in amounts of capital investment, ranging from DDS's 270 million Japanese yen, to DCTh's 29.5 billion yen. Compared to labour-intensive assembly plants, production plants for CPTs, semiconductors and precision components require a much higher level of initial investment. In particular, the production plants established in the latter half of the 1980s boasted the same standards as those in Japan, and reflected a correspondingly large initial investment cost (companies DAK1, DCTh and DLTh, for example). The point to be noted here is not the scale of investment, but rather the accumulated investment, which exceeds the initial investment in almost every case. For example, although DGS's capital was a modest 1.5 billion, over a period of six years the company's accumulated investment was ten times this amount. Since its establishment in 1973, DLM conducted three major reinvestments, transforming itself into a capital-intensive production plant. Our knowledge of these reinvestments, however, is limited. Although data related to the inflow and outflow of direct investments in ASEAN countries is relatively easy to obtain, reinvestment data is difficult to interpret accurately. A close look at the investment pattern of Japanese-affiliated firms in Asia reveals that the initial investments are not followed by larger ones, but by numerous smaller investments as the firm adjusts to market trends. As additional investment in many cases exceeds the capital of the subsidiary, the contributions made by Japanese multinationals may in fact be far larger than formal statistics indicate. Surveys such as this require data that can reveal the actual levels of investment.

The survey included both large firms such as DCTh (almost 20 thousand employees) and small firms such as DFM (280 employees).

DCTh is Thailand's largest Japanese-affiliated firm. It has a complete production system covering everything from materials to processing and assembly of finished products. More than 80 per cent of total production and employees of this company group are located overseas, the highest proportion among the companies surveyed. The composition of the employees by sex at each of the eighteen companies favours females disproportionately. Although the high ratio of female workers is typical of assembly processes in general, it is noteworthy that the ratio of females is smaller in Japanese-affiliated NIEs plants than in ASEAN ones. While around 60 per cent of the work force in Japanese-affiliated NIEs plants is female, the figure is over 70 per cent for ASEAN factories. When the

NIEs experienced labour shortages and an accompanying escalation in wages, they upgraded their manufacturing processes, which boosted the ratio of men, mainly in R&D and maintenance. This is also supported by data on the ratio of direct and indirect workers: the ratio of indirect workers is higher for Asian NIEs.

Total production refers to the annual amount of production at each company. This figure is consistently in the hundreds of millions. A large number of production units is an industry characteristic, since many electronic components, such as coils, capacitors and semiconductor elements, are marketed as sets. Another industry characteristic is strict quality management. If just one unit is defective, the entire set is flawed. Japanese consumer electronics makers owe their international predominance to parts and components makers for producing items in the hundreds of millions while keeping quality assurance at the parts per million (ppm) level. The Japanese-style production system, which involves everyone in the plant to achieve this level of quality, has clearly proved itself. But to create the same system in overseas factories remains a challenge. Plants in free trade zones (FTZs) export all their production to qualify for the benefits available to plants in such zones. These benefits apply not only to direct exports, but also to indirect exports. As long as a manufacturer assembles a product into a set for export, the product counts as an export, enabling the manufacturer to receive tax benefits even if the product is not directly exported. A look at the principal export markets reveals that the supply of offshore products to Japan and other Asian countries has grown steadily. Since 1985, business penetration into Asia has increased. As income levels throughout Asia, including China, have grown, the products produced in Asian factories have begun to be consumed in Asia. The huge demand created by Asia's rapid development is now being met by local Asian plants, which are also sending increasing numbers of exports to Japan.

Looking at the average age of employees, Korean plants have the youngest workers in the Asian NIEs. Taiwan and Singapore both have workers with an average age of 28 or more, but the South Korean average is 24 to 25 years old. The older average ages of employees in Taiwan and Singapore are caused by recent pressures in the labour market resulting from rapid economic growth exacerbated by the distaste by younger workers for manufacturing jobs. In Taiwanese subsidiaries, the older age of employees reflects revisions to that country's labour laws.

After Taiwan implemented a retirement plan in fiscal year 1985, the labour turnover (especially female) decreased, as only workers aged over 50 with at least fifteen years of work experience qualified for the plan.

Accordingly, the average age of the workforce at the production plants rose sharply. In Singapore, which has a serious shortage of general labour, foreign operators occupy 40 per cent of operator jobs. A turnover of foreign workers is generally expected every two years. While this can be an advantage for assembly-orientated plants where fresh young workers are needed, at automated and computerised plants, where accumulated knowledge and experience count, high labour turnover is a major disadvantage.

The low average ages in both Malaysia and Thailand are a result of the high availability of labour in both countries, and the relatively recent appearance of overseas businesses. However, since Malaysia has attracted much direct investment as a result of its favourable investment environment, pressure could build in its labour market. The average age of workers in parent company plants in Japan has passed 35, and the average age at ancillary factories in Japan has also increased sharply. In Japan, where factory workforces are ageing, general electronic component assembly plants which requires dexterous hands and good eyesight is losing its viability.

At 1–3 per cent, the monthly labour turnover in Japan's Asian subsidiaries is high in relation to the parent factories in Japan. Compared with local or other foreign firms, however the rate is low. The effect of labour turnover on local business management is re-examined in Sections IV and V. Since local workers seek to advance by job hopping, the Japanese system of internal promotion and job security may not be entirely suitable for local conditions. However, any overseas plants practising Japanese-style production and with some degree of history behind them usually succeed in retaining their key personnel. But as vital personnel are often scouted by other Japanese businesses setting up in Asia or by other multinational (including Korean and Taiwanese) firms, the problem of retaining trained personnel has become a major issue.

IV SURVEY SUMMARY

Table 4.13 shows through the application scores, the extent to which Japanese-style production is applied. Where scores were low, simple explanations based on interviews have been provided. While the details of the individual categories are delayed until Section V, this section will explore the background to the evaluations resulting in the scores. As mentioned in Chapter 1 of this book, when Japanese-based companies establish overseas subsidiaries, they attempt to transfer the production

Table 4.13   Application–adaptation evaluation form

	Korea	Taiwan	Singapore	Malaysia	Thailand	Average
① Job classification	5.0	5.0	4.0	4.8	5.0	4.8
② Multifunctional skills	2.3	2.7	2.7	2.5	1.8	2.4
③ Education and training	3.5	3.0	3.3	3.0	3.8	3.3
④ Wage system	4.0	3.7	2.7	3.5	2.8	3.3
⑤ Promotion	3.3	4.3	3.0	3.3	3.0	3.4
⑥ First-line supervisor	3.3	3.3	3.3	2.8	3.3	3.2
⑦ Equipment	4.3	4.0	5.0	4.8	4.5	4.5
⑧ Maintenance	3.0	3.3	3.7	3.0	3.0	3.2
⑨ Quality control	3.5	3.7	3.3	3.3	3.3	3.4
⑩ Process management	3.8	3.7	3.7	3.3	3.5	3.6
⑪ Local content	4.3	2.3	3.7	3.3	3.3	3.4
⑫ Suppliers	4.8	3.7	3.7	4.0	4.3	4.1
⑬ Procurement method	3.3	3.3	3.3	3.5	2.5	3.2
⑭ Small-group activities	3.0	3.3	3.0	3.5	2.0	3.0
⑮ Information sharing	3.3	4.0	3.0	3.3	3.5	3.4
⑯ Sense of unity	3.8	3.3	4.0	3.0	3.8	3.6
⑰ Hiring policy	3.3	3.3	2.7	3.0	3.5	3.2
⑱ Long-term employment	3.3	3.3	2.7	3.0	3.5	3.2
⑲ Harmonious labour relations	3.8	4.3	3.3	3.8	3.0	3.6
⑳ Grievance procedure	3.0	3.3	3.0	3.3	3.5	3.2
㉑ Ratio of Japanese expatriates	1.5	1.0	2.7	1.8	1.3	1.6
㉒ Delegation of authority	3.5	3.0	3.0	4.0	1.0	3.5
㉓ Position of local managers	3.5	3.0	4.3	4.0	1.3	3.8

system as used in Japan, on the grounds that the Japanese system can provide a competitive advantage. Part of the reason, however, may be that Japanese managers are simply comfortable with their system.

However, the Japanese system does not remain completely intact when transferred overseas. The average degree of application (the scores) for the twenty-three items (see Table 4.13) shows that the Japanese system is applied at about only half of its Japanese level. Evidently, the system does not travel well across national borders. Although transfers are continuing well in certain categories, in other categories no progress seems likely even in the distant future. We shall briefly examine the reasons for this, looking at both Japanese and overseas perceptions of the problem, and looking ahead to the conclusion of this chapter.

The three main obstacles in applying the Japanese system overseas are:

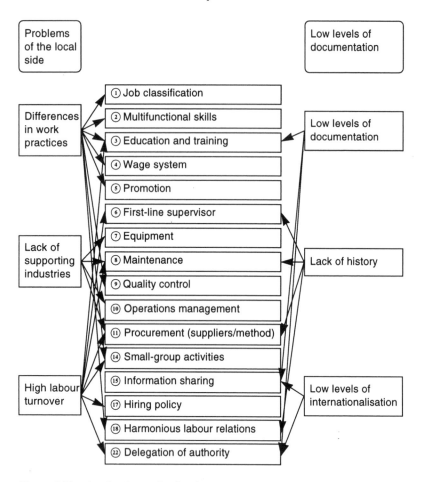

Figure 4.10   Application evaluation form

(i) differences in work practices; (ii) lack of supporting industries overseas; and (iii) high labour turnover.

As shown in Figure 4.1, these three factors have wide influence on the twenty-three categories used for evaluating the degree of application. Looking first to differences in work practices, we can identify three main areas of divergence: (i) limitations in applying the concept of egalitarianism in the workplace, (ii) difficulties in sharing information within the organisation through technological or information circles; and (iii) difficulty in maintaining objective performance evaluations.

The main elements obstructing the implementation of egalitarianism in the workplace are the emphasis placed on educational backgrounds overseas, and the existence of more than one culture within a country. Promotions within the company, career paths, and standards for wage calculations are not based on ability, but on educational background and race, making it difficult for staff to be united and dynamic. While many firms have tried hard to apply the principle of egalitarianism, few have succeeded. The vagueness of job descriptions and unilateral decisions by management to rotate jobs also cause problems. There is a tendency too to treat knowledge acquired through training in Japan or from other outside sources as a personal asset instead of sharing it and this greatly hinders the transfer of technology. As long as work practices exist that prevent workers from being dynamic and united, it will remain difficult for overseas subsidiaries to realise quality levels comparable with those in Japan.

Let us now look at the high labour turnover rate. In every Japanese-affiliated firm surveyed, the high rate of labour turnover seemed to be one of the greatest concerns. First, at the operator level, if a worker quits after acquiring certain experience, productivity must drop. Even in simple operations, experience contributes to higher productivity. Small-group activities are also affected by high labour turnover. Unless a certain amount of technical knowledge is shared by the members over some given period, no real progress can be expected. At one company, the turnover was so high it was not worth the effort to remember anyone's name and it is obviously very difficult to expect results from small-group activities at a company with such a high staff turnover.

However, the most serious problem is the departure of specialists with knowledge specific to that firm. Not only is training wasted, but one of the great pillars of Japanese personnel policies for developing workplace leaders by promoting promising staff up through the ranks is rendered inoperative. The high labour turnover reflects a loose relationship between local staff and the company, or the 'unJapanese' attitudes of local staff to the company. The Japanese are not entirely blameless, however. An egalitarian workplace is not particularly attractive to talented individuals, and does not encourage them to stay. The tendency of the Japanese not to articulate their thinking clearly is another reason for the high turnover. The career opportunities for talented individuals should be clearly defined, and in return, commitments should be extracted from high fliers. This is one way to reduce the labour turnover, though very few Japanese firms seem to realise this.

The lack of supporting industries in Asia is another drain on the overseas firms. Since half or more of the parts and materials are supplied from Japan, the just-in-time (JIT) parts procurement system can never be applied adequately. In addition, the quality and delivery times for parts and materials supplied locally may not be satisfactory. This presents no problem in countries such as Malaysia and Thailand where local suppliers hardly exist and where other Japanese-affiliated firms are the suppliers, but in countries such as Korea and Taiwan where the factories are supplied by locals, the expectations of the Japanese firms and the performance of the local suppliers may not coincide. Although many Japanese-affiliated firms provide technical guidance for their local suppliers, if the suppliers suffer from a high labour turnover as well, the technical guidance may be insufficient. For Asian countries keen to develop their industrial infrastructure, the cultivation of competitive local suppliers can be a strategic goal in itself. But even in places such as Taiwan and South Korea, which have supposedly acquired a certain level of technology, considerable room for improvement remains. Doing business with Japanese firms should provide a good opportunity to learn Japanese management practices, if only for the sake of maintaining the relationship with the Japanese firm. But even at this level, results so far have been quite limited. Japanese managers blame the high turnover of key personnel as well as the 'short-termism' of local managers, and the immaturity of the management system. This problem needs to be studied in greater detail.

The very high score for dependency on Japanese production facilities (4.5) reflects a lack of local supporting industries. With its precision, durability and quality, Japanese-made equipment should give Japanese-affiliated firms a distinct competitive advantage. But managers must also take into account high procurement costs resulting from the strong yen, and consider the recipient country's accumulated trade deficit with Japan as a result of importing capital goods.

Now let us turn to some problems on the Japanese side. First, there is the peculiar Japanese characteristic of low documentation in education and training. As well as a lack of training manuals, there are few written work standards, and few written guidelines on management duties, decision-making and explicit policy and rules in such areas as strategies for subsidiaries. (Perhaps this reluctance to create documentation indicates that Japan is comparatively poor at establishing rules.)

Japanese companies' comparatively low reliance on rule books can also be a strength that allows them to be more dynamic and to rally staff (workplace orientation). Not clearly defining the responsibilities of individuals during on-the-job technical training and enhancement programmes, for example, has proved to be extremely effective. But the problem is not so much formal rules and manuals, or the lack of them, but how the Japanese system, which places supreme importance on continuous efforts to improve standards, can produce the best results in an overseas market where thinking and attitudes are different. Some firms try to adapt the Japanese system to the available technology and local environment. For example, some factories with a high level of mechanisation and device control reinforced their factory off-the-job training in an effort to develop maintenance and molding specialists. Other companies produced manuals and ran proper manual-based on-the-job training programmes. However, ambiguity remains in company management. There is no organised apparatus for handling everyday staff complaints and grievances, and no objective guidelines for appraising the business performance of subsidiaries or their Japanese managers. Since the move by Japanese companies into Asia in the mid- and late 1980s was generally an alarm response to the strengthening yen and not a carefully planned strategy, there was little time to produce manuals and rules for management systems, production transfer, and performance evaluation. The vagueness of management methods should gradually lessen as the new arrivals adapt to their environment, acquire experience in transferring technology, and clarify the strategic position of their new subsidiaries.

The inexperience of the workforce in the overseas factories is another issue. An examination of the categories comprising the Japanese-style production system reveals that each category requires a long period to become firmly entrenched. In particular, management systems (for example quality control and processing control), personnel structures (foremen, maintenance specialists), and small-group activities require time to become well established. Therefore, even if current rates of application are not high, there is a good possibility they will increase in the near future. Of course, a rise in work experience does not necessarily result in a corresponding improvement in rates of application. As local staff become more experienced, however, the Japanese system should become better established.

Japanese parent companies have been slow to internationalise, particularly when it comes to developing foreign language ability. The head offices of Japanese-affiliated firms in the Far East, where English is the lingua franca, are struggling to surmount the language barrier. While everyday communication does not seem to be a problem, conveying the more subtle nuances of advanced technical training or management duties can be extremely difficult. Another problem is the lack of objective standards for evaluating the performance of overseas factories, and the performance of Japanese staff members dispatched overseas. Those playing the main role in the Asian plants, the expatriate managers, are not facing the language issue squarely.

Since the Japanese-style production system is not geared to producing manuals, overseas managerial systems must rely on time-consuming implementation of on-the-job training based on person-to-person contact. This forces the motivation and diligence of individual Japanese managers to play a key role in the transfer of the Japanese system. Japanese multinationals must consider how to motivate their field managers and devise incentives to encourage them.

Four-Perspective Evaluation

In this section we analyse the behaviour of different countries by using Four-Perspective Evaluation (see Table 4.14).

1. The Taiwanese plants focused on transferring methods rather than results for both human and material resources. Compared with plants in other countries, those in Taiwan had the highest application scores for Japanese-style production. Human and material resources were assimilated well into Taiwanese plants, the first to be established in Japan's moves to overseas production. The Taiwanese factories are now technologically and managerially strong enough to be a successful cornerstone in their parent companies' global strategy.
2. In terms of human resources, the South Korean plants resembled Taiwanese plants in their emphasis on transfer of methods. In the area of material resources, however, transfer of results were more predominant. The reason for the higher scores for results in transferring materials lay in the relatively higher number of FTZs in South Korea compared to Taiwan. In addition, the lack of Japanese-affiliated materials and parts makers in Taiwan encouraged dependence on imports from Japan. Another reason for high results scores in materials transfers lay in the absence of government regulations regarding local content in components. A further reason is the difficulty of Japanese-affiliated firms entering an industrial system based on a vertical *zaibatsu* system. Furthermore, the low scores in the Human–Results category were caused by a large number of joint ventures, and relatively low numbers of Japanese staff.
3. For Singapore and Malaysia, transfer of results for both human and material resources scored higher than transfer of methods. This appears to be the result of a high labour turnover and the rush to set up highly mechanised and automated factories. In particular, the factories

Table 4.14   Four-perspective evaluation

Korea				Malaysia		
	Human	*Material*			*Human*	*Material*
Methods	3.5	3.3		*Methods*	2.4	3.3
Results	2.5	4.5		*Results*	3.3	3.9
Taiwan				**Thailand**		
	Human	*Material*			*Human*	*Material*
Methods	3.4	3.4		*Methods*	3.4	2.9
Results	2.0	3.3		*Results*	2.8	4.0
Korea						
	Human	*Material*				
Methods	3.1	3.4				
Results	3.5	4.1				

established in the latter half of the 1980s were supplied with new equipment almost up to the level of the Japanese parent plants. The local workforce was still inadequately trained, however, and Japanese managers were needed to manage the factories. In the future, growing work experience among locals should push scores for transfer of methods ahead of scores for transfer of results.

4.   The Thai factories are similar to those in South Korea, with relatively higher scores in the Human–Methods and Material–Results categories. The success of DCTH influenced the high methods scores in the area of human resources. DCTH employs nearly 20 thousand workers at its Thai factory, but only 167 (0.9 per cent) of these were dispatched from Japan. Fully a quarter of management positions in the factory's forty divisions are held by locals. The trend toward localisation is still continuing. However, with the exception of DCTH company, few local managers understand and practice Japanese-style business management.

In the following section, we select a few items among the twenty-three categories, along with the results of interview surveys.

V   COMPARING CATEGORIES

Job Rotation

The average score of 2.4 for ② Job Rotation is the lowest in any category apart from l₂₁ Ratio of Japanese expatriates. This low score suggests that jobs are fixed, in negation of our earlier assertion that occupational categories are not clearly defined. This score discourages the idea that rotating employees among jobs is the most successful method of strengthening overseas production. While limiting the work range of individual employees enables them to acquire specialised knowledge, it also weakens their ability to cope with problems or change. In particular, in factories that have become highly mechanised and automated, operators should be trained to carry out simple machine maintenance, as a high operating rate boosts productivity. But there is still a considerable gap between such expectations and reality. For example, at DLM, the operators are expected to maintain the machines themselves without the help of technicians. For closely linked processes, operators are expected to be familiar with at least three jobs, though this has been hard to put into practice. Local employees are generally unwilling to perform a wider range of work without financial incentives. In addition, workers tend to see horizontal changes as the equivalent of demotion, which also hinders job rotation. In this respect, however, the Thai plants appear to be different, perhaps because of the more communal style of human relationships in Thailand. There, the workplace supervisor is not just a supervisor of the workplace. The supervisor/subordinate relationship is based on mutual personal commitment transcending any official relationship. Because transferring either the supervisor or subordinate to another factory destroys the informal personal relationship between them, both sides object to the transfer. Furthermore, in female-dominated and manual labour-orientated factories, rotating operators among jobs is viewed negatively.

Education and Training

The average score of 3.3 for ③ Education and training was slightly below the overall average of 3.4. Of the five countries covered in the survey, Thailand boasted the greatest enthusiasm for education, though staff at all of the eighteen overseas factories were motivated to learn.

First, it should be noted that in ASEAN countries, educational exchange between affiliated factories is common. Singapore is especially active in receiving training groups. Company 'B' (a parent company of DBM) Malaysian factory staff are all trained in Singapore, and Company 'E'(the parent company of DES) uses its Singapore factory to train staff for its new plant in China. While 'E's' Chinese engineers were originally trained in Japan, since fiscal year 1992, some have begun training at 'E's' Singapore subsidiary. The engineers dispatched from China to Singapore for two to three months report that the training was much better than that offered in Japan. They faced a language barrier in Japan, and the level of the technology presented at the Japanese parent plant was too high. At the Singapore plant, the trainees did not learn as much technology, but they could communicate in their mother tongue (Chinese) and directly apply in China the technology that they studied. Company 'E' began using its factory in Singapore for training when production began to be transferred to China when the Singapore plants lost their competitiveness. Cases involving transfer of production because of differences in technology levels between regions, and accompanying changes in the country where training takes place, will increase in the future. At Japanese plants, where very sophisticated items are produced and factories are highly automated, there is often a lack of specific knowledge of the products produced at overseas factories. In addition, the relationship between operator and machinery attenuates as automation levels rise. These conditions make Japanese factories unsuitable for training overseas employees. The Asian NIEs factories are ideally suited to take the place of Japanese plants in this respect.

Company 'A'(the parent company of DAK1, DAK2 and DATw) also shifted production from its Taiwan plant to its Malaysian plant. When the Malaysian plant was started up, the Taiwanese technicians were also moved and put in charge of technology. When production is shifted between factories, personnel are often also transferred. The role of such Asian NIEs as Taiwan and Singapore as producers of mass-produced goods diminished with the rising cost of labour in these countries. However, Taiwan and Singapore found a new role as important repositories of accumulated knowledge, and bases for training staff for Chinese and ASEAN plants. Company 'E's' activities are especially interesting here. Company 'E' uses its Singapore plant as a training centre for its young Japanese engineers, since the automation in Japanese factories prevents engineers learning about production processes, flows and technologies. 'E's' semi-automated Singapore plant allows engineers to interact with machinery, making Singapore a good place to learn about the overall production process.

Japanese parent companies play an important role in technology transfers. Even if a subsidiary can produce items independently, it may not necessarily have the capacity to implement the basic changes needed for producing new products or installing new equipment. Therefore, when new products or new equipment are introduced, large numbers of personnel are dispatched from the Japanese parent. In addition, whenever there are ongoing difficulties at a plant or trouble that local resources cannot respond to, Japanese specialists are flown out from Japan.

As a general tendency, the practice of sending staff to Japan for basic technical training is declining, in terms of both the number of missions and the number of personnel sent. For advanced technologies (for example inspection, maintenance, Electronic Data Processing (EDP) and adjustment technologies), however, there is a growing tendency to train local personnel in Japan. Most of those dispatched to Japan are technicians and top specialists from countries such as South Korea, Taiwan and Singapore where the number of high-value-added jobs is increasing quickly.

Company 'C's' (the parent company of DCTH) training programme is second to none in terms of the number of personnel dispatched for training. 'C' has sent 5 thousand staff from Thailand, and 6 thousand five hundred from Singapore, to its factories in Japan, and is a leader in this respect. The company also has a unique method of transferring its technology. Instead of simply transferring production of items no longer made in Japan, as soon as it has confirmed that there is a new product that can be mass-produced overseas, it shifts responsibility for production of that item overseas, consulting closely with overseas employees on any problems in establishing a mass-production system. As soon as the overseas factory is set up, the company establishes a model line at the mother plant in Japan. Then, local staff who will operate the factory are sent to Japan for training on that line, normally for one to one-and-a-half years. During that time, they are housed in dormitories alongside Japanese employees. When the local factory starts up, the line itself and trained staff are transferred back to the overseas factory as a package. This technology transfer, which transfers a large number of personnel as well as a production line, allows the Japanese system to be applied directly and accelerates the start-up of the local factory. The line at the mother plant in Japan can also respond quickly to any trouble or changes that occur in the overseas plant. The local staff sent to Japan find the experience of working in a Japanese factory for a long period of time far more effective than on-the-job training.

Although on-the-job training is the basic method used for technical instruction, off-the-job training alongside on-the-job training is used for specialised fields such as planning, inspection and handling. Many of the companies that have recently set up overseas operations have the problem of local staff not being able to provide on-the-job training. On-the-job training programmes are not well established at Japanese-affiliated firms. And the expertise at the core of the technologies is difficult to express in document form, leaving no alternative except practical training. Under current methods, very little technological expertise is being transferred successfully. After only one or two hours of initial instruction on induction into the company, staff are sent to the production line to work as best they can. In true on-the-job training, however, every individual is set goals to achieve (over a year, for example) and progress is followed up and checked. In Japanese factories, charts indicating individual aptitude and progress are hung at each job site, facilitating the management of individual skills. However, such charts were not witnessed at many of the overseas factories surveyed. The fact that unsatisfactory on-the-job training programmes managed to achieve the results observed suggests that the technical level of many jobs in overseas factories is not very high. However, as we have repeatedly pointed out, the spread of automation and higher levels of added value in products will require higher levels of knowledge and technology than the less-than-satisfactory on-the-job training programmes in use at present can supply.

Using only on-the-job training to teach advanced technology is time-consuming and cannot reach the core aspects of the job. Off-the-job training allows trainees to learn basic principles and rules such as by dismantling and cleaning their machinery. In Japan, the main trend is now towards off-the-job training. Senior workers are encouraged to put their knowledge and experience into writing for the benefit of trainees. Rather than using outside educational institutions for off-the-job training, in-house employees are creating course materials themselves. A good example of this is Company 'L' (the parent company of DLM) Oita factory, where distinctions between engineer, technician and operator became blurred as product and manufacturing technology fused and manufacturing became more automated. This provided an opportunity for the company to systematise off-the-job training to improve the technical training of both operators and engineers. The company established a Semiconductor Technology Training Centre offering three courses: chip manufacturing, maintenance and improvement of semiconductor devices, and a refresher course for engineers. These courses are for eleven, three, and two months, respectively.

The high labour turnover for local staff makes it difficult to increase productivity through active educational and training programmes. Clearly, there is little point in sending staff on expensive trips to Japan if they may leave soon afterwards. There is also the opportunity cost that results from the turnover of such expensively and highly trained workers. Because of Japanese firms' reputation for excellent training, Japanese-trained workers, especially technicians, are headhunted by other companies. Although Japanese-affiliated firms have a gentlemen's agreement not to poach each others' staff, this agreement is not always adhered to. Local firms and multinationals also lure away employees. In Malaysia and Taiwan in particular, where labour shortage is acute and job hopping the norm, retaining key personnel has become a real challenge for Japanese-affiliated firms. In order to combat the high staff turnover, Japanese-affiliated companies have taken such measures as avoiding sending young workers to Japan for training, and simplifying the production process so as to minimise the influence of the departure of staff. But because maintenance of high-level industrial technology requires a certain level of permanent highly-trained personnel, these measures have inevitably resulted in lowering the technology and competitiveness of both the Japanese overseas firms and their host countries. This problem is beyond the control of companies, and requires action by the host governments.

Production Equipment

Scores for this category ⑦ were the second highest of all the twenty-three categories, and second only to ① Job classification. The high 5-point score achieved by Japanese companies in Singapore indicates that their production equipment has reached the same level as that in Japan. Other regions with Japanese firms also show similar scores, indicating very high dependence on Japan for production equipment. Japanese firms have a strong tendency to supply production equipment to their overseas bases. The main reason for this is probably the development of company-specific machinery by electronic components manufacturers to create a competitive advantage.

This practice results in the need to send trainees to Japan for training in the maintenance of this equipment. Since specialised, advanced, company-specific equipment is different from general equipment, only the Japanese plants that developed the equipment can provide the expertise to maintain it.

The level of production equipment within the individual subsidiaries can vary depending on the location: NIEs or ASEAN; the product category: semiconductors, general electronic components, high value-added products, low value-added products; and the strategic position:

processing base or mass-production base. For example, DDTh in Thailand is a sister plant of DDS, and was established with older equipment to produce mainly labour-intensive goods, which were losing their competitiveness. This study clearly reveals that using the latest equipment does not always increase productivity. The key concept is 'optimal equipment'. The appropriate level of production equipment is not determined by the product category or the strategic position of the subsidiary, but by such factors as the quality level of locally supplied materials and parts, wage levels, and the versatility of production equipment. For example, instead of installing state-of-the-art equipment that requires delicate maintenance at an overseas base, it may be better to install maintenance-free machines. It also makes sense not to install specialised equipment for mass production if the plant is only expected to produce a low volume of items. While some countries prevent multinationals from opening plants equipped with used equipment, this restriction can hinder the rational application of technology based on 'optimal equipment'.

That the automation level of overseas affiliates is 70 per cent of the parent plants in Japan reflects the use of 'optimal equipment.' When Company 'L' (the parent company of DLTh) established its CPT factory in Thailand, it originally planned to install the same level of equipment as in Japan. Then, when maintenance training was not as successful as had been hoped, 'L' decided not to install equipment requiring manual operation. The parent plants in Japan can call on maintenance specialists with decades of experience who are able to correct mechanical problems in under a minute. If fixing the same problems overseas can take one or two hours, clearly, the overseas plants cannot sustain the same level of automation as in Japan.

However, dependency on Japan for machinery hinders the development of overseas business because of high procurement costs. With the strong yen probably to stay for a long time, the cost of procuring equipment from Japan will continue to grow. Locally purchased machines can be one-third to a quarter of the cost of those imported from Japan. But, with no high-end local manufacturers capable of meeting Japanese needs, there is no alternative to importing from Japan. In the case of company-specific machines, specifications could be given to local machinery manufacturers for production, but there are few local machine manufacturers capable of this.

Although Taiwan seems to have the most advanced machinery industry in East Asia, by Japanese standards, it lacks precision equipment for manufacturing electronic components. If Taiwan did have this equipment, however, Japanese parent companies would lose revenue. The income Japanese parent companies receive from the sale of equipment to overseas subsidiaries is an important source of income, along with royalties. In countries that severely restrict royalties to Japan, income from equipment sales has strong appeal. Many Japanese parent companies object to local procurement because of loss of revenue.

However, the lack of suitable local equipment is a problem for overseas plants. Along with the next topic of localising component procurement, it ranks as one of the most urgent issues facing Japan's multinationals.

Maintenance

Although the overall average of 3.2 points for ⑧ Maintenance was not particularly high, Singapore's average of 3.7 was noteworthy. The three Singapore plants surveyed (DDS, DES and DGS) produce semiconductors and precision components, and are the most mechanised and automated in the region, perhaps because they have a high maintenance capability.

At advanced facilities, the amount of software used in manufacturing processes is relatively high, but the skill required for such maintenance is even higher. The total preventive maintenance (TPM) programme, which is implemented thoroughly by Japanese producers, is not a special technique introduced from elsewhere, but a necessary adjunct to automation. As mechanisation advances, the operator's job changes from assembly to observation. Inspection and repair of machinery eventually become inevitable. In the earlier mentioned case of Company 'L' this phenomenon resulted in a fusing of the roles of engineer and technician. However, it is unrealistic to expect operators to maintain high-tech machines that use extensive software. In Japan, where high-tech equipment and automation are advanced, the proportion of maintenance specialists is rising rapidly. In some cases, operators are not permitted to participate in maintenance activities. For example, at Company 'G's' Japanese CPT factory, 317 regular full-time staff (72 per cent of the plant's total) are maintenance specialists. The operators are mainly contract or part-time workers, and are not expected to do any maintenance. Admittedly, CPT production is highly technical in nature and therefore requires a larger than average number of specialists. However, the proportion of maintenance workers is increasing steadily at all Japanese electronic components plants.

On the other hand, apart from the Singapore factories, none of the overseas factories has a high proportion of maintenance personnel. Instead, they tend to be predominantly female-staffed, final assembly plants. At most of the overseas factories, machinery maintenance is conducted separately by hired specialists trained in Japan, or performed on-site by Japanese engineers. Many companies, however, still complain about the abilities of their maintenance staff. The number of items produced per worker is lower than in Japan, and the same mistakes are repeated. The knowledge required for machinery maintenance in the 1990s typically takes at least three years to acquire. However, with the high labour turnover in East Asia, personnel training has not been able to keep pace with the growth of the booming economy and its ever-increasing need for investment in capital and new business. In the case of DJM, the operating rate is 10–15 per cent lower than the Japanese parent plant because of a lack of experience among the maintenance staff. 'M' doubled its capital investment over a five-year period, and has not been able to keep up with the growing need for staff training. In Malaysia, where there has been no shortage of labour until recently, the ratio of manual labour was high, and the need to maintain sophisticated machinery was therefore less. However, in the first half of the 1990s, multinationals, including Japanese ones, discovered the country and eventually caused a severe labour shortage. As the newcomers scrambled to automate, maintenance personnel training could not keep up. If China emerges as major player in the future, facilities in the Asian region will have to improve and the lack of maintenance personnel will become even more of a problem.

We have already noted the lack of metal moulding (die-casting) maintenance skills at the Thai plants, and this problem also exists at other plants throughout East Asia. Since metal moulding is a part of manufacturing, moulding maintenance has to be done on site. Metal mouldings can hardly be sent to Japan every time trouble occurs. Some firms such as Company DGS attempt to cultivate highly-trained metal moulders, but very few firms in fact succeed. DGS recruits workers from polytechnic schools, sends them to Japan for a six-month training session, then follows that up with three to four years of hands-on training.

Local Content and Suppliers

The overall average score of 3.4 for ⑪ Local Content and ⑫ Suppliers indicates that 40–60 per cent of materials and machines are procured locally in East Asia (mainly from other Japanese-affiliated firms). The remaining 30–40 per cent are from overseas (mainly Japan). The local content ratio was highest for subsidiaries in Taiwan (2.3) and the lowest for South Korean plants (4.3). The low ratio for South Korea is related to conditions peculiar to that country. South Korea, like Japan, decided in order to promote domestic industry to severely restrict multinationals. As a result, the number of foreign-affiliated firms in South Korea is extremely low compared with other Asian countries. The Japanese affiliated firms included in this survey were mainly allowed into South Korea under its free trade zone arrangements. The FTZ firms have practically no ties with other firms in Korea, and serve as branch factories for the parent factories in Japan, so, they have little alternative but to order from Japan. Japanese companies are in the initial and middle stages in Malaysia and Taiwan, and can therefore still easily procure parts and materials locally, except for some key parts and materials. This is not true of Japanese companies in South Korea, however.

Foreign governments are strongly encouraging more local procurement to redress the trade deficit with Japan caused by dependency on Japanese materials and machinery. For Japanese firms, the strong yen means that procurement costs will continue to escalate, accelerating the switch to local procurement. The problem remains however, whether Japanese-affiliated firms can purchase local raw materials and key parts (such as ferrite, ceramics, phosphors and electron guns) to produce electronic components while maintaining quality and manufacturing precision. Since Japanese assemblers, major users of electronic components, are proceeding with plans to buy locally to cut costs, there should be a large improvement in the amount of local content in the near future.

Among Japanese companies in the ASEAN countries, and perhaps further afield as well, procurement networks are growing. Set makers, the final assemblers, are expanding local procurement. As needs in the initial and middle stages of production became more sophisticated, materials and components makers rushed in to take advantage of the opportunities, and a critical mass of Japanese businesses formed. For example, plans by Japanese medium-sized companies to build a College of Metal Moulding in Penang, Malaysia are taking shape. Metal moulding skills are essential for upgrading the machinery industry, but it is medium-sized Japanese companies that are developing the skilled workers to support this industry. Until recently, Japanese firms brought almost all their metal mouldings from Japan, and employed Japanese workers for maintenance. This college once established, will localise the design and manufacture of metal mouldings. Although 'technology blocks' can sometimes emerge on their own, as with metal moulding in Malaysia, pioneering giants (such as Matsushita, one of the first to set up overseas in the 1960s, and Aiwa), played a large role in internationalising Japanese industry. Such companies, with twenty or more years of experience, helped to develop sheet-metal, press-moulding, and other suppliers. Manufacturers who established overseas plants after the 1985 yen appreciation were greatly helped by the unremarked efforts of these earlier pioneers.

Because overseas suppliers lack adequate technological ability, Japanese firms provide technical instruction. Typically, Japanese firms see this as their duty. Many provide concrete technical and managerial guidance. The technical guidance includes thorough reception inspections and identification of points for improvement. The government of Singapore stipulates as a condition of entry to the country that foreign companies provide technical instruction to local medium sized and small businesses. While the government leaves the method of technical instruction up to the company, Japanese firms usually dispatch engineers to local suppliers and invite suppliers to send staff to them for training. As Japanese firms do not engage in exclusive subcontracting, the results of the training received by the supplier benefit not only Japanese firms but the nation as a whole. Considering the ripple effect of technical instruction throughout the Singaporean economy, Singapore's policy seems to be an intelligent one.

Thus when we consider technology transfers by multinational firms, we must take into account not only direct transfers to overseas subsidiaries, but also the ripple effect of the transfers on local suppliers. A cluster of Japanese companies in the same industry can act like an 'external economy' on the local environment, and have hard-to-quantify effects. Regardless of how high the overseas companies set levels, if those levels apply only to the company, the benefits to the host country are limited. To get the best results, it is necessary to train suppliers and implement programmes that allow technology to ripple out into the economy. But excessively high requirements for local content, restrictions on the percentage of Japanese personnel on the staff, and measures to restrict the importation of machinery from Japan, can in fact restrict the spread of technology by stopping Japanese firms coming into the local marketplace.

VI COMPARISONS WITH JAPANESE FIRMS IN THE UNITED STATES

Table 4.15 compares the application scores achieved by the electronic components subsidiaries in Asia with a report on Japanese semiconductor factories in the United States (Abo, 1994a). In the United States, six Japanese semiconductor companies with seven plants were surveyed, while the Asian survey focused more widely on the electronic components industry, which included three semiconductor companies and three factories. Directly comparing the two surveys might not therefore be

Table 4.15   Comparison between Asian and US plants

	Average of Asian plants	Average of US plants
① Job classification	4.8	2.7
② Multifunctional skills	2.4	2.6
③ Education and training	3.3	3.0
④ Wage system	3.3	3.1
⑤ Promotion	3.4	3.1
⑥ First-line supervisor	3.2	2.7
⑦ Equipment	4.5	4.6
⑧ Maintenance	3.2	2.6
⑨ Quality control	3.4	2.4
⑩ Process management	3.6	2.9
⑪ Local content	3.4	3.7
⑫ Suppliers	4.1	4.4
⑬ Procurement method	3.2	2.3
⑭ Small-group activities	3.0	2.4
⑮ Information sharing	3.4	3.3
⑯ Sense of unity	3.6	2.9
⑰ Hiring policy	3.2	3.1
⑱ Long-term employment	3.2	2.3
⑲ Harmonious labour relations	3.6	5.0
⑳ Grievance procedure	3.2	3.6
㉑ Ratio of Japanese expatriates	1.6	3.9
㉒ Delegation of authority	3.5	4.0
㉓ Position of local managers	3.8	3.9

appropriate. However, the companies surveyed in both the United States and East Asia initially focused on assembly, and both regions underwent rapid automation. In that sense, there is some common ground for comparison. The categories with the largest differences were: ① Job classification (2.1 points difference); ⑨ Quality control (1.0); ⑬ Procurement methods (0.9); ⑲ Labour relations (1.4); and ㉑ Ratio of Japanese expatriates (2.3).

First, let us compare the scores in the Job classification category. In contrast with the Asian workplaces (4.8) where job demarcation is little practised, the Japanese semiconductor factories in the United States (2.7) employ an American-style occupational system, which uses job grades based on job categories. Under the American system, jobs are relatively fixed and not often rotated much. Accordingly, the score for Japanese-affiliated plants in the United States for ② Job Rotation was a low 2.6. The comparable figure for Asia (2.4) was lower, not because of job demarcation but because Asian workers in the overseas factories tend not to learn other jobs unless they offered the incentive of pay increases.

In ⑨ Quality control, there was a difference of 1.0 between USA and Asian plants. The problem areas in the United States result from equipment trouble and operators' response to quality control, exacerbated by a lack of co-operation between sections.

The Asian factories have the similar problems, though in contrast to their USA counterparts, Japanese staff are directly or indirectly responsible for quality, yields and productivity. In Asia, however, local staff play a central role in improving quality. The smaller number of Japanese expatriates in Asia is reflected in the large difference in the scores between the two regions for ㉑ Ratio of Japanese expatriates. As mentioned previously, some companies find local staff are not interested in quality and inspection programmes because of the absence of financial incentives. To achieve quality standards measurable in parts per million, detailed inspections are essential.

In both the United States and Asia, most suppliers to Japanese companies are Japanese or Japanese-affiliated companies. The two regions differ, however, in how the supplies are procured. In the Asian region, Japanese parts and materials makers predominate to form a large supporting sector. Asian supply systems are on the verge of realising just-in-time delivery (Abo, 1994), whereas in the United States, at the time of this survey, Japanese factories were not so close. The situation is the same in the procurement of key materials from Japan. US subsidiaries import 70–90 per cent of key materials from Japan, compared with 40–60 per cent for Asia.

The difference in ⑲ Labour relations is caused by different evaluation standards between the American survey (Abo, 1994a) and our Asian survey. Whereas the previous survey added five points if a firm did not have organised labour, this survey measures actual co-operation between labour and management. The absence of labour unions in USA semiconductor factories gave them an automatic five-point advantage. The Asian plants, where not one case of union-management friction occurred, recorded a low score of 3.6. In reality, however, there is no difference between the two regions in the degree of co-operation between management and labour.

Here, we have examined briefly the major differences between USA and Asian Japanese-affiliated plants over several categories. In conclusion, we shall now point out some of the characteristics of the electronic components industry, including semiconductors. One of the most important points is that in the future, the electronic components and semiconductor industry will be driven by technological changes in manufacturing. The industry has changed rapidly from being female-dominated to male-dominated. In contrast with other industries that rely heavily on assembly (such as automobile manufacturing), the relative number of general operators in electronic component manufacturing processes is declining. At the parent plants in Japan where high-tech, intelligent factories are becoming the norm, general process workers are being replaced by groups of engineers and technicians. For the sake of competitiveness, firms are shifting away from product innovation and low-volume, high-variety production, toward technologies for high-volume mass production. This transition from 'improvement' to 'innovation' forces us to ask whether the Japanese-style production system used in this survey to analyse the success of overseas Japanese companies might require some basic revision. If the results of the new production control technology are transferred successfully to local subsidiaries, what changes would that trigger in the technology exchange process, which is currently based on human resources? We have briefly introduced trends at some representative companies, but to determine whether or not these trends and companies are in the vanguard will require follow up surveys.

Despite the rising number of overseas plants capable of matching the quality of facilities in Japan, Japan's overseas bases are still widely seen as female-staffed assembly plants. It will therefore be important to implement small group activities and enhancement programmes in these plants in the future.

5 Asian Operations of Representative Japanese Multinationals

Toyota Motor Corporation

Kunio Kamiyama

Needless to say, the Toyota Motor Corporation is the largest car manufacturer in Japan. The company was established in August 1937 after the outbreak of the Sino-Japanese War. The origin of Toyota as automobile enterprise, however, dates back to the entrance of Toyota Automatic Loom Works Ltd (established in November 1926) into this industry in 1934. In August 1935, a time when the Japanese auto industry was dominated by foreign capital from US companies such as Ford and General Motors (GM), a decision was made by the Japanese cabinet to establish and promote a domestic auto manufacturing industry. Toyota's decision to enter the auto sector was made when plans for domestic vehicle manufacture became government policy. Toyota was the first company to be licensed under the provisions of the law concerning the manufacture of motor vehicles, promulgated in May 1936. With the support of this government policy, it has since expanded vehicle production, mainly in the field of truck manufacturing. Although Toyota experienced a financial crisis after the Second World War, the company continues to lead Japan's auto industry.

Compared with Honda and Nissan, Toyota's overseas expansion policy appears more conservative. This point is apparent when examining their attitude toward establishing plants in the United States. Honda started manufacturing in Ohio in November 1982, and Nissan set up a plant in Tennessee in June 1983 – in both cases under their own management. Toyota, however, did not start manufacturing in the United States until December 1984, when it began operations at New United Manufacturing Inc. in California, a joint venture with GM. It was not until May 1988 that Toyota established its own plant in Kentucky.

It is often pointed out that Toyota's conservative policy towards foreign investment stems from the 'Mikawa–Monroe Doctrine' created by the major factories concentrated around Toyota city, in Aichi Prefecture, Japan. However, in addition to this, the company's foreign experiences after the war also played a significant role in influencing policy. In 1958, Toyota started knock-down (KD) production of the Land Cruiser in Brazil as part of a rather aggressive transplanting policy. Through its withdrawal from Mexico in the early 1960s, and retreat from Korea, to which Toyota had been exporting KD components since 1966, however, Toyota learned the importance of in-depth feasibility studies before deciding to enter a market, and the value of maintaining stable operations thereafter.

In light of the strong yen in the 1990s, Toyota is having to review its world strategy. Up to this point, there was a tendency for Toyota to avoid establishing local production in areas where it was possible to export Toyota products from Japan. However, it became increasingly difficult to enter local markets successfully unless KD production had already been in operation there, as many developing countries began to introduce import restriction policies and embraced localisation policies. As of March 1994, Toyota's overseas production facilities numbered thirty-five companies in twenty-five countries/regions.

Case studies of three assembly plants in Thailand, Taiwan and Malaysia are detailed in the next section. There are an additional three plants in Indonesia, the Philippines and Pakistan, making a total of six in Asia. Toyota's vehicle sales in 1994 for these areas are as follows: 125 000 in Thailand, 100 000 in Taiwan, 80 000 in Indonesia, 32 000 in the Philippines, and 17 000 in Malaysia. These sales volumes are not yet large, but considering the potential of these markets in the twenty-first century, they are vital to Toyota.

Both domestic and commercial vehicles are assembled in all three plants. The plant in Taiwan was visited in September 1992 and the plants in Thailand and Malaysia a year later, in September 1993. Toyota Motor Thailand Co. Ltd is a joint venture between a local enterprise and Toyota, which owns about 60 per cent of the capital. Employees number 3400 (twenty-three of whom are Japanese); 2500 being factory workers. Production capacity is 107 000 units per year. Assembly Services Sdn. Bhd. in Malaysia is wholly owned by UMW Toyota Motor Sdn. Bhd., in which minor shares are held by Toyota. Employees total 600, including three Japanese. In Taiwan, Kuozui Motors Ltd, 49 per cent of which is owned by Toyota and Hino Motor Co., undertakes painting and assembly processes. Toyota holds a 80 per cent stake in Fung Yong Co. Ltd, which performs pressing and body welding. The two companies share operations, and employees total 1226 and 639, respectively. Thirty-four Japanese are employed at both companies, twenty-two of these being sent from Toyota.

The average degree of application of the Japanese production system based on the twenty-three item, six-group evaluation analysis for the three factories is assessed as follows. Taiwanese plants received the highest score. This score is equal to the score from a survey of auto parts manufacturers in Taiwan, where it was revealed that they had the highest degree of application among sixty Japanese-owned factories. In contrast, the degree of application for the Malaysian factory was low–indeed, considerably lower than the average for ASEAN plants. The factory in Thailand stands in the middle, with a degree of application similar to that of ASEAN plants. The disparity in degree of application stems from various factors, one of which is the date that local production started.

The commencing dates of production for the three plants are as follows: Taiwan – June 1988; Thailand – February 1964; and Malaysia – February 1968. In 1968, Toyota began KD production of the Corona in Taiwan but withdrew in the early 1970s. Then, after joining a government project to establish a plant with an annual production capacity of 200 000 vehicles and later withdrawing from it, in February 1986, Toyota's request to build a factory was approved by the Taiwanese government. The Taiwanese plant was finally completed after long delays, and is Toyota's key factory in Asia. This plant is characterised by its high application of the Japanese system. Having experienced overseas manufacturing in the United States during the 1980s, Toyota's foreign investment policy has become more aggressive and exhibits high adaptation.

In comparison with Taiwan, the degree of application for the two plants in the ASEAN region is low. The lack of inclination towards applying the Japanese system, which covers total factory management and operation, can be attributed to both plants' long histories as KD production factories. In 1970, the Thai government prohibited the importing of completed cars, passing legislation increasing the rate of local content of domestically-produced vehicles. In 1979, Toyota strengthened its local content rate with the addition of pressed parts made by Toyota Auto Body Thailand Co. Ltd. This was augmented by the commencement of engine assembly operations in 1981. As a result, on a monetary basis, local content had reached 60 per cent. Furthermore, in recent years, the trend towards applying the Japanese system, as is the case with the main factories in the ASEAN region, has occurred in the Thai plants. On the other hand, although the company has been making considerable efforts to implement the Toyota production system, such as introduction of quality control or the *kanban* system, the degree of application for Malaysian plants is still low. This is because of the small production scale and the fact that pressed parts have to be imported from Japan. Thus the local content rates remain around 35 per cent. Also, in Malaysia, Japanese management staff do not have the authority to make business decisions. This is one of the main reasons for the low degree of application of the Japanese system in this country.

The following is a more concrete comparison between the three factories with regard to their managerial and operational conditions. Contrary to the US system, job classification in Asian factories is in general less clear and not as strict; thus the demarcation between jobs is very low. This point was confirmed in both Taiwan and Thailand. In Malaysia, however, the British influence on the organisational structure of factories is conspicuous. For example, in principle, the reshuffling of employees is possible; however, in practice, there are often cases where workers reject change. An employee, for example, may refuse to transfer from the paint shop to the assembly line. As a result, there is no systematic strategy to develop multiskilled workers, and changes are made only to cover the duties of absentees within the same work area. In Taiwan, a proposal to foster multiskilled workers was introduced in the same year that the survey was undertaken. In Thailand, factories basically employ the Toyota system but encounter problems because of the long cycle time.

These differences in customs at the shop-floor level reflect the character of the labour unions. In Malaysia, employees are divided into two categories: exempt and non-exempt. Evaluation of union members is prohibited by the union. In Thailand and Taiwan, promotion and wage increases are undertaken as a result of job evaluation. In Malaysia, the union forbids worker evaluations and seeks equality for employees, which is the main barrier preventing the introducing of the Toyota production system.

The following are two ways in which a Taiwanese factory has introduced the Toyota production system successfully. The production control room has a control panel that shows the manufacturing status of all vehicles in the line, from body assembly to final assembly. The manufacturing status is monitored by transferring, by hand, each vehicle's card to the next work station. The progress at each station is reported by the line leaders through an intercom. Progress can be evaluated at a glance. If a car has to be taken off the line because of a fault, the card showing the car's details is also removed. Thus, immediate measures can be taken to meet any changes in job allocation and parts supply that may arise. This production control system can be fed into a computer in Japan. In Taiwan, however, Toyota's production system is carried out by only local employees without the participation of Japanese expatriates. The *kanban* system has also been adopted in the factories. Parts are classified by the colour of the *kanban* (slip) attached to the box: yellow represents CKD parts; white indicates local parts; and red indicates the parts supplied by the four other Toyota affiliated companies in Taiwan. The *kanban* goes back and forth between Toyota and the four local companies. There appears to be a strong intention to further introduce the *kanban* system to the other parts makers in Taiwan.

Other Toyota production systems are also being implemented at Taiwanese factories. In particular, the rapid improvement in shop reform should be acknowledged. An improvement team – composed of members of the maintenance section who participate on a rotational basis and improvement groups in each manufacturing section – plays the central role in improving operations on the shop floor. A further innovation was the establishment of over 100 QC using an 'all-participation' approach that has achieved excellent results. While these improvements in Taiwan still leave Taiwanese factories at half the standard of those in Japan in terms of reform, it is important as an example of successful Japanese reform at an overseas factory.

This high application of the Japanese system in Taiwan is partially supported by the thirty-four Japanese expatriates stationed there. They play very important roles in taking positions on the lines, and not just as co-ordinators, as is often seen in the other overseas factories. In particular, the Japanese employees are allocated general managerial positions. Also, Japanese employees arriving on business trips play a major role, even though their total working days per year have decreased from more than 10 000 days during the start-up stage to 3000–4000 days a year at the time the study was undertaken. Over and above the Japanese influence, however, is the importance of local employee participation in raising the application level of the Japanese system. Education and training will be discussed in the next section.

Taiwan dispatches large numbers of employees to Japan for training: there are generally about fifty trainees in Japan at any one time. A certain level of the Japanese language is the basic prerequisite for entry into this training programme in Japan. In Taiwanese factories, approximately 100 local employees can speak Japanese, an indication of the relationship between training in Japan and a high level of Japanese-speaking ability. Thailand introduced this Japanese training programme in 1991. A group of approximately twenty foremen and twenty group leaders are dispatched to Japan twice a year for a period of three months, and about ten technical staff visit Japan annually for about a year of training. In Malaysia, however, the practice of sending employees to Japan for training is limited. In addition to the above training, local factories have a systematic education programme at each level. The Toyota Human Resource Centre was established within the plant in Thailand in October 1990, and total restructuring of personnel and training was carried out to facilitate the introduction of the Toyota production system.

As was seen above, the factory in Taiwan recorded the highest degree of application, which can be attributed to a strong desire to introduce the Toyota production system. In Thailand, efforts are being made to introduce the system, but the degree of application is still not high because of difficulties characteristic of ASEAN plants. One reason is the difference in production scale; it is not possible for a Malaysian factory to build a full-scale production system when the production capacity of the plant is only 18 000 vehicles a year. Further reasons are labour practices and worker values. In comparison with mass production plants, where automated machines are installed and management techniques and the efficiency of workers play a decisive role in the performance of factories, even the plants in Taiwan and Thailand are unable to gain economies of scale because of the low production volume. Thus, the essential issue is whether or not Toyota's labour management system, which was designed for Japanese factories, will work effectively in transplants where the working conditions are different. For example, applying Toyota's labour management system, which is based on long-term employment, to factories in Taiwan, where frequent job-hopping and a tendency towards self-employment lead to a high job turnover rate (even though the rate has dropped from 20 per cent to 2 per cent per month) could be difficult. To date, there have been relatively few restrictions facing the introduction of the Toyota production system in terms of industrial relations. This is also true in the case of Thailand, with the exception of strong demands for wage increases. Problems remain, however, in practising the Japanese 'all-participation' style of management. For example, differences in the educational background of workers, and segregated cafeterias for workers and management, are two factors working against the realisation of the system. In the case of Malaysia, a different racial structure, diversity in educational backgrounds, and the heavy influence of Western labour practices hamper the introduction of the 'all-participation' style management. The job turnover rate in Malaysia was as high as 5 per cent per month at the time of this survey.

This is the present situation of the three Toyota factories in Asia. The Asian market is becoming increasingly, important and the environment surrounding Toyota's three factories is constantly undergoing change. The implementation of the BBC scheme in ASEAN countries and the growing presence of US and European car makers in the industry are recent examples of change in the Asian market. Close attention should be paid to the rising inclination towards the application of the Japanese system in these factories in the future.

Nissan Motor Corporation

Hiroshi Kumon

I   NISSAN'S POSITION IN THE JAPANESE AUTO INDUSTRY

Nissan Motor Corporation is Japan's second largest auto maker after the Toyota Motor Corporation. Historically, Nissan has two noteworthy features. First, it originally obtained its technology by direct transfer from developed countries through hired engineers and technical tie-ups. Second, it developed its production network through mergers and capital participation.

Nissan's first direct technical transfer from abroad was a prewar purchase of manufacturing facilities from the United States. The company learned mass production techniques from US engineers at the same time. After the war, from 1953 to 1960, Nissan acquired passenger car technology from the United Kingdom by producing Austin cars.

Nissan's first merger was a tie-up with Minsei Diesel in 1950. As a result, Minsei Diesel became Nissan Diesel Motor Co. Ltd, a leading subsidiary of Nissan Motors. In 1966, Nissan Motor merged with Prince Motor Co., and entered into a technical tie-up with Fuji Heavy Industries Ltd. Today, Nissan Motor produces a full fleet of vehicles ranging from passenger cars to commercial vehicles. Its cars cover the whole gamut from small to luxury cars, although it does not produce 'mini' cars – those with less than a 660 cc capacity. Recently, Nissan Motor has restructured radically because of a sudden fall in demand following the collapse of the 'bubble economy' and the rapid appreciation of the yen. In 1995, Nissan closed its Zama plant to cut costs.

II   NISSAN MOTOR'S EAST ASIAN STRATEGY

Assertive internationalisation is another feature of Nissan Motor. In 1957, Nissan formed a technical support agreement with Yue Loong Motor Co. Ltd of Taiwan, and from 1959, began to assemble knock-down (KD) Nissan kits in Taiwan. In 1961, Nissan Motor established Nissan Mexicana S.A. de C.V. of Mexico, which began production in 1966. This was Nissan's first true overseas venture. In the early 1980s, Nissan announced a string of plans to establish foreign operations in Spain, the

United Kingdom and the United States. Nissan's foreign strategy differed according to the location. The auto maker favoured capital participation in Spain, and new plants in the United Kingdom and United States. Since the early 1980s, Nissan has operated major production plants in Asia, North America and Europe. Nissan has also moved some R&D functions into North America and Europe, and has established regional headquarters there. Nissan is the first major Japanese auto maker to achieve a balanced profile across Asia, the United States and Europe, and to have regional headquarters in North America and Europe.

Nissan has production bases throughout East Asia. Its plants in Taiwan, the Philippines, Thailand, Indonesia and Malaysia are augmented by a joint venture in China. Plans have also been made to establish a presence in Vietnam and a technical joint venture in Korea.

Nissan is the first auto maker to develop and produce an exclusively Asian car. Its AD Resort is based on the Sunny AD Van and produced in Thailand, Malaysia, Taiwan, and the Philippines. Nissan also operates a complementary parts supply system among subsidiaries in Asia, using brand-to-brand complementation (BBC). Parts for the AD Resort are supplied by plants in Thailand, Malaysia, Taiwan and the Philippines. In 1993, Thailand and Taiwan began producing the wagon version of the AD Resort, and in 1994, the pick-up version. Malaysia has been producing the wagon version since 1994, and a Philippine subsidiary produces the pick-up version. One of the purposes of a common parts supply system is to standardise manufacturing and quality control among the four Asian countries, and to raise standards to near Japanese levels. The small scale of the project, which produces between 30 000 and 40 000 cars annually, and around 260 parts, is still below the mass production level. The Asian car project is, however, improving technology levels in all four bases so that higher production volumes might be achieved in the future. The Asian car project also seeks to promote complementarity of parts and vehicles throughout the region. Prior to starting production, the managers of the four plants gathered at Nissan's ASEAN Office in Thailand to plan the project. Launching trial production at the four plants simultaneously was a unique experience.

III APPLICATION OF THE JAPANESE PRODUCTION SYSTEM AT MAIN ASIAN PLANTS

Nissan's decision to establish overseas bases is accompanied by a tendency to localise the management of these. In the United States, local managers from Ford played the main role, from deciding on plant location to creating the structure of the company. The Americans actually got the company up and running. In the United Kingdom, Japanese managers initially filled the position of president and other top jobs, but British managers took over, and Nissan's UK subsidiary now has a British CEO. In Asia, too, Nissan pursues a policy of localisation. As it is generally impossible to set up wholly-owned subsidiaries in Asia to produce for the local market, the Japanese generally create joint ventures with local partners and appoint locals to top positions. While this is the usual pattern, when the Japanese parent company places particular importance on the local plant it tends to retain a hold on the reins of management. In Nissan's case, however, the local managers hold the real power at every plant. Even in countries where Nissan needs to remain in control, the local partners tend to wield the real power, because of past factors associated with the company. In such a situation, it can be quite difficult to implement the Japanese production system. However, Asian governments are now changing from a policy of protecting and nurturing local automotive industries, to liberalising and opening their markets. Leaving aside the question of whether they have in fact made much progress in this direction, deregulation is an inevitable corollary of economic development. Accordingly, local plants with Japanese connections are trying to introduce stringent Japanese systems in an effort to become more internationally competitive. Naturally, where Japanese nationals run the company, the Japanese system can be introduced by such managers. But if the local partner holds the power, the application of the Japanese system depends on whether local managers are aware of the need to introduce the system, or whether the Japanese can convince them of that need. In Nissan Motor's Taiwanese and Thai subsidiaries, where the local partners were strong, Nissan tried to introduce the Japanese system without being in control of management. We shall look at the results below. Both Taiwan and Thailand are strategically important for Japanese firms, because the two countries offer the largest markets in East Asia after Korea. Nissan began production in both countries, through technical joint ventures with leading local partners at an early stage.

IV   YUE LOONG MOTOR OF TAIWAN

Yue Loong Motor was established in 1953 by Chinese capitalists fleeing from mainland China. In 1958, the company entered into a technical tie-up with Nissan Motor, forming Nissan's first overseas KD plant. Yue Loong

Motor is Taiwan's oldest automobile company, and has enjoyed a monopoly in its home market for some time. When the government announced its intention to liberalise conditions for foreign firms in 1985, Yue Loong Motor asked Nissan Motor for an injection of capital to strengthen itself against expected competition from imported vehicles and domestic producers. As a result, Nissan Motor now holds 25 per cent of Yue Loong Motor's shares, while the local owners retain management control. Some fourteen Japanese expatriates are employed at the Taiwanese company: one in the position of vice-president, another as a senior manager, and the others as advisers to Taiwanese managers. The top decision-making group is a management board composed of the president, vice-president and seven senior managers, including two Japanese expatriates. As the Japanese occupy only two seats on the board, management control is in the hands of the local partners. In 1989, the company formed a rationalisation section to improve productivity in the face of the fierce competition expected after economic deregulation. The board also asked Nissan to send engineers from Japan to improve standards on the shop floor.

Yue Loong Motor embraced the Japanese production system in 1989. Japanese advisers introduced the '5S' movement to improve quality in manufacturing and to develop multiskilled workers. In quality control, Yue Loong Motor originally used the American system in which products were checked at the final inspection stage and repaired by quality inspectors. When it introduced the Japanese system, the company replaced American QC with Japanese techniques based on improving quality throughout the entire factory. The Japanese approach combined quality checks in an audit room with a process to feed back the results into the manufacturing process. Managers and first-line supervisors gathered at the audit room every morning to evaluate product quality at two stages: pre-repair and post-repair. They then fed the results back to the production line in an effort to decrease both post- and pre-repair defects, clearly delineating the pre- and post-repair processes. All operators maintain personal quality sheets at their workplaces. When a defect is noticed, it is entered in a quality guide sheet and a result check-sheet, in an attempt to build quality into the manufacturing process. When Yue Loong Motor introduced this approach, quality improved remarkably. Defects found in the audit room fell from between twenty and thirty a day, to below ten. While the initiative for the system came from local managers who recognised the need for it, the system was introduced directly by engineers dispatched from Nissan Motor in Japan. However, the Taiwanese and the Japanese sides did not agree over management methods for long. Japanese expatriate managers expressed dissatisfaction when the rationalisation section was absorbed into another division as a result of organisational reforms.

Basically, Yue Loong Motor produces models developed by Nissan, and imports key components from Japan. However, as Taiwan's oldest car maker, it was asked by the Taiwanese government to develop its own model. Yue Loong Motor therefore established a development centre and created a car styled on a Nissan vehicle and using Nissan components. This Taiwanese vehicle is no longer in production. Today, Yue Loong Motor is developing another model, starting with the engine.

V   SIAM NISSAN AUTOMOBILE OF THAILAND

In 1952, a group of overseas Chinese set up an automobile company to import and market Nissan cars in Thailand. This was Nissan's earliest overseas sales company. Then, in 1962, Nissan established a KD plant to assemble cars in Thailand. In 1973, when the government announced a policy to assemble vehicles in Thailand, Nissan built another assembly plant there, this time for both passenger cars and trucks. While the company initially increased sales volume under an aggressive local manager dubbed 'the Automobile King of Thailand', the company's market share dipped because of severe competition with domestic assemblers. Pressed by creditors, the cash-strapped local partner, which suffered a financial crisis in the late 1980s, invited Nissan to inject some capital. To commit strongly to the business, Nissan Motor sought a 40 per cent shareholding. Its partner, however, was determined to remain Thailand's only indigenous auto maker, and restricted Nissan Motor to a holding of 25 per cent. In 1991, Nissan injected more capital, becoming now much more than simply a technical partner. Although Nissan Motor had opened an ASEAN office in Thailand, it left the management of that office to local staff. Nissan led the move to replace family-style management, when it set up a management board as the top decision-taking body of Siam Nissan, and dispatched eleven Japanese staff to serve in the company. The management board consists of an honorary chairman, a chairman, a president, and four vice-presidents. A Japanese vice-president attends board meetings. While this one individual cannot really affect management decisions, Nissan's success lies in setting up a modern democratic body to run the company. Nissan Motor also succeeded in introducing the Japanese production system. Of the expatriates, six serve at the plant, and one assists the local plant manager in plant reform. Whereas previously division and section managers had their own offices and secretaries, section managers and below now work together in an open-plan office, and the company is modifying its management system from a 'top-down' to a committee-style, participatory approach. On the shop floor, the company is establishing precise work standards, implementing the '5S' movement, and strengthening small-group and quality control activities. The results of '5S' activities are announced at each plant, and staff strive to improve results. However, the plant still has a long way to go in its efforts to improve quality and productivity. For example, it is still looking at pre- and post-repair defects in the audit room, and wondering how to feed these results back into manufacturing processes. The company is working particularly hard on ways to increase the rate of cars passing directly through the production line with zero defects.

Mitsubishi Motors Corporation

Hiroshi Kumon

I   MITSUBISHI MOTORS CORPORATION IN THE JAPANESE AUTOMOTIVE INDUSTRY

Mitsubishi Motors Corporation (MMC) is the newest automotive company in Japan. It gained its independence from Mitsubishi Heavy Industries Ltd in 1970, and thereafter developed into Japan's third largest domestic auto manufacturer. Regarding its entry into foreign countries, MMC has almost the same production capacity at related auto assembly plants in East Asia as does Toyota, and since the second half of the 1980s it has also made inroads into industrially advanced countries such as the United States and European countries. In these countries, however, it has lagged behind other major Japanese auto manufacturers. MMC produces various kinds of automobile, such as passenger cars, trucks and buses. The variety of models it produces and its high degree of technical competence is the result of its history as the automobile division of Mitsubishi Heavy Industries.

MMC has increased its share of domestic production, sales and exports in the 1990s, partly as a result of the success of its recreational vehicles. Although its share of production in the case of 4WD vehicles, including trucks and buses, was only 9.9 per cent in 1990, it increased this vigorously to 12.4 per cent in 1994. It also increased sales and exports during the same period, with its share of sales growing from 9.2 per cent to 11.6 per cent and its share of exports increasing from 10.4 per cent to 12.5 per cent. As a result, MMC has firmly secured its number three position in production volume, and is making major strides to catch up to Nissan, which is number two. Production volume (and percentage share) for each company in 1994 was 3.51 million units (33.2 per cent) for Toyota, 1.56 million units (14.8 per cent) for Nissan, 1.31 million units (12.4 per cent) for Mitsubishi, 1.0 million units (9.5 per cent) for Honda, and 0.99 million units (9.3 per cent) for Mazda. In number three position, MMC is thus about four percentage points ahead of number four.

II MITSUBISHI MOTORS CORPORATION'S ASIAN STRATEGY

A distinctive feature of MMC is its early advance into Asia. As did other companies, MMC focused initially on exports as its strategy for internationalisation but, after becoming independent from Mitsubishi Heavy Industries, it turned to Asia to establish local overseas production. It has many subsidiaries in Asia, especially in ASEAN countries, producing not only automobiles but also carrying out the local production of parts to supply its local auto assembly operations. It operates eight assembly plants in seven East Asian and Southeast Asian countries. These foreign subsidiaries are located in Korea, Taiwan, the Philippines, Vietnam, Thailand, Malaysia and Indonesia. In contrast, MMC advanced into the USA and Europe later than the other Japanese auto producers. It was unable to develop its own internationalisation policy freely because its agreement with the Chrysler Corporation, which was concluded when it gained its independence from Mitsubishi Heavy Industries, imposed restrictions on vehicle exports to, and local production in, the USA and Europe. However, after Chrysler fell into a management crisis in the early 1980s, MMC was no longer constrained by Chrysler and began to develop its own internationalisation strategy based on the experience it had accumulated over the years. In 1988, five years behind the front-running Japanese auto manufacturers, MMC began local production in the United States at Diamond Star Motors (DSM), a joint operation with Chrysler. DSM became independent of Chrysler in 1991. In Europe, after negotiations with Mercedes-Benz became deadlocked, MMC decided to begin joint production with Volvo in Holland in 1995. MMC thus possesses local production plants in three major world regions: Asia, the USA and Europe. It also has local plants in the Pacific region, in Central and South America, and in Africa, in the form of CKD.

In the 1970s, following its independence from Mitsubishi Heavy Industries, MMC pursued two different strategies regarding overseas markets: for developed countries such as the USA or European countries, its strategy was to export, but in East and Southeast Asia, it decided to rely on a combination of exports with local production by joint venture or technical tie-ups with local partners. Taking a closer look at its activities in Asia, it can be observed that in 1970, MMC's first technical tie-up was with China Motor in Taiwan. In 1972, it obtained a 15 per cent equity in Chrysler Philippines, as a result of its purchase, together with the participation of local capital and a Japanese trading company. This company is now owned by MMC and one other Japanese firm. In 1973, MMC established an auto parts company as a joint venture with local capital in Indonesia. Thereafter the company turned to auto assembly by producing 4WD vehicles through further investment by MMC. In the same year, MMC concluded a technical tie-up with Hyundai Motor of Korea that resulted in Hyundai developing the first Korean automobile, the Pony, for which MMC supplied assistance in the production of engines. In 1975, MMC entered into a technical tie-up with a Thai auto assembly company. It is apparent from the above that following MMC's independence from Mitsubishi Heavy Industries, its advance into Asia took many forms.

In the 1980s, MMC implemented bold changes in its internationalisation strategy, by actively engaging in local production. At first, it directed most of its attention to Asia. Later, in the second half of the 1980s, it began to advance into the developed countries. Its first local production operations were established in Korea and Malaysia. In 1982, it obtained equity in Korea's Hyundai through an arrangement with the Mitsubishi Corporation, the trading company of the Mitsubishi group. The following year, when Malaysia established its national auto company, Proton (Perusahaan Otomobil Nasional Berhad), MMC participated, in the form of investment through Mitsubishi Corporation. In this way, MMC came to hold equity in the largest Asian auto producer outside Japan, namely Hyundai, and also in the company with the largest production capacity among ASEAN countries, namely Proton. In 1986, after the Taiwanese government changed its policy to approve joint ventures with foreign firms, MMC also obtained a share of equity in China Motor. The next year, it set up an auto assembly plant with a local partner in Thailand. Because of its preoccupation with Asia, MMC lagged behind in its advances into the developed countries. MMC has also taken advantage of its good relationship with Proton in order to facilitate its advance into the Communist countries of Vietnam and China. It has gained permission to begin local production in Vietnam and has plans to enter a joint venture in China.

III   APPLICATION OF THE JAPANESE PRODUCTION SYSTEM IN EAST ASIAN PLANTS

Another distinctive feature of MMC is the organisational form it adopted as it made inroads into foreign countries. In America, Europe and Asia, MMC began to establish and operate plants in the form of joint ventures. In East Asia, these joint ventures can be classified into two types: one is closely affiliated with MMC; and the other initiated by the partner. In the latter case, MMC co-operated in plant operation by complying with its partners' requirements, and such joint ventures have developed successfully into leading national auto manufacturers. The cases in point are Korea's Hyundai Motor and Malaysia's Proton, although China Motor in Taiwan shares certain characteristics. Below, China Motor and Proton will be discussed, as examples of joint ventures initiated by local partners, and MMC Sittipol of Thailand will be described as an example where MMC exerts closer control over management.

IV CHINA MOTOR IN TAIWAN

In the case of the China Motor Corporation, the local partner has assumed managerial authority and MMC provides supports in manufacturing as well as in R&D. Under the direction of competent managers, this company has achieved rapid growth in Taiwan. It was established in 1969 through a technical tie-up with MMC. In 1986, MMC received a share of the equity, of which it currently holds 19 per cent, with Mitsubishi Corporation holding 6 per cent. China Motor in the past produced mainly trucks, but is now beginning to produce passenger cars. MMC has provided design specifications as well as manufacturing guidance. Recently, with the assistance of MMC, China Motor has developed a new truck model.

Since it holds a minority share of the equity, MMC has only dispatched two people to China Motor. One is at the level of vice-president and the other is a quality control adviser. The main managerial positions, from the president down, are filled by Taiwanese.

Since they hold managerial authority, Taiwanese personnel have taken the initiative in applying the Japanese system. This has resulted in a combination of local and Japanese production systems. Wage and employment qualification systems, for example, are essentially Taiwanese. In 1980, they instituted a new wage system, a distinctive characteristic of which is the presence of certain wage incentives. According to this system, there are three components to wages: namely, standard wages; basic wages; and various special allowances. All employees received an equal amount of standard wages. Basic wages are determined by school background and an individual performance evaluation. There are various types of special allowance such as production allowances for achieving a standard production volume, skill allowances for perfect attendance, and a meal allowance. Half the wages are composed of standard wages and the production allowance. In addition, a bonus is closely tied to profit sharing. The amount of bonus for each employee is related to the amount of profit, which is reported to the employees. Therefore variation in wages is determined by employee performance evaluation and company performance.

Employment qualifications clearly distinguish between shop-floor workers and office staff up to top management. Applicants for staff positions must have graduated from vocational college level or above, while shop-floor positions are open to those who have been educated up to the level of high school. Qualification grades are determined for office staff but not for shop-floor workers. In this way, the company makes a clear distinction between office staff and shop-floor workers at the point of hiring. However, it is possible for an experienced shop-floor worker to become promoted to an office staff position.

Concerning quality control, China Motor attached great importance to this activity from the early stages and it has learned quality control techniques from Japanese advisers. MMC's quality evaluations, based on its own world standards, place China Motor's quality in the upper ranks alongside that of MMC subsidiaries. In the area of parts procurement, China Motor implements an hourly delivery system and adopts collaborative organisation between assemblers and parts makers.

V PROTON IN MALAYSIA

When Proton started its operations in 1985, it represented one of the chief segments of the industrialisation policy introduced by Prime Minister Mahathir. It was established as a joint venture between the state-owned HICOM (Heavy Industries Corporation of Malaysia) and MMC. Although developing or newly industrialised countries hope to cultivate a national automobile industry as an export industry and symbol of their successful industrialisation, success does not come easily. This is partly because of scale merits and partly because of the necessity to develop a variety of support industries. A model case for the successful development of such a national industry in Asia is Malaysia's Proton. The company achieved its goal of preferential tax treatment by the government so that it could achieve economies of scale. It also cultivated the development of supporting auto parts industries by purchasing products from them, thus enabling them to continue in operation. However, success was only achieved by virtue of MMC's tenacious support, in the areas of both manufacturing and management, and with the consideration of short-term profit.

The Malaysian government's goal of developing a national auto manufacturing industry by combining government capital and MMC technology in order to establish Proton, constituted a core part of the *Bumiputera* (Pro-Malay) policy of Prime Minister Mahathir. MMC co-operated widely, from plant design to equipment installation, and also contributed design specifications for the Lancer as well as for Proton's Saga. Plant operations were begun under the direction of a Malaysian manager with the assistance of MMC, but lack of experience in plant operation precipitated a management crisis. Consequently, and at the prime minister's request, Japanese managers assumed various managerial roles, including that of company president. They succeeded in restoring the plant to normal operation and in raising the ratio of local content. Since then, MMC has returned the position of president to a Malay national, and has retreated to an advisory capacity, with the help of twenty-four expatriates. The plant has integrated automobile manufacturing processes, such as casting, engine manufacture, stamping, welding, painting and assembly shops. Annual capacity has reached 120 000 units, making it the largest among automobile plants in ASEAN countries. They export products to the UK and Asian countries.

Although aspects of the British labour system, such as job-based wages and an industry-wide labour union, remain intact in Malaysia, Proton has changed such systems at the request of the prime minister: employee wages are graded, and the wage rate varies within each grade. A labour union has also been organised within the company, and small-group activities have been introduced. Shop-floor leaders and managers visit Japan for education and training. When operations were resumed under the direction of the Japanese president, management introduced a performance evaluation system for production workers, and attempted to develop multiskilled workers and establish a system for building quality into the product during manufacturing. The quality control system has not come up to expectations, however, because employees are unaccustomed to the accurate assembly of parts according to work standards. Therefore, management has allowed for a large number of quality control workers to ensure an acceptable level of quality; this has resulted in lower labour productivity than in Japan. Although the Proton has achieved favourable management performance, supported by the reduced tax rate it receives as a national car, it requires ongoing assistance from Japan.

VI   MMC SITTIPOL IN THAILAND

MMC established its local operation, MMC Sittipol Co. Ltd, in Thailand in 1987. It retains managerial authority and holds a 48 per cent share of the equity in that company. The other 52 per cent of equity is held by a local Chinese group. MMC dispatches twenty-nine Japanese personnel to the company (about 1 per cent of the total workforce). These Japanese expatriates are in the positions of president, two out of four vice-presidents, and three out of five senior managers. The company operates two medium-scale plants. The Lardkrabang plant produces commercial vehicles such as trucks (including pick-up trucks) and buses; while the Leamchabang plant specialises in passenger cars, such as new and old models of the Lancer and the Galant. The total annual capacity of the two plants is 130 000 units. Although the new Leamchabang plant has a current capacity of 60 000 passenger cars, this can be increased to 100 000 units. The Leamchabang plant has three shops: namely welding, painting and assembly shops, but no stamping shop. The company produces various kinds of vehicle, from passenger cars to trucks, and is rapidly expanding its market share by adapting to local market demand. It is also the first company within the ASEAN countries to succeed in the export of fully assembled vehicles. MMC in Japan has transferred the entire production of pick-up trucks to Thailand, from which these vehicles are also exported to Japan as well as shipped to the domestic market.

The company has attempted to apply the Japanese production system through the initiative of Japanese management, but problems remain and the functioning of the system must be further improved. It has adopted the same employment qualification system as in Japan, a system which determines basic wages and the promotion route. It has also introduced individual performance evaluations for all its employees. This evaluation partly determines the skill wages, and points accumulated thereby have an effect on promotion. Other elements of the Japanese system, such as multifunctional skills, quality control, small-group activities, and a labour–management consultation system, have also been adopted. Some of these elements differ from the way they are applied in Japan and the Japanese managers are not happy about this. In particular, first-line supervisors do not play a sufficient role in administration, and work standards are prescribed not by them but by staff members. There are also problems with parts procurement, especially quality and delivery. Although many elements of the Japanese production system have been introduced, their working level remains at an introductory stage. For example, regarding multifunctional skills, Japanese managers have introduced individual worker training charts that show each worker's level of skill formation; however, the various shops have yet to implement this measure fully.

Nippondenso Co. Ltd

Du-Sop Cho

Nippondenso Co. Ltd was established in December 1949 following the separation of the electrical components and radiator divisions from the then Toyota Automobile Industries. Since its founding, Nippondenso has supplied Toyota and other automakers with the aim of becoming Japan's premier autoelectric components maker. For this reason it boldly named itself 'Nippondenso', Nippon meaning Japan, rather than 'Toyota Denso'.

Nippondenso has achieved steady growth through the expansion of its core businesses of engine and heater/air conditioner components. In the fiscal year 1994, net sales amounted to 1.25 trillion Japanese Yen, assets totalled 1.33 trillion and employees numbered 41 463, making the company to be one of the world's largest integrated automotive parts manufacturers. Because Toyota Motor Corporation has a 23 per cent equity holding, and accounts for about half of Nippondenso's sales, it goes without saying that Nippondenso is a core member of the Toyota Group. Nonetheless, as it also supplies automotive manufactures throughout the world including the Big Three in the USA, has advanced research and development capabilities, and a strongly independent management. Nippondenso no longer carries the image of being a Toyota subcontractor.

Nippondenso's first major advance was a technical tie-up with German autoelectric components maker Bosch in 1953. Nippondenso did not, however, simply replicate Bosch's technology but used it as a base to develop its own technology, thereby improving its competitiveness. The most well-known feature of Nippondenso's competitive dominance is its establishing of mass production technology. The company's achievement of a defect rate at the parts-per-million level while undertaking the mass production of several thousand different components is outstanding. Innovations such as line automation and precision processing were made possible by an organisation structure that incorporated continual improvement. Preceding Toyota in 1961, Nippondenso received the Demming Award, the ultimate accolade for quality control in Japan. This was further evidence that it had succeeded in creating a system that could consistently maintain a high level of quality. In the following year, the company established a quality control department under the slogan 'Denso Quality'. This department attempted to achieve defect-free production, but soon afterwards it settled for a more realistic goal embodied in the catch phrase 'World Denso, 100 per cent customer satisfaction'.

As Nippondenso's facilities and work practices were geared to using mass-production technology, it experienced a number of problems in overseas operations, where the market scale is much smaller. This issue will be addressed later in this chapter.

At the time of its foundation, Nippondenso was a specialist manufacturer of radiators and autoelectric components, but through the fusion of electronics technology with automotive component technology, new component fields emerged. In recent years, the Communication Instruments Division has expanded the applications of its electronics expertise to produce navigation systems and mobile telephones associated with communications outside of the vehicles.

PIONEERING OVERSEAS EXPANSION

Table 5.1 lists the company's overseas subsidiaries. It should be noted that Nippondenso established its overseas operations before the automotive manufacturers did. Its first overseas facility was a sales operation established in Los Angeles in 1971. New United Motor Manufacturing Inc. was Toyota's first major production facility. Established in 1984, it was a joint venture with General Motors. Toyota's first exclusive production facility, Toyota Motor Manufacturing USA, was formed in 1986. Nippondenso's role in helping this company start full production was considerable. In its international activities, a pattern has emerged in the various automobile manufacturing regions of the world where Nippondenso precedes the entry of major automobile makers, creates a local management structure, then uses the expertise gained to guide the major makers when they begin operations abroad. Conspicuous is Nippondenso's foresight and flexibility in its overseas strategy, which differs slightly from most Japanese corporations who depend heavily on exports. One example is the fact that it has production plants in Korea and China, yet Toyota has not entered either of these markets. A major issue facing the company as it heads into the twenty-first century is to what degree it will be able to unite its twenty-five overseas plants and display its network dominance under the vision of 'Global Denso'.

Table 5.2 details Nippondenso subsidiaries and affiliates in the Asia-Pacific region. Although the Asian automotive industry differs slightly from country to country, the span up to the mid-1970s can be considered the dawn period. For many years, Japanese and some European makers

Table 5.1   Foreign affiliated plants of Nippondenso, as at January 1995

Region	Manufacturing plants	Start of operations	Number of employees	Main products
USA	6	1984	3 870	Radiators, air conditioners, autoelectric components, compressors
Mexico	1	1994	–	Instrument clusters
Brazil	1	1980	997	Air conditioners, compressors, autoelectric components
UK	2	1989	1 440	Radiators, air conditioners, etc.
Spain	1	1989	113	Coils, engine related components
Italy	1	1986	1 164	Air conditioners, heaters, radiators
Australia	3	1972	861	Air conditioners, heaters, radiators, instrument clusters, etc.
Thailand	2	1972	987	Air conditioners, autoelectric components, dies, etc.
Indonesia	1	1975	958	Air conditioners, radiators, autoelectric components, plugs, etc.
Korea	1	1976	909	Instrument clusters
Malaysia	1	1980	820	Air conditioners, autoelectric components, radiators, etc.
India	2	1984	1 093	Air conditioners, autoelectric components, etc.
Taiwan	1	1987	246	Air conditioners, radiators, autoelectric components, etc.
China	1	1994	–	Air conditioners
Total	**24**		**13 458**	

undertook assembly on a complete knockdown (CKD) basis on a small scale. The situation, however, changed dramatically in the 1980s following the progress of industrialisation in many markets. Korea, Taiwan, Thailand and Malaysia embarked on projects to protect and develop their respective automotive industries, leading to a rapid expansion in market scale. Differing from the Japanese, European and US markets, which have virtually reached saturation point, Asian markets have great growth potential and are experiencing increasingly intense competition between rival makers. Not wanting to be left behind, Nippondenso has strengthened its Asian strategy through such measures as investigating the feasibility of establishing an Asian headquarters in Singapore.

Table 5.2 Profile of foreign affiliates of Nippondenso

Location	Name of plant	Ratio of ownership (%)	Start of operations	Sales	Main market
Australia	NDAU	65	1972	247 M Au$	Toyota, Mitsubishi, Daihatsu, Ford, GM
	AAA	100	1989	112 M Au$	Toyota, Mitsubishi, Daihatsu, Ford, GM
	FDI	90	1992	48 M Au$	Toyota, Mitsubishi, Daihatsu, Ford, GM
Thailand	NDT	36	1972	4593 M Bt	Toyota, Isuzu, Mitsubishi, Mazda, etc.
	NDTT	80	1987	63 M Bt	NDT, NDM
Indonesia	NDI	44	1975	353.7 B Rp	Toyota, Mitsubishi, Daihatsu, Mazda, Suzuki
Korea	PSCM	50	1976	67.2 B Won	Hyundai, Kia, Daewoo, Asia
Malaysia	NDM	40	1980	309 M M$	Proton, (Mitsubishi), Toyota, Honda
India	NDIN	37	1984	47 M Rs	Maruti (Suzuki), HH (Honda)
	SUBROS	13	1985	824 M Rs	Maruti (Suzuki)
Taiwan	NDTW	80	1987	3576 M Nt$	Local automobile companies
China	NDSG	30	1994	–	Local automobile companies

Notes:

NDAU	=	Nippondenso (Australia) PTY Ltd
AAA	=	Australian Automotive Air Pty Ltd
FDI	=	Flexdrive Industries Limited
NDT	=	Nippondenso Thailand Co Ltd
NDTT	=	Nippondenso Tool & Die (Thailand) Co Ltd
NDI	=	Nippondenso Indonesia Inc
PSCM	=	Poong Sung Chong Mil Co Ltd
NDM	=	Nippondenso (Malaysia) Sdn Bhd
NDIN	=	Nippondenso India Ltd
SUBROS	=	Subros Ltd
NDTW	=	Nippondenso Taiwan Co Ltd
NDSG	=	Yantai Shougang Nippondenso Co Ltd

Summarising Nippondenso's Asian strategy from the table (5.2), the level of supply to other Japanese companies is striking. Excluding China and Korea, each of Asia's automobile markets are the scene for competition among Japanese makers, which naturally provides Nippondenso with a wealth of business opportunities.

Second, the Company has many minority holdings in Asian joint ventures. This is because the protective nature of Asian markets prevents foreign corporations from holding majority shares in companies. Nonetheless, disregarding Poong Sung Chong Mil Co. Ltd in Korea and SUBROS in India, the Japanese side often holds management power despite the lack of equity. Although cases of failed joint ventures do exist, Nippondenso's superior technological capabilities and management expertise overcome the weaknesses in joint ventures to assure successful management of local companies.

Third, excluding China, Nippondenso completed its overseas plants slightly before the marked intensification of motorisation in Asia in the mid-1980s. It can be said that the company has strong desire for internationalisation. Regarding Chinese market entry, Nippondenso's nimble footwork is conspicuous against the wait-and-see position being taken by most Japanese vehicle makers.

Fourth, in Japan it is said that at least ten years of business experience is essential before the Japanese way of manufacturing can be achieved. But with the case of Nippondenso, it has gained the first-mover's advantage compared with the latecomers.

However, this does not mean that the standards achieved are always satisfactory. Although plants meet basic technological standards, the capacity to respond to change and difficult situations, changing of specifications and the fabrication of moulds requires a higher level of technology that is usually provided by the Japanese parent and the Japanese staff at the local plant. Nippondenso's international vision involves each subsidiary in maintaining its own self-sufficient type of management structure with the aim of forming a worldwide production network where each plant uses its specialised technology to make products that meet global standards. Its Asian operations, however, have not yet reached this stage.

TECHNOLOGICAL TRANSFER TO OVERSEAS SUBSIDIARIES

As mentioned earlier, Nippondenso's production system involves mass production while maintaining high standards of quality. Key factors in transferring this system overseas are; maintaining production levels to enjoy the benefits of mass production, and the training of staff to operate the production lines. Regarding these two points, Nippondenso's head office believes that only in Asia have its plants not reached satisfactory levels of quality and volume.

As with other Japanese corporations, the high level of labour turnover hampers staff training and affects operating efficiency. As operating procedures are not documented systematically in manuals, training by instructors involving teaching by example over a long period of time is essential for Japanese work practices to be introduced on the shop floor. Although it is a commonly held belief in Japan that corporations adapt to improve, this type of thinking is not held universally in other countries. What was striking about Nippondenso's management regarding training was the production of operating manuals that outlined decision-making procedures and work practices appropriate to the characteristics of the particular region.

Although employee training is a problem area, the scale of production is of greater concern. For the automotive industry, the appropriate production ratio of assembly plants to engine plants to components plants is said to be 2 : 3 : 5–10. That is, if the appropriate level for an assembly plant is 200 thousand units, then 300 thousand units are suitable for an engine plant, and between 500 thousand and 1 million units are desirable for components plants. If these levels are not achieved then the benefits of mass production will not be forthcoming. Although this is an example derived from experience, if the ratio has some economic and technological basis, then Nippondenso would need to produce between 500 thousand and 1 million of its main products, such as starters and alternators, at each of its plants. However, discounting China and Korea, Asia's total automobile production totals approximately 1.5 million units, and there are other component makers to consider, so on this basis such a target is unreachable. Even if production levels do not reach optimum levels, by specialising the production process at each plant to form a mutually compensating structure that transcends national borders, profitability should improve. Import tariffs and other restrictions, however, make national borders unnecessarily difficult to penetrate. Within the ASEAN countries, discussion about the introduction of a brand to brand complementation (BBC) agreement whereby tariffs are reduced to a minimum of 50 per cent is taking place, but because the circumstances of each participating country vary, finding an equitable medium is proving difficult.

As it is not possible to establish a mass production system simply by exporting Japanese production techniques, and if intensive production between plants is also not desirable, then the only alternative is to develop a new system that will achieve management goals yet allow the production of many components at low volumes. Nippondenso is addressing this problem through the development of technology for medium-volume production that involves an appropriate mix of manual and automated operations. This system involves maximising the work done by cheap labour and automating the vital quality control processes, such as precision and checking processes. Although this appears to be a step backwards in terms of production technology compared with the high-volume advanced automated plants operating in Japan, creating a system that suits the circumstances of the particular overseas market is the most appropriate solution.

We expected that the subsidiaries would be playing a leading role in formulating work standards, work organisation and the production line layout, and the purpose of our visits to Japanese subsidiaries in Korea, Taiwan, Thailand and Malaysia was to investigate these aspects.

MANAGEMENT OF LOCAL SUBSIDIARIES

Poong Sung Chong Mil Co. Ltd of Korea (hereafter referred to as PSCM) was the only plant in the study where the local partner controlled company management. Irrespective of levels of equity holdings, in the majority of Japanese-Korean joint ventures, the Korean side makes the management decisions, as this is said to improve management performance. The Korean partner is also a component manufacturer with an excellent understanding of Japanese technology, and both sides are satisfied with their relationship.

The establishment of Nippondenso's plant in Korea was also influenced by Toyota's business activities. During the 1970s, Toyota investigated entering the Korean market, starting with the formation of a joint venture. However, political reasons caused the shelving of the majority of the plans, with the only remaining vestige being PSCM, which only supplies Korean manufacturers.

PSCM has adopted Japanese technological methods successfully, and now has reached the stage where production and management could be undertaken adequately even without aid of the three Japanese staff (the lowest number at any of Nippondenso's Asian plants). Although production and management are being undertaken smoothly, its results, however, are not that positive. Despite purchases from Japan that will ensure product competitiveness (such as special materials, custom-made equipment, and electronic circuits), the fact that it is an unaffiliated maker without strong direct links with either manufacturers or suppliers is affecting profitability adversely. With the help of the Japanese head office, PSCM is diversifying into new fields such as engine control fuel systems, and seriously considering supplying the Japanese market, which maintains the world's toughest quality standards. These developments are believed to ensure a bright future for PSCM. Being able to export to Japan is an indication that PSCM has achieved world standards, and this should be an important factor in boosting employee morale.

The establishment of Nippondenso Taiwan, Co. Ltd (hereinafter referred to as NDTW) was also influenced by Toyota. In 1988, Toyota bought a 22 per cent stake in the local automobile company as a starting point for full local production, and NDTW was formed as a backup. By being geographically close to Toyota's joint venture, NDTW contributed substantially to boosting Toyota's market share by ensuring stable quality control and reducing inventory levels by introducing the *Kanban* system. Although NDTW entered the market as recently as 1987, by producing high-value-added products and being protected by high import tariffs, it quickly achieved a high market share and was able to turn a profit in its second year of production. Among the plants studied, the speed of success of this plant is most unusual.

One problem facing this company is that it is operating in a market of less than 500 000 vehicles in annual production. As Nippondenso's production system is not applicable in its original form, the benefits of operating at large economies of scale cannot be expected. When NDTW built a new factory in 1989, a medium-volume production system was investigated and local technical staff inspected the facilities at Nippondenso (Malaysia) Sdn Bhd (abbreviated as NDM) and Nippondenso Indonesia Inc. (NDI). The result was a compact plant where automation had been scaled down and employees appeared to be working in an orderly manner.

Although the Taiwanese labour market will in future pose problems for NDTW, and this company will continue to face setbacks such as the resignation of all the technicians on the primary line, demand for luxury vehicles is increasing, which is positive indication that Taiwan's economy is strong. As the plant emphasises quality over price, it will be able to overcome the problems of small-scale production and growth is expect to be steady.

As with the Taiwanese operation, NDM's greatest problem is that it is operating in a small market. In 1987, this company suffered two setbacks:

a severe drop in demand (130 000 units in the early 1980s compared with 50 000 units in 1987); and the introduction of the Malaysian government's national automobile policy linked to the Proton Project. Temporarily this forced NDM to implement staff redundancies and close down. In Malaysia, with its small population and shortage of labour, labour intensive mass production is an impossibility. Regardless of all these, this company was able to rebuild itself and become profitable. Although it is now focusing on high-end components and expanding its export volume, fears about rising unemployment in Japan may slow the shift to overseas production of high-end products. Because Nippondenso's South east Asian plants have yet to establish a mutually compensating structure, the prospects of expanding exports substantially are slim. As exporting to Japan is an attractive alternative, NDM's Japanese managers are busy formulating plans to develop a cost-competitive medium-volume production system. As current exports to Japan are negligible, however, it is not clear whether the plans will come to fruition. Nevertheless, Japanese corporations as well as the Malaysian government, are implementing employee training, an integral component for setting up a medium-volume production system, so the plan to transform the Malaysian facility to a producer of high-end products may not be altogether a dream.

Of the subsidiaries covered in the study, Nippondenso Thailand Co. Ltd (NDT) was the most active. As a reflection of Thailand's strong economy, demand for cars is continually expanding, as are NDT's results. Because the existing plant is unable to meet the growing demand for components, NDT has secured a site on the outskirts of Bangkok four times the size of its current plant and is rushing to complete new facilities. Another feature of NDT is that it operates Nippondenso's only moulding plant outside of Japan. Because of its advanced nature, moulding technology is an indispensable field, but to date, no other ASEAN country has established such an independent technological base. Although moulding technology causes more concern for Japanese corporations than any other area, Nippondenso is striving to establish this technology overseas to supply the Japanese market with medium-grade moulds. Currently, however, local demand accounts for over half of sales. The technology transfer occurring because the local market is being supplied by the Nippondenso Group other Japanese affiliates and local companies is having a positive effect on the technological level of the local companies.

FUTURE STRATEGIC ISSUES

By benefiting substantially from the expansion of Japan's automotive manufacturers, in particular Toyota, Nippondenso has been able to achieve continual growth as a domestic and international general components maker. With the current friction over the imbalance in the automotive industry between the USA and Japan, the previous strategy of continually expanding exports and market domination is no longer possible. Nippondenso's future growth will depend on its ability to develop products and boost the cost performance of existing products, while capitalising on the high potential growth of the Asian market by seizing the first-mover's advantage.

Having realised the importance of the Asian market, Nippondenso is hurrying to complete a regional headquarters in Singapore and to strengthen ties between the other Asian operations. Although it is limited, the company is moving towards the production of mutually compatible components at its Asian plants. If it were able to create a mutually compensating structure, this would provide great impetus for its global structure, which incorporates an integrated network.

Yazaki Sogyo Co. Ltd

Kunio Kamiyama

The origin of the Yazaki Group headed by Yazaki Sogyo Co. Ltd can be traced back to May 1929, when Sadami Yazaki began selling automobile electric cables. Now consisting of a network of seven domestic and twenty-five overseas factories, the Group's business covers a wide range of products, including wire harnesses, standard electrical cables, vehicle instrumentation, tachographs, gas meters, gas air conditioners, alarms, solar systems, solar heaters and optical fibres.

Since its establishment, Yazaki has focused on wire harness production, and at present is the industry's leading maker. A wire harness can be described as simply a bundle of strands of wire; the number of wires varies according to the type of car, but is generally around several hundred wires. The manufacturing process begins by cutting a length of wire approximately 550 metres long, and placing connectors at both ends. Next, the wires are gathered into the main harness and subharness groups. Although some parts are highly sophisticated, production is basically a labour-intensive process.

Yazaki's aggressive policy in building overseas production bases can be attributed to the fact that manufacturing wire harnesses is labour-intensive. Since Yazaki's establishment of the Thai Yazaki Electric Wire Co. Ltd in 1962, the company has expanded its overseas business aggressively. Thai Arrow Products Co. Ltd's predecessor, a joint venture company with local partners, was established in 1963, and the Taiwan Yazaki Corporation was formed in 1970.

But the distinctive nature of the wire harness lies not only in its labour-intensive production. It is one of the first components to be installed in the assembly process yet, because its shape can be easily changed, it is one of the last components to be designed. Indeed, the wire harness undergoes an extremely large number of design changes as it is adapted to design alterations of other parts during the trial production process. This makes production automation difficult and necessitates flexible counter-measures. These measures, such as labour-intensive manufacturing, short delivery, and immediate compliance with design changes, require flexible production control and effective labour management to be successful. Yazaki has an established system that meets these requirements, making them an industry pioneer. A look at two factories in Asia will explain how this system developed.

One factory is in Ping Tung Prefecture, Taiwan. It began operations in February 1970 with full investment by Yazaki on condition that it exported to the United States. Aided by inexpensive labour, the factory expanded steadily until the late 1980s, when the Taiwanese gen appreciated, thereby reducing labour cost competitiveness. Because of this relative rise in labour costs, the total number of workers in the main and subordinate factories was reduced from over 5000 in 1987 to 2500 in September 1991. By September 1992, employee numbers in the main factory had dropped to 994, and even when workers in the three outside factories and seven work stations were included, the labour force only amounted to 1750 workers.

In addition to these labour reductions, a complete review of the production organisation was implemented and a new emphasis was placed on the introduction of the Japanese production system. This put the company back into the black by the end of 1980s. Within a short period of time, however, it is a complicated task to completely change a factory having a production style and equipment introduced in the early part of the 1970s. The Yazaki operations as of 1992 will be analysed in the following pages.

The majority of the workforce is made up of female, junior-high-school graduates, but more recently about half of the new recruits have been high school graduates. The employees work in teams of ten to fifteen, the smallest unit of a work team. Team leaders are predominantly female, but male team leaders are also employed. A group is formed from three teams and here the leaders are predominantly male: the ratio is seventy-nine male group leaders to thirteen female group leaders. Three or four groups make up one section. Similar to the role of their counterparts in Japan, leaders are required to supervise quality, efficiency, delivery and safety. The level of accuracy, however, is slightly lower.

A newly-hired operator receives three days of routine training, and is then allocated to a line (the shop floor was organised into a line system in 1990). They undergo OJT from team and group leaders. When this survey was conducted in 1991, the introductory training period was only one day, but in 1992 it was extended to a full week. After being allocated to a line, a worker's job assignment is basically fixed. The efficiency level of operators is the same as in Japan for exclusive operations. When, however, workers are required to co-ordinate with pre- and post-operations, the degree of efficiency drops. Along with changing layouts and trying to implant reform consciousness, efforts are being made to increase operational efficiency and flexibility. Because of the rise in labour costs, however, such measures cannot recover the competitive edge of the Taiwanese factory. Job rotation was considered as one of the reforms, but this idea ended in failure as workers demanded wage increases when new techniques were expected to be acquired.

It is important to note that, from the latter part of the 1980s, the company succeeded in reducing production costs by 10 per cent to cover the annual increase in wage costs. None the less in terms of cost and supply of labour, difficulties in maintaining the labour intensive production of wire harnesses in Taiwan while remaining competitive as an overseas base for an extended period of time still exist. In 1992, Yazaki manufactured 240 000 wire harness units, the majority of which were exported to US companies such as Ford and Chrysler. After continued efforts to increase the ratio of domestic sales, the percentage of domestic sales increased from 3 per cent in 1990 to around 10 per cent in 1993 and the aim thereafter was to achieve a ratio of 20 per cent. In 1992, Yazaki held a 40 per cent share of the Taiwanese domestic market.

Although the factory in Taiwan has improved its operations rapidly, the level of efficiency and flexibility does not compare favourably with other overseas Yazaki factories. Even with the remarkable improvements made during the late 1980s, the quality control system has not reached a satisfactory stage, because of more inspection stations and a higher defect rate than in Japan. Superiority over other manufacturers in Taiwan can be attributed to the introduction of 'material–results' aspects from Japan. The Taiwanese factory uses jigs and tools, dies and special machines imported from Japan. In fact, 60 per cent of imported parts and materials come from Japan. This does not pose a problem for the Taiwanese government, as almost all products are for export. Nevertheless, the local procurement rate by production facilities should be increased since the factory is situated in Taiwan, where, unlike in ASEAN countries, a range of strong supporting industries exist. Since it may be difficult to raise local procurement from the present rate of 40 per cent, a reduction in costs will be required. The original new jigs and tools are imported from Japan, but the rate of local procurement in Taiwan is rising. Simple tools and dies are increasingly procured locally; however, sophisticated parts – such as for housing connectors – must be imported from Japan.

Another way to make use of the Taiwanese factory is by sending workers trained in Taiwan to Chinese-speaking areas where growth is expected. The Shantou factory, the second Yazaki factory in China, started operations with the help of the Taiwanese factory in January 1991. This type of involvement for Taiwan symbolises the future of labour–intensive factories in the NIEs.

Another example is the Phitsanulok factory of Thai Arrow Products Co. Ltd. The 'branch factory' style seen here was devised and implemented in Japan. This style, typical of Yazaki, involves establishing factories in rural areas where there is an abundant pool of labour. Furthermore, securing jobs for the local people will help to prevent population shifts to other areas. Factory construction in countries and areas where other companies have not yet ventured, and expansion into even more rural areas, helps to prevent other companies from following suit. Yazaki tries to avoid being influenced by other companies and strives to build factories embracing the Yazaki spirit; the company's motto is 'Supporting local areas'. The establishment of the Phitsanulok factory in an area free of industrial development is a typical example. This factory is Yazaki's third wire harness factory in Thailand. The first was the Bangphli factory set up in 1984. The next was the Chachoengsao factory also established in 1984. The Phitsanulok factory was established in July 1992 and began operating in September 1993. Although it had only one year of operational experience, the degree of application of the Japanese system was considerably higher than in Taiwanese factory and thus production was able to begin roughly on schedule.

The ease with which production began was because of the long operational experience of the other factories in Thailand. As stated before, the earlier form of Thailand Arrow Products Co. Ltd, the parent company of the Phitsanulok factory, was established in 1963. The company originally produced cotton products for export to Japan, but changed its name in December 1977 when it began producing automotive wire harnesses and measuring instruments for automobiles. A related company, Thailand Yazaki Electric Wire Co. Ltd, which mainly manufactures electric wires, began operations in Thailand as early as 1962. At the time of writing, the Yazaki group has five companies in Thailand, employing a total of 12 000 workers.

To aid in the start-up of the Phitsanulok factory, 150 Yazaki employees were dispatched from other plants in Thailand. Initially, eighteen Japanese employees were sent to the factory for a period of three to six months, but from August 1993, the number of Japanese was reduced to six, with a total workforce of 3338. This small number of Japanese expatriates was consistent with other factories. Japanese workers are necessary in areas such as design, production technology and purchasing; however, once the foundations have been established only a few Japanese expatriates are required to remain. The foundation building process takes about ten years and the establishment of the first Bangphli factory took approximately that length of time.

The workforce mainly consists of junior high school graduates, but about 30 per cent are high school graduates or above. The hiring process consists of a test and interview, and there is a four-month probation period for successful applicants. During this period another exam is held, and those who pass become permanent employees. Throughout the four-month probation period, work attendance is closely monitored, and an additional interview with the line chief is conducted. Over 90 per cent go on to become permanent employees, but those who do not meet the standards are not employed. At present, the company faces no difficulty in recruiting workers. One week of off-the-job training is followed by a week of OJT. In the third week, the new employees join the production line and are trained by leaders or subleaders. It takes about three months to become an independent operator; those who cannot adjust during this period usually resign. The job turnover rate of employees, including those during the trial period, is a low 2 per cent per month.

The performance of this newly-established factory is very promising. The method of setting up standard working hours differs from the Japanese mother plant, but within a year of starting production, the index of standard working hours increased from 60 to an estimated level of 100. At the time of the survey, the extent of achievement was 10 per cent below that of other factories, but above the original predictions. The defect ratio in the manufacturing process is still higher than other factories in Thailand, but the ratio has dropped to a level below that of Yazaki's Japanese plants. The secret of this high level of performance lies in the training system.

Training is conducted on a yearly basis, with programmes differing according to employee level. Designed to meet the circumstances of the plants in Thailand, the training programmes were devised at the Bangphli factory. In addition to those undertaken in Thailand, the training programmes conducted in Japan are achieving excellent results. Approximately 240–250 employees per year are sent to Japan, each for a six-month period. The training lines consist of workers only of Thai nationality, as was the case for the trainee operators coming from the Philippines and Portugal. With the competition that arises between the different nationalities, the groups improve to the extent they are on a par with the Japanese workers within a month. Excluding ordinary operators, there is a continual stream of workers coming to Japan for training. Maintenance technicians receive six months' training and computer-related technicians participate in a year-long programme. Since these workers return home with their newly-acquired skills, the local factories are able to maintain a standard matching that of Yazaki's plants in Japan.

Problems remain, however. For example, the multiskilled operating system in operation at other factories in Thailand has not yet been implemented. At the time of the visit, introduction of a job rotation programming was only in the discussion stage. There were thirty-six QC circles operating on a trial basis (the participation ratio is one third), and the goal was to increase the number to a hundred circles within a year. The aim is not for reform on a Japanese-scale level but for an increase in the level of quality consciousness. The suggestions system was already in use, but only 200 suggestions were received each month.

The Phitsanulok factory was established for mass production and at the time the survey was held, the main customer was the European subsidiary of Ford in Belgium; supply to the United States was also being considered. Similar to other Yazaki overseas operations, this plant aimed to supply markets in the developed countries, thus a level of quality equal to that achieved in Japan had to be ensured. Therefore, in Thailand, where the level of supporting industries was inadequate, apart from equipment such as conveyors, which can be procured more cheaply locally, the factory was dependent on Yazaki in Japan for the majority of its resources. This factory's ratio of local content was lower than that of the Taiwan factories. Although the method of improving localisation remains an important issue, with the expansion into China and the slowing down of development at the Taiwanese factory, the Thai factory, which has become the exporting centre for auto parts to developed countries, will remain the centre of attention in the near future.

Matsushita Electric Industrial Company Ltd

Tetsuji Kawamura

The Matsushita Electric Industrial Company was established in 1925 (although its history can be traced back to 1918, when Konosuke Matsushita founded Matsushita Electric Apparatus Works in Osaka) and is now the world's largest consumer electronics company. It has developed into one of Japan's leading multinational enterprises. Its overseas production operations started as far back as the early 1960s, and Matsushita's business operations and foreign subsidiaries now cover almost the entire world. In 1994, overseas operations accounted for 50 per cent of total sales. Overseas production accounted for 32 per cent of its total overseas sales. Matsushita's plan is to produce more than half of its overseas sales abroad by 1996. To organise its worldwide operations, it has developed a 'four-zone' strategy covering North America, South America, Europe and Africa, and Asia and the Middle East. It has also recently opened a division in China. Regional divisions are responsible for the activities in each region. In North America, for example, as of March 1995, Matsushita had twenty-seven subsidiaries, including Matsushita Electric Corporation of America (MECA) as a regional parent company. The Asia and Middle East Division has as many as fifty-four subsidiaries, the largest number of subsidiaries among the 'four zones'. Forty-two of them are manufacturing subsidiaries, most located in Southeast Asia. This demonstrates that Southeast-Asian operations are highly significant to Matsushita's overseas production strategy. In addition to the manufacturing subsidiaries, there are ten sales companies, one R&D, and one service company in Southeast Asia.

Our research project conducted a number of field surveys, focusing on television and to some extent on VCR manufacturing plants at Matsushita Television Company (MTC) in the USA and Matsushita Industrial de Baja California (MIBA) in Maquiladoras, Mexico in 1989; at Matsushita Electric Taiwan (TAMACO) in 1992; and at Matsushita Television in Malaysia (MTV) and National Thai (NTC) in 1993. Television manufacturing is one of Matsushita's major areas of activity, and it has been in the forefront of the company's international production operations.

Although Matsushita's overseas production started in the early 1960s, its overseas production operations continued to be mainly of the import-substitution type. In the early stages, Matsushita's overseas production strategy involved a 'mini-Matsushita'-type operation. This strategy was characterised by local production for the respective domestic markets, which were often protected by high tariffs and other barriers. Matsushita's local production of assembled end products such as TV sets involved no clear intention to export to world markets, or to re-export to Japan. Consequently, they did not make use of the 'free trade zone' (FTZ) system, and most of the operations were organised as joint ventures with the participation of local capital.

In the early 1970s, Matsushita also began to pursue a 'single-item' strategy for the domestic market in each country. In 1972, the company established a joint venture in Malaysia, MAICO, to produce wind-fan-type air conditioners, and another to produce dry cell batteries in India (INN). There were also other subsidiaries in Iran and Latin America. However, in the late 1970s and early 1980s, Matsushita implemented major changes in its international business strategy, in a similar way to did other Japanese electronics firms at that time: they shifted to an overseas production-orientated strategy. This marked the second stage in the development of Matsushita's international business operations. The shift in focus was prompted by a set of adverse conditions that developed after the late 1970s: increased uncertainty of global markets caused by the transition to a floating foreign exchange system, and intensified trade conflict with the US and European Community (EC) countries. At this stage, Matsushita's overseas production was gathering momentum, and Matsushita began to follow a path towards becoming a fully-fledged multinational enterprise (MNE). The start of TV set production in the USA, which was the most important market for Panasonic (a Matsushita brand), highlighted the second stage.

After the late 1980s, the shift to overseas production operations by Japanese electronics firms was accelerated through the effect of the rapid appreciation of the yen against the US dollar, coupled with an increasing labour shortage in Japan. Major Japanese electronics firms constructed new export production bases in East and Southeast Asia. Matsushita opened new production lines for TVs and other end products in Malaysia and other Southeast Asian countries. It also expanded its efforts to cultivate a 'broad procurement' system and reshuffle product line-ups among its overseas production bases. In addition, it reorganised its management structure to become more highly integrated in order to supervise more efficiently its expanded overseas operations. At the same time, Matsushita's traditional strategy of 'mini-Matsushita'-type operations was a facing major change; Matsushita's overseas production operations was by this time entering its third stage.

'Mini-Matsushita' operations, which characterised the early stage of Matsushita's overseas production strategy, made a variety of products for the domestic markets in which they were located. In accordance with its principle of 'one supply base in each country' and a policy for production to be carried out close to the target market, Matsushita built 'mini-Matsushita' ('mini-M') local plants in each country. Sanyo, another major Japanese consumer electronics company, followed suit. A factory complex was organised wherein each product division jointly operated production lines in the same production site. The factory complex manufactured a variety of items to supply each domestic market. Matsushita established several 'mini-M' local plants in Asia: NTC in 1961, TAMACO in 1962, Matsushita Electric (Malaysia) Co. (MELCOM) in 1965, Matsushita Electric Philippines (MEPCO) in 1967, and P. T. National Gobel (NABEL) in Indonesia in 1970.

In the late 1970s, decline in demand caused by the world-wide recession intensified international competition. Japanese electronics firms accelerated export efforts to their major markets, the USA and Europe. Increasing trade conflicts with them, coupled with the appreciation of the yen, added difficulties to Japanese exports, especially to the USA. In the late 1970s, under the Orderly Market Agreement (OMA) with the USA, voluntary export restraints regarding colour TV sets started. In 1974, Matsushita acquired the Quasar division from Motorola and established the Matsushita Industrial Company (MIC). It started local production for the Panasonic and Quasar brands in the USA. However, the USA levied high duties on CRT imports. In 1980, Matsushita established MIBA in Mexico under the Maquiladora system, to supply chassis to MIC and launched TV set assembly there. In this period, Matsushita also built overseas production bases for parts and components, such as Matsushita Electronics (S)(MESA), Matsushita Electric Motor (S)(MEM), Matsushita Denshi (S)(MECS) and Matsushita Technology (S)(MASTEC) in Singapore.

The 'export-base' type of local production, which highlights the phase of Matsushita's overseas production strategy in the mid-1990s, involves the construction of export production bases, especially in Southeast Asia, where labour costs are lower and currencies are virtually linked to the US dollar. This is accompanied by a strategy for the globally 'optimal' distribution of production sites and the development of a 'broad procurement' system. Matsushita is attempting to optimise the procurement of parts and components in an attempt to achieve a reduction in costs. Consequently, Matsushita's overseas production operations are becoming more integrated and organised, which is characteristic of an

MNE. Simultaneously, operations in areas such as Taiwan and Malaysia, which are considered to be strategic for Japanese electronics firms, are undergoing significant changes to their traditional 'mini-M' strategy.

MTV in Malaysia typifies Matsushita's recent 'export-base' strategy. In 1987, the yen rose over the ¥100 to the US dollar benchmark. At the same time, Matsushita's competitors in South Korea, LG and Samsung, were catching up rapidly, and exports from Japan were encountering further obstacles. In response, Matsushita established MTV in 1988, with the aim of creating the 'World's No. 1 Colour TV Plant', and started production there in April of that year. MTV is located in Selangor Shah Alam, a major industrial district of Malaysia. It produces, exclusively for export, a million units of colour TV sets per year, most of which have 21-inch or 14-inch picture tubes, and ships them to the Middle East (30 per cent), Southeast Asia and Oceania (30 per cent), Japan (25 per cent), and Russia and eastern Europe, as well as to Hong Kong. Matsushita continues to produce larger sizes of TV sets in Japan.

MTV enjoys lower labour costs in Malaysia, and the Panasonic brand name has established a strong presence on world TV markets. High quality and manufacturing efficiency are necessary, however, to preserve its edge as an export base in the face of intensified international competition. The application of Japanese-style management and production systems constitutes a basic competitive strategy. Moreover, as our surveys have shown, this strategy is applied not only by Matsushita but by all Japanese firms that have export bases in Southeast Asia. It is easier to apply these Japanese systems in Southeast Asia, where traditional American-style management and work practices are not deeply ingrained. Compared with Japanese-affiliated plants in North America, the plants in Southeast Asia generally receive high scores in our evaluation of their application of the Japanese production and management systems. In fact, MTV is in the group of companies that has received the highest application evaluation; it is considered to be a typical 'application'-type factory.

There is a clear contrast between MTV in Malaysia, and MTC, a typical 'adaptation' type of local production operation in the USA. MTC began operations in 1974 (called MIC at the time) through the acquisition of Motorola's TV division. MTC's application of traditional American-style management and production systems is facilitated by the fact that its operations are limited to assembling TV sets from PC boards and chassis imported from MIBA in Tijuana, Mexico. In contrast, at MTV, the Japanese production system is applied to a plant in which integrated TV set production, ranging from the PC board insertion process to final assembly, is carried out. Complete ownership of MTV also makes it easier for Matsushita to apply Japanese-style management practices to this factory.

The 'mini-M' plants, on the other hand, are all joint ventures between Matsushita and local capital. In Malaysia, MELCOM is one such joint venture. It operates at the same location as MTV and is 43.1 per cent owned by Matsushita.

According to the survey evaluation, MTV received generally high scores for application. In particular, the score for Group II, Production Control, was highest, with Groups V, Labour Relations, and VI, Parent–Subsidiary Relations next highest. For MTV, the scores in these groups were somewhat higher than the average application evaluation scores for Japanese affiliated plants in East and Southeast Asia, and considerably higher than those for similar plants in North America. However, for Group I, Work Organisation and Administration, and Group III, Procurement, application scores were relatively low. It is particularly worth noting that MTV's score for Group I is lower than the electronics industry's average, and lower than the average for all four industries surveyed.

The additional 'Four Perspective evaluation' also revealed that MTV was characterised by a high degree of application in all four aspects. At TAMACO, a typical 'mini-M' plant that has been operating for a long time, a similarly high degree of application was seen in all except the 'human–results' aspect. This demonstrates that at TAMACO, local management succeeded in operating the plant by applying Japanese-style practices, without relying too much on the assistance of Japanese expatriates. In contrast, at MTV, the Japanese system was being applied with a great deal more assistance from Japanese personnel.

One of the most notable aspects of competitive strategy at MTV, as a typical 'export base' operation, is plant facilities and equipment. Production equipment, as well as testing and adjusting equipment, is brought in from Japan, and is either similar to the equipment used in Japan or, in some instances even more advanced. This equipment gives MTV the ability to achieve the standards of quality and efficiency that provide the basis for competitive strength in export markets. Bringing in production machinery and other equipment from Japan is the rule among Japanese affiliated overseas transplants. This equipment incorporates the expertise and technical improvements achieved through long production experience in Japan. This constitutes one of the major vehicles for the transfer of technology from Japan to overseas countries. MTV's competitive edge as an 'export base' depends largely on such advanced equipment and machinery. This equipment is highly computerised. Chassis insertion and mounting processes adopt CIM. Testing and adjustment processes, quality control, information, design and R&D are also computerised. Optical fibre cables interconnect the systems and link the systems to Japan via an on-line network in Singapore. Chassis stockers are even more automated and computerised than in Japan. These advanced systems help to achieve production line management that is as efficient, and product quality that is as high, as it is in Japan. Cheap labour in Malaysia is not the sole source of MTV's competitive edge, although such human factors are, of course, very important.

A key factor in the successful operation of overseas production using advanced equipment and machinery is local maintenance capability. This is typically observed in the now highly automated insertion process of PCB. Matsushita is a leading manufacturer of insertion machines, called Panaserts, which provide Matsushita with one of its competitive advantages. Panaserts, however, require very finely tuned adjustment and a high level of maintenance in order to maintain high quality and efficiency. The high cost of Japanese expatriates underscores the importance of having a local maintenance capability for achieving successful technology transfer and an independent local operation. It is notable that after several years of production experience, local staff are able to conduct most of the equipment maintenance at MTV. In this respect, technology transfer to MTV has advanced to a very high level. Although Japanese expatriate engineers still seem to be indispensable, lead workers undertake ordinary maintenance activities, thus achieving one of the key elements of the Japanese production system. MTV runs a systematic training programme for local engineers and technicians, to enhance their maintenance skills. It sends twenty or thirty local staff members, including engineers and technicians, to mother plants and the Matsushita Training Centre in Japan.

In fact, the MTV insertion process is a little less automated than in Japan. At MTV, 80 per cent to 87 per cent of the parts are automated, while 90 per cent is automated in Japan. The slightly lower degree of automation simplifies maintenance. While the insertion of radial and larger parts requires more manual work, the low cost of labour makes it unnecessary to automate these function, and limitations in local maintenance capabilities make it undesirable to do so.

Quality control is another key factor in preserving international competitiveness. MTV conducts a number of quality control practices, as a result of which the defect rate is even lower than in Japan. In order to achieve one of the main principles of the Japanese production line, namely that no defects are allowed to advance to the next stage of the manufacturing process, MTV establishes a greater number of quality inspection checkpoints, thereby achieving in-process quality assurance, as well as 'block quality assurance'. MTV has also computerised its QC information management. The human factor is generally considered to be important for achieving quality control. In that sense, the application of the Japanese system is significant. At first glance, however, it seems that MTV's high levels of quality and efficiency are largely the result of advanced equipment. This requires a further examination of the application of Japanese human resource management systems at MTV.

Based on the 'Matsushita system', the MTV production system exhibits a somewhat lower degree of application of Japanese 'methods' and represents some interesting 'revised applications' of the Japanese system. For example, MTV produces manuals that detail explicitly standard work practices for many operations. The wage system is a mixture of local Malaysian and Matsushita practices. This demonstrates how Matsushita's 'application' strategy reflects its long experience in overseas production operations. Where necessary, computerisation and automation compensate for insufficient skills in the local workforce in areas such as picture adjustment and testing, as they do in management. In this sense, too, MTV is in the vanguard of Matsushita's current overseas production strategy.

Job assignment is quite rigid on the MTV production line. Their system for developing multiskilled workers seems to differ slightly from the Japanese practice of frequent job rotation and OJT. There seem to be two reasons for this. First, workers in Asian areas have not had much experience with the type of job management associated with Taylorism. Simple job rotation is therefore unlikely to assure strict control over individual work tasks, which is a basic precondition for the development of multiskilled workers. Second, advanced automation has reduced the degree to which the electronics industry depends on manual operations, and this has simplified the jobs of individual workers greatly. There is consequently less necessity for multiskilled workers in this industry than in the auto assembly industry. There has also been a general tendency to separate female workers, who work on production lines, from male workers, who are promoted to technical and supervisory positions. It is more important for female production workers to carry out individual job tasks strictly. At MTV, it is notable that workers insert fewer items into the boards during the manual insertion stage of radial and large parts into the chassis. Workers are trained more systematically there than in Japan, although OJT still plays a significant role.

MTV has introduced small-group activities, and seventy-three QC circles have been organised, with an average of fifteen workers in each.

About 95 per cent of the total workforce participates in these activities, which are conducted during paid working hours. Although there are fewer voluntary activities than in Japan, they are carried out with enthusiasm.

MTV also implements a deliberate employment policy intended to secure highly skilled workers. MTV makes an intensive effort to hold on to such employees and to this end provides considerable welfare benefits. The employee turnover rate is therefore below the local average.

Advanced production equipment comparable to that used in Japan, production line management similar to that in Japan, and the introduction of the basic elements of Japanese style human resources management (certain aspects of which have been revised), enable MTV to preserve its competitive edge as an export production base.

On the other hand, the 'mini-M' local production plants face major revisions under the changing global environment of the electronics business, which, among other trends, is witnessing the advent of the 'export-base' type of operation in Southeast Asia. The 'mini-M' strategy typified by TAMACO's TV and VCR operations will be eliminated. NTC, another 'mini-M' is turning into a production base for electronics parts, such as capacitors and deflection yokes, for export to Southeast Asia, while its TV set and VCR production remains targeted to the domestic market.

TAMACO, established in 1962, is a typical 'mini-M'. With as many as 6000 employees, it makes various products, including colour TVs, VCRs, radio cassette recorders and other audio-visual products, refrigerators, air conditioners, washing machines, electric fans and cooking apparatus (toasters, etc.), as well as electronics parts and components such as flyback transformers. TV production started in 1969, and VCR production in 1984. TV sets and VCRs are produced exclusively for the domestic market, with the exception of a small volume of OEM TV sets that are shipped to South Korea, and the export of some VCRs. However, the business environment changed considerably in the late 1980s. Taiwan's rapid economic growth as one of NIEs, and its increasing democratisation, brought about rapid wage increases. Trade conflicts rose because of an accumulated trade surplus with the USA, and the appreciation of the Taiwan dollar against the US dollar prompted the opening-up of domestic markets. Import duties on VCRs were reduced from 45 per cent in 1986 to 27.5 per cent in 1989. Duty on TV sets was also lowered, to 15 per cent. Competition with imported products increased in domestic markets, which expanded as a result of rapid economic growth. Therefore, TAMACO's TV and VCR business, instead of enjoying the benefits of a protected market, faced new competition from imported products in its own domestic market.

One of the ways in which Matsushita has responded to this challenge has been to strengthen the efforts of application of the Japanese production system at TAMACO. Indeed, the application evaluation score for TAMACO was as high as that received by MTV. Moreover, TAMACO has applied the Japanese system largely through its own local staff. It is also notable that its long operating experience has enhanced the capability of local management. At the same time we can assume that Taiwan's socioeconomic conditions are more suitable to Japanese-style management than are those of the USA or even of Mexico.

Another way that Matsushita responded was to reshuffle its product mix by assigning medium-grade products to TAMACO, high-grade products to Japan, and low-grade products to Malaysia. This strategy reflects the recent competitive advantage of Taiwan in the electronics industry. In the 1990s, Taiwan has improved its capability to make electronics products. It is now the leading supplier of 14-inch TV sets and computer displays. It is also becoming more advanced in electronics parts manufacturing, including that carried out by Japanese firms.

TAMACO produces 14- to 29-inch TV sets, while the larger ones are imported from Japan and the smaller ones from Malaysia. Concerning VCR production, Matsushita is introducing more value-added products. For example, 60 per cent of TAMACO's VCRs are the replay-only type, but 90 per cent of those are the hi-fi type. The remaining 40 per cent are recording-replay VCRs, 60 per cent of which have a *karaoke* function for the Taiwan market. Matsushita is also increasing its R&D activities at TAMACO to promote the design of new, higher value-added products for the Taiwan market, and utilising local parts to reduce costs. Similar moves are also apparent in Malaysia, and at MIBA in Mexico.

These product reassignments and reorganisations at TAMACO are in fact part of Matsushita's global business strategy for creating an 'optimal' production base network. As part of that strategy, Matsushita is also concentrating the production of flyback transformers and toasters in Taiwan.

Concurrently, Matsushita is carrying out a global reorganisation of its parts and components procurement network. It is pursuing a 'broad procurement' strategy to secure low-cost procurement of parts and components overseas. While it is true that 60 per cent of VCR parts and components used at TAMACO are imported from Japan, and that only a negligible volume is procured through 'broad procurement', it is also true that 25 per cent of the value of its TV parts and components are procured through the 'broad procurement' method, and that 50 per cent is procured from local suppliers. Regarding picture tubes, the most important components of TV sets, Matsushita produces high-quality flat-type displays in Japan, 21- to 26-inch normal displays in the USA, and 21-inch displays in Malaysia. Local production activities by Japanese firms have been strengthening the supply capability of electronics parts and components in Southeast Asia, especially in Malaysia. Consequently, MTV procures 99 per cent of its TV parts and components from within Southeast Asia (Malaysia, Singapore and Thailand). The International Procurement Office (IPO) of MTV supplies Southeast Asia-made parts and components to Matsushita's twenty-one TV plants world-wide.

Centring on its production activities in Southeast Asia, Matsushita's overseas production strategy is now becoming more organised and integrated in order to preserve its international competitiveness. Although other Japanese electronics firms are making similar moves, the strategy of Matsushita's TV operations is leading the way. The surge in the value of the yen in the mid-1990s is accelerating this trend.

Sony Corporation

Tetsuji Kawamura

Sony Corporation, founded in 1946 as Tokyo Tsushin Kōgyō, is a leading Japanese consumer electronics manufacturer specialising in the field of audio-visual products. It reported ¥4.0 trillion total sales (US$34.4 billion) on a consolidated base in fiscal year 1993, 80 per cent of which was earned through the sale of audio-visual and other electronics products. Sony has demonstrated innovation in the development of new product technology and firmly established its name as a prestigious brand on world markets, thus providing the company with a strong competitive edge. Sony has ventured overseas, first through the export of its products from Japan to global markets, and now through an enormous manufacturing operations network that has established Sony as one of Japan's major multinational enterprises (MNEs).

Sony, a latecomer compared with other Japanese firms such as Matsushita and Sanyo, began its overseas production in the late 1960s. However, from the late 1980s, its output increased rapidly, especially in the wake of the rapid appreciation of the yen and the increasing labour shortage in Japan. During the course of those years, its total overseas investment in plant and equipment has come to surpass its investment in Japan.

By the early 1970s, Sony had established mainly TV assembly plants but also several electronics parts and components plants in North America, Europe and East Asia. Looking first at East Asia, the Taiwan Toyo Radio Co., Sony's first overseas production plant, was established in 1967. This plant produced mainly radios and tape-recorders. It was followed in 1973 by the Korean Toyo Tsushin Kōgyō Co. (now Sony Electronics of Korea – SEKC), which was established in South Korea's Masan free trade zone to produce electronics parts and components. Turning to North America, the San Diego Mfg Centre was established in 1972 to supply TV sets and other audio products; picture tube production started the following year. In 1974, the Audio Mfg Division opened a plant in Pennsylvania for the production of audio speakers. In Europe, Sony established Sony España in Spain in 1973 to produce colour TV sets, and in 1975 it established Sony-Wega in West Germany for the production of colour TV sets and audio products. At this early stage, Sony's global 'four-zone' strategy was already becoming apparent.

In similar fashion to the other major Japanese consumer electronics manufacturers, Sony's overseas production began expanding rapidly after the late 1970s. It too had to contend with trade conflicts with the USA, especially in the area of colour TV sets, and had to deal with the rapid appreciation of the yen against the US dollar. Sony has developed into one of the more integrated and organised of these Japanese MNEs in the consumer electronics industry. After the late 1980s Sony beefed up its production bases in its main product markets, namely North America and the European Community (EC). The company also transplanted operations for the production of radio-cassette recorders, hi-fi audio products, VCRs and colour TV sets to East and Southeast Asia, and expanded the production of key devices and electronics parts to these regions as well. These moves make it possible to discern three major features of Sony's global competitive strategy.

First, Sony has developed production bases in and for each of its 'four zones', in accordance with a principle of 'global localisation'. At the same time it pursues a 'product demarcation' strategy, aimed at 'optimal production site distribution' world-wide. Second, Sony promotes the overseas production of key devices and electronics parts and components, especially in East and Southeast Asia. Third, and closely connected to these moves, it is strengthening international procurement activities through International Procurement Offices (IPOs) to achieve cost reduction, and in particular as a countermeasure to the appreciating yen. At the time of writing Sony has thirteen transplant operations in North America, comprising eleven in the USA and two in Mexico. It operates twelve transplants in Europe (four in France, three in Great Britain, and others in Germany, Spain and Austria). Now Sony is developing a global 'four-zone' system on a more co-ordinated and organised basis. Asian operations are receiving a greater share of attention as part of Sony's global competitive strategy, not only for the manufacturing of end products and key components, but also for the procurement of parts and components.

Field surveys were conducted at several of Sony's overseas production plants. In particular, these were carried out at the Sony Manufacturing Center of America in San Diego (SMCA) in 1989, the Sony Electronics of Korea Corporation (SEKC) and Sony Video Taiwan (SVT) in 1992, and the Sony Precision Engineering Center in Singapore (SPEC), Sony TV Industries (STI) in Malaysia, and Sony International Singapore in 1993. The characteristic features of Sony's Asian production activities and management situations were analysed by examining the data gathered through these surveys, and by focusing on the 'application' of the Japanese management and production system.

SPEC is typical of Sony's recent overseas operations for the production of key devices and components in Asia, while SVT and STI represent cases of an '(end product) export-base' type of production. SEKC, which was established in South Korea's Masan FTZ (MAFEZ), has been in operation for a long time, also shares characteristics with SPEC. Manufacturing in Japan faces adverse conditions in the form of the high yen and increased labour costs. As NIEs, Singapore, South Korea and Taiwan have been improving their technology, human resources and management capability, and their infrastructure. By making the most of these advantages, SPEC and SEKC are substituting for the Japanese production of key devices and components, and developing into major supply bases for Sony production in Asia, as well as world-wide. They are in a good strategic position with regard to Sony's global competitive strategy.

SPEC was established in 1987 as a wholly-owned subsidiary, and started operations in the same year. Its main products are optical pickup devices, precision dies, floppy disc heads and VCR cylinders. Sony provides 70 per cent of the world's supply of optical pickups for CD players, of which SPEC and SEKC each produce 40 per cent.

One of the most notable features of plant operation at SPEC is its utilisation of advanced technology and highly automated equipment to produce advanced key components and devices. This is typical of current moves in Sony's overseas parts production.

SPEC's automation ratio surpasses 80 per cent. Robots and other advanced automated machinery were brought in from Japan at the very start of operations and set up by Japanese engineers and maintenance specialists. Although local staff are now capable of conducting relatively simple and straightforward maintenance, more advanced maintenance is carried out by the 'FA team'. At this level, assistance by Japanese expatriates seems to continue to be indispensable. In fact, the ratio of Japanese expatriates to total employees is a little higher than at the average Japanese electronics parts plant in this region. However, SPEC's FA division is very competent and is learning to apply *kaizen* activities to its production equipment. SPEC gives various types of technical assistance to Sony's production bases, as well as to other group companies and suppliers in Southeast Asia. Thus SPEC is placed in an important position of mediating Sony's technology transfer to the region. SPEC's FA centre is in charge of software development, engineering design and factory automation. It provides significant technical assistance to local industry, such as TV production in Malaysia. The Die Section supplies precision dies for SPEC itself and for other Sony group companies in the region.

The Mounting and Production System Section furnishes information and expertise, not only concerning factory automation, but also concerning the design of flexible production systems and computerised testing systems.

Singapore is the business centre and operations headquarters for the Sony Group in Southeast Asia, and as such it oversees finance, procurement and logistics, technical assistance and R&D. Sony's six subsidiaries have a combined workforce of 3000 employees, and 300 Japanese expatriate employees and their families live in Singapore. Sony International, founded in 1982, is making full use of the advantages that Singapore offers as a centre for business information, finance and traffic in Southeast Asia. It supervises the export and import activities and logistics of the Sony group. Sony Logistics, established in 1988, functions as a distribution centre for materials and products for Asia and the Middle East, as well as for North and South America. Other group companies are Sony Display, a picture tube manufacturing plant, and Sony Singapore, a sales and service company.

Another interesting feature of SPEC is that it does not have a very high degree of application of Japanese-style human management methods. The evaluation scores obtained from the survey indicated a lower 'application' score than the average in Southeast Asia. In fact it could even be considered an 'adaptation'-type plant. For example, SPEC does not pursue multiskill formation enthusiastically in its training of shop-floor workers. Even in Japan there is some apparent separation of shop-floor workers from technicians or maintenance workers, but this is even more notable at SPEC. This may reflect the 'academic background-orientated' society that characterises Singapore. Wages are determined in accordance with position and there are substantial differences in workers' wage scales according to their different academic backgrounds. It should be noted that SPEC implements performance evaluations (*jinjikōha*), however, it utilises American consultants in the process. The system is more American than Japanese in style. It applies an American evaluation format that contains five grades, with 110 items in each. A worker must sign the evaluation to indicate his or her approval. Attempts are being made, however, to break the academic background orientation. For example, workers are able to be promoted to managerial positions. A certain mixture of Japanese-style elements with local conditions can therefore be observed.

Quality control is crucial for the production of key electronic components, and to this end SPEC has introduced SEDAC, Sony's worldwide 'zero defect' activities, to reduce defect rates successfully. Equipment maintenance is another important factor for reducing defect rates. Although supervisors seem competent enough, the overall quality consciousness on the part of shop-floor workers is said to continue to be insufficient. However, Japanese-style socialising activities help to enhance a sense of unity. These activities include employee trips, family athletics meetings, and a morning ceremony. The company also gives free uniforms to employees. In this respect, the elements of Japanese-style human resources management are being applied at SPEC. This may account for its relatively low employee turnover rate, despite a recent increase in Singapore's labour shortage.

In short, the management and production system at SPEC relies on advanced, automated production equipment and machinery brought in from Japan, while human resources management is similar to American high-tech type, but with the addition of certain Japanese-style practices.

SEKC in South Korea, on the other hand, exhibits different characteristics. It produces similar key components and parts, and is also strongly orientated towards advanced production technology. However, it applies Japanese-style human resources management methods more strictly, and, moreover, entirely through the initiative of local managers. SEKC's long operating experience has to a large extent promoted the localisation of management. It is Sony's second-longest operating overseas production base after Taiwan's Toyo Radio. Production began in 1972 in the Masan Area Free Export Zone (MAFEZ) not long after the zone was established in 1970. It currently carries out the volume production of VCR heads and CD components, including optical pickups and headphone speakers. It also produces CD players, for which it has its own design section. SEKC provides some of its key components to other Korean companies, but most are exported. SEKC commands the largest share of total export value in the MAFEZ. Although the government has permitted SEKC to ship goods, valued at up to 50 per cent of its total exports, to the domestic market since 1991, it remains an export-orientated production base. It exports audio products to Europe, the USA, Japan and other areas, including the Middle East, Latin America and Asia.

Rapid wage increases and the appreciation of the won have been having an adverse effect South Korea's export trade, while at the same time, higher national income has expanded the domestic market. These radically changing conditions are having a considerable effect upon the free trade zones (FTZs) in South Korea. One of the ways in which SEKC has attempted to respond to the challenge that these changes present is by upgrading its products and enhancing local capabilities for advanced process technology and factory automation. Another counter-measure is improving its production system. Its long operating experience provides ample background for applying Japanese-style management methods.

Although key components such as advanced ICs and controllers are still brought in from Japan, the high degree of application of Japanese-style management and production methods help to maintain its competitive edge in export markets. Under the active leadership of the Korean company president, the amount of equipment and the number of Japanese expatriates who specialise in management and who have been brought in from Japan has decreased considerably. The advance in overall localisation at SEKC is a notable feature of this company.

About 70 per cent of SEKC's production equipment is designed and assembled in-house from externally procured parts and components. The company still relies on Japan for machine tools and controllers, but local capabilities concerning production equipment have improved. The FA section has made substantial progress in *kaizen* (improvement activities) related to equipment. The design section has undertaken basic design improvement functions for several years, not to mention its design of key devices. The general impression seems to be that, from a technological standpoint, SEKC has been becoming increasingly independent from Japan. As much as 85 per cent of parts and components is procured locally. SEKC is in the process of shifting supply sources of some key components, ICs and precision presses, among others items, from Japan to South Korea.

Almost 85 per cent of total employees at SEKC are direct workers. Compared with Japan, there are relatively fewer indirect personnel, mainly as a result of fairly active job rotation. This contributes to cutting management costs and is another notable feature of SEKC. This may also be the result of sufficiently strict work management and the generally high work skills of the mostly female shop-floor workers. In fact, ST standards are similar to those in Japan, and its achievement rate is high, even by Japanese standards. There have also been various attempts at simplifying the reassignment of job tasks. Job task reassignment helps to achieve the job assignment flexibility that is necessary for responding to fluctuations in production volume. Also, managers are conscious of and take care to preserve co-operative labour relations, and there are policies specifically created for this purpose. As noted above, quality is crucial in the manufacturing of key devices; however, the quality consciousness and quality skills of shop-floor workers at SEKC are said to remain insufficient. Small-group activities have also been introduced as a part of Sony's world-wide activities, but these have not brought about improvements or been applied at the *kaizen* activity level. Japanese-style QC methods for shop-floor workers are not implemented skillfully at SEKC and, to compensate, it has increased the number of in-line inspections so that it is able to secure defect rates comparable to Japan's.

Although the high degree of localisation of management at SEKC and the substantial application of Japanese-style management methods are notable features of SEKC, the company continues to rely on support from Japan. For example, Japanese technological assistance plays an important role during the start-up of new production. Also, many key components and highly advanced production equipment or ICs are from Japan.

STI and SVT, Sony's overseas production bases of end products, differ from SPEC and SEKC, which produce key components and devices. STI in Malaysia typifies Sony's 'export base'-type production operations for end products in Asia. It was established in November 1987, starting production in May 1988. STI is a wholly-owned subsidiary of Sony and its first and only TV set assembly plant in Asia outside of Japan. STI operates one of Sony's largest colour TV set factories, with as many as 3000 employees, comparable in size to a TV set factory in Mexico. Its main products are the smaller-size colour TV sets with 14- to 29-inch black Trinitron picture tubes, which it exports to areas other than Japan, Europe and the USA, namely to the Middle East (30 per cent), and Southeast Asia (20–30 per cent). STI also produces key components for TV sets, including deflection yokes, flyback transformers, tuners and IF blocks. STI is in fact an integrated TV set production plant. It is similar to Sony's North American TV plants, except that it does not manufacture picture tubes. In-house production of key components helps to reduce production lead time and secure a high level of quality. Picture tubes of 21 inches and below are procured from Sony Display in Singapore, which supplies 70 per cent of the total TV sets produced at STI. Other parts and components are procured within Southeast Asia. IPOs in Singapore and in Taiwan exploit the region as a world production centre of electronics parts and components.

While STI attempts to apply elements of Japanese-style management, it also depends largely on equipment from Japan, and on Japanese expatriates, to fill key positions. In this respect, STI differs substantially, not only from SPEC, but also from SEKC. The application evaluation of STI revealed a degree of application above average for the ASEAN area, allowing it to be categorised as a true 'application'-type factory.

Equipment used for the PC board insertion process is brought in from Japan, two-thirds of it second-hand. In consideration of local maintenance capabilities, the level of line automation is reduced to about 80 per cent. Automatic insertion methods are limited to fairly simple operations, and the greater use of manual insertion reflects the lower labour costs in

Malaysia. The skills of Malaysian workers are said to be high enough for ST achievement to be among the top ranking operations of the Sony Group outside Japan. STI seems to carry out strict job task management of shop-floor workers, probably because of the workers' relatively short working experience. However, they are able to produce 40–50 models on a single line and change models five to six times a day. To a certain extent, shop-floor workers seem to be developing multiskills. STI also puts some emphasis on job rotation. However, because of the link between wages are positions, this is not as easy as it is in Japan.

There is no personal evaluation for shop-floor workers. Key staff such as leads and supervisors, as well as technicians, receive their training through broad job rotation. Although STI pursues 'Sony quality' by applying Sony's world-wide quality standards, small-group activities are limited. Small-group activities that do exist are top-down, conducted within working hours as part of job assignments, and under strong managerial leadership. Technicians and supervisors participate in zero-defect activities, but improvement or *kaizen* activities are mainly led by engineers and managers.

SVT, Sony's VCR assembly plant in Taiwan, is also an 'application'-type factory. While its application evaluation scores are generally as high as those of SEKC, the characteristics of its plant operation practices are midway between those of STI and SEKC. This probably reflects Taiwan's changing economic conditions, similar to those of South Korea, which is another NIE. It also reflects the basic characteristics of SVT as a production base for end products.

SVT was established as a joint venture with a Taiwanese firm in 1984. Initially it produced VCRs for the domestic market, but tariff reductions on VCRs induced by Taiwan's market liberalisation policies in the 1980s led to increasing competition with imports. In 1991 Sony changed SVT into a wholly-owned subsidiary, and shifted the primary focus of its operations on to production for export. SVT has upgraded its products and is trying to make the best use of Taiwan's advantages as a rapidly developing centre for electronics industries. However, adverse economic conditions, such as the substantial appreciation of the won against the US dollar, and the rising cost of labour, accompany the notable economic development that is characteristic of a NIE (similar to the case of South Korea). Consequently, SVT is increasing its efforts to preserve competitiveness by applying Japanese-style management methods and upgrading its products.

Technological dependence on Japan is relatively low, with about half of the parts and components and 30 per cent to 40 per cent of production equipment procured within Taiwan. There is some localisation of management, although not to the extent observed at SEKC, and Japanese-style management methods have been applied to the production line and to labour management to a greater extent than at SVT. The wage system is similar to that of Sony in Japan, with a qualification-rank system (*shokuno shikaku sei*) that has four grades. Shop-floor workers receive performance evaluations, the results of which being reflected in an up to 20 per cent variation in wages. The quality control system is said to be the same as that in Japan and defect rates are lower than in Japan, even with about half as many QC workers. Maintenance technicians are developed internally; however, the job assignments of shop-floor workers are fixed in the short term.

Summing up, there appear to be several salient characteristics of Sony's production operations in East and Southeast Asia. First, Sony has complete ownership of most of its Asian subsidiaries. This gives Sony greater control over plant management at these local production operations.

Second, the production systems are technology-led, especially at SPEC and SEKC, which are the main overseas production bases of key devices and components. Accordingly, Sony is strengthening its efforts to transfer technology and enhance local capabilities in production technology and design. As with other Japanese electronics firms, many crucial aspects of local management and technology continue to require Japanese assistance. However, in South Korea, and to a slightly lesser extent in Taiwan, the localisation of management has progressed well because of long operating experience. In Singapore and Malaysia, however, there is a relatively high degree of dependence on Japanese engineers. Japanese expatriates occupy key posts and play significant roles in top management.

Third, the application of Japanese methods in human resources management varies considerably from plant to plant. Sony seems to have no intention of applying Japanese-style management to all its overseas production sites. In many cases, modified applications and significant adaptations can be observed. While it is true that Sony uniformly applies 'Sony standards' for work procedures and for quality world-wide, it should be noted that the work procedures are modified to accommodate local conditions. There is a general tendency to apply work management of shop-floor workers rigidly, on the basis of which Sony attempts to develop multiskilled workers. Regarding the wage system, SVT in Taiwan applies a system that is similar to the one in Japan, while other locations, such as SPEC in Singapore, where the system is similar to American hi-tech industries, pursue a more job-orientated wage system. Technicians and supervisors are generally trained within the company, but small group activities are typically not conducted in the Japanese style as they are top-down, and as improvement or *kaizen* activities are led by engineers. Japanese-style practices are applied rather more actively in the area of 'Sense of Participation and Unity'.

In recent years, Sony has shifted its business orientation away from one of exporting products from Japan, towards one of rapidly increasing its overseas production. It is becoming a fully-fledged MNE, in pursuit of a global 'four-zone' organisation. The restructuring of Sony's business operations has been necessitated by the collapse of Japan's asset-inflated, 'bubble economy'. Local production and procurement activities in Asia are undoubtedly a cornerstone of Sony's global competitive strategy. Sony is developing export production bases for its major products such as colour TV sets and VCRs in Malaysia and Taiwan, and it is also strengthening cost reduction efforts to procure parts and key components within Asia. Under the leadership of Japanese production operations, the electronics industry in East and Southeast Asia has developed rapidly. At the same time, Sony is promoting the production of key components and devices in the region through the transfer of advanced process technology from Japan. This constitutes another notable feature of Sony's production activities in Asia.

Sharp Corporation

Nobuo Kawabe

Sharp is one of Japan's top comprehensive manufacturers of electrical and electronic appliances. Based on its liquid crystal technology, in recent years Sharp has developed and marketed a number of unique products, such as the Viewcam video camera with an integrated liquid crystal display (LCD), Japanese-language word processors, and the Zaurus, a palm-top computer that uses a pen to input data onto an LCD. Historically, Sharp is known for having produced Japan's first radios, televisions and microwave ovens, and more recently the world's first electronic and solar-cell powered calculators.

While Sharp is now a fully-fledged electronics manufacturer, the company was founded in Tokyo in 1912 as a small-scale processor of metals. The company's name 'Sharp' reflects its development of 'sharp' or propelling pencils.

After the devastating Great Kanto Earthquake of 1923 which destroyed much of Tokyo, the company moved its headquarters westward to Osaka, where it established its Hayakawa Metalworks Research Laboratory to research radio technology. In 1925, when NHK, Japan's national broadcasting station, started radio broadcasts, Hayakawa Metalworks Research Laboratory began producing crystal radio sets and, as early as 1926, exported these to China and other parts of Asia.

In 1932, Hayakawa Metalworks Research Laboratory began to research television technology, and in 1935 became a joint stock company. In 1942, the company changed its name to Hayakawa Electric Works Ltd. and opened a factory for radio parts and components.

Hayakawa managed to ride out the immediate post-Second World War economic confusion in Japan and responded strongly to the 1951 introduction of private broadcasting by developing and marketing a high-sensitivity radio, the 'super-radio', which greatly contributed to the revival of the company's fortunes. In 1952, Hayakawa entered the television market through a technology agreement with US manufacturer RCA, and began selling television sets in Japan one year later. When Japan's economy began expanding rapidly and mass consumerism arrived, the company became an all-round manufacturer of electrical appliances, especially washing machines, refrigerators and electric fans, as it is today.

In 1962, it established a sales subsidiary in the United States and became a full-scale exporter.

In January of 1971, Hayakawa became Sharp. In the same year, the company began researching and developing micro electronics (ME) technology, which it had started to explore in 1964 when it developed an electronic calculator based on transistor technology. Based on its ME technology, Sharp took a further step towards becoming an all-around electronics maker when it began producing electrical home appliances, office automation (OA) equipment, and electronic parts and components. In 1973 Sharp achieved the world's first successful application of liquid crystal technology. This allowed the development of a variety of new office automation equipment and proved to be the cornerstone of Sharp's competitive advantage in the OA field.

In the decade between 1975 and 1985, Sharp launched one successful product after another, both at home and abroad. Beginning with electronic calculators, Sharp moved on to radio-cassette recorders, video-cassette recorders (VCRs), and photocopiers. As a result of this product development, the company greatly expanded its overseas business and rapidly created a dynamic global business strategy. Before this, Sharp had established an overseas production base in 1963 through a technical tie-up with Taiwanese manufacturer, the Sampo Corporation. Sharp went ahead and set up several other production sites overseas: in 1973 in South Korea, the following year in Malaysia, in 1979 in the United States, and in 1985 in the UK.

By December 1994, Sharp had twenty sales subsidiaries in eighteen countries, twenty-seven factories in seventeen countries, four R&D centres in three countries, one overseas parts and components supplier, two foreign finance centres in two countries, and representative offices in eleven countries. Of these, nine overseas sales subsidiaries were located in seven Asian countries, fourteen overseas production bases in Asian countries, one R&D centre in Asia, and one parts and components supplier in Asia. As a result of this expansion of its international activities, by 1995 Sharp's ratio of overseas to domestic production exceeded 50 per cent.

Sharp's general policy for its overseas businesses is something like 'act globally, think locally'. While seeking to become a global player in the industry, the company grounds its management strategies in the various cultures of its overseas bases and stresses the necessity to contribute to the development of local economies and communities. Sharp encourages self-management at its individual overseas subsidiaries, fostering autonomy and stressing independence and uniqueness.

Sharp began to develop a global business strategy based on these principles in the wake of the yen's rise in 1985 and resulting changes in market competitiveness. The first pillar of Sharp's global strategy is the conviction that to deliver products that best meet the needs of local consumers, those products need to be made locally. Especially in the European and North American markets, Sharp's subsidiaries function as 'creative lifestyle focus centres', which means they are constantly monitoring the latest trends in local consumer needs.

The second pillar of Sharp's international strategy is to maintain its domestic production capacity and not allow it to be undermined by the push to offshore production because of the persistently high yen exchange rate. To maintain domestic production, it is essential to develop creative products with high levels of added value.

Sharp's globalisation places increasing importance on Japan's Asian neighbours. For Sharp, the role of Asia in the company's strategy is pivotal. First, Asia as whole is achieving rapid economic growth and developing swiftly into a sophisticated consumer market. Therefore, products manufactured there are made to be sold there. Second, as Japanese production loses competitiveness with the rise of the yen, production in Asia for export on to other countries is rising. The rapid rise in investment in countries such as Thailand and Malaysia following the appreciation of the yen reflects this. Third, production bases in Asian countries are being used as bases for export to Japan as well as to other regions. In 1994, Sharp imported parts, components and finished products worth \150 billion and thus lifted the share of overseas-procured parts and components in domestically manufactured products to 35 per cent.

Clearly, Asia is now Sharp's core production base. It now plays the main role in the company's production activities world-wide, with more than half of Sharp's factories located in the region. Sharp maintains one sales subsidiary and two factories in Thailand, two sales subsidiaries and two factories in Taiwan, one factory in the People's Republic of China, one in South Korea, a sales subsidiary in Hong Kong, four sales subsidiaries and one production base in Malaysia, a sales subsidiary in Singapore, and one sales subsidiary and a factory in the Philippines, India, and Indonesia, respectively. Altogether, Sharp now has nine sales subsidiaries in eight Asian countries, and fourteen factories in eight countries in the region.

Sharp's business activities in Asia differ in several ways from those of other Japanese companies. First, Sharp emphasises the importance of improving Asian manufacturing quality, because Sharp's Asian production bases play a pivotal role in the company's manufacturing activities. Second, Sharp seeks to enlarge the market share of its products and thus reap the benefits of mass production while remaining actively engaged in originating new products. Third, Sharp is conscious of the desirability of improving its brand image. In Asian markets, Sharp's image is perhaps not as good as that of the competitors, Sony and Matsushita, and therefore the company needs to work on improving consumers' perception of it. Fourth, Sharp aims to establish autonomous activities in its various foreign subsidiaries. To achieve this, the company plans to implement design and development at its overseas locations. Fifth, Sharp places great importance on the contribution made by its foreign subsidiaries to local economies and communities. Contributing to the host country is an important aspect of its business activities. For example, each of Sharp's overseas subsidiaries sets aside 1 per cent of its profits for philanthropic activities that benefit the local economy and community. In 1992 and 1994, Sharp's subsidiaries in Malaysia and Thailand were commended for their significant contribution to those countries' exports. On top of this, Sharp's link to two Malaysian universities and the resulting 'Sharp technology lectures' are strengthening the technological base of Malaysia.

Let us now focus further on Sharp's manufacturing subsidiaries in Asia. Sharp has made, and continues to make, Malaysia – where it started local production at three plants prior to the yen appreciation of around 1985 – the centre of its manufacturing activities in the region. The oldest of Sharp's Malaysian subsidiaries is the Sharp–Roxy Corporation, Malaysia Sdn Bhd, which began manufacturing in 1976. This company was established jointly by Sharp and the Roxy Group of Hong Kong, each contributing 40 per cent of the capital, with the rest made up by another shareholder. Sharp–Roxy manufactures and markets radios, tape-recorders, and radio-cassette recorders. The role of the Roxy Group of Hong Kong is limited to owning shares; the group is not actively involved in the management of the company. The Sharp–Roxy Corporation, which at the time of writing employs 3376 people, twenty-one of whom came directly from Japan, is clearly a large-scale production plant. Sharp–Roxy Electronics Corporation Malaysia Sdn Bhd is another joint venture between Sharp, which contributed 50 per cent of the capital, and Roxy Electronic Company, which owns 30 per cent of the shares.

This company produces and markets colour television sets, and fifteen of its 2133 employees came from Japan. Sharp–Roxy Appliances Corporation Malaysia Sdn Bhd began production in 1985 and is a joint venture between Sharp (25 per cent capital) and Technology Resources Industries Bhd of Malaysia (49 per cent). This joint venture employs 685 staff, four of whom are from Japan, and manufactures and markets electrical and electronic appliances. In 1990, in the wake of the yen appreciation, Sharp Manufacturing Corporation Malaysia Sdn Bhd was set up to manufacture and sell VCRs. A 80 per cent-owned subsidiary, this company has 1725 employees, 338 of whom were dispatched from Japan. Clearly, all Sharp's manufacturing plants in Malaysia are large-scale operations that have a major role to play in the company's Asian strategy.

In contrast, Sharp's Thailand-based subsidiaries were all established after the rise of the yen. Sharp Appliances Thailand Ltd (SATL), which manufactures and sells microwave ovens, refrigerators, air conditioners, audio equipment, and facsimile (fax) machines, was set up in 1987. Its large-scale production plant employs a total of 2575 staff, twenty-seven of whom are Japanese. Sharp Thebnakorn Co. Ltd is another venture jointly owned by Sharp (33 per cent capital) and SATL (14.2 per cent). With a total staff of 433, eleven of whom are Japanese, this company produces and sells colour television sets, marketing Sharp products locally.

In Taiwan, in 1989, Sharp established a wholly-owned subsidiary, Sharp Electronics (Taiwan) Co. Ltd, to manufacture and market liquid crystal units for electronic tuners. This company employs 799 people, only seven of whom are Japanese. Sharp Technology (Taiwan) Co. Ltd was set up in 1992 and is 99.95 per cent Sharp owned; the remaining 0.05 per cent is owned by Sharp Electronics (Taiwan) Co. Ltd. Its sixty-six employees, three of whom come from Japan, develop and design IC chips.

In South Korea, the Sharp Korea Corporation was established in 1993 as a joint venture between Sharp, which contributed 50 per cent of the capital, and Lee Kwan Jin, which contributed 22.5 per cent. This company manufactures and markets electronic notebooks, electronic cash registers, calculators, audio equipment, and electronic typewriters. Only one of its 846 employees is Japanese.

In the People's Republic of China, Shanghai Sharp Electronics Co. Ltd was established in 1992 as an air-conditioner-making joint venture between Sharp (40 per cent), Mitsubishi Trading Company (20 per cent), and Shanghai First TV Manufacturing (40 per cent). The company has 517 employees, three of whom are Japanese. In addition, Sharp Office Equipment (Changshu) Co. Ltd, a copier manufacturer and seller, was established as a wholly owned Sharp subsidiary in 1993. Staff number 300, none of whom are Japanese.

In addition, Sharp has joint ventures that manufacture and market electronic equipment in the Philippines; television sets and refrigerators in Indonesia; and colour TV sets and VCRs in India. The establishment of Sharp Electronics (Singapore) Pte Ltd in Singapore deserves special attention. This subsidiary procures packing kits for colour television sets and other materials from international markets.

Thus the characteristics of Sharp's Asian subsidiaries reveal the company's Asian strategy. After the yen appreciation around 1985, Sharp began to evaluate its production sites in Asia within an overall corporate strategy, weaving them into a global strategic approach. Until then, Sharp had seen its Asian subsidiaries simply as suppliers and as export bases, valid though this strategy was at the time. Taking advantage of the different levels of technological capability and industrial depth in individual Asian economies, Sharp rapidly adopted international specialisation in product manufacturing. In the NIEs, such as Taiwan and South Korea, Sharp takes advantage of high levels of technological capability by manufacturing mainly electronic parts and components such as IC chips, or finished products such as electronic notebooks. In Malaysia, Sharp manufactures televisions and audio equipment on a large scale, while in Thailand, the company manufactures products such as refrigerators and air conditioners.

On the management side, Sharp's Malaysian and Thai operations are characterised by a large workforce, a significant number of whom are dispatched directly from Japan. There is a shortage of managers and skilled workers in Malaysia and Thailand who have an adequate understanding of the Japanese production approach, which stresses Japanese-level quality control, and few have the ability to communicate directly with headquarters in Japan. In Sharp's Taiwanese, South Korean and Chinese operations, however, the number of Japanese employees is conspicuously small. Countries such as Taiwan and South Korea have a reservoir of managers and engineers who understand the Japanese approach to management. This is a result not only of the general rise of managerial and technological skills, but also of the historically close relationship of these countries with Japan. The same holds true for the People's Republic of China, which possesses a large number of highly skilled engineers, especially in the field of military technology. Furthermore, not only does China have quite strong legal restrictions on overseas managers working in China, but it also has a considerable number of local managers able to communicate directly with headquarters in Japan.

After further appreciation of the yen from the spring of 1994, Sharp strengthened its overseas production capacity still further. Not only did overseas production volume increase, but the rate of transferring production overseas also speeded up. Whereas, in the past, products were transferred offshore after ten years of production in Japan, now in the 1990s, they are transferred after only three or four years' production history.

The expansion of Sharp's overseas business activities is underpinned by the creation of a management system to co-ordinate global activities efficiently. As early as 1990, Sharp began to create a network to link its overseas operations. Among other things, this network allows interactive reception and placement of product orders, and manages production volume. The company constantly upgraded the network in order to standardise foreign exchange management at its various overseas subsidiaries, establish world-wide product standards, and create an international parts and materials procurement system based on an up-to-the-minute information network. In these ways, Sharp continues to globalise its business activities.

Murata Manufacturing Co. Ltd

Yanshu Hao and Tetsuo Abo

I FORMATION OF AN ASIAN PRODUCTION AND DIVISION OF LABOUR SYSTEM

One of Japan's leading large-scale manufacturers of electronics components, Murata Manufacturing Co. Ltd has been pursuing a policy of overseas production vigorously since the 1970s. As is shown in Table 5.3, in 1972, Murata established its first production plant in Singapore, then added twenty to thirty subsidiaries running manufacturing and marketing operations in ten to twenty countries in Asia, the United States and Europe. Murata's advance into Asia can be characterised as follows.

Form of the advance   All the local plants are wholly-owned subsidiaries of the parent, Murata Mfg Co. Ltd. In fact, subsidiaries established by Murata in other parts of the world also share the same investment profile as the Asian subsidiaries. Wholly-owned subsidiaries were, at first, the best way to achieve a system based on a global division of labour based on

Table 5.3   Outline of Murata's advance into Asia

When	Where	Investment by parent (%)	No. of employees (No. of Japanese)	Type of business
Dec. 1972	Singapore	100	1 170 (34)	Manufacture and sale of electronics components
Oct. 1973	Hong Kong	100	50 (5)	Sales office
Oct.1978	Taiwan	100	366 (8)	Manufacture and sale of electronics components
Dec. 1980	South Korea	100	22 (4)	Sales office
Sept. 1988	Thailand	100	2 750 (31)	Manufacture and sale of electronics
1990	China	100	2 (1)	Office
June 1993	Malaysia	100	–	Manufacture and sale of electronics

Source: Kaigai Shinshutsu Kigo Soran, 1994, Toyo Keizai Shinpou-sha and from the corporate interviews by JMNESG members.

Murata's global investment strategy. Second, this approach maintained Murata's competitive edge and favoured the transference of Murata's unique production system.

Timing of the advance In the 1970s, Murata focused investment on the Asian NIEs, widening this in the 1980s to include the ASEAN community. Thus from the 1970s to the 1980s, a clear shift in investment direction took place, from NIEs to ASEAN. This was closely related to such issues as the stage of economic development of the target countries, market conditions, and labour trends.

Type of advance in Asia The subsidiaries in Hong Kong, South Korea and China are principally marketing branches, while subsidiaries in other countries have both manufacturing and marketing functions. The factory in Thailand focuses on manufacturing and is Murata's largest overseas subsidiary. The next largest is Murata's Singapore factory.

II AN OVERVIEW

The Singapore factory pioneered Murata's local offshore production operations. At a later date Murata opened its Thai plant, which marked the reorganisation of its Asian production and division of labour system after 1985. The Thai factory became Murata's largest overseas plant, followed by its Singapore factory, and the Taiwan plant. These three plants formed the three corners of a triumviral Asian production and division of labour system.

The Singapore factory was opened in 1972, followed by the Taiwan factory in 1978 and the Thailand plant in 1988. This sequence was related to developments in Japan, where soaring domestic wages, labour shortages and the rising yen accelerated the flight of Japanese companies overseas. In terms of local Asian economic development, Murata's moves overseas followed a typical stepped pattern of development. In Asia, economic development was led by the Asian NIEs, with development then spreading to Southeast Asia and on to coastal China. In response to the labour shortages accompanying the sequential development of the Asian economies, Murata widened its production bases to new areas of Asia.

Why did Murata select Thailand as its new production base in 1988? From 1985, appreciation of the yen, labour shortages in Singapore and other problems prompted Murata to create a production and division of labour system in the Asian region. Before implementing the new production base, Murata carefully surveyed several Southeast Asian countries. Indonesia was pronounced unready for such a venture, the restrictions of Malaysia's *Bhumiputra* policy ruled it out as a venue, while poor law and order in the Philippines made that country unattractive. Thailand thus emerged as the strongest candidate. The decision to produce in Thailand was also influenced by Murata's experience with its Singapore plant, where 200 migrant Thai employees had demonstrated their superiority to local Singaporean workers.

Extremely cautious in this new venture, Murata decided to avoid over-centralised Bangkok, finally choosing Lamphun Industrial Park in a depopulated part of northern Thailand. Murata recognised several advantages in locating there. First were the labour advantages: high-quality, cheap labour was plentiful. Where wages in Bangkok were 125 baht a day, workers in Chiangmai, a city near the Lamphun factory, earned 110 baht a day, and daily wages in Lamphun were 102 baht, so Lamphun offered clear wage advantages. The quality of labour in northern Thailand was also high. Workers were conscientious and diligent, and a labour force was easy to recruit. Murata's experience with its plants in the prefectures of Japan's Hokuriku and San-in districts (in the North-western part of Japan) had demonstrated that the work ethic was stronger in remoter regions. Lamphun also offered the advantages of an industrial park. In addition, Lamphun offered special incentives under the

Table 5.4   Outline of Murata's Singapore and Thailand factories

Factory	Thai factory	Singapore factory
Location	Lamphun Industrial Park, Northern Thailand	Pemimpin, Malaysia
Start of operation	August 1988	December 1972
Ownership	Japanese parent 100%	Japanese parent 100%
Products	Ceramic condensers, electronic tuners, VIF units	Chip-layer ceramic condensers, ceramic filters, ceramic resonators
Export destination/ export ratio	80%, 100% (including indirect exports)	50%, mainly to Southeast Asia
No. of employees	2 750	1 170
No. of Japanese	30	34
Male/female ratio	Female workers 99%	
Average age	19 yrs	
Absence	2~3%	5~7%
Monthly staff turnover	2%	2%

decentralisation policy promoted by a Thailand investment committee (BOI). In addition to land acquisition, permits for foreign labour, visas for engineers, and guarantees for remitting funds out of the country, concessions included exemption from import and value-added taxes on machinery, parts, and materials; exemption from export and value-added taxes on products; and exemption from various taxes on domestically produced materials. In addition, BOI agreed not to interfere in labour or environmental issues. As we shall see later, differences in utilising the workforce had a particularly important effect on the application of Japanese production systems.

III   A COMPARISON OF APPLICATION AND ADAPTATION SCORES

Section II described Murata's two largest overseas production centres. This section will examine, in relation to Murata's offshore location policy, how differences such as the length of the overseas presence, location factors, and labour problems had an impact on application and adaptation in overseas production.

A Comparison of Six Groups and twenty-three Items

First let us look at the average applicability of the Singapore and Thailand subsidiaries. As Table 5.5 shows, the Thai factory has an average application score of 3.5 and the Singapore factory an average score of 3.4. The factories were respectively 0.2 and 0.3 points above the average application score of 3.2 for Southeast Asia. Looking at the application characteristics for each group, the average scores for Groups II, III, IV, and VI were identical; only Groups I and V differed. Even given the points differences among the categories inside the groups, the congruence of the group average applicability scores indicates that both the Singapore and Thai factories share a general ability to transfer the advantages of the Murata parent plants to the local setting. Although it might seem an obvious observation to make, few companies could achieve such similar results in differing offshore locations. Murata's success indicates the resolution and consistency of the parent company in its overseas location policy and approach.

The application scores of Groups I and V, however, reveal large differences between the Singapore and Thai subsidiaries. In contrast to Groups II, III, IV and VI, the Singapore plant's score for Group I (Work

Table 5.5   Comparison of application in Murata's Thai and Singapore plants– six groups and 23 items

Application category	Thai factory (T)	Singapore factory (S)	Difference (T–S)
I Work Organisation and Administration	3.3	3.7	–0.4
① Job classification	5	5	0
② Multifunctional skills	2	3	–1
③ Education and training	4	4	0
④ Wage system	3	4	–1
⑤ Promotion	3	3	0
⑥ First-line supervisor	3	3	0
II Production Control	3.5	3.5	0
⑦ Equipment	4	5	–1
⑧ Maintenance	3	3	0
⑨ Quality control	3	3	0
⑩ Process management	4	3	1
III Procurement	4.0	4.0	0
⑪ Local content	4	5	–1
⑫ Suppliers	5	4	1
⑬ Procurement method	3	3	0
IV Group Consciousness	3.0	3.0	0
⑭ Small-group activities	2	3	–1
⑮ Information sharing	3	3	0
⑯ Sense of unity	4	3	1
V Labour Relations	3.5	2.8	0.7
⑰ Hiring policy	4	2	2
⑱ Long-term employment	3	2	1
⑲ Harmonious labour relations	4	4	0
⑳ Grievance procedure	3	3	0
VI Parent–Subsidiary Relations	3.7	3.7	0
㉑ Ratio of Japanese expatriates	2	3	–1
㉒ Delegation of authority	4	3	1
㉓ Position of local managers	5	5	0
Application average by factory 23 items	**3.5**	**3.4**	**0.1**

Organisation and Administration) was 3.7, while the Thai plant's corresponding score was 3.3. This is partly related to the shorter length of operation of the Thai plant. In the case of Murata companies, which demonstrate a strong ability to apply Japanese systems successfully, we can see to some extent a tendency towards a positive correlation between the period of operation and the application of the 'core components' of the Japanese system.

However, the two companies also differ in which elements or groups they emphasise, and what they see as their main aims based on labour and other conditions imposed by the local plant. In the case of Murata's Thai factory, the issue is how to mass produce comparatively standard products in a short time to the highest quality standards and with the highest production efficiency. Accordingly, for Group v (Labour Relations), the Thai factory's application score of 3.5 surpasses the Singapore factory's score of 2.8. The Thai factory's emphasis on assembly and its labour-intensive electronics production technology depends largely on the obedient and diligent young female workforce of the Lamphun region. Murata considered this crucial when it selected the Lamphun factory to take over the labour-intensive production of its Singapore factory. The Thai factory's 0.7 point lead in Labour Relations owes much to the advantages of its northern Thailand location. The economic development of the Singaporean city-state brought about a serious labour shortage necessitating new factories in the ASEAN region and a reorganisation of the division of labour within the company.

The Singapore plant responded to the labour shortage by meeting half of its labour needs by importing migrant workers from Malaysia and other ASEAN countries, but, compared to other countries, Singaporean wages remained high. Establishing a factory in Thailand not only lowered wages, but more importantly, transferring production to Thailand also raised the level of technology at the Singapore plant. Technologically more sophisticated products such as chip layered-type condensers, ceramic filters, or resonators necessitated converting the Singapore factory to a processing plant based on a high level of capital investment. Products that the plant had manufactured previously, such as mass-produced capacitors with leads attached, and electronic tuners, were transferred to the new Thai factory. Thus, trends in local labour altered the division of manufacturing within the company.

Four-Perspective Evaluation

In the Four-Perspective Evaluation, Material–Results and Human–Results showed high application scores. Material–Results at the Singapore plant came close to the perfect score of 5.0 with a total of 4.6, while the Thai plant scored a high 4.3 for Material–Results. These results clearly reflect Murata's strong orientation to transfer systems from its parent plants

Table 5.6   Four perspective-evaluation: comparing Thailand and Singapore factories

Category		Thailand factory	Singapore factory
Method	Human	3.2	3.3
	Material	3.0	3.0
Result	Human	3.5	4.0
	Material	4.0	4.6

directly to its overseas plants. For parts procurement, city-state Singapore offered only a narrow industrial base. Some 20 per cent of components for Murata's Singapore factory were procured in Japan, with the remaining 80 per cent coming from the NIEs and other Southeast Asian countries. Generally, only cardboard was procured locally. The Thai factory, which centred on post-processing, relied heavily on Japan, with 80 per cent of its components pre-processed in Murata's Japanese factories, and 20 per cent of its components obtained from Southeast Asia.

The application score for Equipment was 4.0 for the Thai plant, and 5.0 for the Singapore factory. The basic difference between the two factories was that the Singapore factory was a process-type plant focusing on forward-processing, and therefore needing large-scale capital investment and a higher level of technology. The Singapore's plant's chip layer-type condensers were used in communications systems, VCRs and mobile telephones. The machinery and equipment used in the plant demanded well-trained engineers, a stable power supply, and a level of development commensurate with chemical and other local industries. Much of this machinery and equipment had been transferred first from Japan to Singapore, to Taiwan, and then on to Thailand. As the Thai factory had many cheap and capable female workers, it was able to employ less efficient equipment that was several generations old. As new equipment would have required sophisticated technology to maintain and operate, hardly practical in a plant staffed by inexperienced workers, the Thai plant was well suited for post-processing and other manual tasks. Interestingly, while the use of automated machinery at the Thai plant was 20 per cent below levels for Japan, productivity in manual work, which in Japan was contracted to other companies or taken home by workers, was 20 per cent higher than in Japan.

In Human–Results, application scores were unexpectedly high. The Thai factory, which had not been operating very long, scored 3.5, while the longer-established Singapore factory scored 4.0. Looking at numbers of Japanese employed locally, both factories employed over thirty Japanese staff. While the numbers were almost the same, percentages differed: Japanese people made up 2.9 per cent of the staff of the Singapore plant, which employed a total of 1170 personnel, and only 1.1 per cent of the staff at the Thai factory, which employed 2710 personnel. The labour-intensive Thai factory operated with a very low proportion of Japanese expatriates on the payroll. However, the few Japanese found at both companies filled the top positions and controlled the companies: the presidents and most of the management at both plants were Japanese.

Next, let us look at Human–Methods. The average application scores were 3.2 for the Thai factory, and a very close 3.3 for the Singapore factory. As mentioned earlier, quite different scores recorded in some groups cancelled each other out. The two factories scored, respectively, 3.3 and 3.7 in Group I (Work Organisation and Administration) and, respectively, 3.5 and 2.8 in Group V (Labour Relations). However, in the Methods category, the high score recorded by the Singapore factory in Group I is significant. The Singapore factory was comparatively enthusiastic about developing multiskilled workers, and also rotated jobs. It was also interesting that promotion to the position of group leader required not only work skills but personnel management skills as well. That is, to manage onsite workers comprising mainly migrants from other countries, it was important to develop core figures, mainly group leaders, in the workplace.

In contrast, the Thai factory largely depended on hiring (location) and good labour–management relations. In personnel management, the assessment and promotion systems used by the Murata parent plants were directly translated to the Thai factory. Thailand, which had no experience of large factory production and therefore no established local customs in this area, demanded the direct implantation of a Japanese system. For its wage system, the factory adopted a grade system. Operators were paid by the day, for example, but still graded on a scale of 1 to 3. Base pay was determined by a combination of regular pay increases, length of continuous service, and performance assessment. The interesting point about grading was that each operator's daily performance was plotted on a graph attached to a board beside the operator's machine. This would be unheard of in Japan, where it might be considered to be 'over application' or 'positive adaptation'.

In managing the work site, the Thai factory, whose workforce was 99 per cent female, was extremely thorough in implementing the 5S movement. The following slogans, in the Thai language, were posted on the factory wall: 'Know your duties', 'Maintain discipline', 'Be well behaved' and 'Be on time'. In particular, the use of the women's identification tags was interesting. Operators wore their identification tag, which showed employee number, name, and a head and shoulders photograph, on their left shoulder; those with skills such as soldering or quality control wore the tag on their right shoulder; while permanent staff wore the tag on the chest. The identification tag came in eight colours, with leaders sporting a red L and subleaders a yellow L. Making supervisors conspicuous emphasised their authority and role. This also reinforced workplace management, suppressing chatter on the factory floor, smothering the shared consciousness of those from country villages, and encouraging workers to give their undivided attention to the job. Giving permanent staff and group leaders special identification tags also engendered an elite consciousness. This new system, not implemented previously at any other factory, was applied to over 2000 workers and sought to turn women fresh from country villages into factory workers.

Finally, for Material–Methods, both factories achieved a score of 3.0. Both factories used a similar system of quality control. The concept of 'building in quality' was adopted, but each individual's task was meticulously carried out within the framework of the assigned job. In other words, each person was not required to do more than the specified job. For example, when a defect occurred during the cutting process in the Singapore factory, a Japanese female worker who happened to be present dismantled her machine and checked for the fault, then corrected and reassembled the machine. That could never be expected from a Singapore worker. This reflects a subtle difference in the precision achieved by Japanese workers and the precision achieved by others.

The preceding analysis involved the examination of two overseas Murata factories by comparing their application scores. The clearest characteristic of the two factories was their thorough application of Human–Results and Material–Results. Quality and efficiency were ensured by the leadership of the parent company, through direct control by Japanese managers and dependence on Japan for components. Murata's thorough application of the Results aspects of Japanese practices and systems was selective and flexible in accordance with the Methods aspects of local circumstances and environment. In particular, the different natures of the process-type Singapore plant and the assembly-type Thailand plant were clear. But what was most noticeable in Murata's local Asian production activities was those activities' responsiveness to gaps between Japan's domestic economy and the development of each local Asian economy. Murata provided a typical example of a sequential, mutually dependent development relationship between the various regions of Asia, with industry shifting in a stepped or 'flying geese' development pattern (see Note 1 in chapter 4) from Japan to the NIEs, and from the NIEs to the ASEAN countries.

6 Hybrid Evaluation of Japanese Electronics Plants in Southern China

Yanshu Hao

I INTRODUCTION

In the 1980s, mainly because of the appreciation of the yen and the onset of domestic labour shortages, Japanese companies rapidly shifted production overseas. However, in Asian NIEs such as Taiwan, Korea and Hong Kong, which served as manufacturing bases for Japan, the conditions that had at one time made them favourable manufacturing sites were gradually being eroded as a result of a growing labour movement, labour shortages, and currency revolutions.

In the late 1970s, China established four special economic zones[1] in its coastal areas as part of its experimental introduction of an open market and in order to attract foreign investment. Southern China was not only geographically privileged in being close to Hong Kong and Taiwan, it also enjoyed the advantage of an almost unlimited supply of low-cost, high-quality labour, since all the vastness of China was behind it. These foreign and domestic changes made southern China a new investment destination for Japan and other industrialised nations, and incorporated it in the new Asian triangle[2] consisting of Japan, the NIEs, and China. Southern China became a prominent international manufacturing base by combining foreign capital with low-cost, abundant, good-quality labour, and exporting its products to world markets. Typically, these new types of special industrial areas utilise young people from inland China for short-term labour.

How are the advantages of the Japanese production system, which is based on long-term employment and human resources endowed with a wide range of expertise, applied in these areas? What will the consequences be when these ideas are incorporated into a relatively new production system characterised by its own unique set of circumstances? Can the advantages of Japanese manufacturing technology be utilised properly under these conditions? This study proposes to answer these questions by applying the 'Application–Adaptation' method of analysis.[3]

II AN OUTLINE OF COMPANIES ENTERING SOUTHERN CHINA

It is generally accepted that foreign companies entering Southern China are primarily owned by overseas Chinese (for example, Hong Kong Chinese), and that few Japanese companies are represented in this region. According to an incomplete survey, however, there are over sixty-eight Japanese electrical appliance factories active in this area. Two characteristics common to Japanese companies entering this region explain why the impression exists that there are few Japanese companies. The first is that many companies consign production to local factories and manufacturers. In the past, such local production was not treated as direct investment because, in these cases, Japanese companies do not establish a local corporation, and capital investment takes place in the form of tangible objects such as production facilities and raw material. This paper defines such investment as a form of direct investment used in local production. The second characteristic is that many Japanese companies either channel their investments through Hong Kong, or transfer their manufacturing base from Hong Kong to southern China and leave their head offices in Hong Kong. Statistically, these are treated as being Hong Kong investors. There is no denying that there are numerous factories and investment from companies owned by overseas Chinese from places such as Hong Kong, Macao and Southeast Asia in this region. However, these two characteristics lead erroneously to the impression that there are few Japanese companies in southern China.

Japanese companies operating in this region can thus be characterised as follows:

1. They assume various forms of organisation: namely, independent capital, joint venture and co-operative production, as well as that of consignment production factories.
2. Many of the companies are from Asian NIEs, such as Korea, Taiwan and Hong Kong. The connections that run deepest and are the most complex are those with Hong Kong. In many cases, the head offices remain in Hong Kong while manufacturing plants are set up in southern China.
3. Most of these factories produce parts which are exported to Japan or to other international markets.

4. There are many female workers. The total number of workers in the sixty-eight Japanese electrical factories is 59 143, of which female workers comprise 85 per cent, or 50 271.

5. There were certain peak periods for the establishment of foreign companies in Southern China. The first period was 1987–8, when twenty-four companies ventured into that area, and the second was 1991–2, when sixteen companies established operations. This wave of advancement can be seen as a reflection of yen appreciation and labour shortage in Japan, as well as of wage rises and currency revaluation in Korea and Taiwan. This reveals a close connection between the arrival of these companies and changes in the domestic and international environment.

6. In the 1980s, when the special economic zones were first established, many corporations chose to locate within these special economic zones because of preferential treatment. Later, companies expanded to neighboring areas as a result of China enforcing its coastal area policy and wage increases in the special economic zones.

From the above, it is reasonable to conclude that Japanese affiliated companies operating in this area characteristically established export-orientated factories employing mainly female labour, and that this region could best be described as an international manufacturing base. However, in order to ascertain how the factories are managed, and to determine their characteristics and the extent to which they succeeded in transferring the Japanese production system, it is necessary to examine each of these companies independently. Current conditions at each of the target factories will be looked at next to determine the 'degree of application'.

The companies that are the subjects of this study are shown in Table 6.1. They are five final assembly plants and parts factories owned by Japanese electrical appliance firms, three located in Shenzhen, which is designated as a special economic zone, and two in Panyu, Guangdong, which is near a special zone. Factories A and B had already been visited in October 1990, so the visit in September was the second visit by the researcher. Of the five plants in Southern China, one is a general manufacturer producing AV equipment, calculators and electronic parts; one is a manufacturer of radio-cassette players and colour TVs; and the other three are factories that produce electronic parts. Their products include everything from large parts such as cathode-ray tubes to small components such as coils and magnetic heads.

It may be valuable to describe briefly the circumstances surrounding the arrival of these five companies in Southern China. These are all Japanese

Table 6.1 Profile of Japanese-owned electronics plants in South China

Plant	A 'Export-base type'	B 'One firm, two systems' 'Outward exporting type'	C	D 'Township enterprise type'	E 'International subcontractor type'
Start of operation	March 1983	July 1984	20 May 1989 30 March 1991	1984	October 1990
Location	SEZ Shekou, Shenzhen	SEZ Shenshen	SEZ Futian, Shenzhen	Guangdong Province Shuikengxiang, Panyu	Guangdong Province Shuikengxiang, Panyu
Capital	104 000 HK$	10 000 000 US$	36 000 000 US$		
Mode of entry	Independent capital	Joint venture	Joint venture	Consignment	Consignment
Ratio of capital	100% Hong Kong parent company	50%	Jap. 25%, CH. 75%, 156 000 000 US$	Production	Production
Number of employees Percent. male/female	3 204 (male 542: 17%/ female 2 662: 83%)	1 600 Male/female 3/7	2 452 Male/female 8/2	2 992 female. 2 850 95.3%	700 Female 97%
Average age	23.33 (male 26.01/ female 22.76)	Lifetime employees 37 Temporary contract 20	20	Female 19	Female 18
Number of Japanese expatriates	43 (1.34%)	10 (0.6%)	10 (0.4%)	4 (0.13%)	Expatriates. 3 Temporary 9
Number of Hong Kong expatriates	176			7	7
Production volume (000s units)	Radio-cassettes, motor electronics, parts, speakers, motors, PCBs etc.	CTV, radio-cassettes, TV cabinets	HS colour picture tubes 1 600 000/year	Coils 30 000 000/month	Magnetic heads
Destination	Main exports	For TVs China 30% export 70%	Export 30% China 70%	Japan 70%, Hong Kong 20% Singapore 10%	Japan 100%

Notes: SEZ (special economic zone)
Source: Prepared on the basis of personal interviews

companies that took advantage of an opportunity to shift their factories to Southern China: namely, an opportunity that arose after 1980, when China's open market policy was first implemented, the special economic zones were established, and the southern Chinese economic zone was beginning to form. Companies A and B shifted production from Hong Kong; companies C and E from Japan; and company D from Korea. Company A is an independent capital corporation (100 per cent financed by Japanese firms); companies B and C are joint ventures; and companies D and E are consignment production plants. In terms of the form of investment, two companies (B and C) are partly owned and operated by state-run corporations, and two companies (D and E) are township enterprises. Identified by characteristic features such as type of association with the head office, investment form, co-operative production partners, and import- or export-orientation, the companies can be categorised as follows: Company A is an export-base type; company B a one-firm, two-systems type; Company C an outward-export type; Company D a township enterprise type; and Company E an international subcontractor type. These phrases, and the factors that determine the 'degree of application' for each company, such as the form of and circumstances surrounding the shift in production location, and the location and scale of production, are explained more fully below.

Export-base Type: Company A

Company A is notable as a large, independently capitalised corporation (financed 100 per cent by a Japanese company), and as one of the first Japanese firms to shift its factory to the Shekou industrial area of the special economic zone of Shenzhen, just after the opening of the market. In terms of human resources, the areas of investment and management are controlled directly by the Japanese. In terms of physical resources, parts and raw materials are procured from Japan and other Asian countries via Hong Kong. Its finished products are exported all over the world. Since the company's connections with China are weak, it is heavily dependent on the head office in Japan. This phenomenon, in which foreign countries play a central role in both the procurement of raw material and the sale of the products, is called '*liang tou zai wai*'.[4] The plant maintains close ties with its Japanese head office, and from the Japanese side is seen as one of the strongholds of its global strategy. The characterisation of this factory as a general 'overseas production stronghold' will inevitably influence the degree of application of the Japanese production system.

One-firm, Two-systems Type: Company B

Company B is a joint venture. Company S from Japan invested 50 per cent, and China's state-run K holds 50 per cent. The part of Company K that is not involved in the joint venture remains a state-run enterprise. Consequently, a Japanese–Chinese joint venture and a Chinese state-run enterprise co-exist in a single plant and it is referred to as a 'one-firm, two-systems' type. According to the delegation of responsibility and authority between the Japanese and Chinese sides of management, production, technology and financial management are conducted by the Japanese, while personnel and welfare issues are taken care of by the Chinese. Personnel-related issues and the wage system is managed directly by the Chinese head office. This dual management system has a profound effect on the application of the Japanese production system.

Outward-exporting Type: Company C

Company C is a large, high- technology joint venture established by China and Japan. Their products are cathode-ray tubes for colour television sets. The Chinese side invests 75 per cent, while Japan's Company H invests 25 per cent. This is the lowest share of foreign investment allowed under the Chinese joint venture laws. The factory was built in the special economic zone of Shenzhen as a state project, and is aimed at exporting products outside of China to international markets. However, time is needed for a product to gain competitiveness in the fierce international markets. When research was being carried out at this company the factory was one year old, and since most of its goods were being supplied to Chinese markets, it relied on domestic demand. Further effort will be required before the company is able to fulfill its objectives and start exporting internationally.

Township Enterprise Type: Company D

Ever since the open-market policy was implemented, China's township enterprises have grown larger and stronger. There are several types of township enterprises, of which Company D is perhaps the most typical model in the coastal area. Two parties control Company D: one is Japan's Company M, and the other the government authority P, which is the governing authority of the district in which Company D is located. The two parties have a very simple consignment relationship and share neither ownership nor investment. In other words, P provides the land, buildings, and labour, and Company M supplies the equipment, technology and raw materials. All processed goods are sold and exported by Company M, which pays processing fees to P for the number of workers as a way of compensating P for its contribution. Company D's products are small coil electronic components. There are 2992 workers in total, of whom 2850 (95.3 per cent) are female. In general, it seems that China's township enterprises employ surplus labour in the villages where they are located. This is referred to as 'leaving one's land without leaving one's village'. However, factories for consignment production in southern China deviate from these general models. The female workers in these factories are not from the district in which the factories are located, but rather they are young migrant workers from distant provinces such as Gangxi, Hunan and Sichuan. These workers return to their home provinces after working for two years as temporary contract workers. Therefore, the factories are able to maintain average age of nineteen years for their female workers. These young, obedient workers are well suited for delicate component processing operations. Such characteristics of township enterprises and labour requirements greatly affect the degree of application and adaptation of the Japanese production system.

International Subcontractor Type: Company E

Company E shifted its production to southern China in 1991 and operates in the same factory as Company D. Companies D and E have a consignment relationship in that Company D supplies a part of the premises and labour provided by the P district government to Company E, for which Company E pays manufacturing fees related to the number of workers it uses. Company E handles the technology, job-site supervision, procurement of raw materials, and product sales. Company E has a single consignment relationship with Company D for the utilisation of facilities and labour, and in this way it is able to benefit from Company D's experience in consignment production while avoiding the trouble of negotiating with the P district authorities. This enables the late-arriving Company E to get its production on track quickly. Company E's connection with its Company L head office in Japan is best described as an international subcontracting relationship. The computer disk magnetic heads that Company E produces require a high level of precision manufacturing, which results in stringent labour requirements such as good eyesight and a high degree of manual dexterity. It is an extremely clean job-site at this part of the factory where female workers use microscopes as they engage in extremely delicate operations. Company L, the Japanese electronic components manufacturer, used to order parts that required such delicate operations from domestic subcontractors. However, because of factors such as the high value of the yen and a shortage of labour, it became increasingly difficult for Company L to find domestic companies from which it could order such parts. Japanese subcontractors became unable to recruit female workers in their twenties, and rapid changes in the variety of the products and technical innovations meant that production customisation was not worth the cost.

Southern China, with its abundance of young, good-quality labour, became the site where the most suitable subcontractors were located. Panyu was chosen because its proximity to Hong Kong was convenient for receiving supplies of materials. In this way, Southern China's township enterprises replaced the Japanese subcontractors and became international subcontractors in their own right.

The following section will examine the conditions surrounding the transfer of the Japanese companies' production system to Southern China, and explore the characteristics and degree of application of the production system by comparing it with those that exist in Korea and Taiwan.

III   THE HIGH APPLICATION OF 'MATERIAL–RESULTS'

The most distinctive characteristic of the export-orientated factories in this area is their high dependence on Japan for equipment and parts. In Southern China, the deciding factor concerning whether or not to automate facilities is the extent to which local labour can be utilised. In the independently capitalised Company A, the Japanese personnel with managerial authority decided to start by establishing facilities which depended mainly on manual labour. When export demand for international markets increased and when the workers became more skilled, they gradually introduced automated equipment. Automatic inserters for print bases were installed after four years of operation, and chip mounters were brought in after nine years. Of course, the Japanese companies in this region do not rely exclusively on Japanese machinery. They procure machinery from whatever source is the most advantageous. In Company C, which produces cathode-ray tubes, 70–80 per cent of the main equipment is imported from Japan, but the furnaces are purchased from the UK, and conveyers are procured from China.

Japanese support in terms of production facilities and equipment is without doubt one of the most salient characteristics of Japanese factories operating in Southern China. This is not unlike Japanese factories operating in other foreign countries. However, each factory must decide on how many of its facilities to bring over from Japan, and how best to co-ordinate the use of those facilities with local, low-cost labour. Company D is engaged in the production of electronic parts, for which it relies on the dexterity of its young, female workers, thus enjoying the merits of low-cost labour. In the case of Company E, a manufacturer of high-precision electronic parts, it would not be profitable to automate facilities because changes in the variety of products produced occur frequently, and they engage in the production of a variety of products in small lot-sizes. Therefore, it manufactures its products by relying on manual labour at its overseas factories. It also enjoys low-cost labour, but in a different way from that of Company D.

Japanese factories in Southern China also have a high degree of application for 'parts', similar to their high dependence on Japan for equipment. However, this degree of dependency varies somewhat in accordance with the products manufactured, with the companies to which they sell those products, and with the length of time in operation. Companies A and B both make finished products. However, while Company A procures most of its materials from Japan and other foreign countries, and buys only cardboard boxes domestically, Company B procures 40 per cent of its materials from China. Company B began to increase the percentage of domestic production by utilising cabinets that were made in China. The difference in share of domestic content derives from the fact that the independently capitalised Company A makes products for export to overseas markets, and therefore emphasises the quality of its goods. For this reason, it procures materials that are easily and inexpensively shipped from all over the world. Since it does not sell its products domestically, it is not under pressure from the Chinese government to increase the percentage of domestic production, and is not obligated to support the Chinese parts industry. On the other hand, Company B was promised that if it increased its percentage of domestic production, it could sell 40 per cent of its products domestically. Among Companies C, D and E, Company C imports the most components from Japan, because cathode-ray tubes require numerous parts, and also because it has not been in operation for very long. However, since the goods are very fragile and therefore difficult to ship, and because shipping fees are expensive, this company attempts to procure its parts locally. Company D's products are very small, and the required raw materials, such as ferrite core and bronze wire, are relatively simple. Therefore, it buys the former from Company F in Hong Kong, and imports the latter from Japan. Company E's products are precision-made products, so it imports all the components from Japan. Almost all of the imported parts are sourced from

Japan or from Japanese companies in Southeast Asia. Ten of the fifteen companies that are supplied by Company B, which has a high rate of local procurement, are Japanese companies in China.

As is apparent from the above discussion, Japanese affiliated companies located in Southern China rely heavily on Japan for production equipment and for parts, both of which come into the category of 'Material–Results'.

IV THE TRIPLE STRUCTURE OF 'HUMAN–RESULTS'

In Southern China, Japanese expatriates are relatively few. However, they play a central role in the management of the local factories. The reasons that the 'ratio of Japanese expatriates' is so low can be explained as follows. First, the five companies in Southern China are relatively large, and their average number of workers is around 2000. This reduces the ratio of Japanese workers in these factories. Second, these factories do not require many Japanese engineers because they are mainly engaged in labour-intensive operations. Generally, when a factory is built, or when a new product is introduced, many Japanese are dispatched to the overseas sites but return to Japan once production has begun and is operating smoothly. This further lowers the number of Japanese who stay on as regular employees. Third, many people from Hong Kong occupy top management positions above the level of factory manager. In Hong Kong, the former international manufacturing base, many locals were trained as middle managers, as in Taiwan. Next to Japanese expatriates, these people play the second most important role.

Company A employs forty-three Japanese and 176 Hong Kong Chinese. These represent 1.26 per cent and 5 per cent of the total number of workers, respectively, so the percentage of Japanese is clearly not very high. However, important posts such as company president and division heads are held by Japanese staff. Posts in the next class of management are held by Hong Kong Chinese. In the joint ventures B and C, the company president, division heads and factory managers are Japanese. The difference between these cases and that of Company A is that there are no Hong Kong Chinese in these positions. This is probably because the partner of the joint venture is a state-run enterprise that trains middle management human resources, thus eliminating the need for help from Hong Kong. However, in the township enterprises D and E, the factories were run by Japanese and by Hong Kong Chinese, just as in Company A. In these cases, the factories were located in Southern China, while part of their management was based at their head offices in Hong Kong.

Each company's management form is directly influenced by the high degree of application for 'position of local managers'. Since Company A is financed 100 per cent by a Japanese investor, the Japanese have complete authority over its management. In the township enterprises D and E, while the district government P supplies land and labour, the Japanese look after management. The particularly interesting cases are those of joint ventures B and C.

In the case of Company B, since the Chinese and the Japanese sides each have a 50 per cent share of the investment, their status and managerial authority should be divided equally between them. However, the post of company president, as well as other important posts such as those in technology and finance management, is held by a Japanese expatriate. In time, after several years of technology transfer, the Chinese become factory managers, and the Japanese become advisory assistant managers. Important events affecting the application of the Japanese system take place when the Japanese company president changes. At the time of the first visit to this company, the president had been concentrating on introducing the Japanese style of production management and site supervision. However, at the time of the second visit, there was a new president who was an expert on financial matters. He was concentrating on introducing the Japanese management system in the field of finance. Notably, as time passed, the number of Japanese expatriates increased from seven to ten. Of the three local organisations A, B, and C, Company C is the only one with a Chinese president. This is probably because of a decision made by the Chinese because of the high percentage of investment from the Chinese side. Although the percentage of Japanese investment in Company C is the lowest allowed by the Chinese joint venture laws, Japanese staff are appointed to important posts, for example, in production technology and finance.

In Companies D and E, management, materials and financial matters are handled by their head offices in Hong Kong, and the function of the local plant is limited to production. This is the reason why few Japanese are employed at these sites. Company E's president is Japanese, but the management of production technology and technological guidance is carried out by short-term Japanese expatriates, who are sent from Japan for three months at a time. When a new variety of goods is introduced, or a new line is established, Japanese employees are dispatched temporarily from Japan. Daily management is conducted by Chinese workers from Hong Kong.

As was seen above, the small number of Japanese expatriates posted to Japanese affiliates in Southern China generally occupy important posts in management technology and finance. Among these various companies, however, there are differences in the percentage of Japanese personnel as well as in their particular authority. Production management is handled by Hong Kong Chinese, with local Chinese in charge of personnel matters. This triple structure reflects the general trend at factories in Southern China. The tendency to grant considerable power to a small number of Japanese differs from that of Taiwan and Korea, where localisation is in progress. The reasons for this are that it has only been a short time since the Japanese companies first established their presence in Southern China, that local managers have yet to be trained, and that there is a need for the products to gain strong international competitiveness in a short period of time.

V THE MULTI-TIERED CHARACTERISTICS OF 'HUMAN–METHODS'

Work Organisation and Administration

Aspects comprising the core of the system, 'work organisation administration' will be examined here. This group includes 'education and training', 'multifunctional skills' and 'first-line supervisor'.

Turning first to 'Education and Training', all the companies place an important emphasis on the training of new employees. In the case of Company D, new employees receive thirty-six days of training. The 250 employees gather in a large room where they teach the new junior and senior high school graduates the basic objectives and train them in the required skills. The primary objective of this type of training is not so much the acquisition of job skills, but rather to train these girls, who come from rural farmlands, to sit in their seats all day and concentrate. Once this basic objective is accomplished, the new employees receive training and opportunities to practice basic job skills. Next, the new employees must examine defective products and develop a sense of quality awareness. The female employees who undergo the thirty-six days of training have the correct frame of mind and the skills necessary to become workers, as well as the ability to further enhance their own skills through subsequent on-the-job (OJT) training.

In the case of Company E, job rotation is carried out on the shop floor in order to develop versatile workers who are then posted to flexible production lines.

In contrast to Companies D and E, which carry out an in-house training programme for their exclusively female workers, Company C, which has many male workers, conducts a month of military training for all employees. It is more important for the young male workers from farmlands to be able to adjust to the demands of a highly organised environment in which they have to get up and go to bed at designated times and eat with all their co-workers. After their training, they are posted to various parts of the factory and trained through OJT.

The factories in Southern China send employees at the section chief and squad leader levels to Japan for further education and training, and they also have instructors dispatched from Japan when new factories or new assembly lines are being established. This is the method that is adopted by other Japanese affiliate companies overseas. In the case of Company C, 150 employees were sent to Japan for training when the plant was first established. There were sixty employees in charge of equipment, and thirty in charge of manufacturing. Training was also provided for those in charge of technology management, materials, personnel and finance. They also make use of the facilities and courses supplied by Japan's Overseas Technology Training Association, and they dispatch high-level managers such as the company president, vice president and planning engineers.

Company E organised a local training system when it established computer disc magnetic head production lines, by co-ordinating the dispatch of trainees to Japan with that of engineers from Japan. First, site supervisors, who are Hong Kong Chinese, were dispatched to Japan and trained in the main factory for one month. When they returned to Company E, they instructed five Chinese technicians on how to operate the lines. At the same time, five Japanese instructors were dispatched to China. Through this 'triple combination' instruction system, the female line workers received three months of instruction and training before the line began operating. Because the size of the product is very small, the employees began practising the assembly of large models of the parts. After examining defective products and analysing the cause of the trouble, they reassembled the parts. After three months of thorough training, the line was officially put into operation.

In the case of Company A, which has been in operation for ten years, regular workers receive OJT, while site supervisors and 10 per cent of the ordinary workers receive additional training. It is understood that a high level of training for these workers will be a decisive factor in the transfer of the Japanese production system. Each year of the three-year training programme has a different emphasis: namely, JR (job relation, how to treat people) in the first year; JM (job method, problem solving) in the second year; and JS (job safety) in the third year. The site supervisors and the selected 10 per cent of the workers are efficient and produce high-quality results in their work. Advisers from Japan come to train the Chinese instructors, who then train the workers. Apart from this special training, there are general courses covering matters such as quality control, cost reduction, and computer training. This intensified training for workers who represent the core of the factory can be interpreted favourably as an important method for transferring and stabilising technology.

The second aspect to consider under the heading of 'work organisation and administration', is 'multi-functional skills'. In Japan, companies create versatile workers, who then go on to form the core of the organisation, by avoiding restrictive job classifications and by expanding the spheres of job rotation. This does not, however, necessarily correlate with factories in Southern China. Rather, the factories in Southern China restrict workers to a single operation, and try to enhance the skills, precision and speed of their performance. This is probably because of the belief that it is easier to improve work efficiency and quality by taking into account and adapting to the relevant production technology and the nature of the workforce. In the electronic appliance and parts industry, for example, the nature of the assembly lines suggest that there is little necessity to conduct frequent job rotation. There is also no purpose in conducting job rotation by short-term female workers who leave and are replaced by new employees every two to three years. However, because the products are made for the international market, they change in accordance with international demand. When products change, workers on each assembly line must collectively change their job practices and positions. For this reason, factory workers are expected to acquire new and different skills, and it is important for the companies to train their core workers to be able to adapt to such changes in production operations. The general method, therefore, is to employ smart, promising people and train them to become versatile workers.

The next item, 'first-line supervisor', is concerned with how operations leaders acquire their skills, an explanation of their roles, and of the extent of their authority. Workers at Company A are ranked from the bottom up as production worker, group head, line head, assistant chief, and chief. First-line supervisors include group heads, line heads and assistant chiefs. The first notable characteristic about first-line supervisors at Company A is that there are many women among them. Among the twenty-nine heads of operations in Company A's motor factory manufacturing division, twenty-four, or 83 per cent of the total, are female. This is not surprising, since they were promoted from the position of factory worker, 94 per cent of whom are female. In addition, they have all been promoted internally.

Not only are line operators promoted to be heads of operations, but also to management positions after being recommended at various stages and passing through examinations. A third characteristic is that there are differences between the numbers of years before promotion according to when the employees were hired. Employees who were hired earlier required fewer years before being promoted. Most female workers who entered the company before 1986 spent less than a year before they were promoted to a supervisory position. Worker B, who entered the company in 1983, became a group head after less than six months' employment, while in the case of worker F, it took three years to become a group head. Workers who were hired in 1988 has to wait a much longer time to be promoted. This is probably because there was a need to train the supervisors quickly when the factory was first established and expanding.

The role of the supervisor can be analysed conveniently by examining a typical working day for worker C. Her roles and authority on such a day can be grouped into three parts: (i) production supervision – this includes taking care of changes and problems; (ii) personnel management – she conducts first-stage assessments for bonuses and promotion; and (iii) supervising the daily lives of the workers – she must not only supervise family planning for her married workers, but also supervise the daily lives of the short-term female workers who live in company dormitories. Thus, supervisors have authority over production, personnel and employees' daily lives, and they are essential to Japanese companies in Southern China, whose workers are mainly short-term employees.

Employment and Labour Conditions

Here, I will examine the elements such as 'hiring policy', 'long-term employment', 'promotion', and 'wage system'. Analysis of employment and labour conditions shows that Japanese affiliated companies in Southern China succeed in training core personnel while employing young, low-cost labour.

The item 'Hiring policy' is concerned with the area of recruitment, methods of recruitment, and employment qualifications. While Japanese affiliated companies in Korea, Taiwan, Thailand and Malaysia recruit their workers independently through printed advertisements or by word of mouth, in Southern China, these companies recruit collectively in specially designated recruitment areas. For Company A, one of the first to enter Southern China, the recruitment areas were Shenzhen, which was near the factory, and neighbouring areas such as Baoan, Hueizhou and Donggan in 1983. From 1985–7, the recruitment district expanded to include Guangdong and neighboring Mei county and Zhanjiang. From 1988 it was further expanded to include Hunan, a province far distant from Guangdong. The fact that the recruitment areas were expanded to include surrounding areas indicates that the company had to adapt to changes in the economy, society and labour force of each district. Few Japanese affiliated companies were in operation when Company A was established, because it was immediately after the creation of the special economic zones. There was therefore a surplus of good-quality female labour in the special economic zone that included Shenzhen and the neighboring Baoan district. Applicants always outnumbered job openings ten to one, and the workforce was very stable, with a near zero turnover rate. However, as the number of Japanese affiliated companies, other foreign affiliated companies, Hong Kong enterprises, and other township enterprises increased, the number of applicants decreased and wages rose. Some female workers left for factories that offered higher wages, without waiting for their contracts to expire. Japanese affiliated companies shifted their attention to Hunan province, which was less economically developed than Guangdong, to avoid labour and wage competition. Trial employment of female workers in this area showed that they possessed certain advantageous qualifications: they had high levels of education; could comprehend instruction well; were honest and hard-working; were skilled with their hands; and would remain loyal to one company. Moreover, the labour division of the local government was also co-operative. For these reasons, Company A changed its recruitment area from Guangdong to Huai Hua county of Hunan province. As one of the first Japanese affiliated companies to enter Southern China, it had to adapt its recruitment practices to changes in the external environment.

In contrast, Company C was a latecomer and seems to have been very conscious of particular objectives in selecting its recruitment area. It recruited 1865 factory workers between January 1991, when it was first built and March 1992. Workers were recruited from all of China's eleven provinces and twenty-two districts. The reason it recruited over so wide an area was to compare the quality and aptitude of the workers from different areas. Its young, male workers are temporary employees on five-year contracts. This will be discussed in more detail later. The male workers from these twenty-two districts are 'experimental' workers. In other words, on the basis of their performance, the company intends to select the district in which to concentrate future recruitment of workers who are most suitable in terms of how well they work in an organisation and how well they contribute to factory operations. Companies D and E, on the other hand, recruit their female workers from Guangdong, Guangxi,

Hunan, and Guizhou, which are all far from Panyu, where the factory is located.

In this way, China offers an abundant supply of good-quality labour from among its young school graduates. Japanese affiliated companies, who try to employ suitable workers with an aptitude for the work, therefore have a wide variety of choices. This almost unlimited supply of labour in Southern China also restrains wage rises, thus creating an advantageous environment for capital.

The second aspect of 'Hiring policy' to be considered is recruitment methods. How do these Japanese affiliated companies with factories in Southern China go about recruiting workers from all over China? Unlike in Korea, Thailand or Malaysia, these workers come from places in China that are distant from the factories, so it is difficult for them to apply at the factories in person. Instead, the companies commission the labour departments of each local government to carry out this recruitment.[5] After workers are recruited by the various labour departments they are sent to the factories in a group. In this type of collective recruitment, the company's personnel department informs the local labour department of the number of workers needed, the required qualifications, and the hiring deadline. The labour departments gather qualified recruits and conduct medical and written examinations. They then send the people who pass these examinations to the factories they want to go to. The number of personnel sought at the time of each collective recruitment is around 200 to 300, although this differs according to the needs of the particular company. There are usually about five to six times as many applicants as there are job openings.

Personnel departments of Japanese affiliated companies prefer commissioning local labour departments for recruitment, rather than going directly to each district and doing it themselves. There are three reasons for this: first, local labour departments are more knowledgeable about the local labour situation. Second, parents feel more at ease about sending away their children, particularly daughters of rural families, when they know that the state-organised labour departments are involved. And third, these local labour departments implement various measures for the supervision of the new graduates they send off as migrant workers.

Local labour departments thus serve as an organisational guarantor and supervisor for the migrant workers. This not only secures a stable supply of labour, but also creates an environment in which female employees can work comfortably. For the local governments, this serves as an opportunity to dispatch workers on a regular basis, and provides job opportunities for the surplus labour in the district.

The third aspect of 'Hiring policy' is employment qualifications. In general, successful applicants should have graduated from junior or senior high school, be under twenty years of age, be over 155 cm in height, have perfect eyesight, a high degree of manual dexterity and no physical handicaps. Companies A and C require high school graduates, who are relatively highly qualified. Companies D and E are less strict in their academic requirements. Applicants who fulfill these qualifications may then take an entrance examination at a designated time and place. Applicants who pass this examination receive an interview. General questions asked at this interview concern matters such as family background and reasons for applying. An important factor is points awarded for the impression that the applicant makes upon the interviewer. According to worker R, who entered Company A three years before the survey date, one of the three people that applied passed the written examination but failed the interview. The reasons were unknown, but it was suspected that the applicant received low points for 'impression'. One of the factors influencing the impression applicants make on the interviewer may be the 'attitude' of the applicants. Those applicants who succeed in passing the local selection, the various examinations, and the interview are then employed by the companies.

The next items to be considered are 'long-term employment', 'promotion', and 'wage system'. The Japanese 'long-term employment' system is not equivalent to unconditional long-term employment. The emphasis is on employing the 'right people' for the company. This tendency is especially strong in the electronics industry. Japanese affiliated companies in Southern China are attempting to maintain a young age level in their workforce for the electronic products factories, and at the same time are trying to create skilled core employees for long-term employment. This is accomplished by classifying jobs on the basis of job composition.

Looking first at Company A's employment system, it can be seen that there are four types of employment: namely, permanent, outside, temporary contract, and contract workers. Permanent workers are similar to Japanese staff employees in that they are, in fact, 'life-time employees'. These are mainly middle managers from state-run enterprises, or university graduate engineers. Outside workers are on loan from other companies, and this type of employment is similar to outside workers in Japan. The present emphasis will be on temporary contract workers and contract worker types of employment.

Female workers who enter the company after undergoing a multistaged selection process are first employed on a three-month trial basis. They are then promoted to 'temporary contract workers'. This means that they are temporary workers whose term of employment is limited by contract. The length of that term of employment differs for each company but is usually two or three years. Specifically, the term of employment for Company A is three years; Company B, two years; Company C, five years; and Companies D and E, two years. The need to create this form of employment is related to the Chinese 'family registration system'.[6] After the contract expires, its term can be renewed provided this is in accordance with the needs of the company and the wishes of the employees. However, in many cases, workers return home if they are not promoted. Since the status of 'temporary contract workers' does not enable them to register in the district where the factory is located, they are not permitted to find partners to marriage. Even if they are permitted to marry, they must then leave, since they lack certain family requirements such as suitable housing. Because of these social limitations, most 'temporary contract workers' leave and are replaced after three years. This is why factory workers are always young. On the other hand, very few workers with excellent performance are promoted to become 'contract workers'. Contract workers are quasi-staff employees. If the workers are promoted to become 'contract workers', then they have a chance of being employed on a long-term basis. Therefore, whether or not one is promoted to 'contract worker' is a very important turning point in one's life and career. This promotion enables people to work on a long-term basis, and if they are further promoted later, they are then able to register in the special economic zones. This guarantees that they can work at the companies in these zones.[7] 'Contract workers' also play an important role for the companies. These workers become important core personnel as they acquire a wide variety of skills through long-term employment.

Company C, which employs mostly male workers, has a similar way of classifying types of employment. However, it has a longer, five-year, term for temporary contract workers. This is because of the special needs arising out of its production technology, also the workers' gender. The company observes the performance of its workers for five years, and then selects those whom it considers to be the best workers. It promotes them to 'contract workers' or 'first-line supervisors', giving them a central role in the factory. Meanwhile, it recruits new, young, temporary contract workers. These employee selection systems enable Companies A and C to secure the 'right people' to become important factory employees.

Company B, which is a joint venture, also utilises 'temporary contract workers', but in a different way from Companies A and C. In the case of Company B, Chinese Company K is in charge of matters relating to personnel. The 899 permanent workers who were dispatched from the state-run enterprise contributed greatly to the development of Company B when it first went into operation. However, in the course of time, 'ageing of the workers' became a problem, since these employees are, in fact, 'life-time' employees. This hinders the smooth development of the electronics industry, and the efficiency of factory production suffered as a result. Company B started to deal with the problem of 'ageing' by strategically placing its temporary contract workers according to age. It positions young temporary contract workers, below the age of twenty, in the stages of production where physical strength and good eyesight are required, namely to those stages for which the older permanent workers are not well suited. However, temporary contract workers are only in charge of simple operations, under a two-year contract, with no possibility of promotion. Key factory workers are selected from the ranks of permanent or contract workers. Temporary contract workers are assistants to permanent workers, and they neither have, nor require, opportunities to improve their skills.

Companies D and E were originally township enterprises and most of their employees are from farming areas. Because of this, they are not allowed to establish the official status of permanent or contract workers in state-run enterprises. All their employees can be considered to be temporary contract workers. The problem with this system is that, because of these limitations, few university student applicants aim at becoming permanent workers for the state. This makes it difficult for the company to secure engineers. To employ such people, the Japanese managers have no choice but to provide exceptionally high wages and other fringe benefits. On the other hand, in the case of assemblers, even though employment is stratified as it is at Companies A, B and C, there remains a distinction between the local people and the young female migrant workers, who are known as 'girls from other areas'. Opportunities for promotion are offered more frequently to local people and this creates a gap between the local employees and the migrant 'girl' workers. These migrant workers are on a two-year contract, which they are only allowed to extend up to the time they get married, after which they must return to their homelands.

As is clear from the above, 'long-term employment' is not unconditional. The important issue is whether the companies can employ workers who will become key employees on a long-term basis, and whether they are able to train these workers in a wide variety of skills through long-term employment. Company B's system of employing permanent workers of the Chinese state-run enterprise on a long-term basis is not a Japanese, but a Chinese style of employment. The introduction of short-term 'temporary contract workers', though, may be an application of Japanese style employment. This is similar to the way electronics factories in Japan employ many housewives and part-timers. However, Company B's introduction of the 'dual structure' of employment becomes an obstacle to skill improvement for temporary contract workers because it cuts off their route for promotion. In contrast, Companies A and C, which rely on short-term temporary contract workers, provide more opportunities for promotion. They are able to improve their workers' skills, and thereby contribute actively to the formation of key employees. In Companies D and E, the numerous migrant workers have no hope of promotion, and this keeps skills low among a wide range of workers.

Unlike in Korea, Taiwan, Hong Kong and Malaysia, there is an abundant supply of labour in China, and so there is no need to worry about a long-term employment policy. In China, the emphasis in 'long-term employment' systems is not the actual length of the employment term, but the question of how to best train people to be able to cope with the various production changes and problems that arise. This is closely related to the 'promotion' and 'wage system' that will be discussed below.

All five of the companies in Southern China make use of an internal promotion system. However, the route of promotion may vary according to the different forms of employment discussed above. Company A's group heads and line heads were all promoted from the position of assemblers. The process begins with line heads recommending candidates from among the workers for the position of group head. Then managers above the first level of line heads assess these recommended candidates. There are several criteria for assessment: namely, co-operation, ability, skill level and human relations. If the criteria are considered to be met, then the recommended workers become formal candidates. This is followed by a careful screening of documents. Candidates must then produce a report in which they evaluate their own performance as well as make a proposal for operation plans that they would implement upon becoming group heads. The superiors of the candidates make their decisions, based upon this document, concerning which of the candidates become group heads.

As mentioned earlier, promotion from assembler to group head is of life-changing significance. It is not only a matter of a change in title, but also of a considerable change in status. If they are 'temporary contract workers', they become 'contract workers'. As well as being a form of employment, 'contract worker' is a link in the chain of personnel selection. As 'contract workers', their chances of registering in Shenzhen become stronger, they are guaranteed a company position on a long-term basis and, if they are diligent, there is a possibility for further promotion to the position of line head or even of manager. Being promoted to a group head or a contract worker is therefore an important turning point in their lives. The system is very attractive for the temporary contract workers. They work hard under the internal promotion system so that they can stay with the company and remain in the special economic zones. Those who are promoted to group heads work harder still so that they can register in the special economic zones and be eligible for even further promotion.

In this way, long-term employment begins at the position of contract worker or group head. Skilled factory workers are developed in a system that selects bright, experienced people for promotion. Decisions on how to cope with changes or problems that arise in the factory are made by those above the group head level. Temporary contract workers are in charge of simple assembly-line operations. This multistage selection system forms a hierarchy in which temporary contract workers at the bottom, contract workers are in the middle, and heads of operation at the top. This system ensures a constant supply of young, low-wage assemblers, and yields key factory workers who rise to the top of the pyramid. This type of employee flow is ideal for these companies.

Company B, however, does not have this type of advantageous employee flow. As seen in the discussion about 'long-term employment', only permanent and contract workers are promoted at company B. Temporary contract workers are isolated and limited to a peripheral role, and the source of personnel with prospects for promotion is therefore small. Although Company B also practices internal promotion, university graduate engineers are promoted the fastest. It seems that there is a tendency to value academic over work experience.

At Companies D and E, there is a gap between the position of local and migrant workers, who have little chance of being promoted. There are concerns that this will be an obstacle to the development of personnel with a wide variety of skills.

The 'wage system' is examined next, as part of the overall system for securing and training personnel. The 'wage system' stimulates the workers' will to work, and can be considered to comprise one aspect of the promotion of human resources. The example of Company A warrants closer examination. Company A's wage system consists of basic wages, various benefits, bonuses, and wages based on job class. Basic wages are determined by length of service, thus establishing seniority as an important factor. Benefits are provided for meals as well as to reward diligence and discourage absenteeism. Bonuses are adjusted each month in accordance with the volume and quality of products from each line. This practice is intended to ensure production efficiency and product quality. The amount of the bonus is determined on the basis of the collective achievements of each line. The line head decides how to distribute the bonus according to the results attributed to each worker on an individual basis. The job class component of the wage system is similar to the Japanese 'kyūgō'. According to this system, each job class is graded from one to twenty, and each grade is further subdivided into the ranks A, B and C. Table 6.2 displays the job classes for Company A. Temporary contract workers are classified as grade 0 upon entering the company, and they become grade 1, rank C, after their first year. The base salary differs slightly according to the length of service and the age of the workers. The lowest base salary for someone employed on a trial basis, is 156 yuan, while that of a line head is 260 yuan. In terms of the job class component of the salary, temporary contract workers who are employed on a trial basis received nothing. However, line heads receive an additional HK$300 to HK$350, and division chiefs receive an additional HK$2000. The difference in job class components of the salary, which are much larger than those arising from base salaries, are clearly connected directly with promotions, and are the result of long-term performance assessments. Since this wage system incorporates seniority and assessment factors, it may be appropriate to call it a seniority–job classification wage system. Combined with promotion, this system plays a role in improving workers' skills, and at the same time, it helps to form the corporate employee hierarchy. Also, since most assemblers return to their homelands after three years, it maintains a stable, low-wage group of employees in the company, and safeguards the interests of the core employees.

The salary system of Company D, a municipally owned company, will be examined next. Characteristic of Company D's system are the numerous, quickly changing grades within the wage structure, and the small gaps between each of these grades. In the case of assemblers, their base salaries of 260 yuan does not change at all for the first four years. Beginning in the second year, they receive HK$30 as skill benefits. In addition, however, assessment wages reflect their individual achievements. The assessment salary is very simple; it imposes the ranks of A, B and C on each job class. If a worker is promoted to a position above that of assistant squad leader, his or her salary becomes higher than that of an assembler. If a worker is promoted to a position above that of assistant squad leader, then his or her base salary and overtime pay rises further still. Company D's wage structure shows that it is trying to improve the skills of its employees by taking even small job class distinctions into

Table 6.2   Job classification table for Company A

Position	Grade	Rank	Salary
(Plant) manager	20	A	2 000
	19	B	1 700
Assistant manager	18	C	1 450
Manufacturing manager	17		1 200
Assistant manufacturing manager	16		1 000
Chief	15	A	900
	14	B	800
Assistant chief	13	A	700
	12	B	600
	11	C	500
Line manager	10	A	400
	9	B	350
	8	C	300
Group leader	7	A	250
	6	B	200
	5		180
	4	C	150
Technician	3	A	120
	2	B	80
	1	C	50
New employee	0	0	0

Source: Prepared on the basis of personal interviews.

consideration. Company E utilises a similar wage structure to Company D, but additionally encourages its workers to acquire skills that correspond to the variety of jobs on a production line, and pays 20 yuan in such 'multiple-job' benefits.

At Companies A and D, wage systems are mainly determined by the Japanese. In the joint ventures B and C, however, a large part of their salary systems is based on the salary systems applied at the Chinese state-run enterprises. Company B uses the same personnel management system and wage system as does its Chinese head office. The salary consists of base salary, benefits, floating wages, and overtime pay. Floating wages are linked directly with the company's performance (production volume, product quality, sales). Base salary and benefits comprise 30–35 per cent of total salary, with the floating wage comprising the remaining 65–70 per cent. Seniority is an important factor in determining base salary. Permanent workers with long service receive a higher base salary than temporary workers. The floating wage corresponds to company performance and has little connection with the form of employment. For this reason, temporary workers who contribute significantly to production receive what they deserve for their efforts. This system then attempts to address the fairness issue by recognising the link between identical contributions of many workers and company performance, and rewarding workers for their contribution. Overall, however, there seems to be little incentive for workers to improve their skills.

From the above, it can be seen that these five Japanese affiliated companies in Southern China implement systems with their own distinctive characteristics in order to develop and secure their human resources, and that these systems differ somewhat in accordance with the different conditions under which they operate.

VI   THE REVISED APPLICATION OF 'MATERIAL–METHODS'

The following section examines 'quality control', 'maintenance', and 'parts procurement method', the three items comprising 'material–methods'.

All these companies can be considered 'Japanese' in terms of the emphasis they place on 'quality control' and 'maintenance'. The quality of their products is said to match that of products made in Japan. This is partly because of human factors such as the keen eyesight and skilful hands of the young workers. It is difficult to attribute this high level of product quality to a Japanese-style quality control system within which each worker takes full responsibility for the products of his or her own operation. As will be discussed, efforts are made to improve product quality through supplementary methods.

One method of encouraging quality is the introduction of quality bonuses. In the case of each company, bonuses are determined by a number of quality standards. One of these standards is the proportion of defective products and the rate of insertion mistakes. The companies try to stress the importance of quality by adjusting the amount of the bonuses. Company D applied a very simple method of paying five yuan a month to workers if there were no returned products. A second method of guaranteeing quality is by increasing the number of quality checkpoints within the manufacturing process, and a third method is to increase the number of quality inspectors. Company E's computer disc magnetic head assembly line is a good example. The manufacture of these magnetic heads is a very delicate, high-precision operation. Compared to factories in

Japan, the Japanese affiliated plants in Southern China are characterised by a large number of processes and personnel. Where twenty-one assemblers work at a given production line in Japan, thirty-nine workers, or almost double the number in Japan, are based at the factories in Southern China. There are also more quality inspectors. In one case, seventeen workers check thirty-two quality points for each finished product, in addition to the stationing of quality inspectors. Factories attempt to decrease the occurrence of mistakes by simplifying each operation through manufacturing process fragmentation, and by increasing the number of personnel. The introduction of quality-checking production workers and the increase in the number of final product, quality inspectors creates a dual inspection system which is expected to bring about even further improvements in product quality.

Company B, which produces finished goods, employs thirty inspectors in its quality guarantee division, five times the number employed in a corresponding division in Japan. According to a Japanese employee, the company must maintain strict controls over quality in order to ensure similar quality levels to those achieved in Japan.

As explained above, while quality control in Japan is the result of workers proceeding carefully with their work, in Southern China, an external quality control system is in place. This external system is applied to in-process products by simplifying, or fragmenting the manufacturing process, as well as to finished products. This system is appropriate for these local factories that employ young, female, migrant workers on a short-term basis. It was devised to suit the particular conditions obtaining in these factories while making it possible to maintain a desired level of quality. While this system contributes to higher costs, the relatively low wages in Southern China soften the impact considerably. The companies put a much higher priority on quality control than on personnel costs. This 'quality making' system is different from the characteristic Japanese approach.

'Maintenance' is also affected directly by the employment situation. These companies cannot expect their short-term female workers, who carry out relatively simple tasks, to be responsible for conducting maintenance on production equipment. Therefore, these Japanese affiliated companies in Southern China all rely on specialists to carry out necessary maintenance. For the most part, these five companies utilise an internal training system. At Company C, where most workers are male, the first maintenance crew were employed from outside and sent to Japan to acquire maintenance skills. At the other four companies, where the workers are mainly female, male workers are selected for maintenance crews. In other words, these companies rely on short-term, young, female workers for simple production operations, and they train their male workers to become maintenance specialists, one of the central roles at production sites. The way the factories train the male workers to become skilled maintenance personnel and to serve as the core of the factory is not unlike the system used in Japan. Female workers conduct general facility inspections, or take care of refuelling, but complicated maintenance is left to the male specialists. In especially difficult cases, engineers are sometimes called in from Hong Kong or Japan.

Turning to the 'parts procurement method', it was observed that these companies procure their parts, from 'external' locations such as Japan or Southeast Asia, via Hong Kong, which serves as a trading centre and is extremely advantageous to Japanese affiliated companies in Southern China. In fact, this was one of the reasons Japanese companies entered Southern China in the first place. The high dependency upon external procurement, however, makes it difficult to implement the Japanese JIT system. Procurement methods vary according to the parts involved, as well as to how long the company has been operating overseas. In the case of Company A, which has a long presence in Southern China, most components are procured from Japan and Southeast Asia via Hong Kong; however, it orders easily-manufactured production parts from state-run corporations and Hong Kong factories, in an attempt to increase the rate of local production. It also makes an effort to implement JIT fully, as its subcontractor parts suppliers are situated nearby. Despite differences in degree, companies are making efforts to practice JIT, and there are even signs that some are starting to establish subcontractual relationships.

Company B is trying to increase the percentage of parts produced internally at the final stages of assembly of television sets and radio cassette-players. It manufactures cabinets for its own use as well as for export to Southeast Asia. This policy originated from the Japanese head office's internal personnel division, and increases the percentage of local procurement as well as guarantees delivery dates. Company C, which has not been operating very long, imports most of its raw materials and parts from Japan. Although, in the beginning, it imported all its components from Japan, it has begun to increase the percentage of internally produced parts. It currently manufactures electron guns, deflection yokes and other metal parts within its own factory. Internal parts production reduces the percentage of imports, thus helping to save foreign currency. This company is also considering the procurement of 30 per cent of its panels from a local US company. Overall, the company is actively pursuing a higher proportion of local procurement.

Company E, which produces precision electronic parts, is able to ship its parts by air because of their small size. Taking advantage of this, they practise international JIT in an attempt to reduce the parts inventory and save on related interest rate costs. For example, ¥150 million worth of inventory, at an interest rate of 1 per cent per month, costs the company ¥1.5 million in monthly interest. This is why Japanese affiliates in Southern China try to reduce their inventories. International JIT requires smooth and efficient communication. This is one of the important roles for Japanese affiliated companies in Southern China to fulfill.

As seen from the above, the 'Material–Methods' aspect of these five Japanese affiliates' application of the Japanese system is greatly influenced by employment and training systems, and by whether the workers play important roles in the factories.

VII CONCLUSION

The above analysis of the application of the Japanese production system at the five electrical appliance factories of Japanese affiliated companies in Southern China showed that the average degree of application for all twenty-three items among the five companies located in Southern China was a high 3.2 points. This is only 0.1 points below the average reported for similar companies in Korea and Taiwan, where there is a longer history of local production by Japanese affiliated companies. These firms in Southern China are characterised as export-base, one firm–two systems, outward-exporting, township-enterprise, and international subcontractor types, respectively. There are common points, as well as differences, in terms of degrees of application and adaptation in the local introduction of the Japanese production system among these five companies. For example, all five companies are highly dependent upon Japan for 'material' and 'human' support, reflecting a high application for 'Material–Result' and 'Human–Result'. In other words, these operations introduce 'production equipment' and 'components' directly from Japan, and then export locally-manufactured products. In terms of production, they have a weak relationship with China, but rely heavily on Japan and the international markets. Also, the relatively small number of Japanese sent from Japan play a large role in managing and running the local factories. In short, although there is a low 'ratio of Japanese expatriates', the large role they play in the 'Human–Results' management of the local factories cannot be ignored. Plus, Chinese people in Hong Kong play an assisting role in local production, exploiting the geographical advantage of proximity to Hong Kong. Hong Kong is also significant with regard to the flow of material.

In contrast to the many common aspects in 'Human–Results' and 'Material–Results', there are numerous differences in the areas of 'Human–Methods' and 'Material–Methods'. In 'Material–Methods', the Japanese system is revised and applied to fit the variety of goods the factories produce and employment terms of their workers. On the other hand, the companies have varying characteristics in the 'Human–Methods' area, namely, the recruiting and training of workers.

Company A is most typical. It hires young female temporary contract workers who are replaced every three years. It then selects and promotes temporary contract workers with excellent performance records, to become regular contract workers and even group or line heads. In this way, they cannot only secure young female workers who are highly suitable for the simple operations required in the electronic industry, but can also cultivate skilled core employees, from among their workers, through promotion. This increases the company's ability to handle change and cope with problems. The implementation of a seniority, job-assignment wage system maintains low wages for short-term temporary contract workers, and at the same time stimulates competition among the female workers. Under the multistage selection system, employees work harder and try their best to contribute to the company in order to remain at the factory. This strengthens the company and at the same time develops the skills of the employees in a way that is beneficial to the company. The 'rotary employment system' and the multistage promotion system enable the company to maintain a system with low wages as well as to secure experienced workers. Company C, which hires mainly male employees, implements the same type of personnel training system. At the joint-venture Company B, on the other hand, there is a gap between temporary and permanent contract workers, with the former used simply as low-wage workers, and the latter receiving most of the benefits of personnel training. However, the efficient use of temporary contract workers enables Company B to secure a stable, permanent workforce, as well as to implement a training system for them. Internal personnel training for township enterprises D and E is hindered by the distinction between local employees and migrant workers who 'immigrated' from other areas of China. However, it is the low salaries paid to these 'girls from other areas' that support factory production, securing profitable employment for local workers and making it possible to hire highly-paid Hong Kong managers and university graduate engineers. On the whole, the Japanese affiliated companies in southern

China that were the subject of this study all have an effective personnel training system.

It seems from the above discussion that the Japanese system has the potential for large-scale application in southern China. However, local production by these Japanese affiliated companies is conducted under the direct control of the Japanese production system operating in a unique environment and in a limited area of China. To what extent these conclusions hold for other areas of China requires further research.

Notes

1. The Chinese government established four special economic zones, in Shenzhen, Zhuhai, Shantou and Xiamen, as symbols of China's open market policy.
2. Twv (1992).
3. I participated in research on the Japanese electrical appliance industry, automobile industry, and Japanese companies abroad as a member of the Japan Multinational Enterprises Research Group. In September and October of 1992, the group conducted research in Korea and Taiwan as part of a project entitled 'Transferring Technology to Japanese Factories in Asian Countries'. However, I was unable to enter Taiwan because of procedural difficulties and went directly to Hong Kong and Shenzhen, with the same research framework and objectives. Thus this study is both an element and extension of the group's research. The analysis proposed in this study is based on materials gathered in the two research excursions, unless noted otherwise.
4. The term '*liang tou zai wai*' refers to the 'coastal area strategy' proposed by China's former prime minister, Zhao Ziyang. This means that the sources for equipment and raw material (the 'two heads'), as well as the product market, are overseas, while the manufacturing operation takes place in China. The objective is for China to earn manufacturing wages by this process.
5. In China there is a Labour Service Company within each local labour bureau. This was originally a department dedicated to finding work for the unemployed, including those who cannot find work after graduating from junior or senior high school. Later, it became a department that mediates labour for foreign companies in the coastal area.
6. The Chinese 'family register system' is rather complex. For present purposes, it may suffice to explain that this system was established to restrict the free influx of farmland population into city areas. The requirement for those who work in the state-run firms in the cities is to be registered in the city. Since those who are registered in the farmlands cannot easily transfer to the city, it is difficult for them to become formal company employees. See Tajima (1993) for a more detailed description of the family register system.
7. Interviews with female workers and their parents revealed that many of them do not want to go back to the farmlands once they have entered the companies in the special economic zones. I had the impression that they have a strong desire to leave the farmlands for good.

7 Conclusions and Prospects

Hiroshi Itagaki

I THREE FACTORS DETERMINING THE DEGREE OF APPLICATION

The analysis presented in this book has revealed three factors that help to determine the degree of application of Japanese methods or elements. The first is the strategic factor, or the extent to which application of Japanese methods or elements is considered to be necessary. This is influenced strongly by the technological characteristics of a given industry; that is, whether the industry requires highly skilled employees or can manage with relatively unskilled ones, and whether the skills themselves are important for a wide range of employees or are only relevant to a handful of experts or specialists. Competitive conditions such as market size, degree of protectionism, existence of rivals in the host country, and level of quality demanded by the market are also crucial in determining necessity.

The second factor concerns particular 'attributes' of the Japanese system that determine international transferability. These attributes are described as 'methods', 'result', 'human', or 'material', and include the notions of 'core system' (for example, elements in the Work Organisation or Production Control groups, which are considered to be necessary for the proper functioning of the Japanese system) and 'sub system' (for example, elements in the Group Consciousness group, which play more of a supplementary or support function for the overall system). Every element is a product of the historical, social and economic environment of its home country. Typically, subsystem elements are related directly to behavioural patterns and the value-system of the people in the home country. Core-system elements, on the other hand, are related only indirectly to cultural and social conditions.[1] In general, elements that are directly related to the home country's cultural and social environment are expected to be more difficult to transfer than those that are indirectly related. However, this is not necessarily always the case.

The third factor is the host country environment. Particularly critical is the existence of institutional hindrances to the introduction of the Japanese system, or the presence of an already established production system. Even if elements that are to be transferred are only related indirectly to the cultural environment of the home country, it is difficult to transfer them into a host country where a firmly-established system already exists. In contrast, elements that have a definite cultural component may be transferred easily to the host society, provided that the host country shares certain cultural characteristics with the home country. Furthermore, elements that are unfamiliar to the host country may be transferred deliberately in a different context from that which exists in the home country. For example, some Japanese affiliates in the United States enthusiastically introduce devices that facilitate a sense of unity and egalitarianism, although American society is, in general, strongly orientated towards the individual and towards respecting differences of opinions. They introduce such devices in order to eliminate the gaps between the upper and lower strata of the corporate hierarchy, and especially the disparity between treatment that is accorded to blue-collar and white-collar employees.

Of course, social conditions external to the corporate system, such as social or geographical mobility, income disparities, social gaps stemming from different academic backgrounds and so on are also crucial determinants. The stage of industrial development of the host countries poses a complicated question. Generally, technological transfer into industrialised countries is considered to be more easily accomplished because of abundant managerial resources and well-organised infrastructure. Although this is essentially undeniable, it should also be seriously considered, as emphasised above, that industrial development creates an indigenous management system which hinders the subsequent transplantation of systems that originated in other countries.

II   APPLICATION OF THE JAPANESE SYSTEM IN EAST ASIA: REALITIES, SIGNIFICANCE AND PROBLEMS

The Hybrid Configuration Today

The combination of the three factors described above determines the particular hybrid configuration that exists at the affiliated plants in each host country. Japanese methods in areas such as job classification, the wage system, and education and training, have penetrated Japanese affiliates in Taiwan and Korea. Japanese affiliated plants in those countries are much more orientated towards Japanese methods, with regard to the core system of plant operations, than are their counterparts in the United States. The major reason for the relatively successful application of 'Methods' in Taiwan and Korea is the absence of institutional hindrances or of firmly rooted management systems, compared with the United States. At the same time, it should be noted that factories in Taiwan and Korea already possessed certain organisational elements that resembled Japanese system elements, such as job classification and wage systems.

On the other hand, the localisation of management and managers at Japanese affiliates has progressed further in Taiwan and Korea than in other host countries. This is attributed mainly to the presence of local managers who have a thorough understanding of the Japanese system, and the ability of even middle management to communicate by telephone or facsimile in Japanese with personnel at mother plants in Japan. It is as if some ideal form of management has been realised at these affiliated plants, a form of management composed of Japanese system-orientated operations led by localised management, and sometimes even local managers. Supported by this particular hybrid configuration, some affiliates in Taiwan and Korea are able to achieve the highest product quality and the most efficient production among any Japanese affiliates outside of Japan.

However, when plant operations are examined in more detail, several limitations and problems become apparent. The most significant limitations are discrepancies between formal systems and actual operations. Typical examples are: multifunctional skill formation lags behind the practice in Japan, despite the weak partition between jobs and the introduction of a 'person-centred' wage system, in which wage rates are determined by personal factors and not by job categories; the majority of affiliates display inferior performance regarding in-process defect ratios, compared to their mother plants, although they do implement some formal measures for building quality into the production process; the rate of employee participation, enthusiasm, and achievement of small-group activities has not reached a satisfactory level, although the activities themselves are well organised and well executed. These limitations result from a shorter operating history, greater inter-company mobility of employees, wider social gaps, and a lack of strong motivation to introduce substantial elements of Japanese methods, on the part of the affiliates, through having achieved a certain level of managerial performance with the help of a favourable exchange rate between local currencies and the US dollar, as well as considerably lower wage levels than exist in Japan.

Affiliated plants in ASEAN countries have also not had to contend with obvious institutional hindrances. This is reflected in the high application rating for Job classification among all ASEAN countries, with the exception of Singapore. Nevertheless, the application of 'Methods' aspects is considerably lower than in either Taiwan or Korea. In particular, there is a remarkable difference in the extent to which the core system is introduced. This is mainly attributed to the affiliates' low enthusiasm for introducing Japanese methods, such as expanding the range of jobs for individual employees or having ordinary production workers participate in quality control or maintenance, since they judge that the time is not ripe for introducing such practices. Managerial environments in the host countries, including employees' high intercompany mobility and wide social gaps, also hinder the transplantation of Japanese methods regarding the wage system, promotions, and supervisors. In Singapore and Malaysia, Western influences, such as revealed through job demarcation, must also be kept in mind.

Insufficient application of 'Methods' is supplemented by a higher application of 'Results', in both its 'Human' and 'Material' aspects. This is a characteristic that affiliates in ASEAN countries have in common with affiliates in the United States. The conspicuous feature of affiliates in ASEAN countries is the application of 'Human–Results' elements. The ratio of Japanese expatriates to total employees is as low as at affiliated plants in Taiwan and Korea, and differs markedly from the United States. In contrast to Taiwan and Korea, however, almost all the affiliates in the ASEAN countries station Japanese expatriates at strategic points within the corporate hierarchy, where they exercise considerable authority. Affiliates in the ASEAN countries are strongly characterised by management that is under the control of a small number of Japanese employees. A shortage of managerial talent within these recently industrialised societies, cultural and historical dissimilarities to Japan (in comparison with the cases of Taiwan and Korea), Western influences on those persons with higher academic backgrounds, and linguistic communication difficulties, all result in a lesser understanding of Japanese methods among local managers. Consequently, the presence and strong leadership of Japanese employees is required.

Export-orientated factories in the electronics assembly and parts industries achieve high production efficiency and world-level product quality by virtue of the hybrid configuration mentioned above. This is, for example, evident from the fact that Malaysia is the largest exporter of colour television sets. Of course, affiliates achieve such high efficiency and quality in the production of a limited variety of products, with relatively low added-value. However, export-orientated Japanese affiliates in ASEAN countries do not necessarily adopt the traditional American mass-production system. The major difference is that Japanese affiliates in ASEAN countries operate their factories by emphasising the role of the shop floor, although plant management is under the control of Japanese employees. They have a positive attitude towards rigidly securing product quality and paying meticulous attention to equipment through enthusiastic employee education that extends to production workers.

Contributions to the Host Countries

The kinds of contribution that Japanese affiliates make to the development of the host countries will be examined next. Affiliates contribute in various ways, ranging from increasing production and employment, to earning foreign currency. One of the most important contributions is the continuous transfer of technology,[2] which has stimulated the rapid industrialisation of the East Asian region,[3] and which is one of the most important reinforcements of the 'geese formation' type of industrial development. In contrast, the presence of US affiliated auto and electrical plants that preceded Japanese affiliates embarking upon Asian operations, with the exception of some electronics and semiconductor companies, has become very weak. This is mainly attributed to the fact that, unlike Japanese affiliates, they have not engaged in the continuous transfer of technology because they established those foreign subsidiaries only in order to exploit temporary cost advantages.

There are three aspects to technology transfer, namely, 'material–result', 'material–method', and 'human–method'. First, there is no question that the 'Material–Result' type of technology transfer, such as product technology, and capital goods including equipment and components from Japan, has played a crucial role in the transfer of technology by affiliated Japanese plants to their host countries. Industrial development and increased income in the host countries have forced Japan to develop higher added-value products and innovative production technology, and this in turn has facilitated a transfer of higher product technology and more advanced capital goods. The role of this type of technology transfer is enormous, since 'material–result' transfer has been achieved not only through foreign direct investment but also by way of manufactured imports and technology licences (the latter channel has played an important role, especially in Korea).

Second, the 'material–method' type of technology transfer, which takes place thorough comprehensive production control, is also important. As discussed in Chapter 2, high application for the production control group is common to all the host countries surveyed (see Table 2.2). Of course, this high application is partly the result of transplanting production equipment from Japan, but, it is also necessary for Japanese affiliates overseas to maintain that equipment as meticulously, and to manufacture products with as high a level of quality as possible, given the conditions obtaining in their respective host countries. As mentioned repeatedly, the building of quality into the production process, and the participation in maintenance on the part of ordinary production workers, have not penetrated these factory management systems sufficiently. At the same time, however, we should not forget the extraordinary efforts of Japanese affiliates to control quality and equipment carefully by having employees fulfill individually assigned tasks. The tasks of Japanese expatriate and temporarily dispatched employees are often relevant to these efforts. In various parts of the shop floor at various affiliates, we met skilled Japanese technicians and young engineers who instructed local employees, sometimes through gestures if linguistic communication was not possible. These Japanese employees engage in trouble-shooting activities that the local staff are unable to cope with. In particular, export-orientated affiliates in East Asia typically demonstrate such an attitude. The role of Japanese affiliates in East Asian countries in providing technology transfer through production control can therefore be highly evaluated.

Third, Japanese affiliates educate and train local employees enthusiastically, especially, as mentioned above, by emphasising production control. Not only Japanese expatriates, but also a number of Japanese employees who are dispatched to the affiliates for short-term assignments, train local employees in the operation and maintenance of equipment, in preventive maintenance, in product quality judgement, as well as in product quality and production equipment trouble-shooting. Furthermore, with an emphasis on OJT, affiliates often supplement insufficient training at affiliated plants by sending numerous local employees to Japan for training at the mother plants. During plant observation in Japan, the instruction of trainees from overseas affiliates was observed occasionally. Japanese companies invest a great deal of money and effort in education and training. This type of enthusiasm for education and training is a salient feature of Japanese multinational companies, which seems seldom to be found among their counterparts from other countries.

Fourth, Japanese affiliates are eager to foster the development of local parts and materials suppliers. They discover and develop capable suppliers, often giving them technological assistance in various areas such as product design, production control and quality control, through a long-term relationship. The recent rapid increase in manufactured exports from the East Asian region to Japan can be attributed to the efforts of Japanese affiliates in production control, education and training, and the cultivation of local suppliers. The East Asian region is creating a 'plus-sum' type of trade relationship, where the supply of high-quality capital goods *from* Japan, and manufactured exports including finished goods and components from East Asian countries *to* Japan, provide benefits to both sides. In addition, increased procurement from East Asian countries reinforces the international competitiveness of Japanese multinationals.

Some criticise Japanese companies for their grudging technology transfer. However, such criticisms often stem from misunderstandings about the attitudes of Japanese companies. Attitudes which appear to be 'grudging' technology transfers may, in fact, only be evidence of 'sincerity' on the part of Japanese companies. Many Japanese companies desire to transfer product and production technology that is suitable for assimilation by the host countries, through comprehensive production control and enthusiastic education and training.

Problems

Nevertheless, Japanese multinational companies must face a number of difficulties and limitations. Some of the problems common to Japanese affiliates overseas will be examined below.

One difficult problem faced by affiliates is discovering how to achieve flexible organisations and participatory management on the part of employees, at least a core part of whom develop a wide range of skills as long-term employees, under conditions of high employee turnover and wide gaps between social strata. The higher degree of employee mobility hinders the formation of broad and multifunctional skills, and weakens a sense of employee participation. A lack of multifunctional skills or sense of participation leads to poor co-ordination between different sections, which in turn hampers swift trouble-shooting and makes it difficult to prevent problems.

This leads to a second limitation, which is also a characteristic feature of management at Japanese affiliates overseas. Namely, top-down management is more common among overseas affiliates than it is in Japan, whether these affiliated plants are controlled by Japanese expatriates or by local managers. It is only natural to adopt a style of management where the upper strata of the corporate hierarchy exercises control, when the capabilities of the shop floor to participate in plant management, are limited.

A third limitation is the introduction of equipment and key components from Japan, or procurement from local Japanese affiliated parts suppliers, which plays a crucial role in sustaining product quality and production efficiency at the affiliated plants. In other words, insufficient application of 'methods' is supplemented with application of 'material–result'. In Taiwan and Korea, reliance on 'material–result' is low compared with other Japanese affiliates overseas, since Japanese technology is introduced into locally-owned parts manufacturers and, particularly in Taiwan, a large cluster of parts manufacturers has been formed. Even there, however, the basic tendency to supplement 'methods' application with 'material–result' application is common to other host countries. The bringing-in of 'material–result' by both Japanese affiliates and locally-owned companies contributes to a trade deficit with Japan, and is the source of some discontent on the part of the host countries. Of course, it is impossible for East Asian countries to industrialise themselves at such a rapid speed without the inflow of Japanese capital goods, including advanced production equipment and key components. In the long run, however, there is no doubt that host countries place a greater value on technology transfer that is achieved through 'Method' application.

Finally, another limitation stems from the fact that, in numerous cases, strong authority is exercised by headquarters or mother plants in Japan. Of course, not all affiliates are under the control of the Japanese side. For example, Taiwanese partners exercise very strong discretion in some auto assembly plants. Nevertheless, Japanese headquarters assume strong authority at many affiliates, especially export-orientated plants. This tendency stems from one particular characteristic of Japanese companies, at home or abroad, which is to rely to a considerable extent on human networks within companies and on information shared by employees, rather than on a standardised and integrated mechanism. Even if an affiliate enjoys strong autonomy, there are often cases where Japanese expatriates, who are most familiar with Japanese methods, exercise full discretion.[4]

The negative aspect of this, however, is that strong authority on the part of the Japanese partner, or full discretion exercised by Japanese expatriates, stifles the motivation of local employees and creates difficulties in recruiting and cultivating talented staff. Also, managers of affiliates with Japanese expatriates are unable to make decisions quickly without the appropriate authority. Furthermore, if this type of delegation of authority is maintained, the expansion of an overseas affiliates network imposes too heavy a burden for headquarters in terms of decision-making and information processing, and is likely to impede the efficiency of the entire corporate organisation. Japanese multinationals are therefore cautioned to localise management of foreign affiliates through a stan-dardised managerial system, or to standardise integrating and controlling mechanisms between headquarters and overseas affiliates, as well as among overseas affiliates.

However, it is not that simple. In the first place, all multinationals must address the difficult problem of balancing the need to localise the management of their foreign affiliates to accommodate the conditions of their respective host countries with the need to integrate these local operations into their global overseas affiliate network.[5] Although ideas such as 'a grid structure' (Stopford and Wells, 1972) or 'an integrated network' (Bartlett and Ghoshal, 1987) have been suggested, the details have not been fully articulated. In addition, as their advocates themselves admit, there are actually no companies that have developed such global structures.[6] Moreover, the proposal to standardise corporate management may, in fact, be contrary to the Japanese system itself. It is possible that the facile standardisation of corporate management spoils the characteristics and advantages of the Japanese system, which arises from participatory management on the part of a broad range of employees sharing common information, and from a flexibly organised operation based on multifunctional skills.

IV PROSPECTS

The Changing Setting

Japanese affiliates in East Asian countries still have many problems regarding production efficiency or building quality into the production process. Nevertheless, they are able to achieve relatively strong performance in terms of profitability. This can be attributed largely to a favourable managerial environment with respect to conditions in the local market, wage levels, and domestic currency exchange rates against the US dollar.

In Taiwan and Korea, however, rapid changes in such favourable circumstances have spurred foreign investment by local companies to other Asian countries, to the point where some are anxious about the hollowing out of their manufacturing industries. In fact, quite a few foreign subsidiaries in the export processing zones, including Japanese affiliates, have disinvested because of deteriorating profitability. During the interviews that were carried out as part of the present survey, some managers suggested, 'We shall be compelled to curtail our operations'.

This writer, however, does not consider casual curtailment or disinvestment of production operations to be an appropriate measure in the changing environments, particularly if accumulated capital investment, materials and human resources are taken into account. Some affiliates surveyed in this book established new plants with substantial investment even after mid-1980. If affiliates choose to stay in Taiwan and Korea and to continue full-scale operations, they will be required to introduce Japanese methods in earnest to bridge the gap between formal systems and actual operations. Indeed, some plants, including both Japanese affiliated and locally-owned factories, have already begun to introduce Japanese methods enthusiastically.

Affiliates in the ASEAN countries have delayed the application of the 'Method' aspects of the Japanese system even more than those in Taiwan and Korea. In that sense, the argument of Krugman (1994), that there will be serious limitations on East Asian economic development merely from the expansion of production factors, appears to be valid. However, perhaps Krugman overlooked dynamism with respect to both supply and demand sides in the East Asian region. With respect to the supply side, as already mentioned, more advanced products, production equipment, and production technology have been transferred continuously and accompanied by direct investment from Japan and the NIEs. Moreover, local production by Japanese affiliates may result not only in the transfer of production technology in the narrow sense, but also of management technology in a broader sense. Examples include future innovation in work organisation and long-term relationships between assembly companies and parts suppliers, as demonstrated by export-orientated plants that emphasise the training employees and providing technological assistance to local suppliers. On the other hand, with respect to the demand side, as the fruits of high economic growth are not confined to a part of the higher income strata, but spread to a broader strata including average citizens, the reciprocal effects between economic growth and an increase in the incomes of ordinary people, will create large consumer markets in ASEAN countries.

One of the factors of great uncertainty for the ASEAN countries is China. In the 1990s it is emerging as an enormous target for investment from Japan and the NIEs. Some are afraid that the ASEAN countries will become relatively unattractive host areas, and that the positive cycle of foreign investment, technological innovation, economic growth, expansion of local markets, and further foreign investment will, malfunction. China's presence, however significant, seems often to be exaggerated, at least from the perspective of the medium term. As clarified in Chapter 6, Japanese affiliates in China lag far behind those in ASEAN countries in the area of production technology. Moreover, it is uncertain whether the remarkable rapid growth in foreign investment can be sustained, since various problems, including legal inadequacies and policy discrepancies between central and local governments, have surfaced. Even if foreign investment continued to expand quantitatively, excessive profiteering may impede the steady development of the manufacturing industries. On the other hand, it is not feasible economically for Japanese affiliates to abandon the considerable investment, quantitative as well as qualitative, that they have accumulated in the ASEAN countries. Economic growth and increased levels of income will raise the level of education, which in turn will facilitate higher production technology and management skills. The expansion of the local market itself, which is a result of high economic growth, will attract direct investment to ASEAN countries.

Revised Application

In accordance with these changing circumstances, it is likely that the hybrid configuration of Japanese affiliates will shift towards attaching greater importance to 'Methods' application, particularly as it concerns the core of the system. The more firmly Japanese affiliates desire to establish a production base, the more necessary it becomes to implement Japanese methods. At the same time, it will become more necessary for Japanese affiliates to reduce their reliance on 'Results' application from Japan, in terms of both human and material aspects. Host countries increasingly will request Japanese companies to employ local managerial resources and to procure local components, in order to reduce their trade deficits with Japan and to facilitate the transfer of technology. Japanese affiliates themselves intend to rely more on local managers and local procurement in order to decrease personnel expenses associated with sending and supporting expatriates abroad, within a globally expanded production network, and to absorb soaring costs with a strong yen. In addition, higher application for 'Method' will automatically reduce reliance upon Japan in terms of 'Result'.

Critical tasks for affiliates that attempt to enhance 'Method' application are overcoming those conditions that hinder the implementation of Japanese systems and dealing with the differences between local and Japanese social conditions. Serious differences between these social environments involve higher employee turnover ratios, wider gaps between social strata, and the existence of a manager–worker dichotomy that is imprinted firmly upon the corporate hierarchy. One notable attempt to mitigate differences in managerial conditions is 'revised application'. Accordingly, rather than transplanting certain elements of the Japanese system in their unmodified, native form, attempts are made to transfer the spirit or essence of the system by altering the original form to incorporate elements native to the host countries. This is illustrated by the following examples:

1. Sony Electronics of Korea Corp. (SEKC), which supplies components to plants in Japan and exports finished goods to the US market, achieves first-rate performance in comparison with its sister plants, including Sony plants in Japan, in terms of production efficiency and product quality. SEKC employs only one Japanese expatriate, and the Korean president takes the initiative as company manager. While the manager always communicates with shop-floor workers and is mindful of enhancing a sense of unity among his employees, SEKC seems to adopt more of a top-down orientation in its decision-making than do typical plants in Japan. The president, who used to serve as an engineer in the army, has achieved flexible plant operations by positioning his ex-subordinates at strategic points throughout the company and implementing job rotation for all staff above middle manager, so they can acquire broad experience and knowledge. SEKC is a notable example of establishing production and quality control systems based on the Sony standard, while simultaneously making allowances for Korean-style corporate administration.[7]

2. Matsushita Television Co. (MTV) in Malaysia has attempted to establish a 'universal' management system that is more advanced than revised application. MTV is standardising its corporate organisation and utilise manuals that detail standard work practices explicitly with respect to various aspects of operations ranging from production and quality control to education and training. MTV is seeking to standardise operations and utilise manuals because it expects to employ the latest fully-automated machines, and mass produce one million TV sets a year in a society where tacit communication and mutual understanding are not well established, and where employee turnover ratios are high. In order to construct a 'universal' plant management blueprint – that is, one that is not restricted to the conditions of a particular host country – MTV has incorporated into its operating manuals and standardisation plans not only those management skills that Matsushita has accumulated in Japan, but also its rich overseas operating experience, including its failures. As this ambitious attempt has only to just begun, it is still too early to make any conclusive evaluations. The critical point is whether or not the

standardisation of the management and utilisation of manuals can remain consistent with the flexible co-ordination and co-operation between different sections that is an essential characteristic of Japanese methods. At the time of writing, management under the leadership of Japanese expatriates – that is, high 'Human–Result' application – sustains the flexibility of plant operations.

Whether or not revised application, or a standardised management system, can succeed in transplanting the essential elements of the Japanese system is a question worth asking. Whatever the case may be, such attempts are not limited to Japanese overseas affiliates. The revitalisation of American manufacturing industries, including computer companies and the Big Three auto assemblers, or the 're-reversal' of the Japan–US competitive situation regarding manufacturing, is attributed in no small way to efforts at assimilating elements of the Japanese system. However, American companies seem to emphasise product development process innovation and material and inventory control rather than conditions on the shop floor.

Hybridisation from Both Directions?

'Revised application' and efforts made by US companies illustrate that a certain amount of variation in emphasis will exist from region to region, or from industry to industry, regarding the introduction of the Japanese system. Even under the premise of introducing elements of the Japanese system, how a company orientates its basic managerial approach, between participation at one extreme and top-down management at the other, as it attempts to maximise operating efficiency, depends on conditions in its managerial environment, such as employee turnover ratios and so on.

For Japanese affiliates in Korea, a well-balanced style of management may be one where there is slightly greater top-down decision-making and organisational standardisation than in Japan, but where there is also an attempt to enhance a sense of unity among employees, as well as between the employees and their companies. In Taiwan, affiliates may strengthen foundations by incorporating into their management style advantages of the Taiwanese economy that allow them to develop and manufacture products in quick response to changing market conditions and to gather suitable parts at reasonable cost. At the same time, they should attempt to establish a firm basis for Japanese-style production and quality control. In ASEAN countries, where there are wider gaps between social strata, Japanese affiliates may be required to adopt a stronger top-down orientation in their decision-making, to standardise corporate organisations more strictly, and to promote talented employees more boldly than is seen in Taiwan and Korea.

On the other hand, participation and standardisation within Japanese industry is also likely to undergo a certain amount of change in the future. As mentioned in Chapter 1, it is the opinion of this author that the basic characteristics of the Japanese system, namely multifunctional skill formation based on long-term employment and participatory management, will not easily change, and that any changes that do occur will be relatively minor. However, beyond a core group of employees, it is reasonable to anticipate an increase in the turnover ratio for two types of employee: one is the specialist, and the other is the employee who puts priority on a private life beyond the company to the extent that he or she shuns long-term employment. In addition, the core group of personnel, which at the time of writing consists almost exclusively of male Japanese employees, will become less homogeneous as Japanese companies hire more female employees and foreigners.

Increased heterogeneity and/or mobility among their employees will induce a certain amount of change in the management systems of Japanese companies. Japanese companies will, to some extent, have to decrease the formal and informal information sharing among employees, or reduce their reliance on individual human factors. Japanese companies will also be required to incorporate some elements of standardisation and integration into their managerial principles, even if this means sacrificing their organisational flexibility to some extent. These changes will automatically increase the number of companies that are orientated towards a top-down style of decision-making. It is possible that partial hybridisation in the opposite direction will occur in Japan. In the processing and assembly industries of East Asian countries, including Japan, hybridisation of production systems from both directions may appear, though, of course, the distinctive system features of the respective host regions will remain.

Note

1. Shiba (1973).
2. Cho (1994).
3. Taniura (1990). Ozawa (1979) considers Japanese direct investment in East Asian countries to be an 'intercepter', which transfers modified Western-type technologies.
4. Yasumuro (1982).
5. Bartlett and Ghoshal (1987); and Abo (1984).
6. Stopford and Wells (1972); and Bartlett and Ghoshal (1989)
7. Also see Cho (1993).

Bibliography

Abegglen, James C. and George Stalk, Jr (1985) *Kaisha: The Japanese Corporation* (New York: Basic Books).

Abo, Tetsuo (1984) *Senkanki Amerika no Taigai Tōshi* (US Foreign Investment in the Inter-war Period) (Tokyo: Tokyo Daigaku Shuppankai).

Abo, Tetsuo (1987) 'A Report of On-the-Spot Observation of Sony's Four Major Color TV Plants in the US, UK, West Germany and Japan', in Joop A. Stam (ed.), *Industrial Cooperation between Europe and Japan*, Erasmus University, The Netherlands.

Abo, Tetsuo (1989) 'The Emergence of Japanese Multinational Enterprise and the Theory of Foreign Direct Investment', in Kazuo Shibagaki, Malcolm Trevor and Tetsuo Abo (eds), *Japanese and European Management: Their International Adaptability* (Tokyo: University of Tokyo Press).

Abo, Tetsuo (1992) 'Nihonteki Seisan Shisutemu no Taibei Iten' (Transfer of the Japanese System into the United Sates), in Tokyo Daigaku Shakaikagaku Kenkyujo (ed.), *Gendai Nihon Shakai 7: Kokusaika* (Contemporary Japanese Society 7: Internationalization) (Tokyo: Tokyo Daigaku Shuppankai).

Abo, Tetsuo (ed.) (1994a) *Hybrid Factory: The Japanese Production System in the United States* (New York: Oxford University Press).

Abo, Tetsuo (1994b) 'Sanyo's Overseas Production Activities', in Hellmut Schutte (ed.) *The Global Competitiveness of the Asian Firms* (London: Macmillan).

Abo, Tetsuo (ed.) (1994c) *Nihonteki Keiei-Seisan Shisutem to Amerika: Shisutemu no Kokusai Iten to Haiburiddo-ka* (The Japanese Production System and America: International Transfer of Management Systems and Hybridisation) (Kyoto: Minerva Shobo).

Abo, Tetsuo (1997) 'Change in Japanese Automobile and Electronic Transplants in the USA, 1989–1993: An Evaluation of Japanese-style Management and Production Systems', in H. Hasegawa and G. D. Hark (eds), *Japanese Business in the 21st Century* (London: Routledge).

Adachi, Fumihiko (1993) 'Taikoku Jidōsha Sangyō wo Meguru Sho Mondai' (Various Problems in the Automobile Industry in Thailand), *Ajia Kenkyu*, vol. 39, no. 2, February.

Akamatsu, Kaname (1956) 'Wagakuni Sangyō Hatten no Gankō Keitai: Kikai Kigu Sangyō ni Tsuite' (Flying Geese Pattern of Japanese Industrial Development – A Case Study of the Machinery Industry), *Hitotsubashi Ronsō*, vol. 36, no. 5, November.

Amsden, Alice (1989) *Asia's Next Giant: South Korea and Late Industrialization* (New York: Oxford University Press).

Aoki, Masahiko (1988) *Information, Incentives, and Bargaining in the Japanese Economy* (Cambridge University Press).

Aoki, Masahiko, and Ronald Dore (eds) (1994) *The Japanese Firm: Sources of Competitive Strength* (Oxford University Press).

Aoki, Takeshi (1993) *Yushutsu Shikō Kogyō-ka Senryaku: Mareisia ni Miru Sono Hikari to Kage* (Strategies of Export-Oriented Industrialisation: Light and Shadow in Malaysia) (Tokyo: JETRO).

Asamoto, Teruo (1992a) 'Taiwan niokeru Jidōsha-Sangyō no Hatten to Buhin no Kokusai-Cyōtatsu (Jo)', (The Develoment of the Taiwanese Automobile Industry and Its International Parts Procurement, vol. 1), *Review of Economics and Business,* Kyushu Sangyo University, vol. 33, no. 1.

Asamoto, Teruo (1992b) 'Taiwan Niokeru Jidōsha-Sangyō no Hatten to Buhin no Kokusai-Cyotatu (Ge)', (The Development of the Taiwanese Automobile Industry and Its International Parts Procurement, vol. 2), *Review of Economics and Business,* Kyushu Sangyo University, vol. 33, no. 2.

Asanuma, Banri (1992) 'Japanese Manufacturer–Supplier Relationships in International Perspective: The Automobile Case', in Paul Sheard (ed.), *Japanese Corporations and International Adjustment* (Sydney: Allen & Unwin).

Bartlett, Christopher A., and Sumantra Ghoshal (1987) 'Managing Across Borders: New Organizational Responses', *Sloan Management Review,* vol. 28, Boston, Mass.

Bartlett, Christopher A., and Sumantra Ghoshal (1989) *Managing Across Borders: The Transnational Solution* (Boston, Mass.: Harvard Business School Press).

Bernard, Mitchell and John Ravenhill (1995) 'Beyond Product Cycles and Flying Geese', *World Politics,* vol. 47, January (Center of International Studies, Princeton University, New Jersey).

Buckley, Peter J. and Mark Casson (1985) *The Economic Theory and the Multinational Enterprise* (New York: Macmillan).

Census and Statistics Department of Hong Kong (1992) *Annual Review of Hong Kong External Trade, 1992.*

Chi Schive (1990) *The Foreign Factor: The Multinational Corporation's Contribution to the Economic Modernization of the Republic of China* (Stanford: Hoover Institution Press).

Cho, Du-Sop (1993) 'Nihonteki Keiei Shisutemu to Kokusai Iten ni Kansuru Ichi Kōsatsu' (The Japanese Production System and Its International Transfer), *Sangyo Gakkai Kenkyu Nenpo,* vol. 9 (Tokyo: Sangyo Gakkai).

Cho, Du-Sop (1994) 'Nihon Kigyō no Takokuseki-ka to Kigyōnai Gijutsu Iten' (Multinationalization of Japanese Enterprises and Their Intra-firm Technology Transfer) *Soshiki Kagaku,* vol. 27, no. 3 (Tokyo: Soshiki Gakkai).

Choi, Dae Won and Martin Kenny (1995) 'The Globalization of Korean Industry: Korean Maquiladoras in Mexico', unpublished paper.

Chushō Kigyō Chōsakyokai (1992) *Ukeoi Bungyou Kozo no Kokusai Hikaku* (International Comparisons in the Division of Subcontracted Labor) (Tokyo: Chusho Kigyo Chosakyokai).

Clark, Kim B. and Takahiro Fujimoto (1991) *Product Development Performance: Strategy, Organization, and Management in the World Auto Industry* (Boston, Mass.: Harvard Business School Press).

Cole, Robert E. (1979) *Work, Mobility, and Participation* (Berkeley, Calif.: University of California Press).

Corbo, Vittorio and Sang-mok Suh (eds) (1992) *Structural Adjustment in a Newly Industrialized Country: The Korean Experience* (A World Bank Book) (Baltimore, Md: The Johns Hopkins University Press).

Council for Economic Planning and Development (CEPD) of the Republic of China (1993) *Taiwan Statistical Data Book 1993* Taipei.

Dertouzos, Michael L., Richard K. Lester and Robert M. Solow (1989) *Made in America: Regaining the Productive Edge* (Cambridge, Mass.: MIT Press).

Doner, Richard F. (1991) *Driving a Bargain: Automobile Industrialization and Japanese Firms in Southeast Asia* (Oxford: University of California Press).

Dore, Ronald P. (1973) *British Factory–Japanese Factory: The Origins of National Diversity in Industrial Relations* (Berkeley, Calif.: University of California Press).

Dobson, Wendy (1993) *Japan in East Asia, Trading and Investment Strategies* (Singapore: ISEAS).

Economic Planning Agency of Japan (1994, 1995, 1996) *Statistics on the Overseas Economy*, Tokyo, January.

Ernst, Dieter (1994) *What Are the Limits to the Korean Model?: The Korean Electronics Industry under Pressure* (Berkeley, Calif.: University of California Press).

Ernst, Dieter and David O'Connor (1992) *Competing in the Electronics Industry: The Experience of Newly Industrializing Economies* (Paris: OECD).

Fourin (ed.) (1995) *2000 nen no Kankoku Jidōsha-Sangyō* (The Korean Automotive Industry in 2000) (Tokyo: Fourin).

Fucini, Joseph J. and Suzy Fucini (1990) *Working for the Japanese: Inside Mazda's American Auto Plant* (New York: The Free Press).

Fujimoto, Takahiro (1994/1995) 'Nikkan Jidōsha-Sangyō no Keisei to Sangyō-Ikusei Seisaku' (Industrial Evolution and Industrial Promotion Policies: A Korea–Japan Comparison in the Automobile Industry), *The Journal of Economics*, The Society of Economics, University of Tokyo, vol. 60, nos. 1, 2 and 4.

Gipouloux, François (ed.) (1994) *Regional Economic Strategies in East Asia* (Tokyo: Maison Franco-Japonaise).

Gupta, Vipin and Hiroshi Kumon (1996) 'A Dynamic Model of Japanese Investment System: A Comparative Investigation of Japanese Hybrid Factories in Asia, Europe and America', *Journal of International Economic Studies*, Hosei University, no. 10.

Hagiwara, Yoshiyuki (ed.) (1994) *Minshushugi to Keizai Hatten* (Democracy and Economic Development) (Tokyo: Tokyo Daigaku Shuppan-kai).

Hartland-Thunberg, Penelope (1990) *China, Hong-Kong, Taiwan and the World Trading System* (London: The Macmillan Press).

Hashimoto, Jurō (ed.) (1995) *20 Seiki Shihonshugi 1: Gijutsu Kakushin to Seisan Shisutemu* (Capitalism in the Twentieth Century, vol. 1: Technological Innovation and Production Systems) (Tokyo: Tokyo Daigaku Shuppan-kai).

Hattori, Tamio (ed.) (1987) *Kankoku no Kogyō-ka: Hatten no Kōzu* (Industrialisation of Korea: The Whole Picture of Development) (Tokyo: Ajia Keizai Kenkyujo).

Hattori, Tamio (1988) *Kankoku no Keiei Hatten* (Managerial Development in Korea) (Tokyo: Bunshindo).

Hayashi, Chūkichi (1989) 'Higashi Ajia Jidōsha Sangyou no Hatten to Kokusai Bungyō' (The Development of Automobile Industries in East Asia), Yachiyo Gakuin University, *Keizai keiei Ronshu*, vol. 8, nos 1 and 2, March.

Hirakawa, Hitoshi (1992) *NIEs: Sekai Shisutemu to Kaihatsu* (NIEs: World System and Development) (Tokyo: Dobunkan).

Hodgkin, Thomas (1975) 'Some African and Third World Theories of Imperialism', in Roger Owen and Bob Sutcliffe (eds) *Studies in the Theory of Imperialism*, 2nd edn (London: Longman).

Horii, Kenzō (ed.) (1991) *Mareisia no Kōgyōka: Tashuzoku Kokka to Kōgyōka no Tenkai* (Industrialization in Malaysia: A Multi-racial State and the Development of Industrialsation), Institute for Developing Economies.

Humes, Samuel (1993) *Managing the Multinational: Confronting the Global–Local Dilemma* (New York: Prentice Hall).

Hymer, Stephen Herbert (1976) *The International Operations of National Firms: A Study of Direct Foreign Investment* (Boston, Mass.: MIT Press).

Hyun, Young-Suk (1991) *Kankoku Jidosha Sangyoron: Gijyutu Hatten Nikansuru Jissho Bunseki* (The Korean Automotive Industry: An Empirical Analysis of Technological Development) (Tokyo: Sekai-Shiso Sha).

Ichimura, Shinichi (ed.) (1988) *Ajia ni Nezuku Nihon-teki Keiei* (Japanese Management Established in Asia) (Tokyo: Toyo Keizai Shinposha).

Imada, Pearl and Seiji Naya (1992) *AFTA, The Way Ahead* (Singapore: Institute of Southeast Asian Studies).

Imai, Kenichi and Komiya Ryutaro (eds) (1994) *Business Enterprise in Japan: Views of Leading Japanese Economists* (Cambridge, Mass.: MIT Press).

Inoue, Ryuichiro, Shujiro Urata and Hirohisa Kohama (eds) (1990) *Higashi-Ajia no Sangyō-Seisaku: Aratana Kaihatsu Senryaku wo Motomete* (Industrial Policy in East Asia: Search for New Development Strategy) (Tokyo: JETRO).

Institute of Developing Economies (ed.) (1980) *Hatten-Tojyō Koku no Jidōsha Sangyō*, (The Automotive Industry in Developing Countries) (Tokyo: Institute of Developing Economies).

Institute of Social Science (University of Tokyo) (ed.) (1990) *Local Production of Japanese Automobile and Electronics Firms in the United States: The 'Application' and 'Adaptation' of Japanese Style Management* (Tokyo: Institute of Social Sciences, University of Tokyo).

Institute of Southeast Asian Studies (1993) *Regional Outlook* (Singapore).

Islam, Lyanatul (1992) 'Political Economy and Economic Development', *Asian-Pacific Economic Literature*, vol. 6, no. 2, November.

Itagaki, Hiroshi (1989) 'Application–Adaptation Problems in Japanese Automobile and Electronics Plants in the USA', in Kazuo Shibagaki, Malcolm Trevor and Tetsuo Abo (eds), *Japanese and European Management: Their International Adaptability* (Tokyo: University of Tokyo Press).

Itagaki, Hiroshi (1994a) 'A Comparative Study on the Japanese Production System Employed at Affiliated Electronics Plants in the United States and Taiwan', in Hellmut Schutte (ed.), *The Global Competitiveness of the Asian Firm* (London: Macmillan Press).

Itagaki, Hiroshi (1994b) 'Nihon no Jidousha-Denki Kojo: Nihon Kōjō no Moderu' (Japan's Auto and Electronics Plants: A Model of Japan's Plants), in Tetsuo Abo (ed.), *Nihonteki Keiei-Seisan Shisutem to Amerika: Shisutemu no Kokusai Iten to Haiburiddoka* (Japanese Production System and America: International Transfer of Management Systems and Hybridization) (Kyoto: Minerva Shobo).

Itagaki, Hiroshi (1995) 'Nihon-gata Seisan Shisutemu no Kokusai Iten' (International Transfer of the Japanese Production System), in Juro Hashimoto (ed.), *20 Seiki Shihonshugi 1: Gijutsu Kakushin to Seisan Shisutemu* (Capitalism in the Twentieth Century, vol. 1: Technological Innovation and Production Systems) (Tokyo: Tokyo Daigaku Shuppan-kai).

Itagaki, Hiroshi (ed.) (1997) *Nihonteki Keiei-Seisan Shisutemu to Higashi Ajia: Taiwan, Kankoku, Chūgoku ni Okeru Haiburiddo Kōjō* (The Japanese

Production System in East Asia: Hybrid Factories in Taiwan, Korea and China) (Kyoto: Minerva Shobō).

Itami, Hiroyuki (ed.) (1991) *Nihon no Kagaku Sangyō: Naze Sekai ni Tachiokuretanoka* (The Japanese Chemical Industry: Why Does It Lag Behind in International Competition?) (Tokyo: NTT Shuppan).

Janelli, Roger L. and Dawnbee Yim (1993) *Making Capitalism, The Social and Cultural Construction of a South Korean Conglomerate* (Palo Alto, Calif.: Stanford University Press).

Japan Auto Parts Manufacturers Association (1994) *Kaigai Jigyō Chōsa* (Survey of Overseas Activities) (Tokyo: Nikon Jidōsha Buhin Kōgyōkai).

Japan External Trade Organization (JETRO) (1985) *Kaigai Tōshi Hakusho* (White Paper on Foreign Direct Investment) (Tokyo: JETRO).

Japan External Trade Organization (JETRO) (1986) *Kaigai Tōshi Hakusho* (White Paper on Foreign Direct Investment) (Tokyo: JETRO).

Japan External Trade Organization (JETRO) (1987) *Kaigai Tōshi Hakusho* (White Paper on Foreign Direct Investment) (Tokyo: JETRO).

Japan External Trade Organization (JETRO) (1988) *Kaigai Tōshi Hakusho* (White Paper on Foreign Direct Investment) (Tokyo: JETRO).

Japan External Trade Organization (JETRO) (1989a) *Ajia Sangyō Kakumei no Jidai: Nishi-Taiheiyō ga Sekai wo Kaeru* (An Era of Asian Industrial Revolution: The Western Pacific Region Is Changing the World) (Tokyo: JETRO).

Japan External Trade Organization (JETRO) (1989b) *Kaigai Tōshi Hakusho* (White Paper on Foreign Direct Investment) (Tokyo: JETRO).

Japan External Trade Organization (JETRO) (1990) *Kaigai Tōshi Hakusho* (White Paper on Foreign Direct Investment) (Tokyo: JETRO).

Japan External Trade Organization (JETRO) (1991) *Kaigai Tōshi Hakusho* (White Paper on Foreign Direct Investment) (Tokyo: JETRO).

Japan External Trade Organization (JETRO) (1992) *Kaigai Tōshi Hakusho* (White Paper on Foreign Direct Investment) (Tokyo: JETRO).

Japan External Trade Organization (JETRO) (1993) *Kaigai Tōshi Hakusho* (White Paper on Foreign Direct Investment) (Tokyo: JETRO).

Japan External Trade Organization (JETRO) (1994) *Kaigai Tōshi Hakusho* (White Paper on Foreign Direct Investment) (Tokyo: JETRO).

Japan External Trade Organization (JETRO) (1995) *Kaigai Tōshi Hakusho* (White Paper on Foreign Direct Investment) (Tokyo: JETRO).

The Japan Multinational Enterprise Study Group (1993/1994) 'Kankoku Taiwan ni Okeru Nihon-gata Seisan Shisutemu: Nikkei Jidōsha/Denki Kōjō no "Tekiyō" to "Tekiou"' (The Japanese Production System in Korea and Taiwan: 'Application' and 'Adaptation' of Japanese Affiliated Auto and Electronics Plants), *Shakai Kagaku Kenkyu*, vol. 45, nos 3 and 5 (Tokyo Daigaku Shakai Kagaku Kenkyujo), Tokyo.

Jomo, K. S. (1985) *The Sun Also Sets: Lessons in 'Looking East'*, INSAN, KL.

Kamata, Satoshi (1982) *Japan in the Passing Lane* (New York: Pantheon).

Kamiyama, Kunio (1990) 'Nihonteki Chingin Shisutemu ni tsuite' (On the Japanese Wage System), *Keizai Ronshu* (Ōita University), vol. 41, no. 5.

Kamiyama, Kunio (1992) 'Makiradora ni Okeru Nikkei Denki Kigyō' (Japanese Electronics Plants under the Maquiladora System), *Josai Daigaku Daigakuin Kenkyu Nenpo*, no. 8.

Kamiyama, Kunio, Hiroshi Ueda, Taku Ohshima and Masataka Ikeda (eds) (1995) 'Jidōsha Sangyō' (The Automobile Industry), in The Society for Industrial Studies (ed) *Sengo Nippon Sangyoshi* (The History of Postwar Japanese Industry) (Tokyo: Toyo Keizai Shinpōsha).

Katō, Takehiko and Mitsusumi Kubota (1989) *Kankoku Jidōsha-Sangyō no Subete* (The Korean Automotive Industry) (Tokyo: Nihon Keizai Tsushin Sha).

Kawabe, Nobuo (1991) 'Fukugō Bunka ni Okeru Nihon-gata Keiei: Mareisia no Nikkei Kigyō' (Japanese Style Management in Complex Cultural Backgrounds), *Waseda Shogaku* (Waseda University), nos. 345 and 346, Tokyo.

Kawakami, Momoko (1995) 'Taiwan Jidōsha-Sangyō Niokeru Nihon-Kigyo Karano Shihon/Gijyutsu no Donyū' (The Role of Japanese Capital and Technology in the Development Process of Taiwan's Automobile Industry), *Ajia Keizai* (Institute of Developing Economies), vol. 33, no. 10.

Kenney, Martin (1995) 'Learning and Coping with Competitive Pressure: The Korean Electronics Industry at the Dawning of the 21st Century', unpublished paper.

Kenney, Martin and Richard Florida (1993) *Beyond Mass Production: The Japanese System and its Transfer to the U.S.* (New York: Oxford University Press).

Kim, Yong-Ki (1995) 'Kankoku Jidōsha Sangyō no Rōshi-Kankei: A Sha no Seisan Noritsu Kanri to Seisan Noritsu wo Meguru Rōshi-Kōbō' (Workers' Challenge to the Authoritarian Productivity Control: The Case of the Automobile Industry in Korea), *The Journal of Economic Studies*, The Society of Economic Studies, University of Tokyo, no. 37.

Kim, Yung-Hoo (1994) 'Nihon Keizai no Kaikaku to Shin-Ajia' (Japanese Economic Reform and New Asia), *Sekai*, April.

Klintworth, Gary (ed.) (1994) *Taiwan in the Asia Pacific in the 1990s* (St. Leonards: Allen & Unwin).

Kobayashi, Hideo (1992) *Tōnan Ajia no Nikkei Kigyo* (Japanese Affiliated Companies in South East Asian Countries) (Tokyo: Nihon Hyoronsha).

Kobayashi, Hideo and Takushi Hayashi (1993) *ASEAN Shokoku no Kōgyōka to Gaikoku Kigyō* (Industralisation in the ASEAN Countries and Foreign Enterprises) (Tokyo: Chūō Keizaisha).

Kodama, Toshihiko (1995) *Kankoku Kōgyōka to Kigyou Shudan: Kankoku Kigyō Shakai no Shakai-teki Tokushitsu* (The Industrialisation of Korea and Enterprise Groups: The Characteristics of Korean Corporate Society) (Tokyo: Gakubunsha).

Kogut, Bruce (ed.) (1993) *Country Competitiveness: Technology and Organizing of Work* (New York: Oxford University Press).

Kohama, Hirohisa (ed.) (1992) *Chokusetsu Tōsi to Kōgyōka* (Foreign Direct Investment and Industrialisation) (Tokyo: JETRO).

Koike, Kazuo (1988) *Understanding Industrial Relations in Modern Japan* (London: Macmillan Press).

Koike, Kazuo and Takenori Inoki (1987) *Skill Formation in Japan and South East Asia* (Tokyo: University of Tokyo Press).

Kojima, Kiyoshi (1978) *Japanese Foreign Direct Investment* (Tokyo: C. E. Tuttle Co.).

Kojō, Katsuji (1991) 'Taiwan ni Okeru Jidōsha Sangyō no Genjō to Buhin Chotatsu' (The Present Situation of the Automobile Industry and Sourcing of

Parts and Components in Taiwan), in Kayoko Kitamura (ed.), *NIEs Kikai Sangyo no Genjo to Buhin Chotatsu* (The Present Situation of the NIEs Machinery Industry and Sourcing of Parts and Components) (Tokyo: Institute for Developing Economies).

Kojō, Katsuji (1994) 'Indonesia/Malaysia no Jidōsha Sangyō to Buhin Chōtatsu' (The Automobile Industry and Sourcing of Auto Parts in Indonesia and Malaysia), in Yoshinari Maruyama (ed.), *Asia no Jidosha Sangyo* (Automobile Industry in Asia) (Tokyo: Aki Shobo).

Krugman, Paul (1994) 'The Myth of Asia's Miracle', *Foreign Affairs*, November/December.

Kubo, Shinichi (1993) *Sengo Sekai Keizai no Tenkan: ME-ka Nies-ka no Senjō de* (The Post-War World Economy in Transition: Towards ME and NIEs) (Tokyo: Hakuto Shobo).

Kumagai, Fumie (1994) 'Amerikajin Jūgyōin no Genchi Nihon Kōjō Ninshiki: Haikaku Bunkaron-teki Kōsatsu' (The Understanding of Japanese Affiliated Plants by American Employees: A Comparative Cultural Study), in Tetsuo Abo (ed), *Nihonteki Keiei-Seisan Sisutem to Amerika: Sisutemu no Kokusai Iten to Haiburiddoka* (The Japanese Production System and America: International Transfer of Management Systems and Hybridisation) (Kyoto: Minerva Shobo).

Kumazawa, Makoto (1989) *Nihon-teki Keiei no Meian* (The Light and Dark Sides of Japanese Style Management) (Tokyo: Chikuma Shobo).

Kumon, Hiroshi (1992) 'Taiwan no Nikkei-Jidōsha Kōjyō' (Japanese-affiliated Automotive Plants in Taiwan), *Society and Labor*, Hosei University, vol. 39, no. 2/3.

Kumon, Hiroshi (1994a) 'International Transferability of the Japanese Production System: Japanese-affiliated Auto Plants in the U.S.A., the U.K. and Taiwan', *Journal of International Economic Studies*, Hosei University, no. 8.

Kumon, Hiroshi (1994b) 'Japanese-affiliated Automobile Plants in the United States and Taiwan', in Hellmut Schutte (ed.), *The Global Competitiveness of the Asian Firm* (New York: St Martin's Press).

Kumon, Hiroshi (1996) 'Kankoku Jidōsha-Sangyō ni Okeru Nihongata Seisan Shisutemu no Dōnyū ni Tsuite' (The Adoption of the Japanese Production System in the Korean Automotive Industry), *O'Hara Institute of Social Research Journal*, no. 450.

Kwon, Heok Tae (1994) 'Kankoku to Datsu-Shokuminchi-ka Katei' (South Korean Economy and Decolonialism), in Tadao Furumai (ed.), *Tohoku Ajia-shi no Saihakken: Rekishizo no Kyoyu wo Motomete* (Rethinking of East–North Asian History) (Tokyo: Yushindo).

Lewchuk, Wane (1987) *American Technology and the British Vehicle Industry* (Cambridge University Press).

Maruyama, Yoshinari (ed.) (1994) *Ajia no Jidōsha Sangyō* (The Automotive Industry in Asia) (Tokyo: Aki-Shobo).

Matsui, Mikio (1998) *Jidōsha Buhin* (Automotive Parts) (Tokyo: Nippon Keizai Shinbunsha).

Ministry of International Trade and Industry (MITI) (1986) *Tsūshō Hakusho* (White Paper on Trade and Commerce) (Tokyo: Tsusho Sangyo Sho).

Ministry of International Trade and Industry (MITI) (1994a) *Dai 5 Kai Kaigai Jigyō Katsudō Kihon Chōsa* (The Fifth Basic Survey on Business Activities Abroad) (Tokyo: Okurasho Insatsukyoku).

Ministry of International Trade and Industry (MITI) (1994b) *Fukousei Bōeki Hokokusho* (A Report on Unfair Trade Practices) (Tokyo: Tsusho Sangyo Chosakai Shuppannbu).

Miwa, Yoshirō (1990) *Nihon no Kigyō to Sangyō Soshiki* (Companies and Industrial Organisation in Japan) (Tokyo: Tokyo Daigaku Shuppankai).

Mizuno, Junko (1993) 'Kankoku Jidōsha Sangyō ni Hinshitsu Furyō no Kabe' (The Obstacle of Low Quality in the Korean Automobile Industry), *The Economist*, 21 September.

Mizukawa Susumu (1993) 'Tojōkoku no Jidōsha Sangyō: Kankoku wo Chūshin to Shite' (The Automobile Industry in Developing Countries: Focus on Korea) (Tokyo: Senshu Diagaku Keizaigaku Ronshu).

Monden, Yasuhiro (1983) *Toyota Production System* (Atlanta: Institute of Industrial Engineering).

Morris, Jonathan (1991) *Japan and Global Economy* (London: Routledge).

Mukaiyama, Hideko (1993) 'ASEAN ni Okeru Sapōtingu Indasutori: Tai no Jirei' (The Development of Supporting Industries in the ASEAN Countries: The Case of Thailand), *Kan-Taiheiyo Bijinesu Joho*, vol. 14, Tokyo.

Murakami, Yasusuke (1992) *Han-Koten no Seiji Keizaigaku, Gekan: 21 Seiki Heno Josetsu* (The Anti-Classical Political Economy, vol. 2: An Introduction to the Twenty-first Century) (Tokyo: Chuo Koronsha).

Murakami, Yasusuke and Thomas P. Rohlen (1992) 'Social-exchange Aspects of the Japanese Polotical Economy: Culture, Efficiency, and Change', in Shunpei Kumon and Henry Rosovsky (eds), *The Political Economy of Japan, vol. 3: Cultural and Social Dynamics* (Palo Alto, Calif.: Stanford University Press).

Muraoka, Teruzo (1986) 'ASEAN, The Regional Economic Collaboration in Perspective', Occasional Papers, General Series no. 3, February (Centre for Contemporary Asian Studies, The Chinese University of Hong Kong).

Muraoka, Teruzo (1991) 'Pursuing the New International Economic Order: Overseas Investment and Trade of Japan, The Asian NIEs and ASEAN', in Jonathan Morris (ed.), *Japan and the Global Economy* (London: Routledge).

Nakamura, Tetsu (ed.) (1994) *Higashi-Ajia Shihonshugi no Keisei* (The Formation of Capitalism in East Asia) (Tokyo: Aoki Shoten).

Nitta, Michio (1988) *Nihon no Rōdōsha Sanka* (Worker Participation in Japan) (Tokyo: Tokyo Daigaku Shuppankai).

Ogawa, Eiji and Takao Makito (eds) (1990) *Ajia no Nikkei Kigyō to Gijutsu Iten* (Japanese Affiliated Companies in Asia and Technology Transfer) (Nagoya: Nagoya Daigaku Shuppankai).

Okumura, Hiroshi (1984) *Hōjin Shihonshugi* (Corporate Capitalism) (Tokyo: Ochanomizu Shobo).

Ono, Koichi and Yumiko Okamoto (eds) (1995) *EC · NAFTA · Higashi Ajia to Gaikoku Chokusetu Tōshi: Hatten Tojyōkoku he no Eikyō* (EC, NAFTA, East Asia and Foreign Direct Investment: The Influence on Developing Countires (Tokyo: Institute for Developing Economies).

Ono, Taiichi (1978) *Toyota Seisan Hoshiki: Datsu Kibo no Keizai wo Mezashite* (Toyota Production System: Seeking the Post Economy of Scale) (Tokyo: Daiyamondosha).

Ozawa, Terutomo (1979) *Multinationalism, Japanese Style* (Princeton, NJ: Princeton University Press).

Ozawa, Terutomo (1991) 'Structural Upgrading and Concatenated Integration' in Denis Simon (ed.), *Corporate Strategies in the Pacific Rim: Global versus Regional Trends* (London: Routledge).

Piore, Michael and Charles Sable (1984) *The Second Industrial Divide: Possibilities for Prosperity* (New York: Basic Books).

Porter, Michael E. (1990) *The Competitive Advantage of Nations* (New York: The Free Press).

Sasaki, Takao and Hideki Esho (1987) *Nihon Denki Sangyō no Kaigai Shinshutsu* (The Japanese Electronics Industry Abroad) (Tokyo: Hosei Daigaku Shuppankyoku).

Sei, Koichiro (1987) 'Kankoku Jidōsha Buhin Kogyō no Genjō to Tenbō' (The Present Situation and Future Prospects of the Korean Automobile and Parts Industry), *Keizai Kenkyusho Nenpo*, no. 9 (Kanto Gakuin University).

Sei, Koichiro (1989) 'Taiwan Jidosha Buhin Kogyo no Seisan-Taisei to Gijyutu-Suijyun' (The Production System of the Taiwanese Automobile Parts Industry and Its Technology), *Keizai Kenkyusho Nenpo he* (Kanto Gakuin University).

Seki, Michihiro (1993) *Furusetto-gata Sangyō Kōzō wo Koete* (How to Overcome the Problem of the Full-set Type of Industrial Structure) (Tokyo: Chuou Koronsha).

Shiba, Shoji (1973) *Rōdō no Kokusai Hikaku: Gijutsu Ikō to Sono Hakyu* (International Comparison of Work: Technology Transfer and Its Diffusion) (Tokyo: Toyo Keizai Shinposha).

Shimada, Haruo (1988) *Hyūman-uea no Keizaigaku: Amerika no Naka no Nihon Kigyō* (The Economics of Humanware: Japanese Affiliated Companies in the USA) (Tokyo: Iwanami Shoten).

Shirai, Taishiro (1982) *Gendai Nihon no Rōmu Kanri* (Labour Management in Contemporary Japan) (Tokyo: Toyo Keizai Shinposha).

Small and Medium Enterprises Agency (1995) *Chūshō Kigyou Hakusho* (White Paper on Small and Medium Businesses) (Tokyo: Printing Office of Ministry of Finance).

Stopford, John M. and Louis T. Wells (1972) *Managing the Multinational Enterprise* (New York: Basic Books).

Suehiro, Akira (1995) 'Ajia Kōgyō-ka no Dainamizumu' (The Dynamism of Asian Industrialisation), in Akira Kudo (ed.), *20 Seiki Shihonshugi 2: Haken no Henyo to Fukushi Kokka* (Capitalism in the Twentieth Century, vol. 2: The Transformation of Hegemony and Welfare States) (Tokyo: Tokyo Daigaku Shuppan-kai).

Sumiya, Mikio, Sin-kei Ryu and Jaw-Yann Twu (1992) *Taiwan no Keizai* (The Ecoomy of Taiwan) (Tokyo: Tokyo Daigaku Shuppankai).

Sung, Yun-Wing (1991) *The China–Hong Kong Connection* (New York: Cambridge University Press).

Suzuki, Naotsugu (1991) *Amerika Shakai no Naka no Nikkei Kigyō: Jidōsha Sangyō no Genchi Keiei* (Japanese Affiliated Companies in US Society: Local Management of the Auto Industry) (Tokyo: Toyo Keizai Shinposha).

Tajima, Toshio (1993) 'Chūgoku Shakai ni Nani ga Okiteiruka' (What is Happening in Chinese Agricultural Area ?), *Sekai*, October.

Takamiya, Makoto (1979) 'Conclusions and Policy Implications', in Susumu Takamiya and Keith Thurley (eds), *Japan's Emerging Multinationals: An International Comparison of Policies and Practices* (Tokyo: University of Tokyo Press).

Takanashi, Akitan (1994) *Kawaru Nihon-gata Koyō* (Japanese-style Employment Transforming) (Tokyo: Nihon Keizai Shinbungha).

Takeuchi Junko (1996) 'ASEAN Toshi to Genchi Sapōtingu Indasutōrizu' (Investment in the ASEAN Countires and the Development of Supporting Industries), *Kankyo Bujinesu Joho*, vol. 3, Tokyo.

Tanaka, Hirohide (1988) *Nihonteki Keiei no Rōmu Kanri* (Labour Management in Japanese Management) (Tokyo: Dobunkan).

Taniura, Takao (ed.) (1990) *Ajia no Kōgyōka to Gijutsu Iten* (The Industrialisation of Asia and Technology Transfer) (Tokyo: Ajia Keizai Kenkyujo).

Tejima, Shigeki and Hiroyuki Nakajima (1995) '1994 Nendo Kaigai Chokusetsu Tōshi Ankēto Chōsa Kekka Hōkoku' (A Report of a Survey Based on Questionnaires about Foreign Direct Investment in 1994), *Kaigai Toshi Kenkyujo Ho*, vol. 21, no. 1, January, Nihon Yushutsunyu Ginko Kaigai Toshi Kenkyujo, Tokyo.

Tokunaga, Shigeyoshi, Masami Nomura and Atsushi Hiramoto (1991) *Nihon Kigyō-Sekai Senryaku to Jissen: Denshi Sangyō no Gurobaruka to 'Nihon-teki Keiei'* (Japanese Companies – Their World Strategies and Practices: Globalisation of the Electronics Industry and 'Japanese-style Management') (Tokyo: Dobunkan).

Torii, Takashi (1990) 'Jidōsha Sangyō: Puroton Sha to Bumiputora Seisaku', (Automobile Industry: Proton and Bumiputora Policy), in Kenji Horii (ed.), *Marēshia no Kōgyōka: Tashuzoku Kokka to Kōgyōka no Tenkai* (Industrialisation in Malaysia: The Evolution of Industrialisation in a Multi-ethnic State) (Tokyo: Institute of Developing Economies).

Totsuka, Hideo and Ken Hyodo (eds) (1991) *Jidōsha Sangyō no Tenkan to Sentaku: Nihon no Jidōsha Sangyō* (The Transformation and Choices of the Auto Industry: The Japanese Auto Industry) (Tokyo: Nihon Hyoronsha).

Tōyō Keizai Shinpōsha (1994) *Kaigai Shinshutsu Kigyō Sōran* (Directory of Japanese Affiliated Companies Abroad) (Tokyo: Toyo Keizai Shinposha).

Twu, Jaw-Yann (1967) 'Sengo Taiwan Keizai niokeru Shihon Chikuseki Katei' (The Process of Capital Accumulation in Post War Taiwan (Formosa)), *Keizaigaku Kenkyu* (Society of Economic Studies, Tokyo Daigaku), no. 8, January.

Twu, Jaw-Yann (1988) *NICs: Kōgyō-ka Ajia wo Yomu* (The NICs: Examining Industrialised Asia) (Tokyo: Kodansha).

Twu, Jaw-Yann (1990) *Tōyō Shihonshugi* (Capitalism in the East) (Tokyo: Kodansha).

Twu, Jaw-Yann (1992) 'NIEs Ron kara Mita Chū-Tai Kankei' (The Relationship between China and Taiwan on NIEs Theory), *Keizai Kagaku*, vol. 39, no. 4.

Twu, Jaw-Yann and Jun Kitahara (eds) (1991) *Ajia NIEs to Daisansekai no Hatten* (Asian NIEs: Implications for Third-World Development) (Tokyo: Yushindo).

Uchida, Kastutoshi (ed) (1994) *Kokusai-ka no Naka no Nihon Keizai* (The Japanese Economy in Globalisation: The Japanese Role Played on the Asian Economic Rim) (Kyoto: Minerva Shobo).

Wang, Nian-Tzu. (ed.) (1992) *Taiwan's Enterprises in Global Perspective* (New York: M. E. Sharpe).

Watanabe, Toshio (1979) *Ajia Chūshinkoku no Chōsen* (The Challenges by Asian Middle-Advanced Countries) (Tokyo: Nihon Keizai Shinbunsha).

Watanabe, Toshio (1990) 'Nishi-Taiheiyō Shin-Chōryu: Kōzō Tenkan no Rensateki Keiki ni Tsuite' (A New Trend in the West Pacific: the Sequential Changes of the Structure), *Kaigai Toshi Kenkyu* (Japan Export Import Bank), vol. 16, no. 4, April.

Weiss, Julian (1989) *The Asian Century* (New York: Facts on File).

White, Michael and Malcom Trevor (1986) *Under Japanese Management: The Experience of British Workers* (London: Heinemann).

Womack, James P., Daniel T. Jones and Daniel Roos (1990) *The Machine That Changed the World* (New York: Macmillan).

The World Bank (1993) *A World Bank Policy Research Report: The East Asian Miracle: Economic Growth and Public Policy* (New York: Oxford University Press).

Yamashita, Shoichi (ed.) (1991) *Transfer of Japanese Technology and Management to the ASEAN Countries* (Tokyo: University of Tokyo Press).

Yamashita, Shoichi (1994) *Foreign Direct Investment and the Process of Technology Transfer* (Hiroshima: Hiroshima Daigaku Nenpo Keizaigaku).

Yanagimachi, Isao (1994) 'Nikkan Jidōsha Buhin Sangyō no Risutorakucharingu: Arata na Kyōsō Senryaku to Shitauke Kōzō no Saihensei wo Megutte' (The Restructuring of the Japanese and Korean Automobile Parts Industry: New Competitive Strategies and Reorganization of Subcontracting Structures), *Nagoya Shoka University Ronshu*, vol. 38, no. 2, March.

Yasumuro, Kenichi (1982) *Kokusai Keiei Kōdōron: Nichibei Hikaku no Shiten Kara* (The Behaviour of International Management: A Comparison between Japanese and US Companies) (Tokyo: Moriyama Shoten).

Yoon, Jin-Ho (1995) 'Kankoku ni Okeru Nihonteki-Seisan-Hōshiki no Dōnyū to Rōdōsha' (Adoption of the Japanese Production System in Korea and Its effect on Workers), *Ohara Institute for Social Research Journal*, no. 439.

Yoshino, Michael Y. (1976) *Japan's Multinational Enterprises* (Cambridge, Mass.: Harvard University Press).

Yun, Hing-A (1995) 'Volvo in Malaysia', in Ake Sandberg (ed.), *Enriching Production: Perspectives on Volvo's Uddevalla Plant as an Alternative to Lean Production* (Aldershot: Avebury).

Index

391